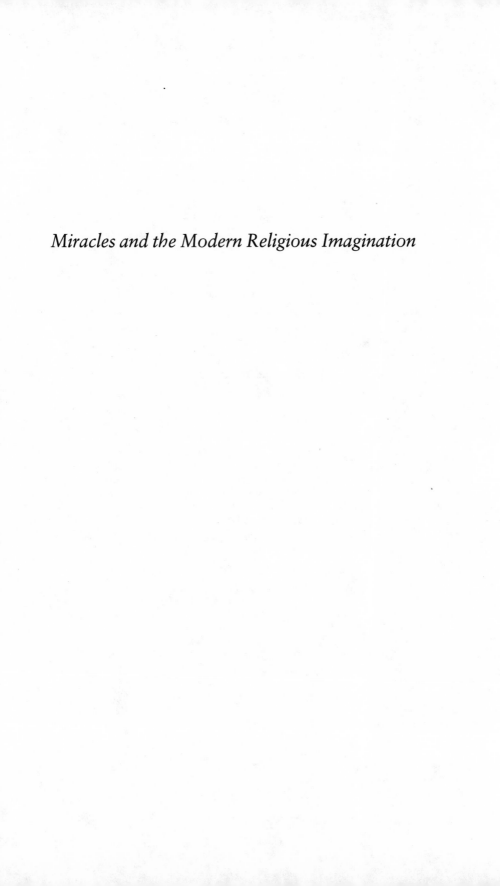

Miracles and the Modern Religious Imagination

ROBERT BRUCE MULLIN

Miracles and the Modern Religious Imagination

SAINT FRANCIS SEMINARY
St. Francis, Wisconsin

Yale University Press
New Haven and London

Set in Sabon type by Keystone Typesetting, Inc., Orwigsburg, Pennsylvania
Printed in the United States of America.
Library of Congress Cataloging-in-Publication Data
Mullin, Robert Bruce.
    Miracles and the modern religious imagination / Robert Bruce Mullin.
      p. cm.
    Includes bibliographical references and index.
    ISBN 0-300-06696-1 (cloth : alk. paper)
    1. Miracles — History of doctrines — 19th century. 2. Miracles —
  History of doctrines — 20th century. I. Title.
    BT97.2.M85 1996
    231.7'3 — dc20   96-13505
                                        CIP
A catalogue record for this book is available from the British Library.
10 9 8 7 6 5 4 3 2 1

In Memoriam
Sydney E. Ahlstrom (1919–1984)
Scholar, Mentor, Friend

Contents

Acknowledgments

To undertake a project of this scope would have been impossible without the help and assistance of many. The helpful insights of Winthrop Hudson, George Marsden, Brooks Holifield, Daniel Walker Howe, J. C. D. Clark, Ronald Numbers, William Hutchison, Peter Hinchliff, Mark Hulsether, Jay Dolan, Donald Gerardi, Allen Guelzo, Diana Butler, Moody Smith, Robert Hambourger, David Austin, Douglas Jesseph, and James VanderKam have guided me through a number of tricky questions. Members of the Ecclesiastical History internet list (moderated by Gregory Singleton) have also kindly answered numerous queries. In their own way, the prodding of students at North Carolina State University, the University of North Carolina–Chapel Hill, and Duke University have forced me to clarify my (at times) hazy ideas. Finally a special thanks goes out to those who have offered critical readings of the manuscript. My colleague Cynthia Miller graciously applied her expert editorial talents to the entire manuscript. Russell Richey, Grant Wacker, Reginald Savage, William Adler, and Dwight Peterson also have read all or parts of this work in various stages. The sharp eyes and astute comments of all of these individuals have saved me from both errors in fact and infelicities of expression. The staff of Yale University Press must also be acknowledged. Senior editor Chuck Grench has been patient, yet encouraging, and my copy editor, Julie Carlson, has smoothed many a rough passage. My heartfelt thanks go out to all these individuals.

The high quality and overwhelming helpfulness of the Triangle area libraries (D. H. Hill at North Carolina State, Davis Library at University of North Carolina–Chapel Hill, and the Perkins medical and divinity libraries at Duke) have allowed me the luxury of doing much of my research in residence. The interlibrary loan department at D. H. Hill was consistently helpful in locating obscure titles. I have also been helped by the libraries of Harvard, Yale, Princeton Seminary, General Theological Seminary, Nashotah House, Episcopal Divinity School, and Union Theological Seminary, as well as the New York Public Library (and in particular Warren Platt), the Boston Public Library, the Library of Congress, the library of the British Museum, the Bodleian library, and the Pusey House Library (and in particular, its librarian Father Kenneth Macnab). These trips were made possible by the gracious hospitality of many, and I would like to thank Tim and Joanne Caffrey for their kindnesses during trips to New England, Bob Wright and Bill and Carmela Franklin for their assistance during numerous visits to New York, and to the staff of the Pusey House for making my stays at Oxford both productive and enjoyable.

Portions of chapters 3, 4, and 7 have appeared in different forms in essays published in *Church History* and *Anglical and Episcopal History*. I am grateful to these journals for their permission to use these materials.

On the practical level a number of institutions have made this work possible. The Department of Philosophy and Religion here at North Carolina State has provided me the time and resources to undergo this project. The College of Humanities and Social Sciences has made available to me travel funds and time away from other duties, for which I am sincerely grateful. An extra special thanks, however, must go to the Louisville Institute for the Study of Protestantism and American Culture and the Pew Evangelical Scholars Program. Together these institutions allowed me the time and resources to finish this long undertaking. Jim Lewis at Louisville and Michael Hamilton at Pew were uniformly helpful at every turn. Words cannot express the gratitude I feel for these two institutions and their commitment to religious scholarship. I hope that this volume is up to the high standard of scholarship they represent.

The dedication of this volume reflects my great debt to one of the fine scholars and teachers in religious history. It was he who first aroused my interest in the topic, and his example has always inspired me in shaping any historical inquiry.

Finally I must acknowledge the support and understanding of my wife, Viola, and daughter, Elizabeth. Through all of the ups and downs of this project, they have been patient and encouraging. I am sure that for them its completion does seem like a modern miracle.

Introduction

Ideas, unlike people, do not have obituaries when they die. Rather, after having had vital and influential lives during which they influence the shape of human discourse, they may pass away silently and largely unnoticed.

On one level this is a study of the collapse of a religious idea, namely that of a limited age of miracles. For over three hundred years, English-speaking Protestants agreed upon a basic understanding concerning the miraculous — miracles were essential for both the revelation of the Bible and the establishment of the Christian church, but after the completion of the scripture they ceased to occur. When it emerged at the time of the Reformation, this belief in a limited age of miracles served a variety of functions. First, it helped define a crucial dividing line between Protestants and Roman Catholics. Whereas Catholics concerned themselves with the "superstitious" miracles of the saints and martyrs, Protestants emphasized only the biblical miracles. Second, it anchored the unique authority of the Bible over both ecclesiastical tradition and other religions. The Bible was authoritative because it rested upon true miracles. Finally, it allowed Protestants to combine a belief in biblical miracles with a vision of a regular and orderly nature. From the sixteenth century to the nineteenth century, this confidence had a prominent role in the Protestant world view. By the middle of the nineteenth century, however, the idea of a limited age of miracles came increasingly under attack, and by the end of the eighty-year period that forms the core of this study (1850–1930) it had lost its hegemonic role in English-speaking Protestantism.

The story of the "decline" in the idea of the miraculous throughout the nineteenth century is a common part of many histories. In the way the story is usually told, David Hume in his inquiry "Of Miracles" is credited with giving a fatal blow to any evidentialist claim for miracles, and the growing awareness of the uniformity of nature is seen as having made the idea of a miracle ever more problematic. Furthermore, as philosophers and scientists were raising intellectual problems, theologians began developing an understanding of religion that made the idea of miracles religiously pointless. Through these forces, a belief in miracles was slowly but surely squeezed out of the modern world view. According to the standard picture, this development was constant and inevitable. As one nineteenth-century commentator observed, "The plain fact is, that the progress of civilisation produces a certain tone and habit of thought which make men recoil from miraculous narratives with an instinctive and immediate repugnance."[1] According to this view, an interest in miracles was a thing of the past. Intelligent persons might continue to use the term, but it had become divorced from its traditional meaning. Where an interest in miracles continued, it reflected retrogressive cultural and intellectual tendencies.

An assault upon the miraculous is indeed part of the intellectual history of the nineteenth century, and it did contribute to the collapse of the idea of a limited age of miracles. But this traditional viewpoint, I shall argue, fails in two crucial regards. The first is that the story was not one of slow evolution but instead of punctuated equilibrium. Religious intellectuals did not slowly and inevitably give up their belief in miracles; on the contrary, the idea had remarkable tenacity among theologians. Indeed, as I show in chapter 6, it was not until the 1890s that any significant number of English-speaking religious leaders felt able to begin to question the miraculous, and the debate raged well into the twentieth century. The picture of inevitable evolution hides the real nature of the debate and obscures what in fact did propel the argument forward.

More importantly, the traditional picture fails to address a countervailing movement during these years of increased interest in the miraculous. If in some circles the idea of the miraculous was being discarded, in others it was paradoxically gaining in importance. In particular, an interest in modern miracles grew markedly during these decades. Whereas some writers began to call into question the miracles of the gospels, other individuals began to claim that these miracles could be found in the present. Furthermore, this interest in modern miracles was not confined to the margins of Anglo-American society but included philosophers, preachers, professors, and playwrights. Finally, the renewed interest in modern miracles was in many cases connected with the attack upon the miracles of the Bible. Both John Henry Newman in England and Horace Bushnell in America recognized that the only way to preserve the biblical miracles was to abandon the idea of a limited age of miracles and reopen the case for modern miracles. The credibility of all miracles was being challenged by modern critics. As Bushnell wrote, "If miracles are inherently incredible . . . nothing is gained by thrusting them back into the remote ages of time."[2]

Third (and most tentatively), this study suggests that this debate over the miraculous may be one of the principle divisions in religious thought since the mid 1850s, replacing the traditional Protestant-Catholic tension. Many students of late-nineteenth-century religion have noted that something important transpired during these years that altered the religious landscape in a profound way. Within the study of American Protestantism, a split between conservative and liberal — often defined by differences over the authority and inspiration of scripture — usually has been assumed. Indeed when I began this study I took for granted the conservative-liberal model. But I have become convinced that the debate over the miraculous and the spectrum of attitudes outlined in chapter 7 were far more important in transforming religious life than the issue of scripture per se. Finally, as I suggest in the epilogue, this pattern of responses may also help us to make sense of the religious discussion of the late twentieth century, where the issue of the miraculous has reappeared.

The full pattern of the debate over miracles can only be seen by exploring a number of different questions and sectors of the religious community that have heretofore been viewed separately. The multifaceted interest in miracles during these years is like a jigsaw puzzle — individually the pieces are enigmatic, but examined together they show a strong pattern. Accordingly, I have attempted to look simultaneously at the debates over biblical criticism and the interest in modern signs and wonders, particularly religious healing. Likewise I examine a group of individuals — such as the theologian Horace Bushnell, the Protestant faith healer John Alexander Dowie, the psychical researcher F. W. H. Myers, and Catholic defenders of the healings at Lourdes — who are almost never studied together. Finally, to grasp the larger effect of the debate, I shall move beyond the technical questions of scholars and theologians and explore how the issue of the miraculous was taken up by novelists and playwrights. Indeed, what I offer here is a picture of a discussion that in key ways transcends the division between high culture and popular culture and places philosophers like William James and playwrights like William Vaughn Moody in conversation.

A complete study of all the facets of the question of miracles and the modern religious imagination would necessitate a study far longer than this. Accordingly I have attempted to limit the topic in a number of ways. Because this is a narrative intellectual history, I have framed my exploration of the issue of miracles as an intellectual question. Why did persons choose either to reject or embrace the miraculous during these years, and what were the ramifications of their decisions on their view of nature or history? I am interested not simply in the fact that a given individual had an opinion on the miraculous, but also in what that opinion meant to a framework of belief. Accordingly, although the renewed interest in religious healing generated an immense amount of testimonial literature as to the reality of miracles, I have chosen to concentrate only upon that portion of this literature that described the meaning of miracles for these believers.

Second, I have limited the scope of the study to the debate within the Christian context. The question of miracles was of course a concern for many other individuals, but by limiting the study largely to members of Christian communities I can focus on how the question of miracles was tied to other religious concerns, most particularly the person of Jesus. Again and again the discussion of miracles was to return to the larger question of who was Jesus and what was the nature of his ministry. For this reason, when discussing the debate over biblical miracles, I have tended to explore the miracles associated with Jesus rather than those of the Hebrew scriptures, as these were religiously the most crucial for Christians. Miracles were entwined within the gospel portrait of Jesus, and Christian critics were loath to criticize them directly until the figure of Jesus could be protected. Furthermore, I have not included examinations of the new religious movements of the nineteenth century such as Spiritualism, Christian Science, and New Thought, except to the extent that these movements prodded Christian writers to reexamine questions such as religious healing. I have also not included to any degree the philosophical or scientific critics of the miraculous, except insofar as their arguments provide a context for the Christian response. Furthermore, among the Christian communities I have largely focused on the historic English-speaking Protestants. Because the idea of a limited age of miracles emerged as a point of division between Protestants and Roman Catholics, however, I have included a discussion of Catholic understandings of the miraculous, as well as Protestant responses to Catholic claims.

Third, we are concerned here with the miraculous as a religious question. The subject of miracles has of course been approached from other perspectives, such as that of science and philosophy. But I shall argue that the tenacity of the idea of the miraculous lies in the fact that it is linked in the religious imagination to a number of cherished beliefs such as the reality of a spiritual realm, the meaningfulness of prayer, and the ability of a personal God to respond to the world. Whereas outside of a religious world view the idea of a miracle might appear meaningless, from within it is not. One reason for the intensity of the debate (which I shall explore) is that the persons in this study all recognized the weight miracles had for religious individuals.

Fourth, the focus of my study is, broadly speaking, the relationship of the thought of key intellectuals to the middle-class literate public, both lay and clerical. Part of my concern is with major thinkers like Horace Bushnell, William James, John Henry Newman, and Charles Gore, all of whom made important contributions to the modern understanding of the miraculous. Yet the discussion of miracles took place not only in theological journals but also in secular periodicals such as the *Century Magazine,* the *Literary Digest,* the *Nineteenth Century,* and even the *Ladies Home Journal.* Both parts of the discussion must be kept in focus. I acknowledge that by concentrating on these subjects I may have accentuated the pattern of rise and decline. In other groups an interest in the supernatural or paranormal has been much more constant.[3]

Further, because I am attempting to describe a public debate, I have tended to pick up the discussion when it reached a certain popularity. Faith healing undoubtedly was practiced throughout nineteenth-century America, but the public discussion of it emerged among Protestants in the 1870s and peaked in the 1880s. My focus on the public debate has also led me at times to emphasize some now little-remembered figures. In my treatment of the 1920s debate over faith healing, for example, I have put more emphasis on James Moore Hickson than on the now more famous Aimee Semple McPherson, because it was the ministry of Hickson and not that of McPherson that catalyzed public discussion within the middle class.

Finally I have attempted to interpret this debate as one within the Anglo-American world, and I have tried to integrate the discussions in Britain and America. What emerges here is a powerful Atlantic community of thought, and one in which Anglicanism was a key conduit. The British and American debates were of course not identical, and I have attempted to note how and why they differed, but they were interrelated. Books and authors crisscrossed the Atlantic. To tell the story from a narrowly American perspective — and hence to avoid the contributions to the American discussion of such figures as John Tyndall, Mary Ward, Percy Dearmer, and Maude Royden — would fail to do justice to the complex nature of the debate. Although the study ultimately focuses on the American situation, it is placed in the context of a larger English-speaking discussion.

One final task remains. What do I mean by a miracle? Here we must acknowledge that this is a surprisingly difficult question, particularly when the question is directed to modern miracles. In a world in which the word *miracle* can be attributed to everything from soap flakes to sporting teams, does the term have any core meaning? As I shall show, during the years under consideration large-scale discussion over a precise definition of miracle occurred, but no unanimity was ever achieved. In a miracle, principles of science, history, and theology meet, and each of these fields have their own criteria for what truly constitutes a miracle. My notebooks bulge with over forty-eight separate contemporary definitions of the term, all slightly different as to how a miracle is to be related to nature (that is, science), to the human condition (that is, history), and to any alleged divine purpose (that is, theology). Rather than employing any of these individual definitions, I have instead created my own functional definition based on the following three criteria.

For an event to be considered a miracle, it must first be understood as an intervention by God into the world of humanity or nature. William James, for example, in the conclusion of his *Varieties of Religious Experience,* contrasted two models of supernaturalism: a "refined" supernaturalism and a "crass" or "piecemeal" supernaturalism. In the former, the spiritual always existed behind the world of nature, while in the latter the spiritual interfered causally in the course of phenomenal events.[4] The latter idea of an intervening causality is one essential principle of a miracle. Thus refined supernaturalism, which sees the presence of the divine in nature but not intervening causally, is excluded from my definition. In this way, I bracket the vexing question of the relationship of a miraculous event to the laws of nature. Proponents of the miraculous differed as to whether a miracle must be understood as a violation of a law of nature, but they all agreed that it was an intervention.

Second, for an event to be a miracle it must have some public character. By this I mean that a miracle is never merely a private or personal experience, but is rather an event that has importance to a larger community. The idea of testimony is a central part of a miracle, whether biblical or modern. The act of reporting the event — whether as a personal witness in a faith healer's tent or in the pages of a scholarly journal dedicated to psychical research — acknowledges the public importance of the occurrence.

Last (and perhaps most controversially), a miracle within the Christian context is almost always seen as an action by God that is in some way connected to the great events recorded in scripture. Virtually all of the claims of modern miracles included in this study can be seen as alleged reverberations of the biblical miracles. The crowds at Lourdes, or those gathered around healers such as Charles Cullis, John Alexander Dowie, or James Moore Hickson, looked for healing because healing was part of the original message of their religion.

I have purposely attempted to keep my definition broad while suggesting that there is still something distinctive about a claim of a miracle. A broad definition allows us to treat in tandem groups that had fundamentally different theological interpretations of the miraculous — such as Catholics, faith healers, and early-twentieth-century seekers of supernatural evidences — and exclude those who while using the term had a very different conception of it. Furthermore one may also note that these three criteria delineate the critical intersection of science, history, and theology. To allege that miracles are real is to assert that outside of the phenomenal world there is a personal reality that intervenes within the phenomenal world. It is to maintain that these interventions are important to the believing community and to imply that these interventions highlight the nature of the received faith. Cast in such categories, it is little wonder that miracles have been both important and hugely controversial.

Considering the topic of this study, the reader might rightfully inquire as to my own position on the miraculous. Personally I accept the great miracles of the Bible and remain open to the existence of postbiblical miracles, but as an individual the miraculous does not play an important part in my beliefs. In this way I differ from almost all the persons in this study who were passionately involved (pro and con) in the question. I hope I have been fair to them all.

A Limited Age of Miracles?

Although this study is principally a tale of the nineteenth and twentieth centuries, it rests upon a larger story of the place of the miraculous in Christianity. The persons I shall consider were passionately interested in earlier discussions, and indeed claimed that their particular insight reflected the classical position. Hence this opening chapter offers a brief overview of the question of miracles in the Christian tradition.[1]

An Age-Old Discussion

If members of the Christian community over the centuries have been unable to agree about the place of miracles in their religion, this inability has no more than reflected an implicit ambiguity in the Christian scriptures themselves. Jesus in the New Testament, for example, is pictured as the worker of remarkable signs and wonders, and when the followers of John the Baptist inquire of him, he directed them to report the wonders they had seen: "The blind receive their sight and the lame walk, lepers are cleansed and the deaf hear, and the dead are raised up" (Mt 11:5). Yet at other times Jesus derides an appeal to signs. "Why does this generation seek a sign?" he is recorded as asking. "Truly, I say to you, no sign shall be given this generation" (Mk 8:12). Nor was the most famous of the apostles any clearer. To the Corinthians, Paul listed the "working of miracles" as one of the "spiritual" or charismatic gifts of the Holy Spirit for the common good of the community (1 Cor 12:10). Yet only a few paragraphs later he discounted the gift of miracles as paling before the greater gift of love ("If I have all faith, so as to remove mountains, but have not love, I am nothing"). Likewise at the beginning of that same epistle he contrasted the clamoring after signs with the proclamation of the good news: "For Jews demand signs and Greeks seek wisdom, but we preach Christ crucified, a stumbling block to the Jews and folly to Gentiles" (1 Cor 1:22–24).

The message of the New Testament seems to be that the "signs," "wonders," and "mighty works" (the actual biblical terms for miracles) were both crucially important yet beside the point. They were closely associated with Jesus and the apostles, but both he and his followers at times dismissed them. Nor is the New Testament any clearer about their continuance. Paul seemed to imply that the gifts of the Spirit (including healing and the working of miracles) would pass away "when the perfect comes" (1 Cor 13:10). But John records Jesus as promising his disciples, "He who believes in me will also do the works that I do; and greater works than these will he do" (Jn 14:12). It is not surprising that different persons have interpreted the biblical record in radically different ways.[2]

A similar ambiguity concerning the miraculous continued in the early centuries. Apologists like Justin Martyr and Hillary of Poitiers appealed to the miracles of Jesus as evidence of his power, but others such as Tatian and Athenagorus put comparatively little stock in them. Likewise whereas Origen attempted to interpret miracles in keeping with the orderliness of nature, Tertullian proclaimed them as witnessing to the omnipotence of God. Finally, on the question of postbiblical miracles, there was still more unclarity. A writer such as Irenaeus could report contemporary miracles while downplaying them.[3]

Students of the early church note that the way in which people understood miracles underwent a significant change during the fourth century. In the decades after the conversion of Constantine, not only did an interest in contemporary wonders surge, but also the tenor of the discussion shifted. Rather than seeing miracles as continuing signs of Christ's victory, Christians began instead to value miracles for themselves and to regard them as part of the sacralization of the Roman Empire. Writers like Eusebius began to interpret miracles as reflections of a heavenly power brought to earth for the sake of the earthly church. As one scholar noted, "The miracles establish the Christian commonwealth, and they function to support it."[4]

In the Christian understanding of the miraculous, no person was more influential than Augustine of Hippo. Augustine became the authority to which later writers would always return. His writings on the miraculous are weighty and have inspired much (and not always concurrent) scholarship, but for our purposes Augustine's contributions were to offer a definition of the miraculous and a framework for understanding postbiblical miracles. For Augustine there was only one miracle—creation. All of creation was in some ways miraculous because it reflected the creative nature of God. Thus the commonly held distinction between nature and miracles was that in the latter the wonder was made explicit. Miracles were miraculous because of the effect they produced. The only reason why we do not see nature itself as miraculous is that it is always present. Accordingly, miracles were not contrary to nature (*contra naturam*) but only *supra-naturam,* or outside of what human beings know of nature.[5]

But Augustine also testified to the growing interest in contemporary miracles in the fourth century. Early in his career he argued that miracles had passed away. "Miracles were not allowed to continue to our time," he explained, "lest the mind should always seek visible things." But by the end of his life his mind had changed. In his *Retractions* he included a defense of contemporary miracles. Furthermore in Book 22 of the *City of God* he listed many modern miracles. They were not "so brilliant and conspicuous" as those of the apostles, but were nonetheless real. "For whether God Himself wrought these miracles by that wonderful manner of working by which, though Himself eternal, He produces effects in time; or whether He wrought them by servants . . . nevertheless these miracles attest to this faith which preaches the resurrection of the flesh to eternal life." Thus the effect of Augustine was to suggest the religious significance of miracles and to emphasize the interconnectedness of biblical and postbiblical miracles.[6]

This fourth-century development was part of a larger phenomenon in late antiquity that associated the miraculous and holiness. The holy man (or person) was reflected in works of miracles and wonders. Relics, tombs, and shrines of saints were seen as places where the divine and mundane realms met, and the miracles associated with them were understood as signs of the transcending of the two realms. The association of miracles and holiness was given official sanction in Latin Catholicism by the eleventh century when the canonization of saints was formalized. Ironically, however, as popular interest grew in the miracles of saints and holy persons, other practices were becoming routinized or sacramentalized. For example, in James 5:14 there was an enigmatic command: "Is any among you sick? Let him call for the elders of the church, and let them pray over him, anointing him with oil in the name of the Lord." Whereas in earlier centuries this passage had been understood as a direct promise of physical healing through the Spirit, by the sixth century the anointing it commands was increasingly understood by the church in sacramental rather than charismatic ways. The nineteenth-century discussion over how God mediated grace — whether regularly through church and sacrament or dramatically through charismatic figures — was to be only part of this much older controversy.[7]

Another understanding of the miraculous was to be found in Thomas Aquinas.[8] For Aquinas the context of the miraculous became not the religious wonder it produced, but its relationship with nature. He understood a miracle to be something that happened outside of the order of nature. And, he added, "If some event should occur outside the ordinary course of things with respect to any particular thing in nature, this would not be enough to make it a miracle — otherwise someone throwing a stone up in the air would be working a miracle. . . . It is for this reason that a miracle is defined as an event that happens outside the ordinary processes of the whole of created nature."[9] To what degree there was a fundamental difference between Augustine and Aquinas has been a matter of debate, but taken together they have usually been offered as two alternative ways of understanding the miraculous. Many of the participants of the late-nineteenth-century discussion argued for a return to an Augustinian view of miracles.

The relationship of miracles to the supernatural would be a late-nineteenth-century problem; the sixteenth century was far more concerned with the association of miracles with holiness. The belief that miracles and wonders were allied with holiness continued to thrive in medieval Christianity, and it was intimately associated with the cult of the saints. Sixteenth-century Catholics continued to emphasize the interrelationship of miracles and holiness. As the Jesuit Robert Bellarmine explained, "The eleventh note [of the church] is the glory of miracles. They are however sent for two reasons. First they are necessary for new faith or for extraordinary missionary persuasion. Secondly they are efficacious and sufficient because . . . they cannot be among the adversaries of the true church and [show] that the true church is among us."[10]

The debate over miracles was to enter a new phase with the advent of the Reformation. Catholic apologists regularly pointed to the existence of miracles within their communion as a sign of its sanctity, and conversely the absence of miracles among Protestants as a sign that Protestant churches were not true churches. In turn, very early in the Reformation period a large-scale Protestant rejection of postbiblical miracles began to emerge. In part this rejection occurred because miracles were associated with the idea of holy places, the cult of the saints, and the doctrine of transubstantiation. All were viewed by Protestants as superstitious at best and as more probably emanating from diabolical forces than divine. Ecclesiastical miracles were "lying wonders," and Martin Luther, for example, pointedly rejected them. Miracles and pilgrimages were a "tom foolery" of the devil for "chasing people hither and yon."[11]

But the Protestant position rested on a second assertion. As John Calvin argued, miracles served primarily to confirm Christian doctrine and accredit its bearers, and therefore they were subservient to scripture. The believer's confidence should not rest on signs and wonders, but rather upon the promise of God in the sacred text. Hence ecclesiastical miracles were not only fraudulent or diabolical, but they were unnecessary. As Calvin explained in the preface to his *Institutes of the Christian Religion,* one should not expect to see miracles occurring within Protestantism, because "we are not forging some new gospel, but are retaining that very gospel whose truth all the miracles of Jesus Christ and his disciples ever wrought serve to confirm." Protestantism, having no new gospel, needed no new miracles.[12]

Throughout Calvin's writings one finds an exegetical schema that emphasizes a limited age of miracles and the subservience of miracles to the scriptures themselves. According to Calvin, God never allowed true miracles to overshadow the sacred text, hence "we may easily gather how foolishly the Papists deal, when . . . they endeavor to lead the world away from the reverence of God and the gospel by bare miracles." He went on to explain that the extraordinary spiritual gifts listed in 1 Corinthians 12 were temporary gifts for the building up of the early community; however, they had long ago passed away. Indeed part of Calvin's criticism of such Catholic sacramental practices as confirmation and unction was that these were originally charismatic gifts rightly associated with signs, but now had become ossified in ritual. Sacramental ritual was the bare shell of a once true and miraculous gift. Calvin did acknowledge that occasional wonders were recorded among Roman Catholics, but these, he insisted, were counterfeit miracles. These wonders were ultimately diabolical, in his view, because they attempted to drive a wedge between the believer and the Bible.[13]

For a variety of reasons the Reformers in England were greatly attracted to the apologetic of a limited age of miracles, and at least one scholar has suggested that the development of a strict cessationist view concerning miracles was a peculiar product of the English Reformation.[14] Much of the prestige of the old faith had rested on the miraculous. For example Thomas à Becket, associated with the shrine at Canterbury, was claimed to have effected over seven hundred miracles within fifteen years of his death.[15] Accordingly, English Reformers joined the attack on ecclesiastical miracles. John Jewel, the sixteenth-century apologist, dismissed the alleged miracles occurring among Roman Catholics in foreign missions as probably feigned and in any case irrelevant for determining true doctrine. Likewise, the proto-Puritan John Hooper could argue, "I believe . . . the gospel in the very time by God appointed was confirmed and approved by heavenly miracles, as well as by Jesus Christ himself, . . . and that after such a sort . . . there is now no more need of new miracles; but rather we must content ourselves with that is done, and simply and plainly believe only the holy scriptures . . . watching and still taking heed to ourselves, that we be not beguiled and deceived with the false miracles of Antichrist, wherewith the world at this day is stuffed." Particularly here in Hooper one sees how the two parts of the Protestant apologetic — the limiting of miracles to the establishment of the gospel order and the dismissal of later miracles as lying wonders — became fused.[16]

Throughout the seventeenth century the question of the miraculous became one of the key disagreements between English-speaking Catholics and Protestants. The religious turmoil of Stuart England, Roman Catholic writers argued, stemmed from the clamor of competing sects. Only when a true church was acknowledged could religious peace ensue, and "it is . . . absolutely necessary to have that happie Society clearly marked out, wherein Divine Faith is taught, but no mark can be more palpable . . . than glorious Miracles, God's own Seals, Christ's own Cognisances, and the clearest Characters of Apostolical Doctrine." A church without the testimony of miracles was as "dark a thing as a Sun without light."[17] Indeed at times the issue was not merely one of theory, but of practice. In the early years of the Restoration a priest, referred to as J. O. F., performed a number of remarkable cures around London — each involving the second Duke of Buckingham and a number of persons associated with James, Duke of York — in the hope of leading England back to Rome. Allegedly the blind received sight, the dumb, hearing, and the lame, mobility. According to one Roman Catholic contemporary, not only did these miracles attest to the truth of Rome, but the rejection of this ministry bespoke the spiritual emptiness of Protestant England. "Wo be to the Sectaries," he wrote. "For if amongst the Turks and Infidels had been wrought the Miracles, that have been done amongst them they [would have] done penance in hair-cloth and ashes long ago."[18]

These debates demonstrated, furthermore, that the Protestant apologetic possessed key difficulties. Perhaps the most fundamental was the need to distinguish between miracles and other activities of God in the world. Although they rejected the ecclesiastical miracles of Roman Catholics, seventeenth-century Protestants were fascinated with the idea of divine providence. Providence, or the means by which God governed and sustained the world, was usually subdivided into two classes: general providence, or the general ordering of the world, and special providence, in which God exercised care for specific individuals and groups.[19] The line between miracle and special providence was never clear-cut. The English nation, for example, saw in the storms that dashed the Spanish Armada nothing less than the intervening hand of God. Similarly, volumes such as Thomas Beard's *The Theatre of God's Judgements* and William Turner's *A Compleat History of the Most Remarkable Providences* offered to an eager public (on both sides of the Atlantic) a panoply of wonders. These collections included not only stories of comets and thunderstorms, but tales from church history like that of the African confessors who continued to confess after their tongues were cut off. Because this account was usually considered a miracle, the question returned: how did miracles and wonder working providences differ?[20] Nor was this merely a question of the past. By the middle of the seventeenth century, defenders of the Reformation position confronted a growing Quaker community that proclaimed an outpouring of grace into the world that was perilously similar to the traditional view of ecclesiastical miracles. In the face of Quaker as well as Catholic miracles, the task of distinguishing between miracle and providence became even more urgent.[21]

To see how American Puritans attempted to maintain the distinction, one might turn to the figure of Increase Mather. In 1684 Mather published *An Essay for the Recording of Illustrious Providences. . . Especially in New England*. He had solicited from fellow clergy stories of wonders and providences, and in publishing these accounts characterized them as "Divine Judgements, Tempests, Floods, Earthquakes, . . . Strange Apparitions, . . . Witchcrafts, Diabolical Possessions, Remarkable Judgements upon noted Sinners: eminent Deliverances, and answers to Prayer." An evaluation of Mather's "illustrious providences" reveals two key points. The first is that even as late as the end of the seventeenth century the terms "miracle" and "providence" had not yet taken on their precise meanings. Mather occasionally used the terms interchangeably, and even in combination.[22] A second is that the conceptual difference between providence and miracles is most vividly illustrated by Mather's pointed contrast between Puritan New England and Roman Catholic practices. Thus in the context of a discussion of how God answered the pious prayers of the people of New England by bringing them rain, he recorded a very different type of incident: "Jovianus Pontanus reports, that when King Ferdinand besieged the city Suessa, all the waters in the cisterns being dried up, . . . the Popish Priests undertook, by conjuration, to obtain Water." The Roman Catholic clergy, the account continued, placed a consecrated eucharistic host in the mouth of an ass, and then buried the animal alive in front of the church doors. "As soon as these rites, so pleasing to the Devil were finished, the Heavens began to look black . . . and anon it rained, and lightned after a most horrendous manner."[23]

The Roman Catholic miracle was everything Protestant providences were not. It involved vain rituals and sacred objects rather than godly prayer. It focused on the miracle workers (the "Popish Priests") instead of the providential action of God. Lastly, the miracle operated on the level of manipulation and control rather than supplication. The most striking aspect of Mather's view, however, is that for him the Roman Catholic miracles were real, but diabolical. Devils were the power behind Catholic miracle claims, and therefore preternatural rather than supernatural. This emphasis upon the diabolical also ironically allowed Mather to suggest one final distinction between Protestant stories of providences and Catholic accounts of miracles. Because the same God who caused the providences also directed and governed the course of nature, providences were seamlessly woven into the natural order. Mather told a story of a starving shipwrecked victim who was fed by flying fish that lept into his boat. This event, Mather argued, was both providential and at the same time in keeping with the regular actions of a flying fish. Indeed, in his *Essay* Mather showed interest in both wonders and the order of nature. In contrast, the diabolical forces that empowered Roman Catholic miracles could not weave their wonders into the course of nature but instead had to impose them upon nature like crude, misfitting patches. The inferior nature of diabolical miracles made them easily recognizable as more crudely supernatural than true wonder-working providences. The former, Mather concluded, were to be rejected, even those recorded by Augustine in Book 22 of the *City of God*.[24]

Miracles and the Protestant Enlightenment

But by the time of Mather the intellectual currents were changing, and these changes would shift the locus of the miracle debate. Mather's concern for things diabolical began to decline by the end of the century. To use David Hall's phrase, by the end of the century one began witnessing the "dissolution of the lore of wonders." There continued to be an interest in magic and wonders among large groups of people, but among learned writers the idea began to have less and less weight. This transition had a decided effect on the discussion of the miraculous. The Anglican divine William Fleetwood, for example, writing in 1701, argued that God alone could author miracles. The devil was unable to perform them; accordingly, a sober and prudent observer could easily distinguish between a true miracle and a false one. As a result of this reconceptualization, Catholic miracle stories began to be viewed more as the product of superstition and ignorance than of diabolical action.[25]

Not only were demons falling out of favor, but so too was special providence. As Francis Bacon had earlier observed, the very idea of a special providence was a subjective category and was difficult to make sense of rationally.

As he noted in *Novum Organum,* "[I]t was a good answer made by that man who, on being shown a picture hanging in a temple of those, who having taken their vows, had escaped shipwreck, was asked whether he did not now recognize the power of the gods. 'But where are the pictures of those who perished after taking their vows?'" An intellectual corollary of this argument would involve a slow shift in apologetical literature away from an emphasis upon special providence in favor of general providence. By the early eighteenth century, even Calvinist theologians such as Samuel Willard placed more emphasis on God's concurrence with nature than upon his interventions. The idea of special providence always found a place among theologians and preachers, but the lament of John Wesley at the end of the next century — "The doctrine of a particular providence is absolutely out of fashion in England" — was beginning to be evidenced by the early eighteenth century.[26]

Both the deemphasis upon the demonic and the growing emphasis upon general providence were part of a wider late-seventeenth-century trend toward seeing the world as operating in a more orderly and mechanical fashion, and thus as more open to mechanico-scientific models of analysis. Whether this trend was uniquely advanced by English-speaking Protestants has been a subject of great debate, but many of these Protestants came to view a limited and distinct age of miracles as crucial in reconciling the reality of biblical miracles with the idea of a world governed by law.[27]

All of these trends called for a new reinterpretation of the meaning of miracles. One sees elements of a new approach to the miraculous in the writings of the Dutch jurist and theologian Hugo Grotius. His *De Veritate Religionis Christianae* offered a rational defense of Christian revelation and emphasized greatly the role of miracles. As he explained, nothing ensured the testimony of divine providence as well as did miracles and prophecy; religions that did not possess them either died away (as in the case of the religions of antiquity) or had to be maintained by force (such as Islam). Miracles were necessary to persuade the first generation to accept the claims of Jesus. For Grotius, the apostles were like solid Dutch burghers, who approached religion with common sense. They embraced Jesus because "by diligent inquisition, such as becomes *prudent men in business of the greatest concernment,* they had found the same was true and verified by sufficient witnesses, which was spread abroad of his miraculous works." Like solid merchants, their prudential faith was only given upon the evidence of miracles. Grotius's use of the category of rational persuasion would echo throughout the discussion of miracles for centuries. It was a particularly appealing image to a society emphasizing prudence and persuasion. But for Grotius the role of miracles was also circumscribed. Miracles occurred only to establish the claims of religion (such as with Moses or

Jesus), or at times when the very existence of true religion was being challenged (such as in the time of Elijah). The universe of Grotius was rational and orderly, and its very orderliness highlighted the evidential value of a miracle.[28]

The theme of the persuasive nature of miracles was also taken up by John Locke. Both in his *Essay Concerning Human Understanding* and more particularly in his posthumous *Discourse on Miracles*, Locke suggested that miracles served to persuade individuals that someone was a messenger from God. "To know that any revelation is from God, it is necessary to know that the messenger that delivers it is sent from God, and that cannot be known but by some credential given him by God himself," he explained. Unlike rational religion, which could be known rationally, revealed religion rested upon evidence, and for Locke miracles were a crucial part of this evidence. As he wrote, "This is the proper case of *miracles,* which . . . do not only find credit themselves, but give it also to other truths, which need such confirmation."[29]

In his *Discourse* Locke also turned to the question of competing miracle claims. What if two competing revelations were each supported by miracles? The rational believer, he explained, would have no problem adjudicating such competing miracle claims, because true miracles would have surer evidence and the message they were associated with would be of a greater concern. Locke's confidence in classifying miracles was undoubtedly made easier by his curt dismissal of claims to miracles in other religions. "For what the Persees say of their Zoroaster, or the Indians of their Brama (not to mention the wild stories of the religions farther east) is so obscure, or so manifestly fabulous, that no account can be made of it."[30]

But if Locke's contemporaries were little concerned with the challenge posed by non-Christian miracles to the biblical events, they were keenly aware of the issue of modern miracles within the Christian faith. The wonders appearing among the persecuted religious communities of France — first among the Camisards as recorded in Francois Misson's *A Cry from the Desert: Or Testimonials of the Miraculous Things Lately Come to Pass in the Cevennes* (1707) and later among the Jansenists as recorded in Louise Basile Carre de Montgeron's *La Verité des Miracles Opéras à L'Intercession de M. de Paris* (1737) — became a key weapon in the Deist critique of biblical miracles. A Deist such as Thomas Chubb could argue that the miracle accounts of the Camisards were more probable and based on better evidence than those of the New Testament, and that this fact militated against the credibility of any miracle claim. As Peter Annet dryly observed, "The miracles of one party are never owned by another."[31]

Defenders of biblical miracles were forced to address the claims of the French miracles, and in their writings one sees how far the discussion of postbiblical miracles had evolved since the time of Increase Mather. The stories coming out of France were dismissed as superstitious, based on flimsy evidence, and as representing in all likelihood the product of benighted imaginations, but they were almost never condemned as diabolical. Whereas Mather could admit to the reality of Catholic miracles while condemning them, eighteenth-century writers had to refute their very existence, and to do this they were forced to rely upon rational and skeptical grounds.[32]

Locke would make one other mark on the debate over miracles. The Protestant position had never been clear concerning when the age of miracles had ended. Even if miracles had been performed to secure the gospel, when was the gospel secured? For a variety of reasons, defenders of the established Church of England desired to see the age of miracles continue through the early centuries of the Christian era. Part of the Anglican apologetic against both Rome and Geneva lay in an appeal to the sub-apostolic church. Writers such as Ignatius of Antioch, Irenaeus, and Polycarp testified to the importance of episcopacy. They also recorded miracles and acts of wonder. To undermine their testimony concerning the latter was to implicitly threaten their value as defenders of the episcopacy. Likewise many Anglicans (particularly High Church Anglicans) held a view of church history that saw the early centuries as a golden age in which the nature of the true church could be found. This golden age for them began to erode in the fourth century with the growing power of the bishop of Rome. Hence High Church Anglicans tended to distinguish between the miracles of the second and third centuries, which they accepted, and later ones, which they rejected.

This theological issue became entangled in politics by the 1690s. Should alternative forms of Christianity be legally tolerated in England? Certainly not, argued some High Church divines. In order for truth to prevail, Jonas Proast argued, it needed external support. During the early centuries this support took the form of miracles, which served to identify the true church. Miracles were an essential part of the divine dispensation until the legal establishment of Christianity under Constantine, when they passed away as no longer necessary. But at no point, according to this view, would God allow the church to be without signs of authority.[33]

Locke, who had argued for toleration in two previous letters, turned in his *Third Letter for Toleration* to the question of post-apostolic miracles. Proast's view of the early expansion of the church, he argued, was fundamentally wrong. The vast majority of converts during those years never witnessed any miracles. They were instead converted through the preaching of the apostolic witness, or "miracles at a distance." As Locke went on to explain, the situation of the early centuries was much like that of later eras. Persons in the early church had the witness of the apostles concerning the miracles of Jesus, and that alone persuaded them to believe. The pre-Constantinian church expanded without either miracles or the authority of law. The implications for religious toleration need not concern us, but what is important is that the political issues of his day led Locke to dismiss any appeal to postbiblical miracles. "He who will build his faith or reasonings upon miracles delivered by church-historians, will find cause to go no farther than the apostles [*sic*] time, or else not stop at Constantine's." No rational line could be drawn on the question of the miraculous except at the juncture of the biblical and postbiblical.[34]

The attempt to demarcate an absolute line between biblical and all postbiblical miracles was even more boldly drawn fifty years later by Conyers Middleton in *A Free Inquiry into the Miraculous Powers* (1749). Middleton's volume was a fundamental assault on the credibility of all postbiblical miracles, and it rested upon both a distaste for Catholic miracles long present within English-speaking Protestantism and an Enlightenment skepticism of the miraculous. Rather than seeing figures such as Clement, Ignatius, and Polycarp as either godly or sober, he dismissed them as benighted: "The ancient Fathers . . . were extremely credulous and superstitious; possessed with strong prejudices and an enthusiastic zeal, in favor, not onely of Christianity in general, but of every particular doctrine, which a wild imagination could ingraft upon it; and scrupling no art or means, by which they might propagate the same principles."[35]

As this quotation implies (and as biographical studies of Middleton confirm), key to the author's agenda was a Latitudinarian critique of many of the dogmas of the early centuries.[36] In this way Middleton was at one with a larger trend among eighteenth-century Anglican Latitudinarians to abandon an appeal to the early church in favor of a simple appeal to scripture. Accordingly he was vehemently attacked by High Church contemporaries.[37] But for our purposes Middleton was important neither as a Latitudinarian nor as a crypto-Deist. Rather, by combining Protestant and Enlightenment principles, Middleton pushed the idea of a limited age of miracles to its logical conclusion. In his vision of history there was no gray area in which the sacred merged into the profane; there was no twilight of the supernatural. The line between biblical and postbiblical history was precisely drawn. The biblical world stood as a unique dispensation in history when things occurred that were unimaginable at any other time. Such a view of history, if troubling to some High Church Anglicans, reflected the growing marriage between Protestantism and Enlightenment among many Anglo-American Protestants. As other scholars have noted, by the end of the eighteenth century American reformed Protestants were moving toward a synthesis of Enlightenment presuppositions and Reformed Orthodoxy, in which a radically defined limited age of miracles was to play a central role. Whereas an appeal to early church miracles would be virtually unheard of in early-nineteenth-century American Protestantism, the radical limited age of miracles would become the standard assumption. It is one of the ironies of our story that the writings of Middleton, forged in the crucible of Latitudinarianism and crypto-Deism, would be appealed to by conservative American Protestants 175 years later.[38]

Middleton, like Locke, surrendered the entire history of the sub-apostolic church to Rome. The early church witness was a classic slippery slope leading to Rome. After reading *A Free Inquiry,* some, like the young Edward Gibbon, accepted the logic and embraced Roman Catholicism. If the choice was Rome or a rejection of the early church, Gibbon explained, he had to choose the former, because "I still revered the character . . . of the saints and fathers whom Dr. Middleton exposes; nor could he destroy my implicit belief, that the gift of miraculous powers was continued in the church, during the first four centuries of Christianity." Gibbon's attraction to Rome was brief, and he is better remembered for his caustic interpretation of Christianity in his *Decline and Fall of the Roman Empire,* in which he delighted in highlighting the credulities and superstitions of the early church. Yet even here the question of the postapostolic miracles could not be ignored, and as a historian he readily admitted to the quality of evidence for the tongueless African confessors.[39]

The idea of a radically limited age of miracles, and the marriage of Protestantism and the Enlightenment that it reflected rested, however, on a precarious base, namely the willingness to distinguish between the plausibility of biblical events and that of nonbiblical events. It was precisely this point that David Hume challenged in his famous discussion of miracles in his *Inquiry Concerning Human Understanding* (1748). As is well known, Hume's essay has two parts. In the first he argues against miracles from probability. Because miracles were violations of a law of nature established by the "uniform experience" of humanity, he explained, no testimony is ever sufficient to establish a miracle "unless the testimony be of such a kind that its falsehood would be more miraculous than the fact which it endeavors to establish." It is his second argument, however, that is more important for our purposes. In order to illustrate his assertion about the improbability of miracles, Hume proceeded to put the Protestant argument for a limited age of miracles on its head. He offered three postbiblical miracle stories: healings associated with the Roman emperor Vespasian, the regeneration of the leg of the doorkeeper of the cathedral of Sargossa (Spain), and healings associated with the tomb of the Jansenist Abbé Pâris in early-eighteenth-century France. Middleton had also appealed to the case of Abbé Pâris, for it was widely discussed in eighteenth-century England; but he had used it to discredit the claims of postbiblical miracles.

Hume, however, argued that the "evidences and authority" of the accounts of the French miracles surpassed that of any biblical miracle. The evidence was particularly impressive because it included testimony from some Jesuit authorities who were the arch enemies of the Jansenists. Hume's implication was clear: if the better attested postbiblical miracles were to be rejected, then the biblical ones should be jettisoned.[40]

Hume's argument provoked a number of responses that recognized the weight of both his historical argument and his philosophical one. Just as earlier writers had done with the similar Deist criticism, Protestant critics of Hume used Protestant-Enlightenment categories to refute Hume's historical arguments—in particular, the miracles of the Abbé Pâris, which were recognized as being the weightiest. In their responses one encounters an attitude of skepticism that would often be directed against the healings of Jesus in the next century. As the Baptist John Leland wrote, the Jansenist miracles had little in common with biblical miracles. At best all they could offer were healings and "miraculous cures, which alone considered are the most uncertain and equivocal of all miracles. Diseases have often been surprisingly cured without anything that can properly be called miraculous in the case." Just because the cure was remarkable and inexplicable, it was not necessarily a miracle.[41]

One of the most systematic (and popular) defenses of the biblical miracles was offered by William Paley in his *View of the Evidences of Christianity* (1794). Paley's volume was in keeping with the general thrust of Enlightenment Protestantism. He invoked a metaphor that had been often used by eighteenth-century apologists: The evidence for Christianity must be evaluated in the same manner as any court would evaluate evidence. The apostles were the chief witnesses of the resurrection, and as men of common sense they were sober and sure witnesses.

Paley next attempted to defend the uniqueness of the miracles of Jesus. He had little interest in the older Anglican concern for defending the miracles of the sub-apostolic church. Rather he attempted to establish a rationale for determining true and false testimonies concerning miracles that would affirm biblical miracles and invalidate all others. Any valid miraculous event, he contended, had to be attested to by witnesses of a high moral character who were close to the event in both time and place. Furthermore, a testimony was considered more certain if it involved an unwavering assent to the claim, such as a willingness to undergo suffering in maintaining it. The apostles' willingness to die for their belief in the resurrection thus gave to their testimonies a strong credence. Paley also attempted to purge from any consideration of miracles all cases that might be seen as simply relative or subjective in their nature. He excluded from consideration, for example, all "visions and voices" and all cures that might have their root in "hypochondrial and nervous complaints." He explained, "I have not mentioned claims to inspiration, illuminations, . . . internal sensations or consciousness of being acted upon by spiritual influences, good or bad; because these, appealing to no external proof . . . form no part of what can be accounted miraculous evidence." By these criteria the gospel miracles, resting upon the testimony of the apostles, were clearly superior to all other alleged miracles, including those offered by Hume. Yet even Paley was forced to admit that the evidence for the miracles of Abbé Pâris was very strong and could also meet these standards. As a loyal Protestant he rejected them, yet the only grounds he could offer for their rejection was that they were not "unequivocal."[42]

Paley's *Evidences* was a key part of the late-eighteenth-century apologetical defense of Christianity, and along with his equally famous *Natural Theology* became one of the standard volumes for Protestant divines. In America, William Ellery Channing referred to the work as an inestimable "classic"; in England, it was required reading at Cambridge until the end of the nineteenth century.[43] In important ways Paley's two works paralleled each other. Miracles affirmed the truth of scripture just as the order and beneficence of nature affirmed God as its creator. Both sets of evidences served to persuade the modern individual of the reasonability and truthfulness of both natural and revealed religion. Both works, one should also note, depended upon the Protestant view of the limited age of miracles. For Paley, God's love and goodness was demonstrated through general providence — the laws by which the world was governed — and not through any special providences, as had been so important for Mather. Happy shrimp and juicy peaches (to mention two of his most famous examples) bespoke the glory and beneficence of God, rather than dramatic or providential answers to prayer. Similarly it was precisely because Paley's natural universe was so orderly and purged of miracles that the miracles of Jesus stood out as such clear evidence of his authority.

It is hard to overestimate the importance of this twofold apologetic, both in refuting Deists and Free Thinkers and in providing the intellectual substance of what is still generally called in America the Second Great Awakening.[44] American Evangelicals and Unitarians, in spite of their differences on other issues, could unite on the question of the evidential value of miracles. From the pulpit of Yale College, Timothy Dwight could instruct his students, "A miracle becomes a proof of the character, or doctrine, of him by whom it was wrought." From a very different pulpit the Unitarian William Ellery Channing dedicated his 1821 Dudleian Lecture to a defense of the miraculous. For Channing, Christianity was inconceivable without the miraculous. "Christianity is not only confirmed by miracles, but is in itself, in its very essence, a miraculous religion. . . . Its doctrines, especially those which relate to its founder, claim for it the distinction of being a supernatural provision for the recovery of the human race." The Episcopalian Charles P. McIlvaine put the case even more simply. Jesus appeared as the ambassador of God, but "before we can be justified in receiving those communications as a divine revelation, we must know the credentials of the ambassador." His miracles were a crucial part of his credentials. Throughout Anglo-American evangelical culture during the early years of the nineteenth century, wherever the battle against Deism and skepticism was fought, there was an appeal to the evidence of miracles.[45]

The concept of miracles, however, continued to pose another problem. How could God be the supreme architect and governor, yet suspend his own perfect laws in the doing of miracles? Did God, like Homer, occasionally nod? One writer who attempted to answer this question was the mathematician Charles Babbage, in his *Ninth Bridgewater Treatise*. The *Bridgewater Treatises* had been published during the 1830s to elucidate aspects of the "power, wisdom, and goodness of God, as manifested in Creation." The problem of miracles was not part of the general plan of the series, but Babbage, who had recently invented a "calculating engine" (an early computer) offered in his treatise a scientific defense of miracles. He argued that miracles were not violations of the laws of nature, but were rather preprogrammed variations. As he explained, it was possible to program his calculating engine "so that it shall calculate any *algebraic law whatever*: and also possible so to arrange it, that at any periods, *however remote*, the first law shall be interrupted for one or more times, and be superseded *by any other law*; after which the original law shall again be produced, and no other deviation shall ever take place." In his view, God programmed miracles into nature with similar skill. Furthermore Babbage also employed his "calculating engine" to test the validity of Hume's skepticism about human testimonies concerning miracles, and showed through elaborate algebraic tables that there was greater possibility that Jesus rose from the dead than that six eye witnesses could all be mistaken. Thus, he declared, the resurrection could be evaluated scientifically. Babbage would not be the last person to attempt to solve with cutting-edge technology those problems that had stymied mere historians and theologians.[46]

But a closer look at the religious temper suggests that all was not well with the Protestant position. As early as 1801 William Emerson, father of Ralph Waldo, complained that "the age of miracles has passed away" leaving the ministry without those supernatural gifts it had once enjoyed. Across the Atlantic the father of Frederick Temple, the future contributor to *Essays and Reviews* and Archbishop of Canterbury, although a loyal churchman, admitted private doubts about the miraculous.[47] Furthermore, if private doubts were occasionally recorded, far more public were the troublesome reports of modern wonders. In Britain the religious movement associated with Edward Irving involved the apparent reappearance of the long-dormant supernatural gifts. These attracted the attention of many, including the Scottish theologian Thomas Erskine, and were avidly discussed on both sides of the Atlantic.[48] In America, the new religious movement of Joseph Smith also claimed a revival of the gift of healing. Although both movements and their claims of miracles were largely rejected by Protestant commentators, they nonetheless raised anew the sufficiency of the schema of history that posited a prescribed age of miracles.[49]

A Controversy in Massachusetts

The question of miracles, however, emerged as a full-blown controversy in the English-speaking world not in Old England, where it had been debated for a century, but in New England, where it surfaced as one of the crucial parts of the Transcendentalist controversy. During the late 1830s, Unitarians and Transcendentalists battled over the meaning and reality of miracles. Upon reflection it is hardly surprising that it was in this community that the first conflict emerged. Boston Unitarians were perhaps the American religious community most dedicated to the Enlightenment Protestant emphasis upon the evidential quality of miracles.[50] The writings of Locke, Paley, and other British proponents of Enlightenment Protestantism composed key parts of their intellectual canon. Furthermore, by the 1830s the liberal view of the inspiration of scripture held by many Unitarians ironically wedded them even more closely to the evidentialist value of miracles. Andrews Norton, for example, in his *Evidences of the Genuineness of the Gospels,* readily dismissed any doctrine of biblical inerrancy and acknowledged that even the gospels contained interpolations. According to this perspective, the Bible was not an infallible book, and was not self-authenticating. Instead, the authority of the Bible stemmed from the true and reliable account of the revelation of God, and in particular its account of Jesus, the man sent from God. For Norton the miracle stories were an essential part of this picture. "Any account of our Saviour, upon the supposition that he was not a teacher from God endued with miraculous powers, must be almost wholly conjectural." Having rejected the idea of textual inerrancy, he rested the authority of the Bible upon the accuracy and veracity of its contents, and this included the miracle stories.[51]

In contrast, the young Transcendentalists such as George Ripley, Orestes Brownson, and in particular Theodore Parker were embracing intellectual trends that would find fault. both philosophically and exegetically, with the Enlightenment Protestant view of miracles. As eager devotees of the new philosophical themes being sounded by European Romantics, they found the views of God and nature upon which the idea of the miraculous rested sterile and cold. Like English Romantics such as Samuel Taylor Coleridge, they saw the power of religion as appealing directly to the intuitive Reason and had little patience with appeals to "evidence." Furthermore, they — and particularly Parker — followed the new approach to biblical interpretation coming out of Germany that challenged the approach of scholars such as Norton.[52]

The story of the Transcendentalist debate over miracles has been told often, and the details of the narrative need not concern us here.[53] But the content of the criticism, particularly as reflected in the thought of Parker and Ralph Waldo Emerson, is important because it rested upon a number of assumptions that dealt a critical blow to the idea of a limited miraculous dispensation. Conflicting views of God, humanity, religion, and history lay behind the debate over miracles.

What was wrong with the accepted view of miracles? What was right with it? countered Emerson, in his famous Divinity School Address. "[Jesus Christ] spoke of miracles; for he felt man's life was a miracle, and all that man doth, and he knew that this daily miracle shines, as the character ascends. But the word Miracle, as pronounced by Christian churches, gives a false impression; it is a Monster. It is not one with the blowing clover and the flowing rain." Like other Romantics, Transcendentalists rejected the idea of a watchmaker God· who designed nature but was present in it only secondarily in form and design. As Emerson noted in the same famous sermon, when we view nature correctly we see that "one mind is everywhere active, in each ray of the star, in each wavelet of the pool." Rightly understood, God was not an architect who occasionally repaired his creation; rather he was at one with all that existed. The miracle as it was commonly understood was a "monster" because it presupposed an absence of God from the world.[54]

Likewise the Transcendentalist critique focused upon the view of humanity assumed in the evidentialist interpretation of miracles. As an empiricist, John Locke had posited a mental tabula rasa as the fundamental human consciousness. External sense impressions affected the mind and formed ideas. As others have noted, there was a connection between his view of psychology and his emphasis on miracles. The evidence of miracles inclined the mind to accept ideas that it otherwise could not discover or recognize. The Transcendentalists, in rejecting Lockean psychology, also revolted against the Lockean view of the function of miracles. They argued that the mind possessed a creative and spiritual function and that the human sense of dependence, for example, led to an intuitive awareness of the presence of God. "The knowledge of God's existence," explained Theodore Parker, "may be called in the language of philosophy, an intuition of REASON, or in the mythical language of the elder theology, a REVELATION FROM GOD." The intuition of Reason was the true revelation of God. Because the human mind was always open to things spiritual, the older idea of a division between nature and supernature had to be rejected. The metaphysics of the old supernaturalism had taught that human beings were helpless in their efforts to understand religious truth without the help of miracles. They deny "that by natural action there can be any thing in man which was not first in the senses; whatever transcends the senses can come to him only by a miracle." The idea that God had to convince human beings of truth by means of miraculous evidence was furthermore monstrous in its implications concerning human nature. It assumed that human beings had no power within themselves to recognize moral and religious truth, or that humans knew that there was a "God, and a distinction between right and wrong only by hearsay, as they know there was a flood in the time of Noah." If Christianity were true, then its truth stood independent of all evidences, even the person of Jesus. As Parker explained: "The good life of a teacher proves nothing of any speculative doctrine he entertains, either in morals or mathematics. A man would be thought insane who should say Euclid's demonstration of the forty-seventh problem was true, because Euclid lived a good life, and raised men from the dead; or that it was false, because he lived a bad life, and murdered his mother. If Christianity be the absolute, it is independent of all circumstances; eternally true, as much before its declaration as after it is brought to light and applied to life." True religion needed no miraculous evidences to convince human beings to accept it.[55]

In his *Discourse,* Parker divided the religious world into three parts: the "Naturalism" of the Deists, the "Supernaturalism" of traditional Christians, and his own Transcendental "Spiritualism." Although critical of both of the first two, he poured perhaps the greatest scorn on those Supernaturalists who argued that the age of miracles was over. Not only did they, like other Supernaturalists, picture human beings as senseless clods until instructed by miracles, they believed that miracles had ceased. They removed God from the world and banished him to a remote age. The present generation was to have no sense of the presence of God in the world: they were to rely instead upon past relics of the divine presence. According to this view, scoffed Parker, those of the nineteenth century have been "born in the latter days and dotage of mankind, and can only get light, by raking amid the ashes of the past, and blowing its brands, now almost extinct." The Protestant understanding of miracles had made God absent from the world, and this effect lay behind the crisis of faith among modern believers. Even the venerable Protestant idea of providence was receding. "The modern notion of special providence, wherein God acts without law or against law, is the most spiritual and attenuated form of the doctrine of miracles, the last glimmering of the candle before it goes out" explained Parker. The presence of God was being lost to the modern world, and the theology of miracles was in large part to blame.[56]

From one perspective the rhetoric of the Transcendentalists, although more boldly stated, is in keeping with the old Augustinian emphasis that miracles were an issue of perspective — that a godly person would see the hand of the divine as much in the natural processes of fermentation as in the miracle at Cana. But clearly Parker, at least, wished to go further. He did not want to reconceptualize biblical miracles, but to replace them with his view of a God-filled nature. Thus he combined his philosophical and religious arguments with a critique of the historical reliability of biblical miracles. He combined elements of Hume's argument about the difficulty of accepting testimony concerning miracles with arguments drawn from German biblical scholars such as W. L. De Wette and D. F. Strauss concerning the weakness of the historical evidences for biblical miracles. Legendary miracles were so interwoven into the narratives that they could provide no historical evidence for any alleged supernatural event. Finally, like earlier writers, Parker contrasted the weakness of the historical evidence for biblical miracles with the better evidence of postbiblical miracles. He particularly relished twitting his Protestant audience by noting that the historical case for the long-despised medieval ecclesiastical miracles was stronger than for those of Jesus: "I do not hesitate in saying that there is far more evidence to support the miracles of St. Bernard than those mentioned in the New Testament." Indeed, he went on, there was more evidence for the "wonders of the invisible world" that had so fascinated their Puritan forebears than there was for biblical miracles.[57]

In the final analysis, Parker's criticism of the miraculous was connected with his concern to identify the best of Christianity with "universal religion." An appeal to miracles was part of the infancy of all religions, or to the age of "fetichism" when human beings only dimly understood God and nature; it must give way in the present. Yet always for Parker the miracles of Jesus were troublesome not only because they were mere fetiches, but because they were an annoying reminder of the particularity of historic Christianity. They inevitably pointed again to the biblical question, "What manner of man is this?" The miracles of Jesus were one of the two pillars (along with the judgment of God) upon which the idea of a supernatural Christianity rested. Together they were the "Jachin and Boaz" of the theology, and both had to be replaced.[58] It was over this question of the distinctiveness of Christianity that the "Second

Unitarian Controversy," in which the Boston Unitarian community distanced itself from Parker's radicalism, was fought. Indeed the ire was so strong that as Parker lay dying in Florence, Italy, the alumni of Harvard Divinity School voted down a motion to convey sympathy.

The Transcendentalists' challenge to traditional Christianity was answered by many writers, but perhaps most famously by Andrews Norton. In *A Discourse on the Latest Form of Infidelity,* Norton took aim both at the Transcendentalist attempt to bring together God and nature as well as their disparagement of miracles. "The denial of the possibility of miracles," he argued, "must involve the denial of the existence of God, since if there be a God, in the proper sense of the word, there can be no room for doubt, that he may act in a manner different from that in which he displays his power in the ordinary operations of nature." Because God was rational, the world was ordered and regular. Because he was personal, there were miracles. And because Jesus was from God, he was the author of miracles. Upon these three principles Enlightened Christianity rested. All three worked together to support a confidence in the reality of the Protestant Christian faith. To abandon these principles was to lose the force of Christianity. In another place Norton spoke darkly of forces at war with these principles. Catholicizing trends associated with the Oxford movement were surfacing and "many of the clergy . . . have turned about and are travelling back into the dark region of implicit faith, Jesuitical morality, and religious formalities." In other places, "speculists . . . have abandoned religion itself, and whose only substitute for it [religion] . . . is an unsubstantial spectre which they have decorated with its titles." Still others had rejected Christianity as a system of truth all together and reduced it to a mere "system" that was "useful to the community." True religion, Norton insisted, had to have a rational and firm base. "The convictions which rest on reason are of very different efficacy from the impressions produced through prejudice, imagination, or passion," he explained. Such a faith had to rest on miraculous evidence.[59]

Despite the vigor of the intra-Unitarian debate, in the short run the Transcendentalist critique of the miraculous did little to shake the beliefs of other communities in the reality of the miracles of scripture.[60] This should not be surprising. The old understanding of the miraculous, resting as it did on the limited age of miracles, was not yet seen to be in crisis. Few members of the Christian communities perceived any threat to the reality of miracles from either science or history. It would not be until after mid-century that such a threat would emerge. And as I shall suggest in subsequent chapters, later writers, even while admitting to the need to reconceptualize the idea of the miraculous, took far more care than did Parker to preserve the authority of the gospels and the person of Jesus. In this sense the Transcendentalist debate over the miraculous was a "tempest in a Boston teacup."[61]

Summary

Although the preceding survey simplifies and foreshortens what is a far more complicated question, it provides a historical context for the discussion that emerged by the 1860s. As we have seen, the idea of a limited age of miracles emerged at the time of the Reformation as a key element in the Protestant anti-Catholic apologetic. By the eighteenth century, though its anti-Catholic function continued, the concept had been modified significantly to meet the needs of Enlightenment Protestantism. First, the age of miracles was circumscribed and became reduced to the era of the apostles. Second, the function of miracles was seen as persuading the first generation of the truth of the claims of Jesus. Among later generations, miracles still had authority and served as evidence of the truthfulness of revelation in much the same way that the course of nature was seen to demonstrate the order and goodness of God. By the early nineteenth century, the idea of a limited age of miracles served to reconcile a continuing emphasis upon the importance of the biblical miracles with an acceptance of an orderly and rational universe. As such it served as a central part of the Protestant apologetical arsenal.

But the entire Protestant discussion of the miraculous rested precariously upon a willingness to divide history into a biblical epoch and a postbiblical epoch, each having distinctly different rules of evidence and probability. It was this final assumption that was to give way after mid-century. Its demise would not only lead to a reevaluation of the evidential quality of biblical miracles, but would also eventually open anew the question of the validity of postbiblical miracles.

The Rise of the New Debate over Miracles

According to the details of the will of John Bampton, lectures (or more properly, sermons) were to be delivered each spring on certain prescribed topics of Christian divinity at St. Mary's Church for the benefit of the entire Oxford community. For the year 1865 the Rev. James B. Mozley had been chosen as the Bampton lecturer. Mozley, whose fame (if any) now rests upon his associations with his tutor and brother-in-law John Henry Newman, was then viewed as one of the highly respected theological voices of the Church of England. His topic was to be miracles. Mozley recognized, however, that his would not be an easy task because, as he explained to his longtime friend R. W. Church, "the difficulty is in dealing with something so informal and unexpressed and indefinite, as what constitutes the real objection to miracles in doubting minds. The *formal logical answers* have been given over and over again, and with great force, but the minds whom they intended to convince do not care the least about them." He concluded, however, that he would try to say something new.[1]

To begin a discussion of the "new" debate over miracles with Mozley's Bampton Lectures may strike the modern reader as odd or quixotic. His tome is now seldom if ever read, and in the few theological surveys of the period he is routinely dismissed.[2] Yet Mozley's lectures are a bridge between the old and new debates. Not only in his discussion of the miraculous but more particularly in the controversy that his book provoked, one can observe some of the developing dynamics that characterized the new debate.

New Challenges to the Old Position

Lying behind Mozley's studied prose lurked an awareness that the inherited Protestant position on miracles was being challenged by critics on a number of fronts, and that the nature of these challenges must be discussed, albeit briefly. This challenge was evidenced most dramatically in the increasing willingness by many to question the miracles of scripture. Thirty years earlier D. F. Strauss had published his *Life of Jesus,* the English translation of which, as Owen Chadwick has observed, can be seen as launching the modern divinity debate within England. Likewise in 1863 there appeared an English translation of Ernest Renan's *Vie de Jésus,* with its evocative description of a nonmiraculous Jesus. Even closer to home and of more immediate importance was the 1860 publication of the collection *Essays and Reviews,* and in particular Baden Powell's contribution "On the Study of the Evidences of Christianity." *Essays and Reviews* is usually considered by historians of biblical studies as representing the first stirrings of the new critical spirit in British scriptural studies.[3] The essays treated the whole gamut of issues then troubling English religious divines. But Powell's was the most radical and threatening to the Protestant miracle argument in particular and to the established religio-intellectual order more generally. Indeed only Powell's untimely death in 1860 prevented his greater fame as well as a probable charge of heresy.

Powell, Savilian Professor of Geometry at Oxford, launched a direct attack upon the century-old belief by English-speaking Protestants that miracles are the chief foundational evidence and pearl of great price of Christian authority. His essay offered both a critical survey of the earlier debate and a new understanding of the true nature of Christian evidence. Every discussion of evidence, he observed, was tied to the historical assumptions of the age that produced it. In the early church, for example, the validity of a piece of evidence was tied to "prevalent modes of thought" — that is, philosophical and theological assumptions — rather than to any strict investigation of the alleged facts. During the Middle Ages, questions of evidence were overshadowed by the greater claims for an infallible church; and during the preceding century, during which Paley "reigned supreme, the acknowledged champion of revelation," the overarching concern was the differentiation between biblical miracles and later ecclesiastical ones. There was no one absolute and unchanging criterion for evaluating Christian evidences. The modern generation, hence, had to confront the fact that the age of Paley was over. In one sense the great question confronting nineteenth-century believers was not Deism versus Jesuitism (as it had been during the previous century) but rather how to determine the true place of divine activity in the laws of nature. "In an age of physical research like the present," Powell explained, "all highly cultivated minds and duly advanced intellects have imbibed . . . the lessons of the inductive philosophy, and have, at least in some measure, learned to appreciate the grand foundation conception of universal law."[4] All educated individuals recognized the persuasive power of reasoning inductively from the natural order of things, and accordingly no alleged evidence of historical or physical accounts could any longer be automatically accepted as was the case in earlier times. One might recall that the locus of the debate between David Hume and opponents such as Paley had been the comparative value of laws of nature and of testimonies concerning exceptions to these laws. Paley had offered his famous appeal to his twelve witnesses of character in order to defend the veracity of miracles attested to by apostolic testimony. The advance of the knowledge of nature that had occurred since Hume's argument, Powell implied, had clearly shifted presumption in favor of law and away from testimony. A knowledge of the natural world had already led intelligent individuals to reject out of hand claims for modern miracles (and here he alluded to the pointed rejection of Irvingite miracles). Should it not also affect one's evaluation of the historical claims of the Bible as well? "The enlarged critical and inductive study of the natural world," he argued, "cannot but tend powerfully to evince the inconceivableness of imagined interruptions of natural order or supposed suspensions of the laws of matter."[5]

According to Powell, modern believers must seek for evidence of the divine in the moral realm rather than the physical. By relocating the search for evidences of the divine away from the realm of the physical, religion and science would no longer be in conflict. "It was formerly argued that every Theist must admit the credibility of miracles," Powell wrote, "but this, it is now seen, depends upon the nature and degree of his Theism, which may vary through many shades of opinion."[6] In support of his claim, Powell appealed to the "highest spiritual purity" of the American Transcendentalists Ralph Waldo Emerson and Theodore Parker, in addition to his own countrymen F. W. Newman and John Sterling. What the age called for, he concluded, was not external evidences and authorities but moral authority.

Arguably many of the ideas and themes of "On the Study of the Evidences of Christianity" are not original, and the modern scholarly reader can hear echoed in Powell's prose arguments that originated not only in Hume but in Spinoza and the English Deists. But Powell's status as a clergyman of the established church, his familial connection with a respected high church family, and his earlier close association with such proponents of the old natural theology as Archbishop Richard Whately all contributed to the scandal surrounding its publication. And its presence in the eyebrow-raising *Essays and Reviews* assured that his challenges to the traditional argument would be placed on the agenda of future apologists. No future writer on miracles could ignore the threat to miracles posed by inductive reasoning.

Nor could scholars ignore Powell's second criticism: that physical evidences were not only philosophically untenable but religiously gauche. What indeed was the purpose of miracles? Here we should note the role of Emerson and Parker in Powell's justification of a miracle-free Christianity. The American Unitarian and Transcendentalist critique of traditional Christian teachings was well known in British circles, and others have noted the role played by New England opinions in forging liberal Anglican religious thought.[7] Indeed Powell's reliance upon Emerson and Channing reflects a curious fact about the interrelationship of the Atlantic intellectual community. Just as American novelists were all too familiar with the necessity of gaining a reputation in Britain as a precursor to success in their native land, so too were American religious scholars well aware of their British audiences. American Protestants were often more influenced by New England critical ideas mirrored through England than by any direct contact with them. The Atlantic would be an intellectual neighborhood with all different patterns of criss-crossings.

If Powell offered a critique of the subject of miracles from the left, many were challenging the Protestant compromise from other directions. Was the age of miraculous occurrences indeed limited solely to the biblical era? As we have noted, during the 1830s Edward Irving and his followers had caused great consternation in the religious public with their claim to possess the gift of miraculous tongues, and the Irvingites were still a point of discussion thirty years later.[8] Similarly during the early 1860s the popular press of England was alight with stories and accounts of proponents of Spiritualism and their belief that the heavens were no longer silent.[9] Indeed, some writers claimed that Spiritualist evidences could be used to defend Christianity from the skepticism of Baden Powell.[10] Nor could Mozley ignore his family connection to the miracle debate. In 1843, while still trying to cling to his inherited Anglicanism, Mozley's brother-in-law John Henry Newman published his *Essay on Ecclesiastical Miracles,* raising anew the question of post-biblical miracles. Must we not take seriously, Newman argued, the evidence for these later miracles?[11] For Newman this was not merely a theoretical question, and in the *Lives of the English Saints,* which he and his compatriots at Littlemore wrote, miracle stories played a significant role. Mozley was aware that for some these stories were part of the path to Rome, yet for others the talk of such topics as the wonders of St. Anthony had the reverse affect, and in a case like that of James Anthony Froude drove them away from traditional Christianity all together.[12]

Finally there were those who rejected the old arguments not in the name of science or Catholicism, but because of the new study of comparative religions. Since the late 1840s Friedrich Max Müller had been on the scene in Oxford, arguing that one must study religions from a comparative perspective.[13] As knowledge of other religions began to accumulate, the question of the relationship between Christian miracle claims and those found in other religions became more pointed.

Defending Miracles at Oxford

All of these factors provided the context for Mozley's Bampton Lectures of 1865 and are reflected in some of the themes he chose to emphasize. In part the lectures, when viewed as a single work, do cleave closely to the older Protestant argument that Christianity to be believed had to be proved, and that the testimony of miracles provided this proof. On this level, "the book is the last statement, by a great English Protestant theologian, of a world of divinity which henceforth vanished . . . it is a watershed in Christian thought. . . . No divine of the first rank could ever argue the case as Mozley argued."[14] In contrast to the position found in Powell, Mozley asserted that proof was necessary because of the very nature of a revealed religion. Revelation offered the world new knowledge, and this knowledge could only be appropriated as a gift. But such was the gap separating God as he truly was and the human understanding of him, that not only were divine truths undiscoverable by human reason (hence the necessity for their revelation), but they could not even be affirmed or validated by unaided human reason. Human reason lacked the capacity for recognizing intuitively the revealed nature of spiritual truth. Throughout human history the question had always been from whence came the authority for a claim, and for Mozley this authority lay in miracles.

Miracles were by no means the only way, nor even the principle way, in which God dealt benevolently with the world. Mozley acknowledged the important role of special providence — of divine intervention in a nonmiraculous way (such as a recovery from sickness). The answering of prayer was a high and loving work of God, but it should not be confused with his working of miracles. In special providences the ultimate cause might indeed be God, but his activity in the chain of causation was either remote or hidden. Such actions were at best "invisible" or partially visible miracles, and as such they were always ultimately subjective. Some might see a divine hand in these actions, whereas others might see only the working out of chance. Hence, in Mozley's view, one must never conflate special providences and miracles. If the former were subjective, the latter had an objective quality. It could indeed be a point of debate or interpretation whether one recovered from illness as a result of prayer or by the workings of nature alone, but such ambiguities vanished when a person rose from the dead.[15]

The authority that miracles offered, he added, was not only objective but also targeted one part of the religious community. The great majority of persons might easily accept a religion on the authority of tradition or sentiment, but a critical few always desired a stronger proof of authority. It was to these critical few, and not to the great majority, explained Mozley, that miracles were addressed. Their witness was a validating credential that persisted from age to age and was always available for study and examination.

Mozley in turn carefully distinguished "authentic" miracles from the alleged miracles of both history and the present. And here the issues of objectivity and certainty also played a key role. Biblical miracles were lodged in an individual person and testified to that person's authority by, among other things, being always successful in achieving their goal. When Jesus in the gospels said, "Rise up and walk," the person ineluctably walked. Such was not the case among the so-called ecclesiastical miracles trumpeted by John Henry Newman. Even defenders of these miracles admitted that there were ambiguities about them. They were not associated strictly with an individual but only generally with classes of individuals (such as the saints), and their results, far from being absolute, were occasional and serendipitous. Whatever these ecclesiastical happenstances might be, they failed to measure up to the expectations for a true miracle. At best they might be special providences, and at worst they were products of the erroneous linking of saintly sanctity and supernaturalism.

Mozley was even more pointed in his criticisms of modern miracles. These modern "marvels" paled in comparison with the great events of scripture, and did not even attempt to measure up. "The system knows what it can do and keeps within a safe line," he explained. "Miraculous cures, vaticinations, visions, exorcisms, compose the current miracles of human history; but these are just the class which is most susceptible of exaggerating colour and interpretation, and most apt to owe its supernatural character to the imaginations of its reporters."[16] He reserved a special ire for the "miracles" of the Spiritualists, because they appeared to be brought about for no high or revelatory reason but for little more than "curiosity and amusement." All in all, Mozley believed, pious believers in miracles need have little fear of critics either from the right or the left.

These are of course traditional positions, and if this were the sum total of Mozley's lectures they would have little import for this study. Within his volume, however, Mozley made three new and important contributions to the miracle argument that combined to nudge the debate away from its carefully worn course.

Mozley's first contribution involved the relation of miracles to both reason and natural law. How could one answer the claim that a knowledge of the laws of nature, grounded in the scientific method of inductive thinking, made a belief in miracles dubious? The inductive principle, he explained, was in actuality tightly circumscribed. Its proper function was the pursuit of individual facts. Unfortunately, the human mind all too often abused the inductive method and attempted to draw from it broad generalizations about the nature of the world. An appeal to a prescriptive law of nature was the most blatant of these generalizations. Such generalizations, however, were inappropriate in Mozley's view, and any reliance upon them in the process of inductive reasoning was an invalid *petitio principii,* which assumed the principle one set out to prove.[17] People were understandably attracted to these generalizations because they made life practical and livable, but "it does not belong to this [inductive] principle to lay down speculative positions, and to say what can or cannot take place in the world."[18] The great weakness of the inductive principle was that it succumbed to the dictates of the imagination. It all too easily could assume that the small corner of reality known through it could prescribe the nature of the unknown. Reason always recognized the tentative quality of inductive reasoning; imagination, in contrast, often became so fixated upon the tangible nature of inductive knowledge that it lost sight of its limitations. The logical culmination of this assumption was materialism ("Materialism itself is the result of imagination, which is so impressed by matter that it cannot realize the existence of spirit").[19] The fixity and regularity of nature might indeed be a psychological necessity for human beings on the practical level, but ultimately no rational account could be given for such a notion; it rested at best upon prejudice, or a "vague, indefinite, expectation." Furthermore, the inductive method always possessed the potential for reverting into a pathology. Indeed, Mozley argued, much of the criticism of miracles that is based on a dogmatic assumption about the regularity of nature is pathological. Our existence in a small segment of nature, of which we have but a limited knowledge, should give us pause before enumerating what was possible and what impossible, not lead us to rush headlong into claims that cannot be rationally justified.

Contemporary commentators recognized that Mozley's arguments ironically bore close parallels with the skepticism of David Hume.[20] In his long appended notes to his lectures, Mozley acknowledged his indebtedness to earlier philosophical discussions.[21] In Mozley's writings, however, the skeptical tradition was turned away from its usual attack upon miracles and directed against their scientific critics.

Mozley's second contribution was to connect explicitly miracles and doctrines to the social power of Christianity. In his view, the witness of the church in history could not be separated from its supernatural foundation. The ethical vision that Jesus set forth, and that by universal consensus had transformed the world, was tied to its authority. As he explained to his friend R. W. Church, "The practical force and success of Christianity has depended on certain motives, which motives have been supplied by certain doctrines, which doctrines could not be proved without miracles."[22] A manifestation of a true miracle gave to a religious community a sense of assurance that was beyond measure. "[A] religion founded on miracles as compared with a religion founded upon evidences of a God in nature, has a much superior motive power in the very fact of its supernatural origin. . . . A supernatural fact, a communication from the other world, is a potent influence; it rouses, it solemnizes; it is a strong motive to serious action."[23] He contrasted (in albeit a typical English Victorian way) the histories of Christianity and Islam. The reality of the resurrection gave to Christian doctrine and social teaching a far greater rigor than that found in Islam. A comparison of Muhammad and Paul showed that the latter was more critical of human sinfulness, yet more optimistic about human potential. A miraculous faith opened for its believers understandings to which natural human intuition was blinded. It was this Christian ethic, according to Mozley, that had transformed the world, whereas the Islamic ethic only confirmed the human predicament.

Mozley's third contribution linked the question of miracles with the larger issues of the nature of God and the possibility of prayer. It was impossible to divorce miracles from the Christian view of God. Nature might display the order of God, but only miracles illumined his personal nature. Their witness possessed a "ghostly force" that nature alone could not have. A miracle "speaks to us of a power out of this order of things, of will, of Moral Being, of Personal Being in another world."[24] The great contribution of miracles to true religion was that they directed the believer past nature to the personal reality beyond it. As such, miracles were intricately entwined with prayer itself. Prayer, as well, connected human beings to the personal, willful, and moral reality of the universe. They both witnessed to a personal God's involvement in the world.

Mozley went on to observe, however, that prayer and miracles were also linked by certain shared problems. From the perspective of the world, both were seen as stumbling blocks. "The primary difficulty of philosophy . . . [in] relating to the deity is action at all." That God might exist or at some primordial time have created the cosmos was an idea not uncongenial to the workings of philosophy, but that God might act and willfully intervene in the world boggled the philosophic imagination. It was for this very reason that the concept of God in the ancient religions was actually far closer to that found in the modern philosophy of the nineteenth century than to that represented in Christianity. As he explained, "The God of ancient religion was either not a personal Being or not an omnipotent Being, the God of modern religion is both."[25] Unaided human knowledge could not conceive of the unity of personality and omnipotence; hence philosophers jettisoned the former for the sake of the latter—but the various religions of the world were forced to choose between them. Biblical revelation united these concepts and displayed God both as the omnipotent creator and sustainer of the world and as a loving parent. Thus, Mozley concluded, the idea of God for modern Christians was ironically more "primitive" and "childlike" than any found in the ancient world. Both the ideas of miraculous intervention and prayer as personal communication presupposed this primitive and childlike idea of God.

Particularly with regard to this last point, one hears in Mozley the echoes of Henry Longueville Mansel, one of the great figures at Oxford of his age, whose 1858 Bampton Lectures had caused a heated discussion that had continued for years.[26] Mansel had argued that Christians, when they talked about God, depended upon the revelation of scripture because human reason could know nothing about God in and of himself. The ambiguity of philosophical language, accordingly, ought to be eschewed by the Christian theologian in favor of the simple and direct language of the Bible. Mansel's thesis is far more involved than this, and Mozley admitted that parts of the argument possessed serious problems, but on the need for maintaining the biblical image of God as a personal Father Mozley was in decided concurrence.[27] Mansel's writing formed the backdrop for Mozley's striking elevation to truth of the "primitive" and "childlike" language of scripture over the categories of philosophy.

We should be careful not to press any case of intellectual causality here. As important as Mansel might be for the Oxford community, much of the appeal of his message was undoubtedly his reaffirmation of the old Pauline theme that the Christian message was a "folly to the Greeks" (1 Cor 1:23) and therefore had to be interpreted by means of its own categories, not those imported from worldly philosophy. As others have noted, the British religious scene in the late 1850s witnessed a renewed interest in the literal interpretation of scripture.[28] In this general sense the appeal to the independent authority of scripture would be sounded regularly throughout the period of this study. But one important fruit of this understanding is that it made biblical imagery more central. If all one could know about God was what he had revealed, the biblical images themselves take on crucial importance. And an honest perusal of scripture shows that the same revelation that called God "Father" also made claims and promises about God's involvement in the world through continuing healings and miracles. If the appeal to the "folly to the Greeks" bolted the door to left-leaning critics of miracles, it left the door ajar for proponents of miracles on the right.

It was particularly Mozley's critique of the authority of inductive reasoning and his linking of miracles and prayer that reshaped the miracle debate. His movement of the discussion away from the traditional philosophical foci (those points that he dismissed as "formal logical answers") was widely followed. So too would others return, though in ways very much at odds with Mozley, to his claim that it was indeed the question of "imagination" that separated proponents and critics of the miraculous.

Miracles and Prayer

Mozley's subtle recasting of the miracle debate provoked many responses. Most were positive, but no one challenged him more pointedly than did the British physicist and apostle of the scientific method, John Tyndall. Even the briefest of biographical sketches of Tyndall makes clear that his was a very different world from that of Mozley or even Powell.[29] Born in Northern Ireland to a shoemaker–leather dealer father, Tyndall's upbringing was not on a par with the national clerisy, but with minor provincials at best. Largely self-taught, Tyndall's career wagon from very early on was hitched to the new empirical sciences. Throughout the 1850s and 1860s he had slowly built up his reputation in a corner of the emerging scientific establishment, which was only beginning to challenge the traditional religious order for the role of the true guide of the nation.

Mozley's arguments were open to scholarly criticism on a number of fronts: his scriptural exegesis skirted problems over the distinction between miracle and providence, his philosophical presuppositions were vague, and his historical generalizations were ripe with ambiguities. Yet Tyndall's criticism did not focus primarily on any of these problems. Instead Tyndall wrote with the passion of a prophet—defending the validity of the scientific method and pouring scorn upon its critics. "Miracles and Special Providences" burns with a moral passion in its defense of the principles of scientific inductive reasoning. Mozley, one recalls, had directed much criticism to the presumptions of the inductive method, and against these criticisms Tyndall spared no quarter. His opponent, he suggested, was a clerical dabbler, willing to besmirch the great engine of modern progress for the sake of a few biblical passages (and, by implication, the social status of their clerical interpreters). Mozley's attack on induction and his defense of miracles might be clever, argued Tyndall, but it ignored the undisputed accomplishments of the scientific method: "The eloquent pleader of the cause of miracles passes over without a word the *results* of scientific investigation, as proving anything rational regarding the principles or method by which such results have been achieved." Any proper evaluation of the scientific method, Tyndall explained, ought not to focus on the sophistical arguments of preachers but the real fruits of induction. Retelling the story of the deeds of Torricelli, Pascal, and the others who helped establish the theory of barometric pressure, Tyndall argued that the scientific method involved a constant weighing, testing, and judging of conclusions as well as strong cooperation among the researchers who worked together to advance human learning. The same could not be said for theologians who spent their time in idle speculation. Past ages might have been content with unbridled speculations concerning reality, but the nineteenth century wanted to know about its world. "The inductive principle is founded in man's desire to know — a desire arising from his position among phenomena which are reducible to order by his intellect," declared Tyndall.[30]

Many have noted that of his generation Tyndall was perhaps the most dedicated to the creed of Victorian scientific naturalism, and his essay is almost a classic formulation of this attitude. Woven into the essay, however, are not only intellectual and professional concerns but personal memories as well — particularly of his Ulster upbringing. Here as elsewhere Tyndall pointedly clumped false religion, superstition, and Rome as the enemies of the scientific vision. It was by no means accidental that he included in his critique of Mozley an account of ignorant Tyrolese peasants offering their silver and gold to shrines for the Virgin Mary in thanksgiving for "special providences" received. Playing upon the Protestant sympathies of his readers, his point was clear: such an attitude was superstitious and contemptible. But was this outlook any different from the Protestant belief in special providences?

Tyndall went on to answer two of Mozley's other points. The first concerned Mozley's invocation of Humean skepticism to challenge the confidence in the natural order, a confidence that was presupposed in the traditional critique of miracles. Mozley had argued that because all scientific knowledge was inductive, or empirically grounded, it was always advancing. Consequently no law of nature could exclude the possibility of miracles. Tyndall slyly noted, however, that skepticism was a sword with two edges, and here it cut far more deeply into religious beliefs than it did into scientific presumptions. Because miracles were usually understood as violations of the natural order, it was unclear what possible meaning "miracle" could have if nature were in fact as open as Mozley suggested. Were these alleged events not at best merely parts of unexplained nature?

> It appears to me that when he infers from Christ's miracles a Divine and altogether superhuman energy, Mr. Mozley places himself precisely under this condemnation. For what is his logical ground for concluding that the miracles of the New Testament illustrate Divine power? May they not be the result of expanded human power? . . . [A] period may come when man will be able to raise the dead. If this be conceded . . . it destroys the necessity of inferring Christ's Divinity from His miracles. He, it may be contended, antedated the humanity of the future; as a mighty tidal wave leaves high upon the beach a mark which by-and-by becomes the general level of the ocean.[31]

If human knowledge of nature was always advancing, it was not sufficient to prove that an alleged "miraculous" event had in fact occurred; it now became necessary (and by implication, for Tyndall, impossible) to demonstrate that such an occurrence was indeed supernatural, that is, outside of the course of nature. It was, for the proponents of miracles, an impossible situation. One could only know that an event was a miracle if it were supernatural or violated the order of nature. Yet the order of nature, in its entirety, was always unknowable. Hence, miracle and supernatural were meaningless categories.

Here in Tyndall one sees the beginning of the formulation of an argument against miracles that we may call "the new Humean argument." Hume's original argument, which presupposed the knowability and fixedness of the natural order, had been that claims for miracles were invalidated by the known regularity of nature. Now miracles were to be rejected for the opposite reason — that human knowledge of nature was so finite that no event could ever be certified to have fulfilled the criterion of violating it. What was now seen as ultimately problematic was not the event itself, but its classification as supernatural or miraculous. T. H. Huxley, in his study of Hume, offered the most succinct statement of this new attitude. As he explained, no event was so extraordinary in character that it necessitated invoking a supernatural explanation: "If it be said that the event exceeds the power of natural causes, who can justify such a saying? The day-fly has better grounds for calling a thunderstorm supernatural, than has man, with his experience of an infinitesimal fraction of duration, to say that the most astonishing event that can be imagined is beyond the scope of natural causes."[32]

This new argument played a very important role in the discussion of miracles during the next forty years, and it would in large part replace the original Humean argument. The confidence it assumed about the human race's ever-expanding understanding of natural phenomena played well in the context of late Victorian culture by combining an empirical openness to new phenomena with an a priori assumption of the uniformity of causation. Furthermore it allowed the critic of miracles to assume a pleasingly moderate persona. Individual miracle cases need not be accepted or rejected outright; they could instead be bracketed in the hopes that with the expansion of human knowledge there would come a time when their meaning would become clear. To a certain degree one can see in the new Humean argument Huxley's category of agnosticism, as an alternative middle ground between belief and denial, being extended to the debate over miracles. And here too such a stance struck a responsive chord in late-nineteenth-century culture. Indeed, as we will see, its attractiveness was not limited to those outside of the Christian communities, and the new Humean argument would be accepted by a large number of religious figures and play a crucial role in their critique of miracles.

Tyndall also found fault with Mozley's defense of the necessity of miracles, and here he employed the same religious grounds to which others had already appealed — the superiority of the moral witness over the supernatural witness. For Mozley, one will recall, miracles were necessary to prove a revelation, because human reason was incapable of evaluating the truthfulness of revelation itself. Tyndall viewed such a line of reasoning as preposterous. If human beings had any connection with the divine, it was through their moral sense, and any Christian authority must necessarily rest upon this intuitive moral sense. Here Tyndall drew his support not from philosophical argument but from the witness of scripture itself. He cited the story of the calling of Matthew in which Jesus attracted the disciple through his moral authority and not his miracles, and he claimed that this was the true message of the scriptures. Mozley's Bampton Lectures, according to Tyndall, did not reflect the message of Jesus but that of his opponents, who cried out (Mt 4:6): "If thou be the Son of God, command that these stones be made bread."[33] It is clear that underlying Tyndall's argument was a vision of Jesus far different from that offered by Mozley. Other scholars have discussed the persuasive power of the new biographies of Jesus that were beginning to appear during these years.[34] In volumes like Renan's *Vie de Jésus* and John R. Seeley's *Ecce Homo,* there emerged a picture of Jesus in which the supernatural was stripped away to expose his fundamental humanity and moral power. It was to such a picture that Tyndall appealed, and from this perspective the clamor for miracles was a sign not of faith but of unbelief.

Tyndall's essay can be seen as part of a larger effort to separate the spheres of religion and science, and in this regard it is connected with his notorious attack upon petitionary prayer. Just as Mozley had linked miracle and prayer in a common defense, so conversely did Tyndall see them as both open to the same critique. For centuries one of the duties of the clergy of the established church had been to intercede with God in behalf of the nation in times of plague, pestilence, and famine. Throughout the 1850s and 1860s, however, some liberal Anglican clergy (in particular Charles Kingsley and A. P. Stanley) began publicly expressing their uneasiness about their duty to offer such prayers (and in one case additional prayers for the restoration of the health of cattle). Among those who defended these clerics was Tyndall. Petitionary or intercessory prayers were no more defensible than those Roman and heretical claims for modern miracles that Protestants had found so offensive. Tyndall argued, "Those . . . who believe that the miraculous is still active in nature, may, with perfect consistency, join in our periodic prayers for fair weather and for rain: while those who hold that the age of miracles is past, will, if they be consistent, refuse to join in these petitions." True Protestantism should eschew such a view of prayer in the same way that it had long ago rejected the appeal to miracles.[35]

These prayers were false, however, not only because they were "Romish" but because they were unscientific as well. Here Tyndall grounded his charge on an appeal to the principle of the conservation of energy. As a physicist he had long been interested in the working out of this theory, developed during the middle years of the nineteenth century, which posited that the universe possessed a finite amount of energy that could neither be added to nor subtracted from. Without a violation of the principle of the conservation of energy, the very possibility of a divine interference within the natural realm was scientifically unthinkable. "No power can make its appearance in nature," he explained, "without an equivalent expenditure of some other power." The conservation of energy created a hermetic separation between God as an active or willful being and the world; God could neither create new energies nor affect the course of nature without violating one of the foundational principles of science. Accordingly, all actions in the natural order were by definition acts of nature and hence reducible to natural cause — "the Proteus changes, but he is ever the same; and his changes in nature, supposing no miracle to supervene, are the expression, not of spontaneity but of physical necessity."[36] For Tyndall, individuals were confronted by two alternative pictures of the universe: one governed by regularity and law and the other overseen by will. No compromise was possible between these two visions, and all intelligent persons needed to ask themselves which picture was a more accurate reflection of reality.

In a curious way one finds here in Tyndall the converse of Mozley's appeal to imagination. Much of the force of Tyndall's argument lies on the level of imagination. He implicitly confronts his readers with an unfathomable problem. Once one has accepted the intellectual presuppositions of nineteenth-century science, how could one picture a divine intervention into the physical realm? Was not, he seemed to ask, an event such as the multiplication of fish and loaves, or the creation of new matter out of nothing, literally unimaginable for an educated individual, as was by extension any divine intervention into the natural order? Throughout his controversy with Mozley, Tyndall relished his role as the commonsensical Englishman.

Against this background came Tyndall's famous call for the "prayer gauge." In 1871, as Edward, Prince of Wales, grievously suffered from cholera (a disease that had claimed his father a decade earlier), a distraught Queen Victoria requested her clergy to pray for her son's recovery. The great majority of them dutifully did so, and, after a period, the prince's health was restored. In recognition of his deliverance, a great service of thanksgiving was held at Westminster Abbey, and there Victoria and her leading clergy assembled — without, significantly, the presence of the leading representatives of the Victorian scientific establishment. Tyndall was not amused, and he proceeded to publish a series of articles that questioned whether prayer could have any influence on the physical order of things. Does prayer, he asked, "invoke a Power which checks and augments the descent of rain, which changes the force and direction of winds, which affects the growth of corn and the health of men and cattle — a Power, in short, which, when appealed to under pressing circumstances, produces the precise effects caused by physical energy in the ordinary course of things"?[37] If so, he argued, this assertion must be empirically tested to "confer quantitative precision on the action of the Supernatural in Nature." Because one of the common ends for such prayers was the recovery from sickness, he proposed that the efficacy of prayer be put to the same sort of test that any other proposed medical remedy would be asked to undergo. Two identical wards should be established in a hospital with patients similar in age, sex, and other outward attributes. One ward would be dedicated to healing through prayer, whereas the other would serve as a control group. "When a very large number . . . has been thus dealt with, the results are compared, and the value of the remedy can be definitely expressed; that is, its influence above or below that of the old treatment, as the case may be, will appear in the per-centage of recovery, or of other results."[38] Only by means of such a gauge could the objective individual determine whether prayer had any influence in physical cures.

Tyndall's recommendation became one of the great religious controversies of the 1870s. A few dismissed it out of hand. "It has been proposed that we erect two hospitals," wrote one critic, "in one the patients are to be 'physicked' and in the other 'prayed for.' Evidently the proposer had need of both remedies."[39] Others, particularly in America, found it more disturbing than amusing. Soon after publishing his call for the prayer gauge Tyndall began an American lecture tour, and controversy followed him wherever he went. Methodist and Presbyterian publications attacked him; prayer meetings were held in both Boston and Philadelphia for his salvation; the Episcopal bishop of New York refused to attend a banquet in his honor; and Tyndall often found himself attacked from pulpits.[40]

The controversy surrounding Tyndall's prayer gauge suggests that he had touched upon a tender topic within English-speaking Protestantism. As we have suggested, a rather complicated and distinctive set of compromises had been carefully worked out in the years since the Reformation. One principle of these compromises was that biblical miracles were to be accepted as authentic but later miracle claims were to be rejected. A second principle was that God no longer acted in the world in a miraculous fashion, but still acted providentially. Thus Protestant apologists believed that they could both cooperate intellectually with a scientific world view (because nature was seen to be governed in a regular or law-like way) and maintain a place for prayer. They were confident that no conflict need exist between true science and true religion.[41] Tyndall upset the applecart. By yoking prayer to the issue of miracles, and in blaming the former for problems associated with the latter, he struck at the careful compromise that had undergirded this Protestant position. For Tyndall, neither the miracles of the biblical epoch nor the life of prayer could be granted a protected status; both were to be weighed by the laws of evidence that governed all other claims about the natural order. As such, Tyndall undoubtedly succeeded in leading many to take a more critical stance toward the question of the miraculous. Yet, as I shall suggest, such attacks had the opposite effect on others. If the idea of prayer possessed the same difficulties as did the question of modern miracles, the converse was equally true—that is, modern miracles were no more problematic than prayer itself. Thus the traditional Protestant position found itself potentially weakened from both sides.

The Debate Goes Public

It was the publication of two other works, however, that brought the scholarly debate over the miraculous to the attention of the general public. In 1874 a massive two-volume, anonymous work appeared under the title *Supernatural Religion,* and in 1888 the novel *Robert Elsmere* was published. Both created a sensation in the general public.

Supernatural Religion is one of those maddening volumes of scholarship that is evocative and challenging, yet riddled with errors. For over a thousand pages, its author pontificated on a myriad of topics all loosely connected with the question of the supernatural. The difference between its approach and tone and that of clerical authors on the same subject electrified many readers. Writing in the *Fortnightly Review,* John Morley waxed enthusiastically over it. In his view, the arguments of its author were "by far the most decisive, trenchant, and far reaching of the direct contributions to theological controversy that have been made in this generation."[42] For years the book was the talk of the British religious world and was considered one of the great radical attacks on dogmatic religion. The anonymity of its author gave the work an added mysteriousness, and it was not until over twenty years later that its author was finally identified as W. R. Cassels, a retired Indian merchant. Until then it was something of a parlor game for Victorian literati to speculate as to the identity of its author.

Supernatural Religion is an extended critique of the traditional claim that Christianity was a supernaturally anchored religion. "Christianity must either be recognized to be a Divine Revelation beyond man's criticism, and in that case its doctrines must be received even though Reason cannot be satisfied, or the claims of Christianity to be such a Divine Revelation must be disallowed, in which case it becomes the legitimate subject of criticism like every other human system."[43] Such were the only alternatives, and for Cassels only the latter was defensible. In the early chapters he followed the traditional path for such a volume: challenging the careful arguments of Mozley and others who had defended miracles, defending Hume's arguments against his clerical critics, and maintaining the reality of the order of nature.

Yet what was new and radical in Cassels was his shifting of the argument to the question of the historical reliability of the biblical narrative itself. For almost two centuries the argument over miracles had focused on such key philosophical categories as the definition of a miracle and the meaning of the law of nature. The present generation, however, demanded a different type of discussion. "The time is ripe for arriving at a definite conviction as to the character of Christianity. There is no lack of material for a final decision, although hitherto they have been beyond the reach of most English readers, and a careful and honest examination of the subject, even if it be not final, cannot fail to contribute towards a result more satisfactory than the generally vague and illogical religious opinion of the present day."[44] For this material Cassels appealed to the new scholarship coming out of Germany, particularly that associated with the Tübingen school. Proponents of the Tübingen school (most notably F. C. Baur) were insisting that the New Testament could only be understood in light of the broader history of the primitive church, and in particular the conflict between Jewish and Gentile elements. The scriptural books that the church now possessed, Cassels maintained, were the product of this conflict, and not, as earlier writers had assumed, the result of an outpouring of divine grace and apostolic good will. Hence the books of the New Testament ought to be investigated within this new historical framework vis-à-vis both their dating and interpretation.

This new perspective provided a fatal blow to the carefully maintained distinction between biblical and postbiblical miracles. After surveying first-century Jewish views on demons, witchcraft, and sorcery Cassels concluded that the biblical epoch, far from being an age of enlightenment preceding a superstitious postbiblical age, was itself an age of superstition. Similarly, parallels between biblical miracle stories and those recorded in the early church undercut the traditional privileged status reserved for the former. It might indeed be true, as earlier apologists for the biblical miracles had claimed, that the story of the miraculous resurrection was promulgated almost immediately by the early followers of Jesus, yet "the miracles recounted by St. Athanasius and St. Augustine . . . were likewise proclaimed with equal clearness, and even greater promptitude and publicity at the very spot where very many of them were said to have been performed, and the details were more immediately reduced to writing."[45] When the protective exceptionalism usually assumed concerning the biblical miracles was removed, they were seen to testify not to divine revelation but to human ignorance. Indeed they were much like the alleged miracles one found peppered throughout history, and like them were most probably products of superstitious epochs and cultures. Appealing to his audience's anti-Catholic prejudices, Cassels observed that miracles are only to be found where enlightenment was not: "[They] are now denied to places more enlightened than Naples or La Salette."[46]

For most of the two volumes Cassels went to great lengths to attack the trustworthiness of the historical records of the gospels, and to argue, à la the Tübingen school, that the scriptures were the theological product of a later age. Yet toward the end of his second volume he asked the question: if all this were true, what remained of Christianity and the figure of Jesus? Here Cassels argued in turn that the new historical scholarship allowed for a successful freeing of Christianity from a bondage to the supernatural. The new scholarship concerning the early Christian centuries, and in particular the rediscovered testimony of figures such as Papias showed that the gospels as they existed were far less reliable as historical guides than had been previously thought, or than English biblical scholars had assumed. The gospels of Matthew and Mark could no longer be identified with apostolic eyewitnesses; Luke was avowedly the work of merely a compiler of traditions; and John could make no claims as a work of historical record. The gospels, as they existed, contained no account of a miracle attested to by an eyewitness, and hence earlier apologists such as Paley had seriously erred in anchoring the authority of scripture upon the testimonies to miracles. The real power of Christianity lay in its noble morality, not in any supernatural evidences, and nowhere was this truer than in the figure of Jesus. "Morality was the essence of his system; theology was an afterthought," Cassels argued.[47] The later ecclesiastical tradition had transformed Jesus in a way reminiscent of the way in which the mob at Lystra had tried make gods out of Paul and Barnabas in the Book of Acts. But a purely moral gospel message stood as a true alternative to ecclesiastical dogmatism and supernaturalism.

Cassels's *Supernatural Religion* is at best a flawed work, and its obvious limitations deeply damaged its importance within the scholarly community. Although a number of scholars addressed it, none did so with the deadly accuracy of J. B. Lightfoot, canon of St. Paul's Cathedral and professor of divinity at Cambridge. Among the names that came up in the guessing game over the authorship of *Supernatural Religion* was that of the dying Connop Thirwall, bishop of St. Davids, who had earlier translated works of Friedrich Schleiermacher. Angered by the slander to the reputation of the dying Thirwall, as well as attacks made in the volume upon the scholarship of his colleague B. F. Westcott, Lightfoot responded with the fury of a scholar scorned. In a series of essays he attacked *Supernatural Religion* on a number of fronts. Perhaps his easiest task was to show that its author was a dilettante when it came to knowledge of the ancient languages and the history of the early church. At best, Cassels reflected the questionable dogmatic assumptions of the Tübingen interpretation of the early record, and all too frequently he did worse by misreading and mistranslating basic sources. Perhaps the nadir of the debate occurred when Cassels, responding to the charge that he must not have read one of the sources that he cited because it baldly contradicted his argument, demanded an apology. Lightfoot dryly noted that he would apologize if desired, but if Cassels had indeed read the work in question he laid himself open to a far more damaging charge.[48] After Lightfoot's pummeling, no one could doubt the superiority of the don over the dilettante when it came to the technical questions of language or history.

Lightfoot went further, however, and argued that the positive religious solace Cassels offered his readers was equally flawed. And here one can hear Lightfoot speaking not as a scholar but as a teacher of young men. It was not enough that Cassels had challenged the scholarly expertise of the British academy, he was undermining the moral fibre of British youth. In Lightfoot's view, Cassels had blithely assumed that one could jettison with impunity the supernatural and still understand the world to be shaped by moral purpose and governed by a benevolent Father God. "The demand is made that we should abandon our Christianity on grounds which logically involve the abandonment of any belief in the providential government of the world and the moral responsibility of man," wrote Lightfoot. Such a compromise might suffice for a generation already shaped by the authority of scripture, but not for the rising generation. "[T]he pupil, having thrown off his Christianity, too often follows out the principles of his teacher to their logical conclusions, and divests himself also of moral restraints, except so far as it may be convenient or necessary for him to submit to them."[49] Speaking as a proper Victorian cleric, Lightfoot argued that any attempt to separate surgically Christian morality from Christian religion to save the former was doomed.

Together with Westcott and their colleague F. J. A. Hort, Lightfoot was one of the famous "Cambridge triumvirate." The triumverate were the leading English biblical critics in the late nineteenth century, and they represented the "sober" and "prudent" British response to the new trends in biblical scholarship. As we will see in chapter 6, their agenda was not merely to refute the radical biblical criticism of the German Tübingen school and to defend the comparative antiquity and fundamental historicity of the New Testament text, but also to salvage the gospel miracles. Lightfoot's critique of *Supernatural Religion* was part of this larger agenda of protecting the figure of Jesus along with his miracles.

Lightfoot's assault on *Supernatural Religion* was devastatingly thorough. One scholar's observation — namely that after it had been leveled the book, albeit read, "ceased to count with serious students" — is the generally accepted scholarly interpretation of the episode.[50] Such an observation is undoubtedly true, but perhaps it is less meaningful than it seems. Other scholars have observed that the theological faculties of English universities became more conservative between 1860 and 1885, in part as a reaction to *Essays and Reviews*. Whenever a spark of continental radicalism landed, it was quickly and carefully extinguished by the "careful" and "sober" English scholarly community. The formal scholarly reaction to Cassels's volumes reflected this mind-set. Yet if it was comparatively easy to show that Cassels was a bungling amateur when it came to scholarly questions, it was far more difficult to exorcise the larger and very real questions he raised, albeit imperfectly. The book's popularity perhaps stemmed from Cassels's very willingness to address those problems about the miraculous that many of his contemporaries apparently shared. As at least one reviewer observed, the wider public often seemed more conscious of these problems than did the (overwhelmingly clerical) scholarly community: "Theology is now for various reasons almost exclusively studied, in England at any rate, by those whose interest in it is professional, and consequently the few serious performances which come now and then from the press in this department are really no more than official apologies, and cannot be looked upon as disinterested inquiries scientifically conducted." All too frequently when persons from outside the academy had attempted to raise foundational questions, their works flourished for a time as "nine day wonders" but were eventually silenced by the clerisy, who buried them under the weight of ponderous Hulsean and Bampton Lectures. But these larger questions could not ultimately be kept at bay in this way; they were continually being raised. Such was the real value of *Supernatural Religion*: " The writer, whoever he may be, has . . . a keen hold of the real issues on which the whole matter must turn."[51] These large questions had to be addressed, not avoided by means of scholarly footwork or even learned refutations.

These themes reemerged with a vengeance somewhat more than a decade later with the publication of the novel *Robert Elsmere* by Mary Arnold Ward (who was always referred to as Mrs. Humphry Ward). A few biographical details may suggest a connection between Ward's life and her work. Through her grandfather, Thomas Arnold of Rugby, and uncle, Matthew Arnold, she was linked to one of the most prestigious families in English-speaking religious high culture. Yet her own father, also a Thomas Arnold, had an ambiguous relationship with this familial heritage. Twice he abandoned his family's religious tradition and converted to Roman Catholicism because he was attracted by, among other things, the Catholic understanding of the miraculous. These actions not only created domestic discord (his wife was so incensed that at the service for his reception she threw a brick through the church window), but caused religious discord within the larger Arnold family. Mary Ward spent many of her formative years near Oxford, where she was influenced by the liberalism and historicism of Mark Pattison. There she met and married Humphry Ward, and there too she became familiar with the ideas and individuals who would appear in *Robert Elsmere*. Oxford during this period was viewed as a battleground between proponents of the traditional faith and advocates of newer and more liberal visions. As Ward later described it: "The Oxford of thought was not quiet; it was divided. . . . Darwinism was penetrating everywhere; Pusey was preaching against its effects on belief; Balliol stood for an unfettered history and criticism, Christ Church for authority and creeds; Renan's *Origenes* were still coming out, Strauss's last book also; my uncle was publishing *God and the Bible* in succession to *Literature and Dogma*; and *Supernatural Religion* was making no small stir. And meanwhile what was beginning to interest and absorb me were sources — testimony."[52]

Many a young scholar's career was irrevocably affected by choosing among these bewildering options, and a loss of faith in this context was common.

Indeed in this story of the loss of traditional faith Mary Ward was perhaps typical. Her belief in the truthfulness of dogmatic Christianity had already been weakened by the general discussion of the time when in 1877 she was invited to contribute to the *Dictionary of Christian Biography*. While involved in this research on the Ostrogoths of Spain, she reached the conclusion that the early testimonies vis-à-vis miracles were "non-sane." No person could be a student of history and still take literally the ancient accounts.[53]

These doubts finally took literary form in *Robert Elsmere*. The latter is the story of a minister, his crisis of faith, and the results of this crisis. Its plot revolves around three central characters: Elsmere, the minister; Catherine, his wife and the representation of traditional piety; and Roger Wendover, the squire and scholarly skeptic.

Students of the novel have observed that it is divided into three sections, each with a distinct focus and geographical location, but for our purposes the second and third sections are of most importance. Here Ward offers a dramatic presentation of the loss of traditional faith. Elsmere, like his authorial creator, begins to doubt the reality of miracles when he takes up the study of history. After reading various lives of the saints, histories of the ancient councils, and accounts of the many supernatural wonders described, he finds his traditional faith sorely shaken. On relating one such story to his wife Catherine, she responds, " 'What extraordinary superstition! . . . A bishop, Robert, and an educated man?' Robert nodded. 'But it is the whole habit of mind,' he said half to himself, staring into the fire, 'that is so astounding. No one escapes it. The whole age is really non-sane.' 'I suppose the devout Catholic would believe that?' 'I am not sure,' said Robert dreamily."[54] Elsmere's conversations with Squire Wendover exacerbate these doubts. Wendover (a name Ward ironically took from a medieval chronicler of miracles) argues that one can never properly study the biblical narrative without a firm grounding in the rules for historical evidence: "To plunge into the Christian period without having first cleared the mind as to what is meant in history and literature by the 'critical method,' which in history may be defined as the 'science of what is credible'; and in literature as 'the science of what is rational,' is to invite fiasco. The theologian in such a state sees no obstacle to accepting an arbitrary list of documents with all the strange stuff they may contain, and declaring them to be sound historical material, while he applies to all of the strange stuff of a similar kind surrounding them the most rigorous principles of modern science" (317). From the perspective of the historical method, the Bible's picture of a supernatural Jesus rested on a very sandy foundation. Elsmere, unable to answer the squire's arguments, after a struggle abandons his traditional faith and surrenders his ministry in the established church.

Ward clearly had her intellectual scores to settle in this section. She heaped contempt upon the Cambridge triumvirate whose "responsible exegesis" isolated and protected the image of the supernatural Jesus from his critics. "Westcott, for instance, who means so much nowadays to the English religious world, first isolates Christianity from all other religious phenomena of the world, and then argues upon its details. You might as well isolate English jurisprudence, and discuss its details without any reference to Teutonic custom or Roman law!" (354) Her novel is filled with characters based on Oxford personages such as Mark Pattison (the model for Wendover) and the Hegelian philosopher T. H. Green (the model for Mr. Grey), as well as such stock figures as ascetic Tractarians and amoral French women. All of this added color and spice to her story.

Yet like Cassels in his *Supernatural Religion,* Ward was not content merely to attack the old dogmatic religion. In the last third of the novel, Robert dedicates himself to the message of the simply human Jesus and preaches this message to the working classes of London. The results were overwhelming; when stripped of its supernaturalism the figure of Jesus took on a new power, and Elsmere is able to establish a "New Brotherhood." As in all good Victorian novels of this sort Robert dies at the end, but not before he is reconciled to Catherine (who had opposed his religious development). The success of Robert's new London ministry leads Catherine herself to move away from her own dogmatic traditional faith, and after his death she carries on his work. It is also clear that for Ward the third section of her novel was not a judgment merely upon the dogmatic faith of Catherine, but upon the skepticism of Wendover as well. The squire's critical scholarship might have emboldened him in his study, but it haunts him in his bed chamber and eventually drives him mad. The contrast between Elsmere and Wendover was clear; doubt was not to be an end in itself but a catalyst to a new faith.

Robert Elsmere took the English reading public by storm. Part of its appeal is undoubtedly the attractiveness of its characters and the charm of the plot, which is engaging enough to hold a modern reader's attention. But it was the broader questions woven into the simple story that provoked the greatest interest. By her own admission the novel was didactic in purpose, using fiction to create a wider audience for her ideas. She had labored to describe in "simple, sensuous, passionate," and pictorial terms the great religious crisis of her age, and whether by planning or chance, the timing of her novel could not have been better. The critical questioning that one saw reflected in the 1870s in *Supernatural Religion* had sufficiently filtered down to the general reading public by the 1880s to create a great market of interest. As one scholar has observed, if Ward had published her work a decade earlier it would have appealed to only a few persons, and if she had published a decade later it would have been passe; as it was, the novel created a sensation.[55]

Numerous reviewers, both pro and con, noted the parallels between *Elsmere* and *Supernatural Religion*. The novel was able to play upon a number of strands of protest against the prevailing religious attitudes, including those set forth by Ward's own uncle. Her connection with the famous name of Arnold, and Matthew Arnold's own contributions to the critique of miracles — particularly his *Literature and Dogma* — added to the seriousness with which both readers and reviewers took the novel. In one of his naughty (but not completely unfair) bon mots, Oscar Wilde observed that for many of her readers, Ward's novel was *Literature and Dogma . . .* without the literature. The novel also benefited from the criticism it received. William Gladstone, longtime champion of both Oxford and Anglicanism, saw the novel as a scurrilous attack upon both institutions, and wrote a long and critical review of it.[56] Other reviewers also found fault with Ward's interpretations, but despite (or perhaps because of) these reviews the book became the talk of the land. There are comparatively few first novels that can count as its reviewers a former prime minister (Gladstone) and a future archbishop of Canterbury (Randall Davidson). Whatever the explanations, within a short time between thirty and forty thousand copies had been sold in Britain, and numerous stories circulated about the pains to which people were willing to go to get a copy of the book.[57]

Commentators noted that the key issue of the book was the miraculous, and in particular the possibility of purging the miracles from the gospels. This was also a theme emphasized by Gladstone in a private discussion with Ward. "If you sweep away miracles you sweep away the Resurrection!" he exclaimed.[58] Yet if the popular response to *Robert Elsmere* was surprising in Britain, it was astonishing in America. There it became a runaway best-seller, and estimates of its sales range upward to 200,000 copies.[59] Within a short time, the novel became the best-selling book in America since *Uncle Tom's Cabin*. A number of factors contributed to the book's enormous success. The lack of international copyright laws allowed the novel to be sold in pirated editions at a fraction of the price of an English edition (and eventually allowed it to be given away as a sales promotion for Balsam Fir Soap). Likewise, the notoriety the book had received in Britain, often communicated to the public in such colorful headlines as "WEG on Bobbie" (that is, Gladstone on Elsmere) stimulated American curiosity. Finally, the timing was right. As libraries grew at an increasing rate to meet the literary needs of the middle class, *Robert Elsmere* became a favorite volume for their collections. In an 1893 survey of American libraries' most popular circulating novels, *Robert Elsmere* made the list of 30 percent of those institutions responding.[60]

What is interesting about the response in America, however, was its spontaneity—hardly any intellectual spadework had preceded it. Unlike England, America, as we will see, had not participated to any degree in the debate over miracles discussed in this chapter. To be sure, Tyndall's advocacy for a prayer gauge had excited alarm among the clergy, and there had been some scholarly discussion of Strauss and Renan's *Life of Jesus,* but the level of interest in the subject in the decades before the publication of *Elsmere* was far less than in Britain. One sees this in the American reaction to *Supernatural Religion.* The volume had been a cause célèbre in Britain in the 1870s and had continued to be discussed in the years following. Memoirs of the times allude to its influence, journals were peppered with discussions of it, and a number of important volumes were written to attack its claims.[61] In marked contrast, the volume elicited no real response in America. Occasionally one finds a journal noting its publication, but no major discussion of its arguments took place.

Thus the publication of *Robert Elsmere* came upon America like a bolt from the blue. From one coast to the other, Americans clamored for copies of the novel. Contemporary commentators noted furthermore not merely the degree of interest, but also the nature of the interest. In America, unlike in England, the book was viewed not so much as a popular novel but as "an oracular pronouncement on God and human destiny." Oliver Wendell Holmes, for example, was so impressed with *Robert Elsmere* that he wrote Ward a letter of praise describing her work as a " 'medicated novel' . . . the most effective and popular novel we have had since *Uncle Tom's Cabin.*"[62] Like Harriet Beecher Stowe, Ward was praised for using fiction to introduce fundamental questions to the general reading public.

But still one must return to question of why *Supernatural Religion* and *Robert Elsmere* provoked such different reactions within the American reading public. Part of the explanation is undoubtedly the differing genres of the two works. The scholarly (or pseudo-scholarly) *Supernatural Religion* was off-putting to a general reader in a way that Ward's novel was not. But perhaps something had also changed between 1874 and 1888. Writers at the time as well as recent scholars have noted that for the American public the decade of the 1880s witnessed a crucial turning point in the understanding of the nature of the Bible.[63] During this decade the early proponents of higher criticism began arguing that the Bible ought to be studied like other historical works. According to the traditional picture of this period, the spirit of historical criticism was quickened in the graduate seminars of Germany, moved from there to the seminaries, and gradually made its way into the pulpits. Yet the great interest among laypersons in *Robert Elsmere,* with its popularized Tübingen-ism, suggests that the interest in attempts to apply the historical approach to scripture did not simply come from the top down. As I shall suggest in the next chapter, as liberal theologians during this decade attempted to formulate their understandings on such questions as the person of Jesus and the authority of scripture, they were forced to answer not only the criticisms of their more conservative colleagues but also the more radical views of Ward's popular novel.

The *North American Review* dedicated a substantial article, which included contributions by many individuals, to discussion of the impact of *Robert Elsmere*. In the differing responses one hears the echo of the earlier debate over *Supernatural Religion*. On one extreme were the comments of Julia Ward Howe. Howe, who had combined her old abolitionist zeal with a passion for freeing religion from enslaving dogma, praised the work. "I know of no story since *Uncle Tom's Cabin,* whose appearance had excited so much comment [and] intellectual interest of so high a character." For her, the novel illustrated the fundamental conflict between the "miraculous" and "ethical" bases of religious belief, and as such set the agenda for the future discussion of the role of religion in the world.[64] Others who were more sensitive to the theological and scholarly difficulties that lay behind Ward's narrative were less enthusias-tic. The Congregationalist minister Joseph Cook criticized the novel for incor-porating the same problematic German scholarship that had earlier found expression in *Supernatural Religion*. Americans were quickly catching up to the British debate.

The regular comparison that was made by writers between *Robert Elsmere* and *Uncle Tom's Cabin* merits one final observation. *Uncle Tom's Cabin,* one must remember, was more than just a novel attacking slavery. Another impor-tant objective was to question how intelligent and moral individuals could tolerate such a horrible evil. In this regard the novel has a decidedly anticleri-cal air. Stowe pictured her clerics as intellectually hidebound and morally obtuse — so concerned with the letter of the scripture that they were oblivious to reality. In the famous slave-catching scene in chapter 12 it was the minister, not the slave catcher, who attempted to defend the morality of slavery on biblical grounds. Moral direction in the novel came not from ministers but from women, slaves, and children. Stowe, as the wife of a professor of biblical interpretation, was well aware that the traditional scholarly approach to inter-preting scripture was at odds with the cause of abolition.[65] The novel ren-dered judgment on a theology divorced from reality. Although never explicitly stated, such a judgment is implied in the praise heaped upon *Robert Elsmere*.

It, too, offered an understanding of reality that was missing in the theology of the times.

Summary

By the 1880s the discussion over miracles had gone far afield from its earlier confines. No longer was it tied to narrow questions of metaphysics and logic: instead, the debate was increasingly linked to scientific issues such as the conservation of energy and the relationship between the biblical era and later history. Furthermore, as a result of both Mozley and Tyndall, the discussion had become part of the larger question of prayer and divine affectation of the natural order. Finally, the debate over miracles was beginning to be associated with a broader reformulation of the Christian message. The old Protestant wall that had served to separate biblical miracles from all others had been broached at a number of places, and in these breaches lay the seeds for a fundamentally new rendering of the question of how to frame the miraculous.

3

The Miracle Question in America, 1860–1885

George Bernard Shaw's famous witticism that Britain and America were two nations separated by a common language was as true for the question of miracles as it was for questions of politics and culture. During the thirty years under discussion, Americans, like their British contemporaries, grappled with the diverse implications of the miracle debate and the challenges posed by such figures as Strauss, Renan, and the authors of *Essays and Reviews,* but the American context would always influence their response. A close examination of the American debate reveals that it evolved in two phases, one during the 1860s and a second during the 1880s. The fundamental differences between these discussions illumine the changing context of the miracle controversy.

Holding Yet Modifying the Line

Debate over the miraculous was of course nothing new in America, but a new phase of the discussion began by the late 1850s. Heretofore it was easy enough to dismiss such questioning as a peculiarity of Boston Unitarianism — as perhaps a malady associated with the confines of Harvard College. *Essays and Reviews,* Renan's *Vie de Jésus,* and Strauss's *Leben Jesu,* which emanated from three of the leading nations of Europe, impressed upon the theological community the seriousness of the challenge, and over the course of a decade a flurry of theological responses appeared. The theological agenda of key American theologians was to attempt to modify the inherited position on miracles by moving it away from evidentialism and by linking the question of miracles more closely to the character of Jesus. Three of these individuals (Henry Boynton Smith, George Park Fisher, and James McCosh), although they represent leading intellectual institutions of the time, are of only passing importance. The last, however, Horace Bushnell, in his volume *Nature and the Supernatural,* offered perhaps the major theological contribution of mid-nineteenth-century America to the miracle debate and proposed a bold rethinking of the question of both biblical miracles and modern miracles.

One distinctive feature of these writers is that they chose to focus not on the question of miracles per se, as did their contemporaries in Britain, but instead on the broader issue of the supernatural, of which the miraculous was only a constitutive part. For American Protestants the central issue was the defense of the distinction between the natural and supernatural orders. Whereas Transcendentalists like Emerson and Parker might challenge the fundamental distinction between nature and the supernatural, American Protestants continued to emphasize the reality both of a nature governed by regular laws and of a supernatural realm lying above and beyond it. The dogged defense of the distinction between natural and supernatural may also reflect a key aspect of American religiosity. As many others have observed, America understood itself as a "Christian" nation in a far different sense than did the nations of Europe. Its faith was tied not to an ancient constitution or to some recorded history stretching back over a millennia, but to nature itself. Nature rather than history inspired American Protestant writers of the mid-nineteenth century. Appeals to the Scottish commonsense philosophical tradition and a Baconian vision of science, which made up the content of countless collegiate lectures, all turned on the importance of nature. But it was always a nature in which the supernatural had a crucial place. Indeed the supernatural gave meaning and comprehension to nature in the way that revelation gave meaning and plot to history. Nature interpreted in the light of an overarching supernatural reality was filled with light and verity; when viewed otherwise it was but a sea of minutiae. Furthermore this popular view of nature was seen to be in harmony with the scriptures. Hence the reality of the supernatural was to be defended at all cost.[1]

One sees this theme emerging in Henry Boynton Smith, a New-School Presbyterian professor of theology at Union Theological Seminary in New York. In a series of essays published in various theological journals over more than a decade, he took aim at the challenges posed by Strauss, Renan, and the authors of *Essays and Reviews.*[2] Much of his discussion involved the issue of the supernatural. The true nature of Christianity could be succinctly stated: it was a "specific divine revelation, supernatural in its origin, announced in prophecy, attested by miracles, recorded in inspired Scriptures, centering in the person of the God-man, and having for its object the redemption of the world from sin."[3] According to Smith, each of the modern critics of the traditional formularies was guilty of perverting this fundamental understanding. The contributors to *Essays and Reviews* were dismissed as "the new Latitudinarians of England" and were criticized both for their scholarly errors and logical inconsistencies. Strauss and his followers were chastised for assuming a view of history that excluded miracles, prophecies, and all other supernatural occurrences on a priori grounds, "although they grant, that the books themselves claim to contain both miracle and prophecy."[4] Throughout his discussion, however, Smith emphasized the interconnectedness of the miraculous to the larger question of the supernatural, and put little weight upon the role of miracles as primary external evidences. He had little sympathy with the traditional Protestant evidential argument. Paley and other evidentialists, in his view, had failed to recognize the true foundation of Christian authority, which was internal or intuitive, and had instead emphasized the external evidences of miracles. The emphasis on miraculous evidence was an accident of the eighteenth century. In most periods of Christian history the internal evidences were always preferred to the external evidence of miracles. But when Hume and the Deists had attacked them in order to challenge the idea of divine agency, Christian apologists found it necessary to defend them. For a century miracles were a battleground over the larger questions of the veracity of the idea of a personal God and the trustworthiness of revelation. "The real question was, not merely that of the evidences of revelation, but whether deism or even atheism was to triumph over Christian theism,"[5] Smith argued. Later apologists, however, became so fixated on the defense of miracles that they lost sight of the subsidiary function of the argument. Yet in Smith's view they were not alone, and modern critics, such as Baden Powell in *Essays and Reviews,* were also guilty of this error. Powell mistakenly believed that by challenging the miracles of scripture he undermined the Bible's authority as a supernatural book. Yet he and the others failed to understand that the primary witness of the reality of the supernatural was the character of Jesus. Jesus was not a person who did supernatural acts, but was himself a manifestation of the supernatural. Critics like Renan might have believed that by eschewing the miraculous they exorcised the supernatural from Christianity, but all such attempts would fail. Smith challenged, "To deny the supernatural is easy, to disprove it is difficult. . . . The supernatural has been chiefly argued in relation to miracles; but there is a higher form of it, and a weightier question, that relating to the person of our Lord as its embodiment and incarnation. This book [*Vie de Jésus*], if it proves anything, proves that naturalism cannot reconstruct, without falsifying, the life of Jesus."[6] According to Smith, a true portrait of Jesus was inherently supernatural, and miracles followed from the supernatural character of Christ rather than proved it.

Smith's elevation of the character of Jesus as the cornerstone of the supernatural nature of Christianity was not unique, and students of nineteenth-century theology will undoubtedly find the theme familiar. Many writers were calling for a renewed emphasis upon the centrality of the character of Jesus as the cornerstone of Christianity as well as for a movement away from the older appeal to external evidences. In England, Samuel Taylor Coleridge had protested against any evidentialist appeal to miracles and had advocated resting Christianity upon its appeal to intuitive reason. Similarly in Germany, Karl Ullmann, Isaac Dorner, and other representatives of the so-called mediating theological tradition (all influenced to a large degree by Friedrich Schleiermacher) called for such a new approach to overcome the old stalemate between supernaturalism and rationalism.[7] Their theme of shifting the focus of Christian apologetics away from doctrine and toward Christianity as a principle of life, as well as their emphasis upon the doctrine of the incarnation, found strong support among mid-century American writers.[8] None of these writers wrote extensively on the miracle question in particular, but in Britain Richard Trench's widely circulated *Notes on the Miracles of Our Lord* did examine the question. Trench believed that the true proof of Christianity was "not logical and single, but moral and cumulative," and was tied to the encounter with the figure of Christ.[9]

The Yale church historian George P. Fisher, in *Essays on the Supernatural Origin of Christianity* (1866), likewise strove to link the question of miracles to the broader issue of the supernatural. Like Smith, Fisher argued that the real question confronting the age was the supernatural nature of Christianity, or whether the origin of the religion of Christ was "of heaven or of men." The debate over miracles was but a part of this larger question. The problems modern critics found with miracles, according to Fisher, stemmed not from any theory of physical nature but from their failure to accept the reality of a personal God. Once one accepted the existence of a personal God, the problems surrounding miracles vanished. If the world was ordered and governed by a personal God, miracles were never "afterthoughts" but were part of the divine plan. "In short, miracles are fully accordant with the laws of the Universe, or of the universal system which includes God."[10]

When Fisher turned next to discuss the purpose of the miraculous, his affinity with the views expressed by Smith became even clearer. He too rejected the earlier assertion that the truth of Christianity needed external miracles to validate its claims for truth, and asserted instead that it was intuitively affirming. The occurrence of miracles did not prove revelation, he explained, but only highlighted it by drawing the attention of those who might otherwise have passed it over. Miracles were, for Fisher, the equivalent to boldface type in printing, helping the eye to focus on the fundamental thrust of the text. As such, they were acts of divine condescension showing and illuminating the nature of God, not in any rational or logical way that might serve as a basis of proof, but in an evocative way. Hence they could never in and of themselves create belief where the seeds of faith were not already present.[11]

But on two points Fisher would not bend. The first involved the abandoning of interventionist categories to understand a miracle. Some philosophers argued that the old distinction between primary and secondary causality, or the direct intervention of God in the world versus divine action through the forces of nature, could no longer be maintained. Miracles, accordingly, should not be distinguished from any other activity of God in the world. Fisher would have none of it. "A miracle," he explained, "is an event which the forces of Nature or secondary causes, operating thus under the ordinary Divine preservation, are incompetent to produce." A miracle was by definition extraordinary.[12]

Nor would Fisher ultimately reconsider the possibility of postbiblical miracles. By implication, both Smith and Fisher had opened the door for the possibility of examining these later miracles. Both men, having rejected the old argument that miracles attested to revelation, and having insisted instead that they were signs of the true revelation, confronted the obvious question: why, then, should miracles be limited to the biblical epoch? Was there not a continuing need for highlighting and elevating Christian truth in the present, particularly on the mission field, where such highlighting would be a great boon? Although maintaining that postbiblical miracles were not to be rejected out of hand, Fisher in fact granted them very little credence. He dismissed accounts of postbiblical miracles due to a lack of evidence: "A defect in the character of the testimony, in the habits of careful observation, or of trustworthy reporting . . . prevents us from giving credit to the Catholic miracles." Nor did he admit that one should expect to find miracles on the mission field. Fisher continued to employ a model of sacred history that was sharply delineated between the biblical era, in which revelation was received, and all later history when this salvational knowledge was merely diffused. Miracles were necessary to the former era, but not to the latter; although the first generation needed miracles to accomplish their tasks, the modern church did not need them. "The origination of Christianity, a method of salvation, is beyond human power; not so the propagation of the religion which is once so communicated," Fisher argued. "We agree that the general method of the Divine government is that of leaving men to discover for themselves what the unaided human faculties are competent to find out." The true proof of Christianity at that time was the "operation of Christianity in the world."[13]

As one sees in Fisher's writings, a three-hundred-year-old pattern was difficult to break. Despite his pointed rejection of the evidentialism of eighteenth-century apologists like Paley, under the patina of his new theological themes lay the old view of a limited age of miracles. Miracles continued to be connected with the origins of scripture and the foundation of the church. The question of modern miracles drew him back to the safe harbor of the traditional Protestant argument.

The last of the commentators, James McCosh, fits only partially into our discussion. When he wrote *The Supernatural in Relation to the Natural,* he was a Scottish philosopher then teaching in Ulster. Yet considering his significant American career as president of Princeton University (1868–1888), his importance as both an evangelical leader and a philosopher, and his later fame as a reconciler of Christianity and Darwinism, he merits discussion here.

It was both as a church leader and a philosopher that McCosh commented on the question of miracles. He was well aware of the philosophical criticisms of the miraculous implicit in works such as *Essays and Reviews.* But he was equally cognizant of the great popular interest in miracles. Although he rejoiced, for example, at the religious revival that swept through Ulster in the late 1850s, he recognized that it was carried along by a flood of popular religious enthusiasm and a series of remarkable miraculous-like occurrences. Like Jonathan Edwards a century earlier, McCosh wanted to affirm the reality of this religious experientialism while guarding against its excesses.[14]

The Supernatural in Relation to the Natural strove to find a middle path between those individuals smitten by the supernatural and those who in the name of the new pantheism desired to excise all talk of miracles from Christianity. In McCosh's view, both opponents of miracles and devotees of modern miracles erred in their understanding of the supernatural by equating it with the idea of God's activity in the world. Nature and supernature, he explained, were equally arenas of God's activity. He likened the world of nature to an island. Just as an island was self-contained, consistent, and understandable in its own terms while surrounded by a larger ocean, so too was the relationship between nature and the supernatural. Nature was surrounded by the ocean of the supernatural. Both, however, were part of the wider providence of God, and hence whereas it was proper to distinguish between nature and supernature, one could not make a distinction between the natural and the divine.

Natural events were produced by natural causes, yet these causes were ultimately from God.

> It is not a miracle when a tower stands, nor is it a miracle when it falls and kills "thirteen" persons, while others may escape. It is not supernatural, but natural, when the ship sails along buoyantly in the favourable breeze; and it is not supernatural, but natural, when it is wrecked by a storm which arose, as it passed a rugged coast, and drove it upon the rocks. It was certainly by the appointment of God, but it was quite by natural agency, that ninety-nine persons in the ship perished, while one was saved; it behoves that one to bless the Lord for his wonderful escape, and his gratitude should not be lessened when he discovers that God has accomplished it by a particular whirl of wind, raising a fortunate wave which brought a fragment of floating wreck to him, and drove it on the shore as he clung to it in despairing agonies.[15]

The distinction between miracle and providence still played an important role for McCosh. God's normal relationship with the world was providential. In contrast, a miracle, as a truly supernatural action, was by definition an intervention — an action by an agent beyond the natural.

But why, he proceeded to ask, did God perform special supernatural actions or miracles, and did they not imply imperfections in the divine ordering of nature? To answer this question, McCosh offered a refinement of the old notion of miraculous dispensation. In the divine ordering of the world there was both a regular system of nature and of supernature. The supernatural system — only partially comprehended by humans — was no more serendipitous than the system of nature, but rather operated as part of the great plan for the redemption of the world. Accordingly, the question of supernatural interventions was directly involved with God's plan of salvation. Miraculous interventions were never acts of pure volition but always served the larger purpose of manifesting divine love and restoring peace and holiness. Using the miracles of the Gospels (and by no means even all of these) as paradigms, he suggested that the higher function of these events could be seen in the words used to describe them: power, sign, and wonder. In McCosh's words, "His 'powers' were not displayed in such acts as making rivers run back to their sources; or in causing the heavenly bodies to wander from their spheres, or in spreading wasting and destruction." Jesus' miracles restored order where disorder had prevailed. In this regard the most typical of miracles were the healing accounts; they testified to the linking of love and power, as well as revealed a crucial truth about the plan of salvation. Like Fisher, McCosh was only willing to acknowledge that miracles were evidences in a limited sense. They functioned in tandem with other parts of the Christian revelation; they affirmed the truthfulness of the doctrine, and they were attested to by the doctrines. As with an arch, each stone supported the other, but the key stone for McCosh (as it was for Fisher) was the character of Jesus. In his ministry, as recorded in scripture, Christ "accomplished, as God commonly does in his providence, two ends by one and the same means: — he showed that he came to this earth gifted with Divine power; but he showed too, that he came filled with Divine Love."[16] Although miracles did not prove the truthfulness of the ministry of Jesus, they were ineluctably associated with it.

Finally McCosh turned to the question of postbiblical miracles. To evaluate them, he suggested that there might exist a third category along with the natural and the supernatural: the preternatural. The preternatural entailed the possibility of supranatural intervention within the mundane world by some other power than God. The alleged accounts of ghosts, demons, and other extranatural occurrences would fall into this category. So too would the whole vast array of alleged postbiblical miracles, as would the alleged wonders of the Ulster revival. But clearly McCosh invoked the category of preternatural not to praise these phenomena but to bury them. Because the supernatural and preternatural were fundamentally different phenomena, he argued, they had to be treated differently.

Here McCosh attempted to provide an answer to the old question posed by David Hume and others: how could Protestants accept the evidence for biblical miracles while rejecting the claims of later ones? One recalls that since at least the eighteenth century, skeptical writers had gleefully criticized the Protestant willingness to dismiss postbiblical miraculous occurrences, many of which were in fact better documented than were the biblical miracles. Baden Powell in *Essays and Reviews* also took up this criticism, and chided the orthodox for their skepticism concerning clairvoyance and spiritual rappings. McCosh argued, however, that miracles, as part of a larger system of the supernatural, had a rational and salvific nature. One could rightly expect to find them at key periods in the history of salvation. For this reason, miracles as supernatural events could be accepted even when the evidence for them was not overwhelming. Because they rationally fit into the larger picture of God's plan, they could be given the benefit of the doubt. Preternatural occurrences could not be privy to such benefit of the doubt. Because they appeared serendipitous rather than connected with any great supernatural system, they hung or fell on the weight of the individual evidence for each alleged case. And in McCosh's view, none of these occurrences could meet this higher criticism.

Thus these three mid-century writers — Smith, Fisher, and McCosh — shared a number of views. They all understood the supernatural to be a foundational element of Christianity that should be defended at all cost. The question of miracles was important for them because it played a role in the larger question of the defense of the supernatural. Second, to a man they were influenced by the themes of the mediating theological tradition, and rejected the old evidentialist apologetics. The authority of Christianity was not tied to its miracles but to the internal authority of the Christian message. Third, these two concerns led them to elevate the personality of Jesus, rather than his miracles alone, as the touchstone of the divine. But we must emphasize that although these writers deemphasized the evidential role of the miracles of Jesus, they continued to defend their reality. Finally, despite their appeal to the reality of the supernatural, they all in their own ways continued to defend the traditional Protestant claim of a limited age of miracles.

Horace Bushnell and Modern Miracles

Of the mid-nineteenth-century American commentators, by far the most famous was the Congregationalist Horace Bushnell. Indeed, Bushnell is perhaps the one theologian whom students of nineteenth-century American religious history may actually have ever read to some degree, and he alone among these individuals is still accorded respect as a theologian. As the author of two of the best-known theological writings of the period (his volume *Christian Nurture,* which criticized revivalism, and his "Preliminary Dissertation on the Nature of Language," which emphasized the symbolic nature of religious language), he is usually pictured as the father of American theological liberalism. Yet he was a far more polyvalent figure and one of his interests was the miraculous.[17]

One factor that differentiates Bushnell from the writers discussed heretofore is that he wrote not as an academic but as a pastor. For over twenty-five years before the 1858 publication of *Nature and the Supernatural,* he served the North [Congregational] Church, Hartford. His ministry there was to a socially rising middle-class congregation, and among his challenges was adapting inherited evangelical understandings to the new Victorian urban environment. One challenge in particular was the question of Christian confidence. Since at least the Great Awakening of the 1740s, New England Congregationalists had emphasized the centrality of the conversion experience for the Christian life. One determinant of whether one was in right relationship to God was the ability to testify to an experience of conversion. Many in Bushnell's flock, and indeed Bushnell himself at least until 1848, had trouble achieving this experiential certainty. His volume *Christian Nurture* outlined the possibility of grounding the Christian life on the nurturing experience of the pious Christian family instead of on a dramatic conversion experience. Throughout his ministry he wrote and preached thoughtfully on the role of personal experience in Christian confidence. Again and again he returned to the question of how one could be sure that God was real.[18]

This pastoral question is one that lies behind *Nature and the Supernatural*. To experience with certainty the reality of the supernatural was a crying need of the day. In a letter to his daughter, Bushnell explained, "We should most naturally expect that God would not hide himself from his creatures. . . . The infidels have said, 'If there be a God, why does he not show himself? Is there anything so important to man to know as God? Why, then, is this kept so ambiguous and dark, when other things are clear?' Are they not right, — that is, right so far as they assume the certainty that a living God will show himself the living God?"[19]

Nature and the Supernatural in many ways fits the broad contours of the discussion as set out by Smith, Fisher, and McCosh. Like these authors, Bushnell revolted against the old eighteenth-century evidentialist apologia. Similarly he took aim against the modern skeptics for their undermining of the true foundation of Christianity. Although his volume was published too early to include Renan in his critique (except in the preface of the 1864 edition), he did address Strauss as well as Theodore Parker. Finally, like the others, Bushnell recognized that the question of miracles could not be divorced from the broader question of the supernatural. Yet Bushnell is far bolder in his willingness to jettison older arguments and set forth new understandings.

Nature and the Supernatural can be divided into three sections: one that deals with the theoretical question, one that considers the figure of Jesus, and one that raises the question of postbiblical miracles. From the outset Bushnell acknowledged that the Christian faith found itself confronted with the great challenge of the "new infidelity" that attempted to strip it of its supernatural content. Not only skeptics and philosophers, but also almost all aspects of modern life — business, medicine, politics — seemed to war against the idea of the supernatural. The great challenge for the church was to defend its reality. Here, however, the church was hampered by a common misconception that had grown up around the supernatural. Earlier apologists had been so careful in protecting and isolating the supernatural that they had ironically succeeded in making it "too fantastic and ghostly to admit a possible defence."[20] In contrast, Bushnell preferred to cast a very broad net around the supernatural. He defined it as that which was not in the chain of natural cause and effect — that which acted upon cause and effect from without. The essence of the supernatural was will or freedom and the affectation of nature. He offered as an analogy the relationship between a ball and a child. The ball was like nature: passive, dumb, and completely dependent upon the forces of nature for its location and movement. The child was like a supernatural force, who through will (or, in this case, a kick) influenced the ball by sending it in a trajectory that left to itself it would never have accomplished. The supernatural acted upon the natural in this same way; when it intervened in the course of the natural it endowed the latter with new thrust and direction. For Bushnell human beings as moral agents were themselves supernatural beings, and even an action such as lifting an arm could be viewed as a supernatural triumph of will over nature.[21] The power of personality and character to move, effect, and indeed even to change the course of nature and history testified to this supernatural basis.

Yet if human beings had the power to affect the natural, so even more did God. God, like humanity, could "kick" nature when he chose and give it altogether new force and direction. For evidence he appealed to the biological theory of the Harvard scientist Louis Agassiz, the leading American biologist during the writing of *Nature and the Supernatural*. Agassiz explained the development of species through a series of special creations accomplished by God: "whole realms of living creatures disappear again and again, to be succeeded by others fresh from the hand of God." These divine interventions within the course of nature that changed the course of life were the divine "kicks." Yet the interventions were more than mere acts of will, particularly in the religious realm; rather they flowed from the divine nature. They were God's response to a fallen world and disordered humanity, and they strove to produce what no mere law of nature could ever bring about. Supernatural interventions were part of the great goal of bringing the created order to its ultimate end.[22]

The second part of *Nature and the Supernatural* focused on the figure of Jesus. Here Bushnell also followed his contemporaries in grounding the witness of Christ upon his character. For Bushnell, one recalls, all character was supernatural, yet the character of Jesus was qualitatively superior to that of any other human being. Bushnell was singularly eloquent in his description of Jesus' personality as the chief evidence of his supernatural nature. Chapter 10 of *Nature and the Supernatural*, "The Character of Jesus Forbidding His Possible Classification with Men," quickly became the most heralded part of the volume and one of the best-known parts of Bushnell's corpus. It was later often reprinted as a separate volume. As one early commentator noted, "It has the finish of a classic, and by frequent republication has already become one."[23] Bushnell here broke decisively from the old argument that tied Jesus' authority to his performance of miracles, and, lifting up a theme that had been touched on by other writers, he made it the central point of his chapter. It was through his *character*, he explained, that Christ's true nature was revealed. "He comes into the world full of all moral beauty, as God of physical [beauty];

and as God was not obliged to set himself to a course of aesthetic study, when he created the forms and landscapes of the world, so Christ comes to his rules, by no critical practice in words. . . . He does not dress up a moral picture and ask you to observe its beauty, he only tells you how to live; and the most beautiful characters the world has ever seen, have been those who received and lived his precepts without once conceiving their beauty."[24]

The character of Christ revealed in the gospels was the greatest of miracles, Bushnell argued. Through it one can see a living embodiment of the gospel message of love, moral beauty, and virtue. This claim would reverberate throughout a generation of Protestant liberals, and it is often used to support Bushnell's appellation as father of American liberalism.[25] But one should note that Bushnell, by linking Christ's authority to his character rather than his miracles, far from rejected biblical miracles; in fact, he gave them new credence. Most immediately Bushnell argued that Jesus' character and moral beauty confirmed his miracles and established a moral distinction between his miracles and purported pagan and Romish miracles. True miracles had to be both physical (that is, stemming from the intervention of a superhuman force within nature) and moral. But Bushnell went further by venturing to suggest a new understanding of the purpose of miracles in the divine economy. Their role lay not in validating revelation, he wrote, but more properly in the practical certainty they offered of the reality of a transcendent God. As he noted, "There is no way to escape the faith of miracles and hold the faith of a personal God and Creator."[26] Miracles served for Bushnell as vivid reminders of the power of the supernatural and of the limitations of the natural order.

One comes then to the last and most controversial section of the volume. Bushnell's new understanding of the purpose of miracles further led him to question the long cherished Protestant rejection of postbiblical miracles. For him, the traditional position was fundamentally flawed, because "if miracles are inherently incredible . . . nothing is gained by thrusting them back into remote ages of time."[27] Hence in chapter 14 of his work Bushnell set forth his claim that miracles, far from having been suspended, have occurred at all times in Christian history. Postbiblical miracles served the same function as biblical miracles in emphasizing the reality of a supernatural deity. Because miracles were "to lift the church out of the abysses of a mere second-hand religion, keeping it alive and open to the realities of God's immediate visitation," they were appropriate during any age.[28]

Underlying Bushnell's claim was a fundamentally different picturing of sacred history than that usually employed by Protestant apologists. Instead of positing an apostolic age of miracles that stood in contradistinction to all that followed, Bushnell offered a dialectical understanding of the activity of the

divine in sacred history. The Christian community historically fluctuated between periods of extreme rationalism, during which God's role in the world
was largely ignored, and periods of hyper-supernaturalism — or "Corinthian-
ism" — when miracles, signs, and wonders were sought after as ends in themselves. The propriety of miracles varied according to the age. During periods
of oppressive rationalism, God would "break forth in miracle and holy gifts,
[to] let it be seen that he is still the living God, in the midst of his dead people."
Conversely, during times of excess when the "sobriety of faith is lost in the
gossip of credulity," miracles, signs, and wonders tended to decline.[29] The
dialectic, however, had been interrupted for some time by the increasingly
more rigid Protestant rejection of postbiblical miracles. This in turn led to two
negative effects. One was that Protestant commentators were forced to employ skeptical arguments in their rejection of modern miracles. Bushnell used
as an example the debate that occurred over the manifestation of healings and
glossolalia in Scotland in the 1830s. Protestant opponents to these excite-
ments were forced to take "precisely the [same] ground as Mr. Hume, as
respects the credibility of miracles performed now" — that is, that any other
explanation was more probable than the miraculous. A second negative effect
was that the Protestant's adamancy increasingly left them with only a secondhand religion that provided no way of satisfying the natural human craving for the supernatural. Thus modern individuals, with nowhere within the
church to turn, began seeking out the modern "sorcery" of animal magnetism,
spiritualism, and ghosts.[30]

Turning from the theoretical issue, Bushnell proceeded to offer a reassess-
ment of several post-Reformation miracle claims.[31] Reaching back to the
seventeenth century, he looked favorably at the accounts, recorded by John
Howe, of spiritual premonitions, divine judgments, and providential escapes
by the Scottish covenanters.[32] He was similarly positive concerning the healings recorded in George Fox's *Journal,* the charismatic gifts exhibited by the
"French Prophets" in early eighteenth-century England, and the oft-disputed
healings associated with the tomb of the Abbé Pâris. All of these examples,
according to Bushnell, possessed the proper combination of moral character
and supernaturalism that allowed them to be considered as modern-day miracles. He furthermore displayed keen interest in the outbreaks of glossolalia
and miraculous healings in Scotland in the early 1830s, associated with the
brothers James and George MacDonald. Indeed, Bushnell, the theoretician on
language, seemed to find great significance in modern glossolalia: "[T]here
is . . . sublimity in this gift of tongues, as related to the great mystery of
language; suggesting possibly, that all our tongues are from the Eternal Word,
in souls; there being, in his intelligent nature as Word, millions doubtless of

possible tongues, that are as real to him as the spoken tongues of the world."[33] Because he viewed all language as symbolic and proximate in meaning, Bushnell found nothing scandalous about this direct language of the spirit. On the contrary, these outbursts, with the spirit "playing the vocal organs of a man," demonstrated the power of the supernatural. The Eternal spirit when it chose could overwhelm the limitations of human discourse just as easily as it overwhelmed the limitations of physical nature through miraculous healings. Bushnell concluded his discussion by offering a series of accounts of present-day miracles, which he himself had gathered. One described how a strange dream led to the rescue of a stranded company of persons at the Carson Valley Pass in California. Others described further occurrences of glossolalia and healings. Lastly Bushnell related an experience of his own in which an uneducated former slave with "a message from the Lord" gave him prophetic rebuke and direction.[34] All of these occurrences, argued Bushnell, testified that miracles were as omnipresent in the modern era as they had ever been.

Bushnell's openness to modern miracles was viewed as a horrible scandal at the time, and was criticized soundly.[35] Similarly, later sympathetic students have usually dismissed his interest in miracles as a product of his unsophisticated philosophical categories. As one biographer explained, "a full doctrine of the divine immanence would have rendered needless many brilliant pages."[36] We should nonetheless pause, however, before unqualifiedly accepting a picture of Bushnell as a frustrated liberal who was condemned by his ignorance of the idea of divine immanence to never grasp the full implications of his own ideas. For if Bushnell was by no means a logically rigorous thinker, we should not underestimate his sensitivity as a religious analyst. Bushnell's defense of modern miracles seems to have been no mere intellectual speculation; rather it stemmed from an awareness of the religious state of his parishioners. This practical consideration is reflected in the final chapter of *Nature and the Supernatural,* where he hinted at the pastoral advantages of his view of miracles.

The first advantage of Bushnell's view was the way in which miracles highlighted the reality of the divine and served as a continual reminder that the God worshiped in the churches was not some dead "metallic meteor" but a vital and active power. Indeed if the intellectual question of the second half of the nineteenth century was the reconciliation of the old scripture and beliefs with the new learning, an important popular theme of religion during this period was the quest for the certainty of a transcendent reality or the vitality of the spiritual world.[37] What evidence did modern believers have that God was real and personal? Throughout *Nature and the Supernatural* Bushnell argued that a religion that had lost its confidence that God acted in the course of history and nature would inevitably succumb to lassitude. This belief lay behind his sharp critique of Emerson and Parker, for whom a belief in an omnipresent spirit rendered embarrassing the idea of immediate and personal interventions. No matter how intellectually neat or interesting the pantheism of the Transcendentalists might be, Bushnell the pastor believed it religiously disastrous. Emerson had rescued the immanence of God through his pantheistic mysticism, but had sacrificed his active personality. Emerson's Transcendentalism was dismissed as a "Bramanism" that might delight the aesthetic impulse, but which had no transforming power. Immanence was not enough; God must be present both in human character and in wonders such as glossolalia, premonitions, and healings. Bushnell's concern with miracles hence reflected his larger concern with the reality of the transcendent.[38]

Second, Bushnell believed that an emphasis upon miracles and the supernatural activities of God in the world could reinvigorate the Christian community. Just as Christianity was suffering from a diet of secondhand experientialism, so too did it suffer from secondhand knowledge. Natural theology, which culled nature for evidence of religious truths but ignored the great outpouring of supernatural "facts" such as "dreams, prophecies, premonitions, visions" and the like, had led even orthodox theology down the road to pantheism. These labors would never provide evidence for a supernatural deity because no God could be proven by an appeal to nature except the God of nature. Using a standard Romantic distinction, Bushnell claimed that if Christianity were to prosper it must not base its knowledge of God upon the "laboratories of our understanding," but rather on the revelation of divine transcendence that our encounter with the supernatural provided.[39]

Clearly, then, Bushnell's interest in the miraculous was central to both his understanding the relationship between God and the world and to his reconstruction of Christian theology. In certain ways his interest can be seen as a counterbalance to his views on language, for if his famous theory of language challenged the reigning biblical basis of Protestant theology, his theory of miracles appears to offer a new foundation. Writing before the great Liberal-Conservative fission over biblical inerrancy, Bushnell argued that the supernatural truth of the gospels lay not in "verbal inspiration," — "no point of infallibility . . . so as to prick and fasten each particular iota" — but instead upon the person of Christ, the reality of his miracles, and the power of the supernatural. Indeed the continuation of supernatural occurrences in the modern age could provide a new empirical basis for Christian understanding. Though no longer linked to revelation as they had been in the old schema, miracles nonetheless did reveal a spiritual reality: "Christ comes into the world from without, to bestow himself by a presentation. He is a new premise, that could not be reasoned, but must first *be*, and then can be received only by faith. When he is so received or appropriated, he is, of course, experienced or known by experiment; in that manner verified — he that believeth hath the witness in himself. The manner, therefore, of this divine experience, called faith, is *strictly Baconian*. And the result is an experimental knowledge of God, or an experimental acquaintance with God, in the reception of his supernatural communications."[40]

According to Bushnell, Christians hence need never be ashamed of religious experience and view it as somehow lower than philosophical knowledge; rather, they should consider it essential. Christian understanding based on supernatural experientialism could provide for the present age a new basis for Christian unity, one equally open to the educated and uneducated, to the rich and the poor.

What does one make of Bushnell's discussion? On one level the question is simple. He clearly rejected the old Protestant argument about miracles and proposed instead a new experientialism. Yet he was never completely clear about the nature of this experience, and because his examples ran the gamut from dynamic personalities to miraculous healings, his writings are open to alternative interpretations. Part of this ambiguity stems from his writing style, which was always more evocative than precise, but it also lies in his reliance on a number of ambiguous concepts in his defense of the supernatural.

One such concept encompassed his definition of the supernatural as a force acting upon causality and his further analogical linking of human will and divine will as supernatural powers. Contemporaries recognized the novelty of this assertion, and its problems. One writer noted, "There is no difficulty in proving that there is a God if men are gods, that there are angels if men are angels, that the Bible is inspired if all great writers are inspired, or that the supernatural exists if we ourselves are supernatural."[41] Through such an argument one could conclude that the human will was elevated to the level of the supernatural and became an icon of the transcendent. Interpreted from the perspective of contemporary Transcendentalism, this elevation of the will to the level of the supernatural seems at one with Emerson's image of the transparent eyeball and in keeping with the interest in philosophical idealism slowly emerging at the time. Yet read from another perspective, Bushnell's analogy is open to a very different interpretation, particularly when one considers what it implied about the nature of the divine will, which was seen to have complete freedom to intervene in the natural. This freedom to intervene lay behind the interest in contemporary miracles.

Bushnell's argument turned upon another radical reformulation: the de facto abandonment of the distinction between primary and secondary causality. As one recalls, the Protestant rejection of postbiblical miracles rested upon a careful distinction between the categories of miracle and providence. Both were from God, but miracles were acts of primary cause, whereas providential events were of secondary cause. An event in which God affected the world through an intervention in nature (such as in turning water into wine) was a miracle. An event in which God affected the world by working through nature (such as guiding a floating branch to a drowning mariner) was merely providential. The distinction between miracle and providence had been crucial for Fisher and McCosh. But Bushnell was willing to jettison it. The fact of affectation, and not the method of the affectation, was for him the benchmark of the miraculous. Accordingly, he lumped together all manner of occurrences in his discussion, from the character of Cromwell to the healings of the Abbé Pâris. All could serve as evidence of the reality of the higher realm. Underlying this entire discussion, however, was a very different understanding of evidence. A key part of the old Protestant position had been that, in contrast to all acts of providence, the testimony of miracles had an objective authority. The image invoked in the eighteenth century, that of a trial of the witnesses, implied that the testimony of the miracles was sufficient to convict Jesus of messiahship in a court of law. This distinction between the subjective witness of acts of providence and the objective authority of miracles was likewise abandoned by Bushnell. The evidential value of all of Bushnell's miracles became to a large degree personal and subjective. Few others might be convinced by Bushnell's account of a "message from the Lord" delivered by the freed slave, but for Bushnell its reality was unshakable.[42]

Personal surety, not public testimony, was the purpose of supernatural occurrences. And here too one could draw widely differing conclusions. For some this blending of primary and secondary causality and subjectivizing of the supernatural effectively removed the question of miracles from public discussion, or at best made any discussion of the miraculous a subset of the larger question of the personal religious experience. Yet others saw Bushnell's recasting of the discussion as justification for a far greater interest in miracles than there had been for centuries. Both are possible readings, and it is not surprising that both later liberals and later Pentecostalists turned to Bushnell for support of their views.[43]

Of course what some critics might fault as ambiguity, proponents might define as comprehensiveness. The decades following the death of Bushnell would witness the fracturing of American Protestantism into various squabbling groups, and, as we shall see, the question of the miraculous was crucial in these divisions. By the end of the century few individuals could be found who like Bushnell were interested in both the symbolic theory of language and incidences of glossolalia. Bushnell's was a road not taken.

A Changing Order

As we have noted, by the early 1870s the questions of miracles and prayer were increasingly being linked. Some religious thinkers, like Bushnell, did so to extend credibility to miracles, but others had a far different agenda. John Tyndall, one remembers, had scandalized the religious community by his common criticisms of miracles and prayer, and these remained to be answered.

Tyndall posed two difficult questions in particular. The first was the question of causality: by what means or force did the divine interfere in the physical? The second was that of evidence: what certainty was there that any such interventions had indeed occurred? His American critics, however, chose to focus not on these challenges but on a number of underlying assumptions. Tyndall's error, argued James McCosh, was his failure to accept the supernatural as an independent realm; instead he reduced it to the category of the natural. Just as one must accept the fundamental reality of nature to undertake scientific inquiry, so too must one accept the reality and suppositions of the religious experience when discussing things spiritual.[44] The natural and the spiritual were both realities, but were different in their essence. Whereas the physical world operated according to the law of necessity, the spiritual world was ruled by will. According to McCosh, human experience illuminated this distinction. All children learned from an early age that one survived in nature by learning its laws but one lived in a family by learning the will of one's parents and trusting in their love. The relationship between God and the believer, in McCosh's view, was far more analogous to that of a parent and child than to a blind law of nature. Hence God did not answer (or refuse to answer) prayer out of some law of necessity, but from will based upon his greater knowledge. McCosh gave as an example the case of Prince Albert of England, who had died of cholera despite the heartfelt prayers of the nation. According to his paradigm, this was not an example of failed prayer, but of a higher divine wisdom, because the prince's death may have dissuaded Victoria from acceding to her advisers' call for intervention in the American Civil War. Because God did not always answer prayer, it was impossible to measure the effectiveness of prayer by means of a prayer gauge.

Mark Hopkins, a noted author and president of Williams College, continued this critique. Human beings knew from experience that will could effect nature, hence a confidence in the efficacy of prayer was tied to a confidence in the personhood of God. Tyndall's error was that he confused prayer and miracle. All divine intervention was supernatural—that is, an intervention of the divine into the natural—but only some of these interventions were miracles. A miracle was a transcending of the law of nature by pure will. Agreeing with Bushnell's claim that all acts of will were in some sense supernatural, Hopkins maintained, in contrast, that simple acts of will could not be classified as miracles because physical measures were employed.[45] God answered prayer, he went on to explain, nonmiraculously: he influenced nature, but did not overturn it. To expect that these subtle manipulations could be measured by the means of a gauge was foolishness. Hopkins put great emphasis as well upon the metaphor of the fatherhood of God, and saw in the divine character the reason why God did not answer prayer by means of miracles. Just as a loving parent balanced a child's desires with the entire household's well-being, so too did God. It would be as improper to ask God to answer a prayer by violating nature with a miracle as it would be for a child to ask a parent to burn down his or her house.

Such responses, whatever their cogency, never fully addressed the central thrust of Tyndall's challenge: whether there was any empirical evidence that prayer affected nature. Both Hopkins and McCosh felt compelled instead to explain the personal experience of prayer—namely, that there was within the human heart a strong impulse to pray, and that confidence in God as father undergirded the confidence in prayer. As in the earlier discussion of miracles, one sees the question of prayer subtly transformed through its linkage with the question of character. Prayer was understood to be an outflow of the human religious spirit as much as miracles were an extension of the character of Jesus. But embedded even in these responses were deeper and more troublesome questions that would come back again in the debate over modern miracles. The resting of the confidence in prayer on the image of the loving relationship between parent and child implied more than either McCosh or Hopkins was willing to grant. It was undoubtedly true, for example, that it would be excessive for a parent to destroy a house to please a child. Yet might not a loving parent do so if the alternative was the death of that child? One of the characteristics of a human parent, ideally, was a love of a child greater than the love of any domicile.

Furthermore the analogy made the assumption of a limited age of miracles far more problematic than it had been earlier. The old Protestant evidentialist argument, despite its obvious problems, was at least morally unambiguous. God intervened in the world, whether miraculously or providentially, for his own sake—whether for the elucidation of revelation or the manifestation of his glory—and the believer had no grounds to expect intervention otherwise.

By linking divine intervention with the parental character of the deity, there always remained the lurking question of the nature of divine goodness. Hopkins's confident assertion that a loving God would not feed his children miraculously while they could feed themselves offered little solace to the starving — particularly when they recalled the abundance of fish and bread provided in the gospels to those who merely missed their lunch. If miracles were not performed for the purpose of revelation, but instead represented an effluence of divine beneficence, what then did they imply about the relative importance of biblical hunger and contemporary hunger? As we will see in later chapters, the early proponents of faith healing offered a very different answer to the question of how God answered prayer.

Embarrassing Yet Necessary Heirlooms

Smith, Fisher, McCosh, and Bushnell all wrote during the middle years of the century, and as I have suggested they shared certain common concerns, not the least of which was a defense of the supernatural. By the early 1880s, however, a great change in the tenor of theological discussion occurred. The defense of the supernatural that had seemed so crucial in the early 1860s was now seen by many as passe. Indeed a word study of one of the better known theological volumes of this latter period, *Progressive Orthodoxy* (a work written by individuals who saw themselves as the heirs of Bushnell), shows that even the term supernatural appears only fleetingly.[46]

This change reflected an intellectual revolution that cannot be understood without some discussion of the effect of Charles Darwin.[47] Darwin's influence upon religion in America is an immensely studied subject and here is not the place to summarize it, but in at least two key ways Darwin's revolution had a decided effect on the question of the miraculous. The first concerned the broad question of the relationship between God and the world. Agassiz's theory of a series of discontinuous special creations could be invoked by a writer like Bushnell to support the traditional view of miracles as divine interventions. Bushnell drew an explicit parallel, for example, between the special creation of species and the miraculous incarnation. If God acted by dramatic intervention to create humanity, it seemed eminently reasonable that he would act in a similar way to redeem the human race. Darwin's vision of evolution, however, posited a uniformity of change and needed no divine intervention. Once one accepted Darwin and his evolutionary paradigm, dramatic discontinuous divine interventions lost their scientific credibility. Nature progressed, according to Darwin's theory, on the basis of uniform law. Scientific explanation accordingly rested upon appeals to uniform causality and not upon appeals to any deus ex machina. The triumph of the principle of uniformitarianism in late Victorian science and the response of Christian evolutionists to this challenge has been well documented: God must be seen as being immanent in creation and a continual presence in nature. Viewed in this way, there was no contradiction between evolution and God's purpose; rather in evolution one saw the working out of God's plan. But if this appeal to divine immanence may have solved the problem of reconciling a doctrine of God and evolution, it dealt a serious blow to the traditional view of the supernatural. Bushnell, one recalls, had likened God's actions in the world to a child kicking a ball. The analogy presupposed that God and nature were sufficiently separate that such kicks could take place. But if one presupposed a far closer or more intimate interconnection, such as that between the mind and the body, any such kicks became conceptually far more difficult.

The second intellectual challenge of this era that must be noted was the question of human nature itself. "What is man that thou art mindful of him?" was a question on the lips of many. Broadly speaking, the crucial religious question during these later decades no longer seemed to be the question of God but instead anthropology, or more precisely, the divine spirit in human nature. One obvious answer to such a question was to look to the figure of Jesus, particularly Jesus as the reflector of true human nature and of the divine spirit. The great interest during these years in lives of Jesus is well attested, and at least one factor in this interest was the vision of Jesus as the revealer of the true nature of both God and humanity.[48] Many writers followed Bushnell in anchoring the authority of Jesus upon his character, but unlike Bushnell, who in turn used Jesus' character to anchor anew the miracle stories of the gospel, this later generation deemed gospel miracles a burden to defend rather than an epiphany to celebrate.

These intellectual currents did much to shift concern away from the miraculous, yet other factors continued to counterbalance this tendency and still reinforce the importance of miracles. The first such factor was the prominent place of the miracle stories in the biblical picture of Jesus. From the virgin birth to the ascension, the incarnation was described in miraculous terms. Furthermore, in the ministry of Jesus accounts of nature miracles, healings, and exorcisms abounded. It was one thing to downplay them; it was far more difficult to deny them all together because it was generally recognized that to excise them from the biblical narrative would irreparably damage the picture of Jesus. There was accordingly little sympathy among writers associated with the evangelical denominations for the radical criticism of Renan and Strauss. Indeed, one characteristic rhetorical stance of progressive scholars was to mediate between Strauss and simple literalism. Miracles still needed to be defended to preserve the figure of Jesus. In this regard Americans paralleled the practice of British scholars.

A second factor militating against a complete acceptance of uniformitarianism was the continuing concern about defending the power of prayer. The controversy raised over Tyndall's prayer gauge was a reminder of the close connection between miracles and prayer. Both presupposed a degree of divine intervention that was at best problematic from a scientific perspective. Yet from the religious perspective the impulse to pray was too fundamental to surrender easily. The notion of petitionary prayer was deeply entwined in common spirituality, and each time a believer repeated the phrase "give us this day our daily bread," she might be reminded of the fundamental belief in God as a loving father who responds to needs. Those who accepted the compromise of Christian evolution strove to answer the perplexing question of how prayer, and in particular petitionary and intercessory prayer, could be justified if uniformitarianism were assumed. Hence despite the intellectual problems involved with them, throughout the 1870s and 1880s both miracles and prayer were recognized as being an inseparable part of the Christian heritage.

Scholarly discussion during the 1880s was characterized by all these new influences. Theologians were especially interested in adapting the Christian theological understanding to the post-Darwinian universe while preserving the biblical portrait of Jesus. Like jugglers, liberal-leaning theologians tried to keep all of their concerns aloft at once. This unfortunately gave to such discussions a frustrating lack of logical consistency. Nowhere does one see this ambiguity more clearly than among the proponents of the "New Theology," as found in the volume *Progressive Orthodoxy*.[49] These writers, who were heirs of the New England theological tradition, attempted to free Protestantism from its Calvinist mold and to recast it in the light of the new evolutionary faith. *Progressive Orthodoxy* has had the reputation of being a bold and revolutionary theological statement, and on many questions this is undoubtedly true.[50] It was critical of the old view of the atonement that saw the divine human relationship in juridical terms; it raised the possibility of universal salvation; it called for a new understanding of the inspiration of scripture as reflective of a developing religious consciousness; and it criticized a literal reading of the Old Testament. Yet the volume was surprisingly circumspect about the figure of Jesus, including his miracles: "The historical proof connecting the sayings *and acts* of our Lord with the recollections of the apostolic circle is unimpeachable. Christian faith confirms it, declaring that the character showing itself in these deeds and words can be no other than that of the superhuman person whom it calls Lord."[51] Jesus might now be called "superhuman" rather than supernatural as he had been earlier, but his deeds as well as his words were considered sacrosanct. Like their British contemporaries, proponents of the New Theology believed that it was possible to invoke critical attitudes regarding other aspects of Christian theology and scripture but still bracket the figure of Jesus. Dominical miracles might no longer serve a positive purpose, but because of their interconnection with the figure of Jesus they could not be abandoned.

This discussion formed the intellectual context for the American debate over *Robert Elsmere*. I have already noted the tremendous popular reception of the novel in America and have hinted at how this popular interest caught the religious community by surprise. On one level, American commentators had little trouble responding to the challenge the work presented. They characterized it as no more than the warmed-over skepticism of Renan and Strauss they had been refuting for decades. As such, they claimed, it was merely another example of the old rationalistic a priori rejection of revelation, miracles, and the incarnation. Instead, they confidently (and quite mistakenly, as we will see in chapter 6) appealed to the younger generation of German scholars, in particular Adolph Harnack, who were believed to be critical of the excesses of the Tübingen approach to scripture.

The American commentators also agreed that the central issue was the miraculous, but here too they faulted the novel. The liberal theologian Theodore T. Munger argued that the novel's skeptical attacks on miracles ultimately failed. Ward had created a straw man. Few if any sophisticated commentators still saw miracles as evidences; hence the characters' loss of faith following a loss of confidence in miracles was deemed far-fetched. Nor did Ward understand the interconnection between the miracle stories and the figure of Jesus, in Munger's view. They were not evidences but part of the same historical cloth out of which the picture of Jesus was derived. It was not that all of the miracles were to be viewed with the same seriousness, but to abandon them all was to open up the gospel to a spirit of skepticism against which nothing could stand, not even *Elsmere*'s religion of humanity. "The author seems to have no sense of the condition in which the New Testament is left after the miraculous element has been eliminated," noted Munger, "how small and contradictory and inexplicable a remainder — a headless trunk, a web without woof, a page with every other line expunged, a book false in the main but possibly true in a few details, the order of human society emerging from an atmosphere of emotional blunders and ignorant fantasies!"[52]

Perhaps the fullest discussion of *Robert Elsmere* was offered by George A. Gordon, minister of South [Congregational] Church, Boston, who was then emerging as one of the leading popular theological voices of the New Theology. With his British background and interest in both literature and philosophy Gordon was a natural commentator on Ward's novel. He praised it for both its literary merits and for its evocation of a faith in God and service to humanity. Yet according to Gordon the novel failed in its portrait of Jesus. For Ward, Christianity seemed to rest on a collection of evidences, and not upon the great evidence or the character of Jesus. Gordon pointedly contrasted the true character of Jesus with the shadow found in *Robert Elsmere*. It is perhaps significant, however, that in Gordon's moving sketch of the figure of Jesus, upon whom the Christian confidence rested, there is no mention of his miracles. It was not that he rejected the miracles, but that they served no purpose at all. As he wrote, "Were I certain, as I am of my own existence, that a miracle had never taken place in the history of the universe, I should still retain my faith in the divinity of Christ."[53] Gordon's views aptly epitomize the position of the New Theologians by the end of the 1880s. Paley was dead and buried. Miracles had no role as evidences; indeed they served no positive religious purpose at all. They were at best embarrassing heirlooms from an earlier age, but at the same time they were necessary heirlooms; they could not be disposed of without threatening the larger patrimony. Hence the role of the theologian was to find an inoffensive place for them among the furnishings of modern Christianity.

Those outside of the psychological world of liberal Protestant theology expressed little patience with such subterfuge. As one individual noted, the intellectual integrity shown by Robert Elsmere when he became a Unitarian was refreshing, and stood in marked contrast with the compromising nature of modern theologians.[54] The famous writer-naturalist John Burroughs was even more pointed. In his voluminous writings, Burroughs had attempted to bridge the gap between the poetic impulse of Transcendentalism and the new Darwinian science, which for him was the crucial intellectual challenge of the age. He soundly took Munger and others to task for avoiding the fundamental issue. Their careful attempts to preserve the veracity of dominical miracles by means of distinguishing them from all later miracles was, in his view, an exercise in futility. The real question raised by Ward was whether one could reconcile a belief in the biblical miracles with a modern approach to history. As historical knowledge advanced, "semitic dramaturgy becomes less and less credible." Educated persons recognized this and hence they were drawn to works such as *Robert Elsmere*. The clergy, however, blinded themselves to this intellectual advance, and hence even the New Theology was a fraud. "I had hoped," Burroughs lamented, "that the New Theology, as it is called, of which Dr. Munger is one of the exponents, had escaped from some of the trammels of the old, but, so far as I can see, its only escape is to substitute some softer literary phrases for the hard old dogmas. At bottom it seems to be about the same thing."[55]

Conclusion

The American Protestant attitude toward miracles underwent a tremendous transformation between 1855 and 1890. By the end of the 1880s there was a general willingness to jettison the last remnants of the old evidentialist apologetic, which had anchored Jesus' message upon his miracles, and to emphasize instead the person and character of Jesus. But as we have seen, this development inspired two fundamentally different trajectories. Among those moving toward liberalism there was a greater tendency to push the question of the miraculous ever further from center stage, while, for a variety of reasons, still holding on to the miracles of Jesus. For proponents of this view, miracles were "baggage," but necessary baggage. In contrast, for persons such as Horace Bushnell, the collapse of the old evidentialist apologetic raised anew the possibility of a religious role for modern miracles as a continuing supernatural presence of God in the world. This latter view would provide a context for a new Protestant interest in divine healing.

4

The Question of Healing

No topic placed the question of miracles and the divine intervention more squarely in the middle of the religious debate than the role of faith and prayer in healing. As one recalls, it was here that John Tyndall had proposed his infamous "prayer gauge" to determine empirically whether prayer could affect the natural order, and the furor his proposal provoked indicated that he had struck a sensitive nerve in the religious system of the age. But the calumnies hurled against Tyndall only exacerbated the question for many. How was God involved in healing, and was this involvement a miracle or at least a supernatural intervention?

Protestants and Health

The traditional Protestant (and to a lesser degree, Christian) teachings on this question were somewhat convoluted largely because the Christian heritage was fundamentally paradoxical. On the one hand, many parts of both the Old and New Testaments described health as a divine blessing. Chapter 53 of Isaiah (interpreted as a messianic prophecy by most Christians) spoke of the suffering servant as one who took upon himself human suffering and "by his stripes we are healed" (Is 53:5). Furthermore, and more pointedly, the gospels pictured Jesus as a healer who offered sight to the blind, wholeness to crippled, and even life to the dead. For generations, devout Christians meditated on such stories as that found in John 9, in which a man, born blind, expressed his faith in the simple words, "Whether he be a sinner or no, I know not; one thing I do know, whereas I was blind, now I see" (Jn 9:25). When they read the history of the early Christian community, recorded in the Acts of the Apostles, Christians observed Peter proclaiming, "Silver and gold have I none . . . but in the name of Jesus, stand up and walk" (Acts 3:6). This ministry of miraculous healing was a key point in the life of the early church.

On the other hand, Christians were all too conscious that few if any stood up and walked, that those born blind continued in their blindness, and that a tension existed between promises found in the scriptures and the ordinary lives of believers. As pastors, theologians, and spiritual directors of various types had long acknowledged, the world as it existed was far more a vale of tears than a place of miraculous healing — and in the final analysis Job with his boils or St. Paul with his thorn in the flesh were more immediate scriptural realities than were the accounts of dramatic healings. Human existence, though laced with happiness, was shaped by pain and suffering, and in the end death awaited all. The chief role of religion was to interpret this suffering, not remove it, and continually to remind its members that this life was merely a foretaste of the next. Nowhere was this attitude expressed more poignantly than in the famous response from the litany of the Church of England: "In all time of our prosperity, in all time of our tribulation, in the hour of death and in the day of judgement, good Lord deliver us."

What then was the place of prayer in sickness and suffering? As the implications for religion of the Reformation were worked out, it was agreed that prayer might serve a variety of functions. Almost all scholars and pastors admitted that at times prayer did seem to work in the same dramatic way as was described in the biblical record — and that health was occasionally restored when no healing could be expected. Protestant history contained some famous examples of unexpected healings that bordered on the miraculous and seemed to be tied to an answer to prayer. The most famous account was probably Martin Luther's healing of Philip Melanchthon, which was often included in pious histories of the Reformation. As Melanchthon lay dying on his sick bed, the account went, Luther pleaded with God to spare his life. Luther's prayer was said to have included the phrase, "Thou must hear and answer me if thou willest to maintain my trust in thy promises." Melanchthon did dramatically recover, and Luther was convinced that his recovery was tied to his prayer.[1]

Far more common was what pastors and theologians labeled "providential" responses to prayer. In these cases health was restored, but in a more natural and less dramatic way. We have already seen how J. B. Mozley referred to these occurrences as "invisible" miracles because no law of nature was violated, and divine activity could only be intuited. To the eyes of the faithful, however, such acts of providence were seen as the answer to prayer. An example of this type of activity was the recovery of the Prince of Wales discussed earlier. Health followed after a season of devout prayer by clergy and laity, and God was given the thanks. It was just such claims of providentialism that Tyndall had taken such glee in exploding. As Tyndall wryly noted, any "answer" to prayer that was merely in the eye of the beholder could provide no confidence for the empirical interconnection between prayer and the restoration of health. Their very subjective nature made them little more than wishful thinking on the part of believers.

Still more frequently, however, prayer seemed not to "work" at all, if work were to be narrowly defined as the restoration of health. People continued to die before their time; many suffered from painful and debilitating diseases; and widows and orphans were still left comfortless. Whatever the efficacy of prayer might be, most of Christian existence suggested that it was not linked to this world. Accordingly much of Christian piety continued to presuppose that spirit of resignation of *de contemptis mundi* that had marked it for a millennium.

New Forces and Factors

This pattern, however, began to change gradually during the last part of the century. Part of this story is well known. The second half of the nineteenth century witnessed the beginning of those revolutions in medicine — ranging from anesthesia and antiseptic conditions to the contributions of Lister, Pasteur, Koch, and others — that were to both transform it and grant it far more public authority and prestige than it had earlier experienced. Coupled with these breakthroughs were equally revolutionary developments in the field of public health in areas such as sewage disposal and water purification. The result was that sickness, pain, and premature death were no longer viewed as immovable points on the human landscape, but as problems that could be removed through human intelligence and ingenuity. To be sure, complete success in this endeavor had not been achieved. Illness continued to plague humankind, and paradoxically, many also spoke of the modern age as more fraught with sickness than earlier eras. But the sentiment expressed by the British essayist W. R. Greg, who wrote of elimination of such modern ailments as heart disease and dyspepsia as a "realisable ideal," characterized the hope of many.[2]

Whether leading or following this larger cultural trend, English-speaking religious writers paralleled these tendencies and expressed a new interest in the role of religion in health. It is difficult to pinpoint why this change took place, but some partial answers can be suggested. In part the change can be linked to the declining power of Calvinism during these decades. Colonial minister-physicians, for example, had interpreted illness at least in part by means of divine providence. But a confidence in providence as an acceptable explanation for the events of the world seemed to wane with the ebbing of Calvinism, and a God who did not will damnation (it could be argued) would in all probability neither will sickness.[3]

One also cannot ignore the influence of the alternative healing methods being set forth in nineteenth-century Anglo-American culture. Particularly in America these healing systems gained great popularity. Samuel Thomson's elevation of botanics or natural cures over chemical medicines, Sylvester Graham's advocacy of dietary reform, and homeopathy were all an important part of the nineteenth-century American discussion of health and wellness. The movements these views inspired emphasized the naturalness of health and described sickness as an aberration. As such, they combined healing with a distinct metaphysical vision of the world.[4]

Still another factor was the growing rediscovery of the pre-Reformation Christian experience. When the Middle Ages began to be viewed (often through the haze of Romantic sensibilities) as an age of faith, what emerged was a vision of a church that ministered to all facets of human existence, including the treatment of illness. In his study of the Middle Ages the American Episcopalian William A. Muhlenberg, for example, was surprised to learn that charity hospitals had been a major feature of the church's outreach, and was chagrined to discover that these charity hospitals had been casualties of the avarice of the English reformers. For many, the older medieval ideal, which bound together rich and poor as well as body and soul, was viewed as a higher Christian vision than the individualism and otherworldliness of nineteenth-century American Protestantism.[5]

A final factor can perhaps best be described as a "mundanization" of the Christian world view, or a shifting of existential concern away from the next world and onto the present. Students of nineteenth-century religion have noted a flurry of influences that enhanced the importance of life in this world — post-millennialism, moralism, reform, and so forth — which together helped make Protestant Christianity far more this-worldly than it had been. A corollary of these influences, however, was a heightening of the perceived importance of the well-being of individuals. Once one's eyes had been opened, one understood that physical welfare was a recurring theme in the Bible. "In reading the Gospels," noted one commentator, "every one must have noticed how much the time of our blessed Lord was taken up with doing good to the *bodies* of men."[6] We have already noted how the miracles of the gospels were increasingly being reinterpreted as reflective of the compassion rather than the power of Christ, but this belief suggested further that the point of the dominical miracles was to relieve suffering in this world, not merely to illuminate the reality of the next.

Yet what place did religion in fact have in healing? One obvious place was in the building and organizing of hospitals. Historians documenting the rise of hospitals in the United States have noted that the "modern" hospital had its origin during the second half of the nineteenth century, and this period also witnessed the establishment of a large number of church or denominational hospitals.[7] As one proponent of religious hospitals stated, the hospital was "the distinguishing institution of Christendom. . . . Even more than places of worship, this was the characteristic mark of a Christianized society. . . . Men were familiar with what answered to churches, but asylums for the wretched were yet unknown in the world."[8]

In Germany there were a number of religious hospitals under Protestant direction, and even in England there were still a handful that had survived the Reformation, but in America during the first part of the nineteenth century the hospital movement had been largely municipal. Yet by the late 1840s one began to see a change. In New York, the Episcopal clergyman William A. Muhlenberg had begun a movement by 1846 to establish a church hospital. The cholera epidemic of 1849 added urgency to the plan, and by 1858 St. Luke's Hospital was established as a charity hospital under the auspices of the Episcopal Church. In 1868, Presbyterian Hospital was founded largely through the impetus of the layman James Lennox, and in 1882, Seney Methodist Episcopal Hospital, helped by the labors of James M. Buckley, was founded in Brooklyn. Other denominations, particularly Lutherans, would also found solid and enduring institutions. One indication of the success of this campaign can be seen in the fact that forty years after the founding of the first Methodist hospital, ground had been broken on seventy-four more.[9]

The founding of hospitals was one thing, but the integration of religion into the process of healing was another. The dedicatory hymn sung at the laying of the cornerstone of St. Luke's announced,

> The leper cleansed, the palsied healed
> Restored the maimed, the halt the blind
> Thy Gospel thus of old revealed
> A Gospel still thy power shall find.

But where precisely did this "power" reside? Despite rhetorical invocations of biblical precedents, none of these hospitals advocated healing in the manner of

Jesus. All were staffed by trained medical professionals rather than by miracle-producing apostles. What made them Christian hospitals and theirs a Christian ministry of healing? One possible answer was in the type of care provided: a care that recognized a patient's spiritual as well as physical needs. "In most hospitals, the advancement of science is the fundamental ground of their existence," Anne Ayres, one of the first sisters, explained, "but St. Luke's, while necessarily subserving the interests of science, has for its generic and formative principle, Christian brotherhood, exemplifying itself in loving, sympathizing care for the sick and needy." In Episcopal, Methodist, and Lutheran hospitals, this spiritual ministry was often a principal responsibility of deaconesses and sisterhoods, who gave to these institutions much of their religious character. "No sisters, no St. Luke's," Muhlenberg admitted. Furthermore, in the case of St. Luke's, a Christian orientation was reinforced by architecture and worship. The hospital, which was significantly of gothic design, had the chapel as its central focus, and all patients and staff attended public worship.[10]

This solution, however, would eventually prove unstable. As George Marsden noted in his study of American colleges and universities, the spirit of secularization and the desire for professionalization were often intertwined at the end of the nineteenth century, and this proved to be true in hospitals even more so than in universities. It is perhaps symbolic that later additions and expansions to many of these hospital buildings were typically done not in the "Christian" gothic style, but in a modern functional style. The centrality of the chapel service likewise declined, and as most of these medical institutions developed, their distinctively Christian nature began to recede in favor of a spirit of general benevolence.[11]

Protestants and Healing through Faith

But there were other ways to imagine a Christian participation in the process of healing, and here one sees the dovetailing of this question of healing with a general interest in modern miracles. The roots of the Protestant interest in divine healing are complex, but at least four need to be mentioned.

The first is the influence of continental Protestantism, in particular, German pietism. The "biblical realism," to use Donald Dayton's term, and the concern for a practical gospel made pietism a rich seedbed for the reevaluation of the ministry of healing. The great Johann Albrecht Bengel, in his *Gnomon Novi Testamenti*, spoke movingly of the gospel promise of healing and referred to the anointing mentioned in James 5:14–15 as "miraculous healing." Bengel wrote, "It even seems to have been given by God with this intent, that it might always remain in the Church, as a specimen of the other gifts: just as the portion of Manna laid up in the ark was a proof of the ancient miracle."[12] A number of other German writers were regularly appealed to, most particularly Johann Christian Blumhardt, Otto Stockmayer, and William Lohe.[13] But it was the healing mission of Dorothea Truedel of Mannedorf that brought the movement its greatest fame in the English-speaking world. In the Swiss village of Mannedorf on the shore of Lake Zurich, Truedel established a clinic for those who seemed to be beyond the help of medical science. In her clinic the biblical promises of healing were invoked, for as Truedel explained, "Could not the same Lord who chose to heal through medicines also heal without them?"[14] Her clinic employed worship, personal visitation, prayer, anointing, and the laying on of hands — though the last two, it was explained in good Pietist fashion, were retained because of their biblical connection and not because they had any alleged supernatural or sacramental efficacy as rituals. Healing came as a result of faith and not from ritual action. Under Truedel's leadership the Mannedorf clinic recorded hundreds of cures, most frequently of epilepsy and insanity, but it also provoked strong opposition from physicians. In 1861 the clinic was even closed by court order, and Truedel was fined one hundred francs, but within a few months it was allowed to reopen. After Truedel's death in 1862, the clinic fell under the direction of Samuel Zeller, and it became then not only a healing spa but a site of pilgrimage for English-speaking Protestants interested in the question of healing.

A second strand of the history of Protestants and healing can be traced through the Wesleyan tradition. When proponents of supernatural healing argued that miracles attended the cradle of every great spiritual movement, they invariably invoked the case of John Wesley. Wesley's and Methodism's relationship to the modern miracle debate is controversial, largely because of the ambiguity of the theological heritage of Wesley himself. Influenced by both Puritanism and Eastern Orthodoxy, as well as by patristic biblical realism and eighteenth-century empiricism, Wesley offered the partisan a number of faces. To further complicate matters, students of Wesley have noted that he displayed great interest in both supernatural and natural forms of healing. In his celebrated Letter to the Rt. Rev. Lord Bishop of Gloucester, for example, he maintained that the gift of miracles described in 1 Corinthians 12, instead of passing away, was still present, and that "God now hears and answers prayer, even beyond the ordinary course of nature."[15] In the same work, he also recounted a case of miraculous healing that he himself had undergone. On the other hand, in his *Primitive Physick* Wesley was far more concerned with folk remedies and the maintaining of health than in supernatural remedies. Both aspects of Wesley's interests can be observed in early Methodism's attitude toward healing, which has been described as a "middle way between natural and supernatural healing" — an approach that attempted to balance both an awareness of the power of grace and the responsibility of medical knowledge.[16] But what Wesley had brought together many later Methodists tried to tear asunder; many of the most vocal participants in the debate over healing were from the Methodist tradition.

Methodism would be a fertile seedbed for the rise of modern healing for one additional reason. A distinctive teaching of Wesley concerned the question of Christian perfection. According to Wesley, Christ's accomplishment was not merely that he offered justification, or the forgiveness of sin, but that he also opened up the possibility for a triumph over sin. The idea of the triumphant or victorious life became an important theme in later Methodism, and placed Methodists apart from religious traditions stemming from the Reformation. Although Wesley himself pointedly excluded "bodily infirmities" from this perfect Christian life, others would raise the question of whether there was a physical corollary to Christ's sacrificial accomplishments.[17]

A third strand of this history can be linked with the excitement associated with the great revival of 1858–59. This revival was important for a variety of reasons. Its vigor, extent, and fruits convinced many that it was a true manifestation of the Spirit — indeed, that it was a symbol of the power open to those who trusted in the Spirit.[18] Allusions to the outpouring of the Holy Spirit at Pentecost abound in both contemporary and later accounts of the revival, and many of the persons involved became more open to the active involvement of the Spirit in daily life. One of the most popular literary works to come out of the revival, William E. Boardman's *The Higher Christian Life* (1858) popularized this idea of the power of the Spirit. The theme of this book was that radical new powers and possibilities were awaiting the faithful believer. The revival furthermore gave a sense of newness and urgency to the religious life and seemed to bind and unite the splintered denominational communities.[19]

Lastly, we must not discount the power of the logic of argument itself. As we have seen, the years under consideration were a time in which the miracle debate was beginning to shift from a Protestant-Catholic axis to a naturalist-supernaturalist axis. The attack upon the idea of the miraculous found in Baden Powell, John Tyndall, W. R. Cassels, and the others had the ironic effect of pushing defenders of miracles to the right. Along with Bushnell, other religious thinkers began to recognize that the crucial issue was no longer the defense of the limited age argument against its Catholic critics, but the defense of supernatural intervention against its modern critics. Bushnell's admission, "If miracles are inherently incredible . . . nothing is gained in thrusting them back into remote ages of time," set the new agenda. Only in this way could the challenge of a Tyndall be answered fully.

The Rise of Faith Healing

The debate over faith healing emerged first during the decade of the 1870s, burned intensely during the 1880s, and by the 1890s was largely transformed. The later phase of the story will be treated in subsequent chapters, but what concerns us here is the debate as it was formulated during the 1880s, because it was during this phase that it was an issue of great contention within the major Protestant intellectual communities.[20]

In many ways one can see the public discussion of faith healing entering into the larger arena through the life and ministry of Charles Cullis (1833–1892), an Episcopal layman and homeopathic physician from Boston.[21] Certain biographical items about Cullis are important both for understanding his activities and as a way of illuminating the world out of which he and the other proponents of faith healing emerged. As a youth he was sickly, and this may have contributed to his lifelong interest in health. After studying at the University of Vermont, he established a successful homeopathic practice in Boston and involved himself in religious causes. The premature death of his young wife led him to abandon his career and dedicate himself to religious service. The result was the founding in 1864 of the Home for Indigent and Incurable Consumptives in Boston.

At first Cullis's Home for Indigent and Incurable Consumptives was one of the most popular religious charities in Boston. Its location in the prestigious neighborhood of Beacon Hill is one indication of its acceptance. Another is the individuals it attracted. At its service of dedication, for example, Frederic Dan Huntington — former Plummer Professor of Morals at Harvard, future Protestant Episcopal bishop of Central New York, and at the time rector of the socially prominent Emmanuel Episcopal Church — took a major part. So too did other leading clergy and laity, including Samuel Kirkland Lothrop of Brattle Street Unitarian Church. Its board of directors included pious and prominent names in Boston society.[22] Part of this wide and genteel acceptance probably had to do with Cullis himself, but a further attraction was the way in which the home used a combination of the theological virtues of faith and love in caring for patients. The treatment of tuberculosis victims, or consumptives, was viewed as an ideal avenue for practical Christian charity. Tuberculosis victims, as sufferers of an incurable disease, were often barred from general hospitals and were seen as being in particular need of the compassion and love offered by a religious institution. For many of its supporters, the home represented the best of the spirit of Christian benevolence, because it helped those whom no one else would embrace.[23] Furthermore, pious supporters were attracted to its trust in providence vis-à-vis donations. The Consumptive Home was modeled from the very beginning after the famous orphanages of George Müller and was financed purely by faith. No funds were to be solicited, but if a need arose, prayer would simply be offered and providence would be trusted to provide the want.[24] This theme of trusting in the Lord to answer the prayer of faith was regularly emphasized in the literature associated with the home. Its annual reports read in some ways like a modern-day version of Increase Mather's *Illustrious Providences* because they were filled with stories of financial crises being overcome at the last moment with the assistance of a benefactor who mysteriously felt called upon to make a contribution of precisely the amount needed to keep its doors open. Yet it is important to emphasize that what was offered by the home through 1872 was charity and compassion, not miraculous healing. Of the 148 patients the home treated between 1864 and 1872, only five were listed as cured. The vast majority either died or were released without having been completely healed.[25]

One sees in Cullis's early ministry the intertwining of a number of the threads already isolated in this discussion. I have already noted the influence of the German pietist tradition on Cullis. The centrality of the chapel at the Consumptive Home, complete with its stained glass windows, is reminiscent of the philosophy of Muhlenberg enshrined in St. Luke's Hospital. Finally one sees a number of elements linking the home to ideas coming out of Methodism and the revival of 1858–59. Cullis had been greatly involved in the revival, and was impressed with its rhetoric of power through the Holy Spirit. He was furthermore committed to the possibility of sanctification. In addition, the concern for "biblical realism" was not lost on him. According to his biographer, Cullis was fascinated by certain biblical promises, particularly that of 2 Thessalonians 2:13, which offered "salvation through sanctification of the Spirit and belief of the truth."

In 1873, however, Cullis's ministry underwent a fundamental transformation. That summer he traveled to Europe and visited Samuel Zeller and the Faith Cure Hospital at Mannedorf, and there he became convinced that healing, and not merely solace, was the core of the gospel message. As he later explained, "It seems to me that Christians are not living up to their gospel privileges when they fail to claim God's promises, not only for spiritual but for temporal blessings, and also for the healing of the body."[26] According to an early biographer, in September of 1873 Cullis began to lay claim to the promise of healing found in the Epistle of James, and shifted the focus of his mission from offering compassion to offering healing. Cullis quickly became the cause célèbre of faith healing, and he set forth its claims not only in his consumptive home, but also in conferences and through publications of the Willard Tract Repository.

The conversion of Cullis to faith healing resulted in a large-scale transformation of his support. Many of his earlier prominent and "mainline" (if the term is not an anachronism) religious supporters began to distance themselves from him. As one contemporary explained, "It is not to be presumed that these persons had any objections to the sick being healed; but this was a strain which their faith was not able to stand, and it is only natural for men to denounce as 'presumption' and 'fanaticism' whatever exceeds their own capacity of understanding and belief."[27] Earlier ecclesiastical supporters like Huntington and Lothrop were soon replaced on the various boards by individuals such as A. J. Gordon, W. E. Boardman, Daniel Steele, and Jacob Sleeper, who were more committed to faith healing and largely independent of denominational authority.

In this reorganization of support, we also catch an intriguing glimpse of the functional limits of the concept of providence for nineteenth-century Protestants. As I have already noted, the distinctions between "general providence," "special providence," and miracle, albeit hard for outsiders to grasp, were foundational to Protestant thinking, particularly to the assertion that miracles had ceased but providence had not. The case of Cullis demonstrates one of these invisible lines. God's work through the intellectual or moral order to inspire someone to write a check or make a contribution was seen as an act of providence, and to trust in such providences was seen, accordingly, to be a sign of faith. In contrast, to claim that God could act through the natural or physical order and restore health was to exceed the limits of providentialism and risk censure.

In the articulation of the defense of faith healing, no single writer emerged as the chief exponent. Instead a number of individuals contributed to the discussion, all linked by common assumptions including distinctive views of history, scripture, and theology.[28]

Perhaps most fundamental of these commonalities was their rejection of the limited age of miracles argument. According to these writers, no belief was so pernicious in obscuring a right understanding of God's relationship with the world than was this mistaken view that miracles have ceased. "The devil has forced upon the world a pet phrase," claimed R. Kelso Carter, "until it has become a proverb: *The days of miracles have passed*: And most people regard this proverb as much more authentic than any old King Solomon ever wrote."[29] The belief in the cessation of miracles stemmed not from the Reformers' faith but rather from modern unbelief. Healings had occurred throughout the history of the church. As one writer noted, "The doctrine of Healing is no new doctrine; it has been in the Church from the earliest ages. It was in the Church in the third, fourth, and fifth centuries. It was known in pre-reformation times.

Luther knew of it when he prayed over the sick body of Melanchthon. Wesley knew of it when he prayed for himself and over others. The Church of England held it. In the first Prayer Book of King Edward the Sixth, in the Office of the Visitation of the Sick, there was a form of prayer for anointing the sick. How we lost it out of the Prayer Book we know not. Perhaps, as we lost faith in Christ as the Healer, we dropped out the form of anointing. Now God is reviving this truth."[30] A faithless generation, however, no longer believed in miracles. As still another commentator noted, "It is not geography or chronology that determines the boundary line of the supernatural. It is apostolic men that make an apostolic age, not a certain date of Anno Domine."[31]

Just as Bushnell had done earlier, these authors offered a schema of divine history far different from that of their Protestant contemporaries. Sacred history was unified by a continuing shower of supernatural blessings and not compartmentalized into two fundamentally distinct dispensations: a supernatural biblical era and a later natural era. Witnesses of these blessings could be found in all ages of the history of the church: Augustine, the Waldensians, Luther, the Huguenots, the Scottish Covenanters, George Fox, and the early Methodists, were all appealed to. Indeed, the purpose of Christ's own miracles was not to testify to his uniqueness, but rather to inaugurate a new relationship between God and the world, and such miracles accordingly were still attainable today.[32]

This assumption flowed into another, which might be called a "new literalism," or a belief that the Bible contained a series of heretofore unclaimed divine promises. Christian life could and ought to lay claim to these promises. As Cullis noted at the beginning of his ministry, "I do and will forever, by God's grace believe every word between these two lids [of the Bible] whether I understand it or not."[33] According to R. L. Marsh, the question of faith healing really boiled down to the question of the authority of the Bible. "It is more than a matter of physical healing: it is a matter of fulfilling the Lord's commission, of obeying His command. If it is once admitted that He sent His disciples forth with the injunction, 'Make disciples of all the nations, . . . teaching them to observe all things whatsoever I have commanded you,' it is no longer a question of whether we can see all His reasons for that command, but of whether He shall be obeyed; just as this same command is a sufficient reason in itself for missionary efforts, even if we do not agree as to all the reasons for such a command."[34] If the Bible were truly the word of God, the argument continued, the promises of health and healing were not temporary but eternal, because Jesus himself proclaimed, "He that believeth on me, the works that I do shall he do also, and greater works than these shall he do" (Jn 14:12).

A question emerged, however, over how far one could push this literalism.

The Bible contained accounts of miracles other than healings, and the same Christ who healed also walked on water and raised individuals from the dead. Were these part of the gospel promise as well, and were ferry boats to be seen then as signs of a lack of faith? Here many of the proponents of faith healing argued that a distinction had to be made between miraculous interventions into physical nature and acts of healing. Healing through faith was not technically a miracle — that is, a sign or wonder — but rather a continuing privilege. "We prefer . . . the term supernatural [over that of miracle] thus placing the healing of the body alongside of the cure of the soul, both being the works of the Holy Spirit," wrote one advocate.[35] Protestant exegetes, according to this view, had erred in lumping together these two types of divine intervention, and this error had led to their assertion of a limited age of miracles. Miracles that superseded the natural order were indeed of a limited scope and duration, but acts of healing were different — they were part of the eternal heritage of the Christian church. It was true that the promise had not been used in many periods of history, but that was because of ignorance or a lack of faith and not because God had withdrawn it. R. L. Marsh likened this untapped power to electricity. Like many of his generation, Marsh was fascinated by the recent discoveries concerning electricity, a force that was rapidly transforming everyday life. Here was an apparently unlimited source of power that had for millennia existed under our very noses and was only now being tapped. So too, in his view, was the divine power of healing: "The divine . . . is all about us, just as electricity it has always been within reach. But just as man must reach out his hand and appropriate the electric power, and turn its currents into necessary channels before it works his will, so must he reach out, take, appropriate, and turn into the necessary channels the spiritual currents of God's life giving forces before they avail for His salvation and blessing."[36]

A third issue involved in the faith healing apologetic was a new view of Christ's work, and, by implication, a new view of the Christian life. Healing was not incidental to the divine-human relationship, but rather foundational. "It seems to me," noted Cullis, "that Christians are not living up to their gospel privileges when they fail to claim God's promises, not only for spiritual but for temporal blessings, and also for the healing of the body."[37] Because human beings have both spiritual and physical natures, and because both had been defaced as a result of the original disobedience, both needed redemption. Thus for most of these writers the redemption of the body from sickness was just as much an accomplishment of the saving work of Christ as was the redemption of the soul from sin. "I believe that Jesus 'bare my sins — all of them — in his own body on the tree,' and I believe that 'he took my infirmities and bore my sickness,' " maintained Kelso Carter.[38] According to Carrie Judd, Christ must be understood as the " 'Great Physician' of your soul and body."[39] The full Christian life involved not only forgiveness of sin but also triumph over sickness. Nothing else should be expected from a loving and all-powerful God.

This view, we should observe, implied an understanding of the Christian life in marked contrast to both the old medieval *de contemptis mundi* and the world of John Calvin. The Christian life was seen not as a vale of tears in preparation for a heavenly reward, but as a glorious promise to be claimed. As Grant Wacker has noted, there is a curious parallel between the early proponents of faith healing and the emerging Protestant liberalism of the time. Both were critical of the older "Calvinistic" tradition for its otherworldliness and its spirit of resignation concerning this life. For an individual such as A. J. Gordon, standard Protestant piety was literally dispirited: "The heresy of death-worship has supplanted the doctrine of resurrection with a multitude of Christians, because they have allowed the partial felicity, the departing to be with Christ, to take the place of the final victory, the coming of Christ, to quicken our mortal bodies by his Spirit that dwelleth in us."[40] The belief that bodily health was one of the promises of divine grace led some of these individuals to some novel interpretations of scripture. Kelso Carter, for example, saw this gift of health in the Old Testament as well as in the New, and argued that the dietary laws found in Leviticus were not cultic but therapeutic. He admitted that he himself still kept them because "I had abundant experience that many of the excluded animals were not good for my digestion."[41]

Lying behind the new view of the Christian life was a view of God that was also far removed from the old Calvinistic deity. The overwhelming love of God, it was argued, extended to our most mundane needs. God "wants to have our bodies a living sacrifice," one writer explained, "that He may dispose of, and care for them; and thus, whether it be the ache of a little finger, or the slightest feeling of depression . . . the Lord is ready to care for it as though it were a matter of life or death, or a matter of the welfare of nations. Our God is not a stern lawgiver; He is a loving, tender, gracious Father." The emphasis upon the benevolence of God that emerged during mid-century to defend the meaning of biblical miracles was now invoked to explain the gift of healing.[42]

As dazzling as this picture might appear to the believer, however, it nonetheless left its proponents with a question to which no easy answer was available. If all this were promised, why did sin and suffering continue to exist? Or put another way, why did a loving God who promised healing not heal? As even Cullis admitted, not all who claimed the gift of healing were healed. Other Protestants could dodge the question by referring to different dispensations in history, and Catholics could claim that healings were merely occasional witnesses to the supernatural nature of the church; these apologists had to face the question head on. As we will see, various answers were in fact offered, but none proved completely satisfactory. The question would stick to the Protestant healing movement like a tin can on a cat's tail.

A final part of the proponents' claim was that the rejection of the gift of healing impoverished the church, and conversely that a revival of healing would empower it. The ministry of healing was unlike any other ministry, in that it brought the minister into immediate contact with the power of Christ. As A. B. Simpson explained, "I never feel so near the Lord, not even at the Communion, not even on the borders of eternity, standing beside the departing spirit, as when I stand with the living Christ, to manifest His personal touch of supernatural and resurrection power in the anointing of the sick." The spiritual crisis of the age could be attributed to the unwillingness to claim the power of the spirit. "For observe what confessions of weakness our Protestant churches are unconsciously putting forth on every hand," wrote A. J. Gordon. "Note the dependence which is placed on artistic music, on expensive edifices, on culture and eloquence in the pulpit; on literary and social entertainments for drawing in the people, and on fairs and festivals for paying expenses."[43]

Many of their writings included personal testimonies as well as arguments from scripture and history, and the testimonies follow a usual pattern. A man or woman, suffering under an illness that has exhausted the abilities of medicine, finally turns to God. There he or she is not only alleved of sickness but is reinvigorated in both body and soul. And here one should note that these testimonies address directly the empirical question that lay at the center of John Tyndall's "Prayer Gauge." Tyndall, one recalls, insisted that any claim for the efficacy of prayer vis-à-vis physical healing had to be empirically verifiable. It was just such empirical evidence that fill the accounts of these writers. Taking up Tyndall's challenge, they proclaimed that an active God did indeed restore health in a way no physician could and that these actions could be the empirical ground of faith. As one speaker at an international conference on faith healing triumphantly proclaimed:

> Twenty years ago, Professor Tyndal [*sic*] proposed . . . to make a challenge to the Christian world to test the power of prayer — a challenge that so many sick people in a hospital should be treated with medicine, and so many in the same hospital with prayer alone — that Christian people should honestly make this test. The Christian Church was then afraid to accept the challenge, but I doubt whether he could make it to-day. I think it would be answered by the testimonies in this place. I think we should have sufficient evidence to show that prayer is a power, a force, an answer — sufficient to prove that Christ is a Saviour of the body as well as the soul.[44]

A dogged empiricism marked their faith. Their appeal was to facts; it was their opponents who ignored these facts in favor of theory. Accounts of healings were rehearsed in their appeals and were treated as true evidences of the reality of the biblical promise. These evidences demanded a verdict, and as Carrie Judd noted, opponents "must either stubbornly refuse to believe in these cases of healing without giving any reasons for their unbelief; or else rightfully ascribe them to Divine power; or (and I shudder at the thought of any one's committing such blasphemy) attribute them to diabolical agency."[45] This radical empiricism is reflective of the long-standing Baconianism so dominant in nineteenth-century Protestantism. As numerous scholars have noted, the argument from Bacon and Scottish Common Sense philosophy was a standard part of the antebellum Evangelical intellectual arsenal. But here Baconianism was employed for a very different purpose. These writers appealed not to evidences from the natural order but to evidences from the supernatural. We have already seen Bushnell invoking Bacon by name in his appeal for these new evidences, and a supernatural Baconianism was to be found in the writings of many defenders of divine healing.

Furthermore, like Tyndall these individuals also recognized that no logical distinction could be made between a traditional miracle and a divine answer to prayer. Each was equally problematic from the point of view of materialists, and each was equally believable for the devout. "To ask God to act at all, and to ask Him to perform a miracle are one in the same thing," wrote one commentator.[46] Supernatural evidences were the manifestation of scriptural promises, and the interrelation of scripture and evidences is the only real basis of faith. "There is no other safety for our faith," explained Cullis, "than the grand and full acceptance of all God offers to His church."[47]

For this reason these authors were more hurt by Protestant criticisms of their endeavors than by those from secular critics, because these attacks from professed believers implied a lack of faith and trust. As Cullis movingly wrote, "I have suffered for this work. . . . I have been opposed and abused, and called all sorts of bad names, for venturing to believe God, and to act upon that belief. Especially from those unbelievers inside the Church, have I suffered persecution: they call my trust in God 'fanaticism,' and the acting-out of my faith 'presumption.' But God has stood by me, and the truth is making its way."[48]

A lack of faith, argued proponents of this new view, was destructive to both evangelism and mission. The missionary thrust of the early church had been empowered by miraculous healings, and as A. J. Gordon noted, "there is really little if any difference between Paul at Melitta and Judson in India."[49] A failure to claim this power seriously hampered modern missionary endeavors. Kelso

Carter, for example, related two accounts from the experiences of missionaries in China. In one, a native woman who had read about the wonderful works of Jesus asked if she too could be healed, but was turned away with the explanation that the age of miracles had passed. In the other, a blind woman who asked the same question was able to receive her sight through the ministry of healing. The latter woman became a believer; the former, although attracted to the Bible, did not. Was it any wonder, he concluded, that modern missions were less successful than those of the apostolic age, when all too often they did not appeal to the same power that inspired the first century? Nowhere was the dichotomy between biblical faith and modern faith more evident than in the area of missions.

Accordingly, these authors saw that the opposition to their views ultimately reflected the emerging theological modernism and its rejection of the reality of the supernatural. It was "unbelief shading off from rationalism to liberal evangelicalism," in the words of A. J. Gordon.[50] A. B. Simpson put it more pointedly: "The Higher Criticism is industriously taking the miraculous from our Bibles, and a lower standard of Christian life is busy taking all that is Divine out of our life."[51] The real issue for them was the reality of supernatural activity in the natural order. And here they agreed with (and often cited) David Hume: to reject modern miracles was fundamentally to undercut the probability of biblical miracles. Their critics, wrote Gordon, "build a portico to 'the school of Hume' from which their pupils will easily and logically graduate from the denial of modern miracles to the denial of all miracles."[52] Modern miracles were a bulwark against skepticism and rationalism.

The logic of the faith healing argument, however, compelled many of its proponents to push it to a controversial conclusion, or to attack medicine and other material means. If healing was like redemption and was tied to faith, then by implication, it ought to follow the rule of faith. A long-standing belief among Protestants was the doctrine of justification by faith alone — that God alone could grant justification; it was not something human beings achieved by their own labors. Indeed some referred to justification as a moral miracle. But what of health? Was the use of medicine a sign of a lack of faith, and hence antithetical to true healing? Some attempted to allow a place for both medical and faith healing, by noting that the Bible spoke of "good and perfect gifts." In this paradigm, medicine was a good gift, whereas faith healing was the "perfect gift." Others were more forthright in their rejection of medicine. A. B. Simpson claimed that the gospel promise was fundamentally one of trust, and to employ medicine for bodily healing showed a failure of faith.[53] Many argued that medicine was not sinful per se, and hence was acceptable for a nonbeliever, but for a Christian it was a sign of unbelief. According to these religious thinkers, faith alone should be the rule for Christian healing, and they scorned those individuals who came to God only as a last resort after having exhausted medical avenues. Such a conclusion was controversial to be sure, because it rejected any compromise with medical healing, but it was indicative of the logic of the faith healing argument.[54]

Proponents of modern healing had one last problem to address: how were they to explain supernatural phenomena and apparently miraculous healings from nonevangelical sources? In addition to the old bête noires of spiritualism and animal magnetism, there were many other healing movements then current, perhaps most famously Christian Science. Despite the fact that A. J. Gordon was probably familiar with the movement (and this familiarity possibly influenced his interest in faith healing) these new healing movements were not to become major concerns for advocates of evangelical faith healing until the 1890s.[55] But the general question was addressed, and much care was taken to differentiate evangelical faith healing from all other types. It was not enough, however, to differentiate these kinds of healing; these nonevangelical phenomena had to be explained. Since the eighteenth century, Protestant writers had easily dismissed these "works" as fraudulent or open to natural explanations, but for defenders of faith healing such explanations seemed to smack of rationalism. Thus they returned instead to the world of Increase Mather and offered supernatural explanations for these works. Phenomena such as those found in Spiritualism were indeed real supernatural occurrences, but they were the "lying wonders" or "works of Satan."

But what of those miracles associated with that other bête noire, Roman Catholicism? As we will see in the next chapter, at the same time that Protestants were debating faith healing there was a great flurry of sensational Catholic healing miracles, including those associated with the shrine at Lourdes. Although some of these writers continued to reject Catholic miracles as nothing more than "lying wonders," a surprising number of others expressed an openness to considering these Catholic miracles and, by implication, to considering the Catholic faith. Stanton, Simpson, and Carter did not lump these Roman Catholic miracles with those of the spiritualists, but saw them as linked to the gospel promise of faith. Catholic doctrine was undoubtedly wrong, they explained, but Catholic faith was real, and God rewarded that faith. No one made this point more eloquently than Kelso Carter.

> God always keeps His word, no matter who claims it. "According to your faith be it unto you," is just as true to a Romanist as a Protestant. God has always "winked at" real unavoidable ignorance. When a Romanist goes to the grotto of Lourdes, and pleads with God for healing, if *faith in God* is exercised, healing comes of course. . . . That there is an immense amount of devout and simple faith in the church of Rome is a fact perfectly familiar to

every well-informed person; and as that faith really *centres* in God, we should not be surprised if it secures its reward. These people have been accustomed to believe that miracles still exist in their church; while we have been brought up on the proverb "the days of miracles have passed." They are therefore predisposed to believe in the supernatural. We are inclined to doubt everything but the material. However much of the corruption there has been and is in the Romish church, she has certainly one virtue which ought to put us to shame — she has not thrown away the last words of Christ, "These signs shall follow them that believe."[56]

For Carter, not only did Protestants have much to learn from their Catholic brethren, but, also, as this quotation implies, the Catholic faith (at least in its valuation of modern miracles) was closer to his own than was the faith of his Protestant critics. This long quotation shows traces of a new attitude, which we can call functional ecumenism, that was beginning to emerge out of the discussion over the miraculous. It involved a common front linking both Catholic and Protestant defenders of supernatural intervention against its critics. For the first time we see evidence of the Protestant-Catholic polarity beginning to give way to a new paradigm.

Both the challenge of skepticism and the belief that the Bible contained promises of untapped powers inspired the proponents of faith healing. Like Bushnell, they rejected the idea of a limited age of miracles and saw modern signs and wonders as a crucial buttress for belief.

The Critics

The faith healing movement created a noticeable stir during the 1880s. The various publications of the Willard Tract Repository were widely circulated. The annual summer faith conventions (most famously at Orchard Beach, Maine) were large gatherings that received much comment in both the religious and secular press. Finally there was a series of larger conferences culminating in a great international conference meeting at Agricultural Hall in Islington, England (a borough of London) in June 1885. In this last meeting, over fifteen hundred individuals from more than nine nations met to proclaim the gospel of health for soul and body. All of these events helped inform the public about the movement.

Yet it must be admitted that most of this publicity was negative, and what emerged as a result was a sustained critique of the assumptions and pretensions of the faith healing movement within Protestant evangelicalism. And no one more deserves the title of nemesis of faith healing more than does the Methodist James Monroe Buckley (1836–1920). His biography is as illuminative of the opposition to faith healing as Cullis's was of its defense. Like Cullis,

Buckley's early life was marked by concerns for health. His father died of consumption while still a young man, and this disease also claimed his uncle and grandparents. Buckley himself suffered from a variety of ailments, including bronchial and pulmonary problems, as well as from the effects of a childhood accident. His health was so precarious that at times during his youth it seemed as if he would die from these disorders. But here the parallel with Cullis ended. Buckley eventually achieved vigorous health not through miraculous intervention but rather through a combination of medicine and vigorous exercise, and throughout his later life he remained devoted to both. As editor for thirty-two years of the *Methodist Christian Advocate,* his denomination's oldest and most influential weekly newspaper, he championed the Methodist hospital movement, and as we have noted was a leading figure in the founding of the first of these hospitals, the Seney Hospital of Brooklyn. As Brooks Holifield has shown, however, the hospital movement for Buckley was more than simply an act of benevolence. It signified a transformation of Methodism and a movement of the denomination away from its earlier, more populist roots, and toward social responsibility and middle-class propriety. All of these factors made Buckley the sharpest and most dogged critic of faith healing. As an evangelical Christian, a modern citizen, and a person concerned with health and healing, he attacked the faith healing movement with gusto.[57]

He was, to be sure, not alone. During the 1880s a score of critics leveled their aim against the movement, and taken together these critics enunciated a position that rested upon a number of exegetical, theological, and pastoral presuppositions far different from those of their opponents.[58] Central to the position of these critics was the continuing importance of the "limited age of miracles" argument. Biblical miracles were the paradigmatic miracles; they defined for believers the nature of a true miracle. All modern miracle claims had to be weighed against these biblical miracles, and when they were so compared they inevitably came up short. Jesus healed all manner of disease and sickness including blindness, lameness, and death, whereas modern healers treated (at best) only some diseases. Jesus healed instantly, and everyone he pronounced healed was indeed healed. No modern healer could make such claims. For Buckley the paradigmatic gospel healing was the story of the restoration of Malchus's ear (Lk 22:51), in which Christ restored a slave's ear that had been severed by one of his disciples. Such a healing was "radical and permanent" and unmistakably supernatural. No modern healer dared to attempt such healing. Indeed Buckley recounted the explanation Brigham Young gave to a young Mormon who traveled from Europe to have a severed leg restored — namely, that he would not heal him because if he did so it would condemn the young man to endure three legs after the resurrection — as typical of the chicanery of modern healers. Modern healers, these writers admitted, might do some good in restoring health, perhaps through the influence of the mind on weak personalities, but this had nothing to do with the mighty acts recorded in scripture. "[True] supernatural interventions are not lavished in unnecessary and wasteful profusion. They come only at the call of need. . . . Only at long intervals, only to usher in some great birth of time, does the creative spirit look through the veil of secondary causes; only at sundry times, and to meet some pressing necessity, does the light shine through the cloud in which it is ordinarily involved."[59]

Nor would these critics abandon the second part of the traditional Protestant confidence — that which linked a miracle-free faith with spiritual maturity and an openness to science. A mature faith did not need signs and wonders. "The church which is hungry for miracles is in her second childhood," explained Marvin R. Vincent.[60] Miracle mongering was the sign of superstition and a weak faith, whether it was displayed by spiritualists, Roman Catholics, or evangelical Protestants.

Another sign of these faith healers' spiritual immaturity, according to their critics, was their misunderstanding of the true nature of religion. Just as a child often thinks only about getting his or her way rather than about larger issues of justice and purpose, so too did the advocates of faith healing mistakenly believe that the goal of religion was getting what one desired in this world. The human race had perenially fallen sway to this delusion. Modern-day Protestants had erroneously thought themselves immune from the temptation, but the emergence of faith healing proved otherwise. At bottom, however, this misunderstanding involved the confusion of religion and magic. As one commentator mused, "We look on this magical theory of religion with something between a smile and a sigh, and though our reverence does not allow us to place it in the list with other more or less harmfull delusions, such as the Sulphur Cure, the Water Cure, and the Grape Cure, we still have the feeling, that the list is not entirely complete without it." But the movement would ultimately pass away as other fads did, and its proponents must be pitied, in the words of one critic, as "the Lord's silly people."[61]

One term that often popped up in these critiques to describe the healers was "quack," and the choice of this term suggests that behind the stated objections may lie other unstated ones.[62] As historians of medicine have noted, these decades were a time in which the medical community struggled to elevate its professional status and to triumph over alternative schools of healing such as the eclectic movement and homeopathy.[63] As physicians succeeded in their agenda, they increasingly claimed a monopoly on the art of healing, and, perhaps not unconnectedly, raised their own social and economic status. The

movement toward professionalization was of course a broad cultural phenomenon in Victorian America, and it involved the delineation of clearly
defined professional spheres in which expertise could be claimed. A corollary
of this professionalization was the concern to protect these spheres from non-
professional interlopers. A person who interfered in another's professional
sphere was a "quack." When one recalls that Protestant clergy were also
undergoing professionalization as they strove to establish their religious expertise in parallel ways (for example, through professional organizations,
raised educational standards, and so forth), the charge of quackery takes on
new significance. The anti-faith healing rhetoric implied a tacit recognition by
the clergy of the physicians' sphere, and a common policing of the professional
boundaries. This nod to physicians by the clergy revealed their assumption
that only by doing so could the religious ministry of the church proceed without conflict in a rapidly professionalizing society — and could the church hope
to appeal to the socially prominent new class of professional physicians.

Yet the greatest fervor was directed against the theological assumptions of
the faith healers and the pastoral implications of these assumptions. One
recalls that many of the proponents of faith healing had argued that healing
flowed from the work of Christ upon the cross and was a promise to the
redeemed community. This was a monstrous charge, according to its critics,
because it implied that sickness existed due to sin or a lack of faith. One critic
complained, "Such a doctrine takes away all blessing and comfort from the
Christian's sickbed, and brands the sufferer with unbelief."[64] Experience
taught that there was no correlation between godliness and health; indeed,
many of the most pious seemed to suffer more than any others. Human suffering must have some moral purpose.

No one made this argument about suffering more forcefully than did the
Free Church Scottish biblical theologian Alexander B. Bruce, whose book *The
Miraculous Elements of the Gospel* (1886) attempted to shore up the traditional Protestant position. In most of the early part of the work, Bruce defended biblical miracles against materialists, pantheists, and such historical
critics as the author of *Supernatural Religion* and explored the meaning of the
miraculous in the life of Christ. By the end of the work, however, he turned to
address the question of modern miracles, and in particular the claim that
healing flowed from redemption. In this section of the book, the scholar receded and Bruce spoke as a former pastor. He described his early ministry
among the poor and destitute on the west coast of Scotland, and observed that
if any community of pious individuals needed healing it was they. "What
would I not have given to have had for an hour the charism of the Galilean
Evangelists, and how gladly would I have gone forth that day, not to speak the
accustomed words about a Father in heaven ever ready to receive His prodigal

children, but to put an end to pain, raise up the dying, and to restore to soundness shattered reason!"[65] But Christian experience has shown that such was not the case; the gospel offered no more a cure for sickness than a cure for poverty.

The pastoral objections that the critics of faith healing raised were powerful, but the critics in turn opened themselves up to a counterobjection. It was true, admitted the defenders of faith healing, that not all who needed healing asked for it, and not all who asked for it received it. Yet could not the same be said about conversion? Evangelical Protestants traditionally maintained that entrance into the community of faith was predicated upon a supernatural awakening, or conversion. All preachers and pastors knew, however, that not everyone who heard responded, and that not everyone who desired to be converted underwent it. Salvation was a supernatural mystery, the intricacies of which were known only to God. Could this not also be the case concerning faith healing? Accordingly, talking about failure rates in healing was as foolish as speaking of failure rates in preaching. The church was not called to be successful, only to be faithful to the biblical promises, and the promises of conversion and healing were inextricably linked. As one Methodist defender of faith healing, Daniel Steele, noted, "We cannot surrender one-half of the supernatural and retain the other half."[66]

This counterargument struck a sensitive nerve, because it was this type of polemic that was leading some within the American Protestant community to abandon the necessity of the conversion experience in favor of an understanding of the Christian life that emphasized nurture and growth. Horace Bushnell's call for *Christian Nurture* was beginning to find acceptance among those moving toward liberal evangelicalism.[67] Many of the criticisms of the conversion experience did mirror criticisms of faith healing, particularly in their reference to the superiority of the natural order and their rejection of systems of supernatural intervention as anti-natural. Although no critic of faith healing combined an assault on healing with a rejection of conversion, defenders of faith healing were not wrong in seeing that the issues were intertwined.

"Our Martyred President"

In 1881 an event occurred that was to become for a decade a focus for the healing debate. In July of that year President James A. Garfield was shot by the crazed office-seeker Charles Giuteau. The Garfield assassination is now at best only remembered as the impetus for civil-service reform, but at the time it sent a shock wave through the public.[68] For months Garfield lingered close to death as the best medical doctors attempted to save him. The latest in modern technology (including an "induction bell" designed by Alexander Graham Bell to locate the bullet) was also employed, but to little avail. Not to be outdone, the religious public did their part as well, and prayers were offered across the nation. Indeed, the excitement in America concerning the assassinated president is reminiscent of the concern in England a decade before over the sickness of the Prince of Wales. Yet the results were not the same. On September 19, despite the prayers, Garfield died. The death of Garfield at the very beginning of his presidency thrust anew upon the religious public John Tyndall's old questions concerning the efficacy of prayer.

The death of the pious President Garfield became a symbolic event that had two radically different interpretations. For the critics of faith healing such as the Methodist writer Luther T. Townsend, it was a pointed refutation of the pretensions of faith healing. If healing were indeed a divine gift, surely a merciful God would have offered it in response to so many prayers. But further, according to Townsend, the death of Garfield helped one understand the mystery of prayer. An individual prayed not to receive some tangible reward but because prayer was instinctive to human nature. The desire to pray was a universal human need and as such could not be stifled. One always had to remember, however, that the answer to prayer was part of a divine mystery and beyond human comprehension.[69] Although never explicitly alluded to, such arguments echo elements found in writers such as Friedrich Schleiermacher: they describe a religious sense or sentiment as foundational to the understanding of religion and move away from the image of a God who intervened in the world even providentially.[70]

Defenders of faith healing reached the opposite conclusion. The fate of the martyred president testified not to the failure of the faith cure, but rather the failure of faith among American Protestants. As A. J. Gordon noted, "We need less praying rather than more; only that the less shall be real, and deep, and intelligent, and believing."[71] They argued that in all the prayer offered for the dying president, the biblical promises were never invoked. Elders were never called; the president was never anointed; his pastor was not even allowed to see him, so surrounded was he by doctors. "We have no knowledge that Garfield ever heard of the faith cure [and] 'without knowledge, there is no ground of faith,'" observed R. L. Stanton.[72] According to proponents of faith healing, the death of the president was a tragedy, but it was a tragedy because believers failed to claim the divine promise of healing.

Conclusion

Many things strike the modern student about this first phase of the Protestant debate over healing, but two aspects of the discussion stand out.

The first is the public nature of the discussion. Much of it took place on the highest levels of both religious and secular publications. R. L. Marsh's work was a Yale doctoral dissertation; Steele was a leading figure at Boston University; the *Presbyterian Review* was a leading denominational publication, and *Century Magazine* was a leading middle-class periodical. Faith healing was not a concern for a small or unimportant subculture, but was an issue at the very center of middle-class Protestant life. Hence what is significant is not that the movement was attacked by critics, but that it was noted at all. In contrast to the later story in which the successors of Charles Cullis, A. J. Gordon, and Daniel Steele spoke from a subculture and were largely ignored by the religio-intellectual community, the claims of the first generation were attacked rather than ignored.

A second factor, following from the first, is that despite the deep rancor, significant common ground united both the defenders and critics of faith healing. Both parties still assumed the importance of both the concept of the supernatural and the historicity of miracles from the New Testament. Indeed, as we have noted, part of the critics' argument was that modern "miracles" undercut the power and uniqueness of dominical miracles. Such agreement should not be surprising. All of these individuals were self-styled evangelical Protestants, and evangelical Protestants before the 1890s were loath to criticize the miracles of the gospel for fear of impugning the authority of Jesus. Outsiders like Mrs. Humphry Ward or John Burroughs might attack the gospel miracles, but no evangelical Protestant could do so. These presuppositions set the ground rules of the intra-Protestant debate, and both sides recognized that the picture of Jesus as the doer of supernatural works had to be defended at all costs. It was for this reason as well that the issue of modern miracles had to be refuted and not merely dismissed.

By the 1890s, however, all of this would begin to change, as Protestants began to find themselves dividing over the question of miraculous. This transformation would fundamentally recast the discussion of both biblical miracles and modern miracles.

5

Catholics and the Question of Miracles

Of the many prominent families of the evangelical establishment within the Episcopal Church, few were as prestigious as the Stones. As leaders in both the pulpit and the academy they reflected the confidence of American evangelicalism. It naturally then came as a great shock when the young scion of that distinguished family, James Kent Stone, formerly president of the staunchly evangelical Kenyon College in Ohio and now president of Hobart College in upstate New York, announced in 1869 that he was abandoning Protestantism to enter the Roman Catholic communion.

Stone subsequently published an apologia, *The Invitation Heeded*, in which he enumerated the reasons behind his conversion. He was attracted to his new church's seeming perpetuity, its sureness of witness, and its vigor in life and mission, all of which he contrasted with the failures of Protestantism. But key for Stone was what he perceived as the growing link between Protestantism and rationalism. Rationalist apologists, such as William Lecky, were right in claiming that the roots of rationalism were within Protestantism. If one searched for the source of this rationalist tendency, Stone argued, it lay in the Protestant suspicion of the miraculous. Protestant rejection "without hesitation and without examination" of all postbiblical or ecclesiastical miracles had unwittingly laid the seedbed for the flowering skepticism of Lecky. "Protestants *began* not as rationalists, but as Protestants," he explained. "They rejected miracles at first, not because they were miraculous, but because they were *Romish*. . . . But what began as illogical Protestantism must end . . . in logical rationalism. The human intellect cannot persist for many generations in palpable inconsistency." In Stone's view, John Henry Newman had been right. Miracles were a sign of God's continuing concern for the world, and to reject ecclesiastical miracles was to open the door of doubt about biblical ones. The Roman Catholic Church both professed and possessed miracles, and was accordingly the true church.[1]

As the case of James Kent Stone illustrates, the question of miracles was by no means a narrowly Protestant issue during these years. Rather, as we have seen, the topic of miracles had profoundly separated Catholics and Protestants in the centuries following the Reformation. The slow transformation of Protestant attitudes regarding the miraculous could not help but undermine some of the older assumptions and raise anew a consideration of Roman Catholicism. Likewise, Roman Catholics struggled to interpret their traditional claims in light of a world far removed from both the medieval period and the Counter-Reformation. The result of all of these questions was that the second half of the nineteenth century witnessed a vigorous discussion among both Catholics and Protestants about the question of Catholics and the miraculous.

The Catholic Theory

As has been suggested, the miraculous had always been understood in slightly different ways by Catholics and by Protestants, and these differences continued to influence the discussion of miracles among nineteenth-century English-speaking Catholics. Missing, for example, were the Protestant scholastic categories of miracle, special providence, and general providence; in their place were older medieval scholastic categories. Thomas Aquinas was usually the starting point. Aquinas, one recalls, had linked the category of miracle to the distinction between nature and supernature, and this understanding continued to find favor among Catholic writers. As one commentator explained, " 'Supernatural' does not denote simply what is above sensible nature, the laws of the visible universe, and the temporal order of the present world. . . . The supernatural is something above the plane of all effects produced by creation. It is a communication of that which naturally belongs within the divine essence, to a term which is without."[2] According to this understanding, God alone could work miracles because he alone was beyond the created order.

Another key part of the Catholic understanding that would continue to be echoed in the nineteenth-century discussion is reflected in another point of

Aquinas's, "We experience wonder when an effect is obvious but its cause hidden."[3] Many Catholic commentators noted that there were two distinct parts to miracle claims: an external factual element, or that which produced wonder, and a theological cause, which elucidated its meaning. The factual element was recognizable by reason alone; it did not require special grace to be understood. Anyone could recognize, for example, the marvel of the Red Sea being split. The second part, however, which dealt with the meaning or significance of the event, was comprehensible only through grace. Thus a miracle was both an exoteric fact in itself and a sign of a greater reality.

Furthermore, stemming from Aquinas was a typology of miracles. Not all miracles were the same. Some events, such as the reversal of the sundial of Ahaz (2 Kgs 20:9–10) were "substantial" miracles—they were recognized by their very nature to be unique and impossible occurrences. Other events, such as the raising of Lazarus, were "subjective" miracles. These events were extraordinary not because of what was done but because of the subject or context in which it occurred. Nature can and does bring forth life, for example, but not among dead persons. Finally, an event such as the healing of Simon Peter's mother-in-law (Mk 1:30) was a "qualitative" miracle. It was miraculous not because of the cure itself (people have been cured in the past) but because of its manner. Later writers such as the Scottish bishop George Hay went to great length to delineate these categories, and they were formalized eventually by Pope Benedict XIV in the eighteenth century. In the proper evaluation of miracle claims, each of these different types of miracles were to be scrutinized according to differing criteria. Thus for example miraculous cures had to fulfill the following circumstances:

> First, That the disease be considerable, dangerous, inveterate, and such as commonly resists the strength of known medicines. . . . 2dly, That the disease be not come to its crisis, in which it is natural to look for a remission of its symptoms and a cure. 3dly, That the ordinary helps of natural remedies have not been used, or at least there be just reason to presume from the time elapsed since taking them, and from other circumstances, that they could have no influence on the cure. 4thly, That the cure be sudden and instantaneous. . . . 5thly, That the cure be perfect and entire. 6thly, That there happened no crisis, nor any sensible alteration which might have naturally wrought the cure. 7thly, That the health recovered be constant and not followed by a speedy relapse.[4]

Most Catholic writers also observed that miracles were outflowings of the supernatural activity of God. They were acts that had their origin not in human faith but in divine will. No person, therefore, could ever expect or claim a miracle, but only could hope and pray for one. God authored the miracle, and the church attested it. Catholics, hence, seemed to be little troubled by the problem that confronted Protestants over why some persons received miracles whereas others did not.[5]

But of course what most distinguished Catholic from Protestant teachings about miracles was their insistence that these supernatural manifestations continue to the present. Modern or ecclesiastical miracles, one recalls, had been a bone of contention for centuries. Unlike Protestants who saw miracles as only serving to validate revelation, and thus as being withdrawn when revelation ceased, Catholics argued that miracles were an outflowing of supernatural power. It was an act of theological presumption to decide a priori (as the limited age of miracles argument did) why God performed miracles and why he had now done away with them.

Although they often chided Protestants for presuming to know God's plan better than God himself, Catholic writers were not themselves averse to discussing the purposes of miracles. One purpose, as John Milner suggested in his famous apologetic *The End of Religious Controversy,* was to illumine the interconnection between the miraculous and holiness. Milner's thesis was simple: where God was present, one should expect miracles. "The whole history of God's people from the beginning of the world down to the time of our blessed Saviour, was nearly a continuous series of miracles. [Hence] . . . we are led to expect that the true church should be distinguished by miracles, wrought in her, and in proof of her divine origin."[6] The power of God at work in the world through his people would necessarily, if occasionally, manifest itself in miracles.

Nowhere was this claim more true, believed Milner, than in the lifting up of saints. Catholic writers like Milner made it clear that the miraculous was not a prerogative of the saints, but an epiphany of their sanctity. In the miracles of the saints one saw a manifestation of the sanctity of the church itself. As Milner explained, "The church never possessed miraculous powers, as in the sense of most Protestant writers [believe], so as to be able to affect cures, or other supernatural events at her own pleasure. . . . But this I say, the Catholic Church, being always the beloved *spouse of Christ,* Rev. xxi.4, and continuing at all times to bring forth children of heroical sanctity, God fails not in this, any more than in past ages, to illustrate her and them by unquestionable miracles."[7] Miracles were a sign of saintliness, and the lives of the saints were filled with such accounts. Perhaps the most famous instance of this for nineteenth-century Catholics was the life of the sixteenth-century Jesuit missionary to the Far East, Francis Xavier. Dominic Bouhours's famous biography of Francis

Xavier included accounts of healings, restorations from the dead, the miraculous speaking in tongues, and other wonders. But included also were some more unusual occurrences such as the following:

> We were at sea, . . . when a violent storm arose, which alarmed the crew. Xavier drew from his bosom a small crucifix, which he always carried about him, and leaned overboard intending to dip it into the sea; but the crucifix dropped out of his hand, and immediately disappeared. It was very manifest that this loss much afflicted him. . . . [Later] Francis and I were walking on shore. . . . [W]e had proceeded about five hundred paces, when we perceived a crab fish coming from the sea, and bearing — suspended in his claws — the identical crucifix that was lost. I saw the crab approach the Father, and stop before him. . . . I joined [Francis] in returning thanks to God for so evident a miracle.[8]

In the life of Francis Xavier, even the animal kingdom witnessed to the power of God in a most romantic way.

Second, the continuing presence of miracles in the world was seen by Catholics as not merely a sign of God's activity, but as a sign of the true church and a rebuke against all imposters. As Stone observed in his apologia, Protestants could not accept Catholic ecclesiastical miracles because they had none to offer in response. To acknowledge Catholic miracles was to admit that Rome was the true church. John England, bishop of Charleston (South Carolina), made the point succinctly: "Miracles are the criterion of truth. . . . [They] are the finger of God, always pointing at the worship that pleases him and to his ever truth teaching Church. 'Dissenters' from the Catholic Church never have had, and never shall have miracles wrought among them. They find themselves as a sole means of escape from the difficulty in which they are placed, obliged to deny that miracles are any longer performed on Earth." Other writers took glee in exposing the circular logic of such Protestant spokesmen as James M. Buckley, who claimed that miracles must have passed away because the Reformers seemed not to possess any.[9]

The Roman Catholic assertion that their present church was to be identified with the church of the apostles did not go unchallenged by Protestants, who argued that there were key differences between the biblical picture and present Catholic practices. It was all well and good, for example, for Catholics to claim that the sacraments of confirmation and unction were scriptural, but why did their present practice differ so from the scriptural record? In the New Testament, both of these practices were accompanied by miraculous occurrences. Why not now?[10] Indeed, if bishops were the successors of the apostles, why did they not still possess the powers of the apostles? James Cardinal Gibbons, in his famous exposition of the Catholic faith, *The Faith of Our Fathers,* addressed this charge by distinguishing between the original powers of the apostles and those of the later bishops, and by admitting no absolute identification between the practices of the first century and those of the nineteenth.

> Those who were confirmed by the Apostles usually gave evidence of the grace which they received by prophecy, the gift of tongues and the manifestation of other miraculous powers. It may be asked: Why do not these gifts accompany now the imposition of hands? I answer: Because they are no longer needed. The grace which the Apostolic disciples received was for their personal sanctification. The gift of tongues which they exercised was intended by Almighty God to edify and enlighten the spectators, and to give Divine sanction to the Apostolic ministry. But now that the Church is firmly established, and the Divine authority of her ministry is clearly recognized, these miracles are no longer necessary.[11]

Gibbons's answer may sound strangely like a contemporary Protestant defense of the limited age of miracles, but it pointed out the need by Catholic apologists to be clear about the differences between scriptural and ecclesiastical miracles.

Miracles witnessed to the true church not only by attesting to its holiness, but to its catholicity as well — or at least to its comprehensiveness. They were a popular and exoteric sign, and they were particularly persuasive for the simple, common people who often witnessed them. A miracle-based religion was a popular religion. Conversely, the rejection of miracles seemed often to reflect a bourgeois sensitivity and a desire to distance oneself from vulgar forms of religiosity. For converts like Stone, part of the attraction of Roman Catholicism was its appeal to the poor and its ability to transcend the class stratification that seemed to plague American Protestantism. Stone was, of course, not alone in this concern for the religion of the lower classes. Many commentators at the end of the nineteenth century warned that Protestantism in Britain and America seemed to be losing its popular base and that the lower classes were becoming unchurched. Catholic writers were quick to pick up this theme and implied that this trend might be due to a preference for effete culture over simple faith. An "ecclesiastical fine gentleman," suggested one Catholic writer, would naturally find little attraction in the claim that God came to the humble and poor and that the Virgin Mary might reveal herself to a peasant girl. "Little wonder . . . that a story of supernatural occurrences in which a poor barefooted peasant-girl was the heroine should be received with incredulity in a circle of the elite of society, in their own opinion also the elect of God, having 'the promise that now is, as well as that which is yet to come.' "[12]

This populist and democratic thrust to the miracle apologetic is even more striking when one recalls the opposite claim by Protestant apologists. James Mozley, one recalls, argued that the evidence of miracles was directed to an elite intellectual audience — to those who were not satisfied with traditional and customary belief. The mass of humanity did not need, nor could they truly appreciate, such appeals. The authority of miracles was accordingly always associated with a comparatively high genre of apologetics. For Catholics, in contrast, an appeal to miracles was a populist appeal to the general multitude. As one writer noted, the learned had many ways to overcome doubt, yet "as surely as Christianity is not the concern for the learned only, there must be another weapon against doubt," and this was the miraculous. Accordingly, all who favored a popular Christianity should look with favor upon modern miracles.[13]

Finally, as Stone implied, miracles seemed to serve still one more purpose — they anchored a belief in the supernatural for a generation succumbing to the disease of rationalism. The spirit of the modern age all too often seemed to be a functional deism that, although it did not deny the existence of God, made all nature independent of him.

Perhaps no one hammered upon this theme more forcefully than did the convert and Paulist Augustine F. Hewit. Like many other early Paulists, Hewit was a convert to Roman Catholicism who had earlier passed through many of the varied religious movements of antebellum American Protestantism. By the 1870s he was convinced that only a vital personal supernaturalism in which God was active in the world could maintain the traditional faith, and Rome alone was able to offer this. According to Hewit, Protestant defenses of the supernatural were doomed to failure. Protestants such as James McCosh might attempt to answer the positivist critique through a historical apologetic, such as by demonstrating the historicity of the biblical miracles, but such a defense was inadequate. The question was not one of facticity but of theory. "We may assert and prove miracles as a fact, but the objections of Positivists to them cannot be scientifically answered till we have proved that they have their law in the supernatural order," he wrote.[14]

Unless it could be demonstrated that miracles existed as a regular part of God's plan and were not merely exceptions to an otherwise perfect order, the supernaturalist position was lost. Catholicism, with its acceptance of a continuing interconnection between the supernatural and the natural, could accomplish this; whereas Protestantism with its a priori rejection of postbiblical miracles, could not. Protestants' prejudice against ecclesiastical miracles made all miracles appear to be fundamentally unnatural: "[Protestants] reject miracles, not because the testimony is insufficient, but because they cannot be admitted without admitting the reality of the supernatural. The prejudice against the supernatural must be removed as a preliminary work, and this can be done only by presenting Christianity as a whole in its unity and catholicity, and showing that . . . the supernatural or Christian order enters into the original decree of God, and is necessary to complete what is initial to the cosmos, or to perfect the natural order and to enable it to fulfill the purpose for which it exists, or realize its destiny or final cause in which is its beatitude or supreme good."[15] Once one accepted that miracles were signs not only of individual sanctity but also of the transformation of the natural order and its movement toward its created end, then miraculous events no longer seemed out of place. A Catholic understanding of the universe provided a place for God's supernatural activity just as surely as the Positivist vision excluded any such activity. Hence the issue, argued Catholics, was not one of science versus religion or history versus legend but of world views. Miracles were public manifestations of the supernatural power of God, and to reject them was to admit a prejudice against the supernatural itself.

A debate from the 1890s illustrates this Catholic presupposition. Throughout the late 1880s and early 1890s, Andrew D. White, former president of Cornell University and paladin of the new science, had been publishing a series of essays titled "New Chapters in the Warfare of Science" in *Popular Science Monthly* that eventually were republished as his famous *History of the Warfare of Science with Theology in Christendom*. In 1891, White turned his attention to the effect of religion on medicine. For White the rise of Christianity had a mixed impact on the rise of medicine. On the one hand, it promoted medicine through its spirit of benevolence; on the other hand, it denigrated medicine because of its teachings on demonic disease and supernatural healing. These latter ideas flourished during periods of ignorance and were always a threat to the spirit of scientific progress. To show how such elements could take root, he offered as an example the life of Francis Xavier. Using the method of analysis common to higher biblical critics, he contrasted Francis's own modest account of his missionary labors with the fantastic stories that developed in the century after his death. These thaumaturgical accretions were recorded in Bouhours's biography, with its accounts of restorations from the dead, miraculous draughts of fishes, speaking in tongues, and stories of "pious crabs." The spirit of credulity allowed these legendary accretions to overcome quickly the original figure of Francis. The thaumaturgical Francis was in turn enshrined in his *Bull of Canonization*. Never one for subtlety, White observed, "[T]here is much food for reflection in the fact that the same Pope who punished Galileo, and was determined that the Inquisition should not allow the world to believe that the earth revolves around the sun, thus solemnly ordered the world, under the pain of damnation, to believe in Xavier's miracles, including his 'gift of tongues,' and the return of the crucifix by the pious crab."[16]

White's critique called forth a number of Catholic responses, most notably from the American Jesuit Thomas Hughes. Much of the discussion involved the inadequacies of White's translations, his misinterpretation of evidence, and other technical issues, but for White's critics another fundamental problem was his methodological assumptions. Like the radical biblical critics Strauss and Renan, White assumed a pattern of religious development that moved from simple moral teaching to supernaturalism and superstition. Having assumed this pattern, he was free to dismiss as "accretions" all texts that disagreed with his schema. He "refuses to look palpable evidence in the face without flinching," protested Hughes. White furthermore refused to consider the possibility that later biographers could be privy to information unavailable to earlier writers, and that this might explain new material. All of these rules made for bad history.[17]

But more than this, in Hughes's view White's attitude suggested a moral arrogance. The biblical critics assumed that in the ancient world fact and pious legend blended together and that early writers were incapable of distinguishing the two. Whatever merit this argument might possess with regard to sources from the second century, it was clearly not true among sixteenth-century writers. The inquiry into the miracles of Francis Xavier had been inaugurated by King John III of Portugal almost immediately after Francis's death, and the inquiry was pointedly concerned with uncovering historical events and not mere legends. To reject the investigators' findings out of hand and to assert that their conclusions were not merely mistaken, but mendacious and willfully misleading, furthermore was to suggest that no Catholic source could be trusted, despite the fact that Catholic moral theology condemned forgery, falsification, and imposture as grievous sins. White seemed willing not only to reject testimony but to blacken moral reputations for the sake of a theory.[18]

The case of Francis Xavier was important for Roman Catholics because of its relatively recent occurrence and the degree of documentation it provided. Unlike medieval stories (or for that matter biblical accounts), the miracles of Francis Xavier occurred in the full light of history. In addressing them it was not a question of "science versus theology" but a willingness to address evidence versus a preference to dismiss it in order to maintain dogmatic beliefs about the function of the universe. This constituted not merely bad theology but also bad science, according to the Roman Catholics. The true scientist, they argued, dealt with what existed, not what they would have preferred to exist. Catholics, and not a person like A. D. White, were the true friends of the spirit of science because they did not approach it with the blinders of anti-supernaturalism.

An American Miracle Account

Of course for Roman Catholics miracles were more than merely a point of debate between themselves and their opponents, whether they be Protestant or Positivist. They were also a crucial part of the faith of everyday members. As Jay Dolan has noted, an openness to the miraculous was an important trait of devotional Catholicism throughout this period. Publications such as *Ave Maria* regularly featured accounts of miraculous healings through the intercession of Jesus, Mary, and the other saints. The sick continued to be cured and the lame healed, often through the vehicle of the rich devotional practices of nineteenth-century Catholicism. Piety, sacrament, and miraculous intervention bound the believer to the supernatural order and thus created a distinctive "household of faith" that included both the natural and the supernatural. But even in the devotional literature, the wider implication of the miraculous was not forgotten. Often these miracle stories were related in the context of beatification claims or the conversion of Protestants.[19]

In other instances the intellectual and popular elements of miracle accounts merged even more closely. Such was the case with the most documented account of a Catholic miracle in antebellum America, the healing in 1824 of Mrs. Ann Mattingly of Washington, D.C.[20] According to the accounts, Mattingly, a young married woman and sister of an early-nineteenth-century mayor of Washington, had suffered for seven years from an "ulcerated back" and a "tumor" the size of a pigeon's egg. Her affidavits claimed that by 1824 doctors had considered her case "out of the reach of medicine." Between four and five o'clock in the morning on March 10, however, she underwent a dramatic recovery. The previous evening she had been so ill that she could barely swallow the holy wafer placed on her tongue, but after receiving the sacrament she rebounded in health. Affidavits were solicited attesting to both her illness and to her recovery, and eventually thirty-five were secured. Bishop John England wrote a report of the occurrence, and in it one can see the important apologetical role of modern healing accounts for Roman Catholics.

England, for example, playfully reminded his Protestant readers of William Paley's elaborate rules for distinguishing false and true miracles. Paley had insisted that a true account should be contemporary with the event; that it should be specific in names, places, and dates; and that the seriousness of the event had to be recognized by its contemporaries. The evidence provided in the case of Ann Mattingly not only fulfilled these prerequisites but provided "as perfect and sufficient a body of evidence as could be required of anything short of absolute scepticism." In England's narrative, one observes the hoary Protestant Common Sense tradition being turned upon itself. Like a lawyer playing to a jury, England took delight in piling testimony upon testimony (all legally affirmed by authorities such as Chief Justice John Marshall) in order to build his case. The only persons who could refuse to accept such plain evidence were those who "would emulate the wisdom of the philosopher who, not satisfied with the evidence of the existence of the sun, by the immediate testimony of all the senses affected by it . . . determined to disbelieve the fact, until he could frame a syllogism."[21] Those in his readership schooled in Scottish Common Sense philosophy, then so strong in American higher education, could not miss the implication. Far from being the stewards of common sense that they thought they were, evangelical Protestants were as addicted to metaphysical speculation and dogmatic assumptions as the worst philosophe.

As we have noted, however, miracles were not only facts to be acknowledged by reason and common sense, but also signs and hence tied to grace and faith. And to many what was most remarkable about events such as the healing of Ann Mattingly was the faith they generated. This outpouring of belief impressed the journalist James Parton far more than all the affidavits combined. In his article in the *Atlantic Monthly* in which he discussed the growth of Roman Catholicism in America, he described the vigorous faith it elicited as its most attractive feature. He began his article with a description of a crowded early morning mass on a cold winter's day in New York City. While the rest of the city slept, these individuals chose to pray, and in their very posture of prayer showed none of the embarrassment with religion and piety that most sophisticated New Yorkers displayed. From prayer, Parton went on to discuss the case of Mrs. Mattingly and the role of the miraculous in Catholic piety. He offered the following reflection on the narrative of Bishop England.

> This narrative illustrates a very important difference between our Roman Catholic brethren and ourselves. A good Catholic, no matter what his rank or culture, believes in such things without an effort. It was not necessary for the faith of Catholics that Bishop England should gather together such a mass of testimony. Three good witnesses would have sufficed quite as well as three dozen. But no amount or quality of testimony could convince a Protestant mind that Mrs. Mattingly's tumor was cured miraculously, and her linen miraculously cleansed. For my part, if the President and Vice President, if the whole cabinet, both houses of Congress, and the Judges of the Supreme Court, had all sworn that they saw this thing done, and I myself had seen it, —

nay if the tumor had been on my own body, and had seemed to myself to be suddenly healed, — still I should think it more probable that all those witnesses, including myself, were mistaken, than that such a miracle had been performed.[22]

Faith, not evidence, divided the Protestant world view from the Catholic, and clearly Parton, although not a Catholic himself, admired the power of their faith. He went on to quote approvingly the Paulist Isaac Hecker: "We do not worship a dead God! . . . We Catholics have a lively practical *faith* in Providence which you Protestants think you have, and have not." Parton concluded his article by prophesying that within a generation or two the Roman Catholic Church would be the dominant church in America. It had a vitality and power Protestantism seemed to be lacking, and one cannot help but see that for Parton part of that power stemmed from the Catholic belief in miracles.[23]

The Dilemma: Lourdes or St. Januarius?

Parton's observations indicate that a chief point of division between Protestants and Catholics was the Catholic faith in a dramatic supernatural reality. The sacred universes of Protestants and Catholics differed as much as a whitewashed Puritan meeting house differed from the iconostasis of a Greek Orthodox cathedral. Miracles were an essential part in the iconostasis, or structuring of the supernatural reality, of the Catholic universe.

Yet just as an iconostasis is made up of the icons of many saints, and some of these might be more attractive than others to the outsider's eye, so too was the Catholic miracle claim made up of many individual claims of greater or lesser attractiveness to English-speaking Protestants. Of these many alleged occurrences two stood out: the apparition of Mary at Lourdes and the liquefaction of the blood of St. Januarius at Naples. These two cases are significant not only in themselves but also because they illustrate the ambiguous attractiveness of Catholic miracle claims for non-Catholics.

The story of Lourdes is of course well known.[24] In 1858 in Lourdes, a small French town in the Pyrenees, Marie-Bernarde Soubirous, the fourteen-year-old daughter of once prosperous but now poor parents, beheld an apparition while searching for firewood and bones to sell. Bernadette (as she is now better known) saw a young woman, clothed in a long white robe and wearing a veil and blue sash, standing in an oval niche or grotto in the rock cliff of Massiabelle. She experienced a total of eighteen apparitions. Although none of her companions saw them, her believability impressed others, and the grotto became a holy spot for thousands. Even more important for the later history of

Lourdes were two details associated with these apparitions. The first was that the woman identified herself as the Immaculate Conception, a designation of the Virgin Mary only recently defined within Roman Catholicism. The second was that a spring emerged (or was discovered), and the water of this spring began to effect miraculous cures. Lourdes quickly became the most famous healing shrine in the Catholic world, and the story of Lourdes and its miracles caught the imagination of the world.

From our perspective two aspects of Lourdes seem particularly striking. The first is how few miraculous healings have actually been recorded there, particularly in contrast to the superabundance of miracle claims made by the Protestant healing movements discussed earlier. As of 1980, of the over five thousand cures recorded by the Medical Bureau at Lourdes, the Roman Catholic Church has acknowledged only sixty-four to have been "miraculous."[25] In large part this can be attributed to the reticence among Catholic authorities to credit cures as being miraculous unless the evidence for them is overwhelming, but it also may reflect a practical implication of Catholics' linking of the miraculous to ecclesiology rather than scripture. Catholics, one recalls, believed that miracles testified to the supernatural reality of God's church. As such their occurrence was serendipitous in nature. In contrast, the Protestant proponents of faith healing discussed in the last chapter tended to anchor faith healing in the eternal promises of scripture, and at times even in the work of redemption itself. If God were true, they argued, then his promises were true. These acts of healing were seen accordingly as part of God's merciful relationship with the world. As such they could rightly be expected to be general in nature. If one were anointed and one had faith, then one should be healed. If healing did not take place, something was wrong because the biblical promise could not be wrong. Catholics on the whole did not reason in this way. According to the Catholic view, the normal way in which God supernaturally related to the world was sacramentally. Miracles were exceptional signs, occasional reminders of the reality of the supernatural. Hence only a few were needed to accomplish this purpose.

A second striking aspect of these events in Lourdes was that they appeared in an age of science, and further that the Catholic Church seemed to recognize and welcome the authority of science. From the very beginning testimonies of medical doctors were solicited to confirm claims of miraculous healing, and by 1884 a medical bureau, which included non-Catholic doctors, was founded to evaluate all alleged healings. The bureau determined whether a cure was genuine and ultimately whether it defied any medical explanation (and could hence be considered a miracle). Although the scientific status of the medical bureau was a continuing source of debate between defenders of Lourdes and its critics, the very fact that such procedures were set up was an acknowledgment of the authority of scientific and medical professionals to decide what was and what was not a miracle.

One of the earliest and most influential accounts of this event was by the journalist Henri Lasserre, who was also one of the persons who claimed to have been healed. Translated into English in 1870, it set forth many of the themes upon which later English-speaking Catholic writers would build.[26] The story of Lourdes, he explained, reflected the age-old struggle between the people of faith and a skeptical elite. That the Virgin Mary should choose to appear to a poor and simple young girl was a stinging rebuke to the pretensions of the rich, cultured, and powerful. Lasserre charged, "The rich form an exclusive circle, which they call 'good society,' and they regard as unworthy of serious attention the existence of the poor. . . . Except [for] a few rare Christians, no one treats the poor man as an equal and a brother. Except the saint — alas! too rare in these days." Whereas the poor believed, the rich and cultured scoffed at the very idea of the apparitions. They rejected even the possibility of such events and sought to find other explanations for the events. According to Lasserre, " 'Hallucination — catalepsy' were now the two grand words of the savants of Lourdes. 'Bear in mind,' they often repeated, 'there is not a single supernatural fact which Science has not fully accounted for. Science is certain: Science explains all.' " Despite their lip service to science, Lasserre argued, a lack of faith ultimately lay behind their opposition. The rich and learned preferred the world pictured by science, in which God made no appearances and did not disturb the peace. Lasserre took glee in describing the attitudes of Baron Massy, the prefect of the Upper Pyrenees. "Miracles having been indispensable to found the church and give it authority, he [Massy] accepted them as a necessity for the period of formation. But, according to his views, God should have stopped there, and been content with this minimum of the supernatural which had been so liberally granted him." Although a sincere Catholic, Massy could not accept the accounts of miracles because they made the world so complicated. God, like the poor, should know his place and not seek to overstep it. Lasserre describes other skeptics announcing at the grotto: "In the name of the king, God is hereby forbidden to work a miracle in this place."[27]

In the end, according to Lasserre, the scientific explanations for the healings (for example, the mineral content of the water) fell apart, and the healings became recognized as witnesses to the reality of the faith: "The supernatural had ceased to be invisible; it was now material and palpable. In the persons of the sick restored to health, and of the cripples to strength, it said to all like Christ to St. Thomas 'See my hands and my feet . . . The supernatural had, as it were, become incarnate in these incurables thus suddenly cured, and attesting itself publicly, demanded explanation."[28]

This account is significant not only in itself but also because the *Catholic World* chose to highlight it. The Paulists who published the *Catholic World* were dedicated to ministering to American Protestants, and indeed many of their leading members, including Isaac Hecker and Augustine F. Hewit, were converts from different traditions of American Protestantism. They were probably not oblivious, therefore, to the power that such themes would have over a Protestant audience. Issues such as the dogmatism of science, the evils of class division and neglect of the poor, the problem of faith, and the search for evidences, were, as we have seen, overriding questions for English-speaking Protestants in the second half of the nineteenth century. Clearly, the faith of Bernadette was seen as an antidote to the Victorian crisis of faith.

Facticity and faith were powerful appeals for a Protestant audience. We have already seen how a Protestant defender of faith healing such as Kelso Carter found himself more in sympathy with the pilgrims at Lourdes than with their anti-supernaturalist critics. Even more surprising, the Rev. Stephen H. Tyng, Jr. also attested to power of these occurrences. Tyng was the son of one of the leading evangelicals in the Episcopal Church and was himself both a leader of the anti-Catholic party of his denomination and an early proponent of premillennialism. Health concerns led him to travel to Europe in 1880. There he visited the shrines of Lourdes and of Knock in Ireland.[29] Soon after he returned, Tyng delivered a Sunday evening sermon, "The Mountain Movers," in which he described his visit to the shrine at Lourdes and praised the people there for their "simple and profound faith." But he did not stop there. The text of his sermon, Matthew 17:19–20, included the famous saying, "If you have faith as a grain of mustard seed, ye shall say unto this mountain Remove . . . and it shall remove," and Tyng argued that faith could truly bring about miracles. He explained, "We shall never know what the powers of the faith are until we find a man who knows all the truths of God and is free from the errors of man. It is this faith at the shrine of Notre Dame de Lourdes and probably at Knock, in Ireland, that is honored by God." The faith and evidences Tyng found there compelled him to affirm the reality of the miracles of Lourdes. "No one dares to deny that multitudes of cures took place there," he preached. "The lame leapt, the deaf heard, the blind saw. It will never do in this generation to deny those well authenticated facts."[30]

Tyng's admission shocked the Protestant population of New York City and delighted Roman Catholic commentators. As the *New York Times* in an editorial admitted, "Lourdes has been of late years a growing stumbling-block in the path not only of rationalists, but of all sincere enemies of the Roman

Church" (enemies that, as the editorial implied, included the *Times* itself). The evil of Tyng's logic, the Protestant community concluded, was that it came dangerously close to legitimating Roman Catholicism.

Tyng may have been unique in his willingness to accept the cures at Lourdes as genuinely miraculous, but many other non-Catholic visitors to the shrine attested to the power and appeal of the pilgrims' faith. One finds a wistful and nostalgic quality in many of these accounts, as if the authors were observing a world in which the acids of modernity had not yet begun to eat away the innocence of the faith. They might often criticize the doctrines they heard, or the commercialism they observed, but not the faith itself, which was quite often pictured in a positive light.[31] The English convert Robert Hugh Benson was even more explicit. Benson, son of an archbishop of Canterbury, noted in his account of Lourdes that there the biblical world took on a reality missing in the proper Anglicanism that his father represented. He felt "that I had been present in my own body, in the twentieth century, and seen Jesus pass along by the sick folk, as he passed 2000 years before."[32] At Lourdes one did not find a dormant religion of the book but a vibrant religion of life.

Lourdes reflected, in many ways, much that was positive and attractive about Catholic miracle claims for English-speaking Protestants. Other miracle accounts, however, exhibited the Catholic claim in a less flattering light, and none more than the "miracle" of St. Januarius (or St. Gennaro). According to tradition, Januarius was the martyred fourth-century Christian bishop of Benvento (Italy). At the time of his death some of his blood was preserved in small vials, and it became an object of veneration. According to the faithful, the blood itself was the substance of a recurring miracle. Eighteen times a year at public ceremonies in the cathedral of Naples, this dried-up blood would reliquify. Aiding the clergy in this ceremony were a group of poor and elderly women, the "aunts" or "relations" (*zie*) of the saint, who took it upon themselves to chastise the saint if the miracle was slow in coming. The miracle of the liquefaction was furthermore seen to have preserved the city from everything from outbreak of cholera to eruptions of Mount Vesuvius.

The liquefaction of the blood of St. Januarius, like the healings at Lourdes, fascinated Protestant commentators, but for fundamentally different reasons. Joseph Addison provided one of the earliest observations of the events in his *Remarks on Italy*. "I had twice an opportunity of seeing the operator of this pretended miracle," he wrote, "and must confess that I think it so far from being a real miracle, that I look upon it as one of the most bungling of tricks that I ever saw." For the next two centuries visitors would come to see the spectacle, and like latter-day Caesars they came, they saw, and they censured. The miracle of St. Januarius seemed to confirm for these observers all of their prejudices about Roman Catholicism. The elaborate ceremony was interpreted as an example of sacerdotal chicanery created to dupe into subservience a benighted and superstitious population. It was "pious mendacity" and "consecrated fraud" for Andrew Dickson White. The fact that the Catholic miracle seemed to be foreshadowed in the ancient temple of Isis discovered in nearby Pompeii only confirmed for others that these practices were far closer to paganism than to Christianity. One commentator wrote: "There was no more priestly jugglery in this pagan temple [of Isis] than is practiced yearly in a Christian church in Naples. The blood of St. Januarius is as much a falsehood as was the voice of Isis. Nor do I believe that her priesthood were, in general, worse in morals than those Roman friars who have continued their practices under another name."[33]

It is not hard to understand why the liquefaction was viewed so negatively. If there were two religious virtues that Protestants valued above all others they were personal faith and divine benevolence. These formed the center of the teachings of Jesus, and made up the core of the Christian faith. Both seemed to be profoundly absent from the liquefaction of the blood. The Naples ritual gave the impression of being a pure spectacle divorced from faith and morality. It appeared much more like fetishism or superstition than the pure religion of the gospels. And finally, national and racial stereotypes seemed to be confirmed. If Protestantism equalled progress, then the farther away one moved from Protestant northern Europe the more superstitious the Catholicism became. Addison for example observed, "The French are much more enlightened than the Spaniards and Italians, on occasion with their frequent controversies with the Hugonots [*sic*]; and we find many of the Roman Catholic gentlemen of our own country, who will not stick to laugh at the superstitions they sometimes meet with in other nations." Januarius represented to the visitor the degenerate nature of Latin Catholicism, or the antithesis of all that Protestants most treasured. Catholic writers, to be sure, adamantly defended the veracity of the liquefaction, but their accounts elicited little if any appreciation among non-Catholics.[34]

Thus the paradox: miracles at the same time testified to true faith and credulity, bore witness to supernatural action and priestly intrigue, and manifested the aura of an age of faith and the superstitions of paganism. How could one make sense of them?

No Catholic writer treated this question as ably as did John Henry Newman. The issue of the miraculous had long been an important one for him. As one recent biographer has noted, early in Newman's career he had been touched by the skeptical argument against miracles, and throughout his career as both an Anglican and a Roman Catholic he strove to answer eighteenth-century critics such as Middleton and Hume. At first he was a loyal defender of the limited age of miracles argument. His "Miracles of Scripture Compared with Those Related Elsewhere" (1825–26), defended the uniqueness of biblical miracles against both skeptics and proponents of ecclesiastical miracles.[35] His Anglican faith, rooted in a vision of history that pitted a primitive Catholicism against medieval and Roman perversions, further reinforced his appreciation of the limited age argument.

As he edged toward Rome, however, Newman not only began to question the reality of any "primitive Catholicism" divorced from later developments, but also to reassess the entire question of ecclesiastical miracles. We have already seen that after his retirement to Littlemore he had dedicated himself to publishing the lives of saints of the British Isles, which included an honest rendering of their miraculous claims. The opposition these volumes engendered contributed to his disillusionment with Anglicanism.[36]

These developments provided the background for his celebrated and infamous "Essay on Ecclesiastical Miracles." The essay, which was originally intended to be a preface for an translation of Claude Fleury's *Ecclesiastical History*, was instead published in 1843 along with his earlier essay on biblical miracles. In it, Newman offered not only a reflection on the nature and meaning of ecclesiastical miracles, but also a reconsideration of such long-discussed alleged ecclesiastical miracles as the tongueless African confessors. Like many of Newman's greatest writings, "Ecclesiastical Miracles" was inspired by the method and themes of Joseph Butler's *Analogy of Religion,* particularly the way it addressed the questions of evidence and belief. Like Butler, Newman recognized that for the great questions of life, including religion, human beings were forced to deal at best with only probable evidence. His essay first attempted to delineate the nature and function of ecclesiastical miracles and to distinguish them from the great biblical miracles. At first glance his essay seems to follow the pattern laid down by earlier Protestant critics. Following Paley, Newman admitted that ecclesiastical miracles were at best "tentative miracles" and were fundamentally different from biblical ones. The latter were consciously wrought and associated with revelation, and as such served to instruct the multitudes. No ecclesiastical miracle could make this claim, and in this sense the early church writers whom Protestants loved to quote were indeed correct — miracles such as those recorded in Scripture had indeed passed away. Ecclesiastical miracles, Newman believed, were but a shadow of their biblical counterparts and served a far more limited function. They were usually directed to individuals rather than to multitudes, and they served merely to strengthen the faith of believers rather than convert unbelievers. They were quixotic in nature, Newman explained: "Ecclesiastical miracles are not so much wrought as displayed, being effected by Divine Power without any visible media of operation at all . . . or by instruments who did not know at the time what they were effecting, or, if they were hoping and praying for such supernatural blessing, at least did not know when they were to be used as instruments and when not." Scriptural miracles were "grave," whereas ecclesiastical miracles were "romantic." The former were perfect like the Garden of Eden; the latter were "luxurious" like the "jungles of Asia."[37]

But if only a shadow they were a real shadow nonetheless. Ecclesiastical miracles paralleled some of the lesser miracles recorded in scripture such as the healing handkerchief of Paul and the stories of Elisha, in Newman's view, and hence they ought not to be dismissed out of hand. The modern believer had to decide upon the probability of their occurrence, and this was tied to evidence. Some accounts that had more evidential support were truly more probable than others, but the absence of evidence — although making a claim improbable — could never in itself disprove a case. The Protestant rejection of ecclesiastical miracles stemmed from its misunderstanding of the true nature of Christianity. In Newman's words, Protestants mistakenly "believe that Christianity is little more than a creed or doctrine, introduced into the world once for all, and then left to itself," unaided by any divine presence or supernatural gift. Christianity, however, was not a dry truth but a dispensation, like Judaism, and the church was the supernatural ordinance of this dispensation. According to this outlook, just as miracles marked the dispensation of Judaism so too did they mark the dispensation of the church. All this did not prove the case for individual miracle stories, which still had to be judged on their evidence and believability. But for the believer the antecedent probability should lie in favor of miracle claims. The inalienable rights of Englishmen ought to be extended to the claims for miracles. Miracles were innocent till proven guilty, and the burden of proof was now with their accusers.[38]

As with so much of Newman's thought, the believer here confronts not a world of black and white but an intricate web of probabilities. Gone is the clearly defined periodization with its true and false miracles. All ecclesiastical miracle claims are shades of gray. But significantly biblical miracles were caught up as well in this web of probabilities. By claiming that ecclesiastical miracles were no more improbable or incredible than the miracles of scripture, Newman was also in effect saying that the scriptural miracles were no more probable or credible than the later stories. All were ambiguous.[39]

As Sheridan Gilley has observed, "The work is as uncomfortable to believers as to sceptics, because Newman's battery of arguments against the sceptics raises as many sceptical arguments as it resolves. Newman's gossamer web of probabilities was unlike either earlier Protestant or Roman Catholic writings, and seemed pernicious to many of his contemporaries." Throughout his career as a Roman Catholic, Newman was accused of obliterating the distinction between truth and falsehood in order to believe more easily the most incredible of teachings, and "Ecclesiastical Miracles" was viewed as a prime example of this pathology. The biblical critic and schoolmaster Edwin A. Abbott wrote of it, "It was one of the most intellectually demoralizing books that I have ever met with. After two or three hours of it, my reasoning faculties seemed to become 'unclean till the even.' It was needful to go wash in a scientific treatise and recover the perception of the difference between truth and falsehood." Others who preferred bathing in scientific treatises had similar reactions.[40]

"Ecclesiastical Miracles," however, should be understood in light of another of Newman's works, his sermon "Faith and Reason Contrasted as Habits of the Mind." There he addressed the arguments of Hume (referred to in the text as only "a well known infidel of the last century") and why the evidence of miracles failed to convince the scientific mind. Hume was correct, Newman noted, in his assertion that the evidence for the miraculous was forever inadequate to compel belief: "Reason weighing evidence only, or arguing from external experience is counter to faith." No amount of empirical evidence would ever produce faith. Faith was not built upon evidence but was instead a "supernatural principle" or presupposition. It existed as a habit of the mind prior to and independent of any examination of the material world. Reason flowed from faith and was not independent of it. The naked reason, such as scientists and skeptics delighted in, was unnatural reason. It constructed an understanding of reality upon only part of the real (that is, the physical and logical), but ignored other equally true realities such as God and the moral sense. Miracles were always problematic to the pure reason because they seemed to contradict what was known of the physical laws of the universe. But once a person came to perceive other realities through faith such as the nature of God and his moral order, those events that apparently contravened the physical law of the universe could be recognized as being in accord with the moral law. Because miracles seem impossible without a prior understanding of the divine nature and the moral law, Newman added that they appear for the sake of believers, not skeptics. "Miracles . . . are not wrought to convince Atheists, and when they claim to be evidence of a Revelation, presuppose the being of an Intelligent Agent . . . [they] are grounded on the admission that the doctrine they are brought to prove is . . . accordant with the laws of His moral governance." His age's problems with the idea of miracles reflected their increasing skepticism, not any advance of knowledge.[41]

But what of the problems of superstition and credulity, seen so graphically in popular devotions such as the liquefaction of the blood of St. Januarius? By abandoning the common room of Oriel College for the world of Roman Catholicism, Newman found himself forced to confront these questions. It was true, he explained, that in the life of his newly adopted church truth and error were inexorably mixed. He freely admitted that in popular devotions such as the reverencing of the relics of some ancient saint, there was at best only a probability that the relics were actually derived from the saint in question. They might be spurious. Yet the church chose nonetheless to permit such devotions. Why? Precisely, he explained, because there was at least some probable evidence on their behalf. If the church could not be sure that the relics were genuine, it could also not be sure that the relics were fraudulent. Furthermore, one could see that the faith of the believers was real, and the church had always maintained that it was better to err on the side of faith. Such was the meaning of the New Testament parable of the tares and wheat; all should be done to preserve the wheat even at the cost of tolerating an occasional tare. Newman went on, however, to observe that there was something pernicious about the concern of the present generation with superstition and credulity. These were not the great sins of scripture. He reminded his readers, for example, about the scene from the gospel (Lk 8:44) in which a woman touched the hem of Jesus' garment to be healed. In her belief that by touching a garment she could be healed "she was under the influence of what could be called, were she alive now, a 'corrupt religion', yet she was rewarded a miracle." Perhaps twitting his former compatriots prejudices, he added that the woman was like a "poor Neapolitan crone, who chatters to the crucifix," or perhaps would participate in those other religious practices of that benighted province. But the scriptures record that her faith was rewarded. Nor did Christ even chastise her for the idolatry implicit in her simple belief that there was a special power in his material clothing. In fact, when Christ chose to condemn idolatry, he directed his wrath to the idolatries of pride and wealth, not the idolatry of ignorance.[42]

Clearly for Newman the revulsion of his generation to credulity was misplaced. Jesus often condemned faithlessness; he never condemned overly faithful impulses or even superstition. Credulity was for him a peccadillo. The church always strove to correct it and keep it under control, but it was far less destructive than the loss of faith that seemed to be overtaking his generation. "Taking human nature as it is," he explained, "we must surely concede a little superstition as not the worst of evils, if it be the price of making sure of faith." These were shocking words in mid-Victorian England, but perhaps even more shocking was their social implication. Despite the prejudices of class and nationality, the educated believer ultimately had more in common with a "Neapolitan crone" than with the most sophisticated of skeptics. The sharing of a common faith was more foundational than any element of superficial intellectual culture.

Modernism, Americanism, and the Miraculous

Although Newman was praised vociferously by American Catholics, and his "Essay on Ecclesiastical Miracles" was regularly cited, the full impact of Newman's thought went largely unnoticed.[43] In large part this was because by the end of the century the focus of many Catholics vis-à-vis the miraculous was fundamentally different from the concerns of Newman.

The question of the relationship between reason and faith is of course an old one in Christianity. Can an unaided human being know anything of the truth of God, and if so, how? Is there a rational foundation for Christian dogma? Such questions had long been dear to Catholic philosophers and theologians. In Catholic theology a traditional distinction had been made between apologetical, or fundamental, theology and dogmatic theology. The former was concerned with grounding the very fact of revelation (often through the help of reason), whereas the latter rested on the authority of revelation. The relationship between reason and faith was further elucidated by other theologians who distinguished between a rational preparation for faith (or a *perambula fidei*) and the supernatural act of faith itself (the *actus fidei*). By the mid-nineteenth century, Catholic theologians began wrestling with the radical transformations of the European world symbolized by Romanticism, the French Revolution, and the new post-Kantian philosophy. Some questioned whether these changes had rendered the older theology unusable. Various alternative schemas were brought forth stretching from theories of ontologism (according to which the human soul had an intuitive perception of God's truth) to fideism (in which no knowledge was possible; faith was the only answer). Although this was largely a continental debate, American Catholics, particularly those converts who had been touched by Transcendentalism, did play a role. In the ontologism of Orestes Brownson, and the emphasis on the internal witness of the Holy Spirit in Isaac Hecker's *The Church and the Age*, one sees two such flowerings.[44]

The question of the relationship between reason and faith was one of the subjects discussed at the First Vatican Council. From the council issued forth the apostolic constitution *Dei Filius*, which propounded the idea of faith as both rational and supernatural, and in turn condemned both rationalism and fideism. It also largely affirmed the traditional scholastic principle that the ascent to faith was not a blind leap but was assisted by unaided human reason.

Most importantly for our purposes, the constitution reasserted that the assent to faith, being reasonable, could be justified by rational arguments based on the "divine facts" of miracles and prophecies: "To the end . . . that the obedience of our faith might be agreeable to reason, God willed to join unto the interior grace of the Holy Spirit external proofs of His revelation, to wit divine works, and chiefly miracles and prophecies, which, as they manifestly show forth the omnipotence and the infinite knowledge of God, are proofs most certain of divine revelation, and suited to the understanding of all."[45] The canons passed were even more explicit: "If anyone says that all miracles are impossible, and that therefore all reports of them, even those contained in sacred scripture, are to be set aside as fables or myths; or that miracles can never be known with certainty, nor can the divine origin of the christian religion be proved from them: let him be anathema."[46]

Although the document made clear that this knowledge was insufficient for salvation, it nonetheless emphasized that an empirical confirmation of belief was necessary and was provided by the signs of miracles and prophecy. Thus the essential elements of the earlier scholastic theology were reaffirmed as was the rational and extrinsic basis for fundamental or apologetical theology.

Yet scholasticism was not the only voice in fin-de-siècle Roman Catholicism, and in the years following *Dei Filius* a spirited debate arose over alternative models for fundamental theology. For some the revivified Thomism of the neo-scholastics seemed too abstract, metaphysical, and a priori. It neither successfully responded to the new challenges of history and science, which, as we have seen, were threatening the certainty about these divine facts, nor met the deep felt spiritual needs of the age. An alternative mode of apologetic was needed.

If one name was associated with this new style of apologetic, it was that of the French lay-Catholic philosopher Maurice Blondel. For Blondel, ultimate truth was not a simple rational process but could only be reached by involving the whole of a person's being. Hence philosophy must be grounded in action. It involved willing and feeling as well as rationally knowing. Blondel explained the implications of his theology for the question of apologetics in his *Letter on Apologetics* (1895). In it he criticized the scholastic approach for its "extrinsicism" and failure to address the actual human condition. He argued that there was an intrinsic need for the supernatural in all persons that ought to be the starting point of apologetics. True apologetical theology worked from the inner self outward toward revelation—not in the reverse as in the neo-scholastics schema. Because in his view a successful apologetical theology could not be grounded on the external appeal of divine facts but should start from human consciousness, Blondel was comparatively indifferent concerning the facticity of the miracle accounts. Like Newman, he argued that miracles in themselves enlighten some but blind others. Human reason could neither validate nor invalidate miracle claims, hence their value was not to prove faith for nonbelievers but to confirm an already existing faith. "Miracles," he wrote, "are truly miraculous only for those who are already prepared to recognize the divine action in the most usual events. And it follows that philosophy, which would offend against its own nature by denying them, is no less incompetent to affirm them, and that they are a witness written in a language other than that of which it is the judge."[47] Blondel provided a markedly different conception of fundamental or apologetical theology. At the time (and ever since) critics have used the terms "immanence" versus "transcendence" to characterize these different starting points, though as other scholars have noted his philosophy can also be seen as harking back to earlier teachings of Blaise Pascal and even John Henry Newman.[48]

The question of this new apologetic was discussed frequently by American Catholics, yet what is surprising is the largely negative response it received.[49] Despite their warm admiration for Brownson, Hecker, Newman, and others who could be seen as forerunners to the movement, American Catholics offered it lukewarm support at best. As one critic noted, despite its appeal to nonbelievers, the new apologetic failed successfully to ground theology. "The first and last aim of the Catholic apologist is to justify belief in supernatural truths — to lay down and build up systematically the logical foundations of faith in a supernatural revelation."[50] If theology is properly a science, believed these Catholics, then it must be based on a sure and objective foundation. The new method might suffice as a subjective apologia, or as a preamble for the faith that might be able to persuade a faithless generation to take religion seriously, but it could never be an objective foundation or ground for constructive theology. Furthermore the testimony of external witnesses was not the church's to give up. God himself had chosen to accredit revelation with these signs, and no true theology could ignore this fact. To abandon this belief, even to win over the present generation of non-believers, would be to sell the church's divine patrimony for a mess of subjective porridge. Even the generally promodernist *New York Review* drew the line at endorsing wholeheartedly the new apologetic.[51]

How does one explain this reticence, particularly since many aspects of the new apologetic seemed persuasive? One factor, as we have already seen, was a continuing recognition of the value of the traditional apologetical or fundamental theology, and its presupposition that the foundation of the "science" of dogmatic theology was rational. But two further factors militated against the new apologetic and both involved, at least in part, questions about the miraculous.

The traditional understanding of miracles, one recalls, interpreted them as both fact and sign, with the fact being exoteric and comprehensible to the natural mind, and the sign being perceivable only by faith. In Catholic miracle claims, the facticity of these claims had played a chief role. The affidavits of Mrs. Mattingly, the physician reports at Lourdes, and other such evidences all witnessed to the objective reality of the supernatural in the natural. For centuries these miracles had been pictured as stubborn facts challenging the smooth dogmatisms of Protestants and naturalists. Critics feared that the new apologetic was all too willing to abandon the objectivity of the fact for the subjectivity of the sign, yet "the mind cannot rest on any object less certain than a fact."

Even more important, this new apologetic seemed to jettison that intellectual certainty and solidity that was so central to the Roman Catholic appeal. Protestantism had been derided for decades for succumbing to subjectivism — it was accused of attempting to anchor itself on the individual interpretation of scripture and personal religious experience rather than upon a sure and solid foundation. In the large corpus of apologetical writings by converts to Catholicism in nineteenth-century America, Rome was often described as a rock of certainty in the vortex of American society. "We know where we stand; whilst rationalists are dodging for a foothold amid quicksands," had long been a proud boast, but one that seemed threatened by the new apologetic. And in the final analysis, the deep-rooted anti-Protestant stance toward the new apologetic was too powerful to be overcome.[52]

The question of the new apologetic leads necessarily into the question of Catholic Modernism, because they are connected, at least in part.[53] Furthermore, because the anti-Modernist oath of Pius X included the attestation "I accept and willingly recognize the external proofs of revelation, that is, the divine facts, in the first instance miracles and prophecies, as most certain signs of the divine origin of the Christian religion, and I hold that they are visible in the highest degree for the intelligence of all men, in every age, including those of the present time," one would naturally expect to find an extended critique of the miraculous in the writings of the Catholic Modernists. But here one is disappointed. Particularly when they are contrasted with those by contemporary Protestant liberal thinkers (to be discussed in the next chapter), it is apparent that the question of the miraculous played little if any formal role in the writings of major English-speaking Catholic Modernists. In their defense of biblical criticism, one finds virtually no assault on the virgin birth such as one finds in Protestant writers, and even in the attacks of a person like George Tyrrell on medievalism there is no criticism of healing miracles. Indeed the Modernist-leaning *New York Review* openly defended the category of the miraculous against radical critics.[54] If, as some have argued, Catholic Modernism paralleled the liberal or modernist impulse within Protestantism, how do we explain this fundamentally different attitude toward the miraculous?[55]

Any answer to this question is conjecture, but certain possibilities do arise. One is that the movement was stymied before such doubts could fully emerge. A number of writers have noted that the heresy condemned under the name of "Modernism" in the encyclical *Pascendi* in 1907 was actually a synthetic comprehensive theological system propounded by no individual Modernist. What were condemned were the (alleged) logical implications of certain principles, and if this is true then the problem of the miraculous might have been a potential issue, but had not yet become a real one. A second possible explanation is that an attack on miracles was consciously held back. In private correspondence, for example, the English Catholic Modernist George Tyrrell was far more critical of miracles than he was in public; he even called them "myths." Likewise Michael DeVito in his study of the *New York Review* demonstrates that the editor of that journal, James F. Driscoll, purposely refrained from publishing more controversial positions in order not to derail the journal's entire agenda.[56]

The difference between Catholic Modernists and Protestant liberals, however, may in fact ultimately reflect the different place of the miraculous in these two communions. The comparative lack of emphasis upon the place of the miraculous in the present life of the church, it will be suggested, helped convince Protestant liberals that the miraculous as a category could be jettisoned from the Christian story without substantially altering it. Miracles truly were (to return to one of the Protestant liberals' favorite analogies) part of the baggage and not the artillery of the church. No real Catholic could believe this. As we have seen, the miraculous was imbedded within the religious life of Catholics, and no simple cosmetic surgery could remove it. It infused the piety and thought as well as the doctrine and practice of Roman Catholicism, and to attack it was ultimately to attack the Catholic system itself. As long as Catholic Modernists understood themselves to be Catholic, the issue of the miraculous was tacitly seen as out of bounds.

An implicit acknowledgment of this need to transform rather than exclude the miraculous is found in one of the few critical discussions of the miraculous by an American Modernist, William L. Sullivan's novel *The Priest*. Subtitled *A Tale of Modernism in New England*, it is in some sense a Catholic *Robert Elsmere*. It tells the story of the ministry of a Catholic priest, Ambrose Hanlon, in a small New England village. It is by no means a good novel. The characters are wooden and the plot contrived, and the attempts for humor, such as when the conservative Catholics regularly refer to the great liberal historian Adolph Harnack as "Hermann," are ham-handed. Nor has the intellectual posturing of the novel aged well. In one dramatic scene Hanlon has his volumes of the Spanish Jesuit Francis Suarez burned. For Sullivan, book burning was apparently a sign of intellectual maturity; for those who have survived the diabolical spirit of the twentieth century, however, book burning has perhaps a less elevated connotation.

But the novel does culminate in two scenes involving the miraculous, as Hanlon wrestles with an understanding of his ministry. The first involves the healing of Mary Kiley, a young woman paralyzed by an accident. Her suffering is a recurring theme in the novel, because her faith was true and deep. Finally she is healed. As she explains: "For some time past . . . a conviction that I should get well had taken hold of me. It grew deeper and stronger every day until it became an irresistible certainty. I knew I should be cured. I felt that God's will was being disclosed to me. I seemed to be drawing on the resources of infinite strength, of God's own infinite life. . . . The very day you left Axton, 'Cured!' 'Cured!' 'Cured!' kept ringing in my ears. I tried harder to direct the current of the vitality I felt pouring into me, into the nerves that were lifeless. I felt wonderfully, awfully near to God, in a kind of ecstasy of confidence, I sat up in bed, I stood upon the floor, and God's merciful miracle was accomplished."

Occurring when it does in the novel, this scene of healing serves to emphasize the reality of faith and the power of true belief over bodily illness. Spiritual power was present and worked through human beings. The power of belief could dumbfound all its rationalist critics. Religion was real. But immediately after this scene, Ambrose receives a letter informing him that his church had been sent regular table wine rather than altar wine from the supplier. This error, the letter went on, probably invalidated all the masses that had been celebrated with the improper wine, and it was suggested that all masses of intention be reoffered. This letter shocks Ambrose as much as Mary Kiley's healing had inspired him: "What disgusting casuistry! What a riot of superstition! Because one wine was one or two per-cent less purely the juice of the grape than the other, therefore the latter could be changed into the blood of Christ, and the former could not!"[57]

The contrast between these two images — the healing of Mary Kiley and the invalid masses — brings one back to the ambiguous appeal of the miraculous in late-nineteenth-century Catholicism. It is in some ways a reiteration of the clash between Lourdes and Januarius. The moral and spiritual power of the healing of Mary Kiley could not help but inspire faith and confidence. It testified to the triumph of spirit over matter and of faith over scientific presumptions. In contrast the "miracle" of the mass, like that of the liquefaction of the blood of St. Januarius, seemed magical, mechanical, and out of place in the modern world.

Once the issue was framed in these terms, the resolution became clear. The end of the novel finds Ambrose abandoning the Catholic priesthood for Unitarianism. Only this different venue could allow the true power of belief to be finally freed from dogma and superstition. This was the path that Sullivan himself chose to take.[58]

A Different Look at Lourdes

The critique of the Catholic system of the miraculous hence was seen not as a rejection of the power of belief, but as its liberation. It was a liberation, however, that had to transcend Catholicism. And nowhere was this theme of the attraction of faith warring against dogma and superstition more powerfully presented than in the most popular late-nineteenth-century account of the events at Lourdes, the novel *Lourdes* by Emile Zola. Published in 1894 and translated the same year, the novel was widely popular in both Britain and America and was even serialized by the *New York Herald*.[59] On one level Zola's *Lourdes* is what one would expect from such a notorious naturalist and opponent of the Catholic Church. From the outset Zola rejected any possibility that the cures of Lourdes could be miracles or that the doctrines could be true. The novelist took great delight in showing the crassness of the place and the credulity of the believers. The plot of *Lourdes* focuses on a series of pilgrims, and in particular, their various reasons for going and their experiences while at the site. One goes to seek a husband for her daughter, others go to achieve financial gain, and still another goes to rendezvous with her lover. It is of little surprise that the volume scandalized pious Catholics and that it was quickly placed on the *Index of Forbidden Books* along with the rest of Zola's oeuvre.

But what is surprising about the volume is the sympathy Zola maintains not only for the pilgrims but for the idea of Lourdes itself. Lourdes for him represented the ambiguous state of the French soul at the end of the nineteenth century: caught between its memories of the ancient faith and its new confidences in reason and science. This conflict is highlighted in the novel's central character, the priest, Pierre Froment. Froment, a child of a pious mother and scientific father, feels his faith ebbing away; he hopes that by making the journey to Lourdes his faith could be restored.[60]

Another factor that makes the novel compelling is that the conflict between scientific reason and faith is played out through striking role reversals. In the scenes between Pierre and the scientists Sabathier and Chassaigne, it is the priest who insists upon reason and comprehensibility, whereas the men of science argue for the mystery of reality and the need for faith. Unlike Pierre who seeks rational meaning, these men are led to Lourdes as simple supplicants by the tragedy and incomprehensibility of life. As Chassaigne counsels Pierre, "You are a priest, my child, and I know what your misfortune is. The miracles seem impossible to you. But what do you know of them? Admit that you know nothing, and that what to our senses seem impossible is every minute taking place."[61] In contrast, anyone who traveled to Lourdes to attain certainty would surely be disappointed. In the chapter "Verification," the author ridicules the vaunted bureau of examination. In their attempts to validate medically a miraculous cure the examiners demonstrated neither good science nor real faith. Their task was worse than worthless because it merely "wounded the feelings of the pious, and failed to satisfy the incredulous." No certainty nor even evidence could be found at Lourdes. Even the "healing" of Pierre's beloved friend Marie could not restore his faith, because it could not remove his doubts or heal his broken spirit.[62]

But again and again Zola returns to the pilgrims themselves, and in their faith, no matter how misguided, he sees a glimpse of true reality. The power of Lourdes, he implies, lay not in its dogmas nor its alleged miracles but in its moral vision. This vision is what brought the pilgrims there. They were "all condemned, abandoned by science, weary of consulting doctors, of having tried the torturing effects of futile remedies. And how well could one understand that burning, with a desire to preserve their lives, unable to resign themselves to the injustice and indifference of Nature, they should dream of a superhuman power, of an almighty Divinity who, in their favour, would perchance annul the established laws, alter the course of the planets, and reconsider His creation!"[63]

Thus in the last chapter of the novel, entitled "The Death of Bernadette — The New Religion," Pierre's struggle between faith and reason culminates in a series of juxtaposing reflections on the phenomenon of Lourdes. On one level Lourdes was a remnant of an absolute faith that was dead and impossible to revive. "History never retraces its steps, humanity cannot return to childhood," Zola preaches. Yet it was nonetheless valuable. Lourdes might be a falsehood, but it was one of those falsehoods that made life possible; hence it should be tolerated. The ambiguity of Lourdes also exacerbated Pierre's own dual makeup. Lourdes was an affront to his own rationality, which was so very much part of his nature. "He had been unable to kill reason and humiliate and annihilate himself. Reason remained his sovereign mistress. . . . Whenever he met with a thing which he could not understand, it was she who whispered to him, 'There is certainly a natural explanation which escapes me.'" But his faith responded that reason was not enough. Pierre hungered for an equality and justice that his reason could never find in passive nature. As long as the soul hungered for more than it could see, it would need places like Lourdes. "Lourdes was a resounding and undeniable proof that man could never live without the dream of a Sovereign Divinity, re-establishing equality and re-creating happiness by dint of miracles."[64] How then could these conflicting claims of his own nature be reconciled? Only by a new religious vision that could acknowledge the realities of both reason and faith. The old religion of Catholicism was an "illusion departing," and a new religion that affirmed the world must arise in its place. But it had to be a religion that allowed for the transformative power of spirit.

It is uncertain whether Zola himself put stock in this final hope of Pierre, but it is clear, as we have seen, that it was one solution to the Catholic paradox of the miraculous. Lourdes had finally freed itself from Januarius. Faith and science, rather than dogma and church, lay at the core of this new religion. The cost, of course, was a rejection of Catholicism as any organized system of belief, and it is not surprising that Catholic writers poured scorn on Zola and his novel. But as we shall see in the next chapter, many of the Protestant liberals and even more of the post-Protestant defenders of the supernatural attempted to follow Zola's path.

This was of course a path Catholics refused to take. Thus after condemning Modernism, Roman Catholics continued in their own direction, defending the scholastic view of the miraculous against liberalism and naturalism. Likewise their distinctive view of miracles as a reflection of ecclesiology gave Catholics a theological vision fundamentally distinct from that followed by Protestant proponents of faith healing and other modern miracles. In the years to follow, Catholics would be observers rather than participants in the great debate.

What About Jesus?
The New Biblical Criticism and the New Testament Miracles

By the end of the 1880s, the storm that threatened to wash away a miraculous Christianity appeared to be receding. The critics of the supernatural had launched their strongest attack, and it had been rebutted. Out of Germany Adolph Harnack acknowledged the excesses of the Tübingen school and urged a more cautious historical approach. In the English-speaking world one found the same spirit, and the radicalism of *Robert Elsmere* appeared to have been a fleeting fancy. Indeed some could not resist a bit of gloating. Robert Elsmere had abandoned his ministry "through the arguments of a book which has not been written, and because of a 'science of evidence' which has not yet appeared upon our planet." But what appeared as a cessation of hostilities was only a lull in the battle, and beginning in the 1890s the English-speaking Christian world became engulfed in a new debate over the miraculous, and particularly over the miracles of Jesus. This debate would complete the fracturing of the Protestant communities.[1]

Holding the Line on Miracles

The heroes of this apparent victory had been the famous triumvirate of Cambridge scholars: J. B. Lightfoot, B. F. Westcott, and F. J. A. Hort. One sign of their triumph over the radical continental criticism was the praise offered to them from the pulpit at their traditional rival institution. All Christians were indebted to the Cambridge scholars, noted one Oxford preacher. "We point with great reassurance to the way in which the Evangelic Record and Apostolic Epistles have emerged from the war of criticism which has assailed them this last fifty years, and we ask where in Europe you will find a criticism so impartial, so free, so strong, so learned as the criticism of those great Cambridge divines to whom . . . the Church of our generation owes the vindication of her Apostolic documents."[2] For Cambridge men to be commended from an Oxford pulpit was praise indeed.

As was noted in chapter 2, the Cambridge scholars had labored both to preserve the integrity of the gospel miracles in the face of the Tübingen critics (and their British popularizers such as Cassels) and to offer an explanation of the meaning of the dominical miracles that avoided both the evidentialism of Mozley and the skepticism of Ward. Some points were to be conceded, some caveats were to be granted, and some ideas were to be reconceptualized, but the fundamental historicity of the miracles of Jesus was to be defended. This agenda continued to flourish in the 1880s. It lay, for example, behind Frederick Temple's famous Bampton Lectures of 1884, entitled *The Relations Between Science and Religion*. These lectures are justly famous for the rapprochement they offered between evolutionary science and Christianity, but one of their major themes is the question of the miraculous.[3]

In his lectures Temple's strategy was twofold. He first offered an olive branch to science. Earlier defenders of the miraculous, according to Temple, had erred in two major ways. They had mistakenly insisted that a miracle was a scientific category. The reality of the miraculous was actually tied to the existence and activity of God, and thus it was ultimately a religious category and not a scientific one. "Science can never in its character of Science admit that a miracle has happened," explained Temple. Because scientists dealt with phenomena of nature rather than ultimate causes, they could never properly conclude that an unexplained natural occurrence was in fact a miracle. Furthermore, earlier defenders of the miraculous had falsely insisted that a true miracle had to be a violation of a law of nature. This assertion not only led to conflicts with those who posited a uniformity in nature, but also failed to recognize that the key essence of a miracle was a willful activity of a personal God in the natural realm. If the key to a miracle was divine will and not violation of law, miracles could just as easily occur through nature as against it.[4]

But if one part of Temple's agenda was to defuse the scientific question, a second was to bolster the historicity of the gospel miracles. He willingly jettisoned most of the miracle stories of the Old Testament, but not those of the New. Unlike the Old Testament accounts that had the tinge of legend, New

Testament miracles were woven into the historical narrative. "It is not possible to get rid of miracles nor the belief in miracles from the history of the Apostles," wrote Temple. "They testify to our Lord's Resurrection as to an actual fact, and make it the basis of all their preaching. They testify to our Lord's miracles as part of the character of His life. . . . It is difficult to maintain even their honesty if they preached the Resurrection of our Lord without any basis of fact to rest on."[5] In Temple's opinion, William Paley might have been wrong in his natural theology, but on this point he was still correct: the gospels made no sense without the miracles.

Temple's lectures reflected the complex nature of the Cambridge mediating position, which conceded to science with one hand and defended the historicity of the gospel text with the other. Although the Cambridge scholars removed the issue of the miraculous from the realm of science, they anchored it in history and morality. A scientist need not accept the idea of a miracle, but a believer must. Even the uniformity of nature to a believer was secondary to the moral purpose of God: "Uniformity has never succeeded, and can never succeed in showing, that the God who made and rules the universe never sets aside a physical law for a moral purpose, either by working through the human will or by direct action on external nature."[6]

The dogmatic confidence of persons like Temple, as we have suggested, reflected the views of Westcott, Lightfoot, and Hort on the gospel miracles. This position in turn rested upon three assumptions.

The first involved the fixedness of the miracle stories in the gospel text itself. The textual labors of Westcott and Hort, which culminated in their famous Greek edition of the New Testament, had demonstrated the unity and comparative antiquity of the New Testament text. The miracles of Jesus could be relegated neither to mythical accretions nor to interpolations. As one scholar noted, "You have in the Gospels and Acts a number of incidents narrated in the same tone, with the same historical and topographic circumstance, and relating to the same historical personages. What reason can be given for calling some of these incidents legendary and others historical?"[7] Only a dogmatic opposition to the idea of the miraculous could try to dislodge the accounts. The concern here was with the historical reliability of the narrative, not with any abstract definition of miracle. As Temple observed, how the events were brought about was a lesser point. The crucial issue was that they occurred in the way described by the evangelists.

A second assumption concerned the centrality of the miraculous in the apostolic preaching. As Temple noted, Paley's claim that the actions of the apostles were incomprehensible without the miraculous occurrences was still true. Miracles may not buttress our faith, but they do form the basis of any understanding of the psychological world of the apostles. "The martyrdom of our Lord's disciples," he explained, "is enough to prove that belief in His supernatural powers . . . was no gradual growth of later times, but from the very beginning [was] rooted in the convictions of those who must have known the truth."[8]

A final assumption of the Cambridge scholars was the unique nature of the New Testament miracles. Unlike the miracle accounts of the Old Testament or later ecclesiastical history, the works of Jesus were not mere supernatural wonders but reflections of his loving nature. There was a wonderful interrelationship between Christ's teachings and works. They cohered as closely as did his divine and human natures, and each testified to the other. Rather than being supernatural, Christ's actions could be seen as mirroring true nature. Present existence was broken by sin, but the miracle stories of the gospels pointed to the hope of a restored nature. "They anticipate a time when moral and spiritual forces shall dominate the material world through and through," explained Charles Gore.[9] On the religious level, miracles served as a testimony of divine love and a witness to the power of spirit over matter.

The attractiveness of this solution was evident. It allowed British scholars to absorb much of the new criticism of the Old Testament yet preserve the reliability of the New Testament, in particular, the figure of Jesus. This answer also meshed nicely with the long-standing British tradition of seeing the New Testament writers as commonsense witnesses to historic events.

This Cambridge mediating position was to be adopted and subtly modified by a group of young Anglocatholics in the famous collection of essays, *Lux Mundi* (1889). The earlier Tractarians had been suspicious of the new biblical criticism, and indeed E. B. Pusey in his commentary on the Minor Prophets assiduously defended the historicity of Jonah and his whale, but these writers attempted to move the Anglocatholic party in the direction of the Cambridge mediating position. Chief among them was Charles Gore, then librarian of Pusey House. Gore, the leading Anglocatholic of his age, was in the early stages of his career as one of the great theological minds of Anglicanism. Having studied with Westcott at Harrow and later with Benjamin Jowett at Balliol, Gore was convinced that a critical approach to the Old Testament was both possible and necessary for the bolstering of credal Christianity. In his "The Holy Spirit and Inspiration," he acknowledged that the Old Testament was developmental and hence imperfect: "It is of the essence of the Old Testament to be imperfect, because it represents a gradual process of education by which man was lifted out of depths of sin and ignorance."[10] The New Testament in contrast was the fulfillment of the divine truth. The core of the New Testament was the incarnation, and the miraculous was a part of this incarnation. This was a theme on which Gore would elaborate elsewhere. The miracles of Jesus reflected the essence of Christianity. Just as the incarnation overturned the dualism between God and humanity, the miracles overturned the dualism between spirit and matter.[11]

But as another contributor noted, if the miraculous incarnation was the foundational Christian doctrine, it was most fully set forth in the dogmatic language of the church itself, particularly in its creeds. The creeds both crystallize and enunciate the faith of the Christian community, and are the means by which Christians interpret the scripture. Dogma was what separated the believer and a skeptic such as T. H. Huxley: one "viewing everything on the basis of the perfect Divinity of the historical Jesus Christ," the other "viewing everything on the basis of the absolute impossibility, or at least the incredibleness, of a miracle."[12]

The argument that the dogmatic faith as recorded in the historic creeds was the proper means by which to interpret the scriptural record was the contribution of the *Lux Mundi* writers to the Cambridge position. For them the creeds provided a simple summary of the foundational teachings of the gospel.

Of course there were other reasons to feel confident that the storm had been weathered. The onslaught of scientific materialism that had seemed so irresistible in the early days of Darwinism seemed to be receding. Darwin himself recognized the inadequacy of natural selection as a sufficient cause, and the neo-Lamarckians increasingly argued for the existence of a spiritual force in the course of evolution.[13] The attempt to reduce human mental action to the material had also not been successful. On the whole, apologists could look out on both a world made safe for the miraculous and an audience now more interested in spiritual freedom than material necessity. Henry Scott Holland noted, "Surely, it is a world that invites miracle: it is a world that is receptive of suddenness and change; it is not finished and rounded off, a thing of stiff, unyielding outlines; it has windows thrown open to the voice of God's cries; and doors wide and free through which His Feet may enter."[14]

All this confidence did not imply that the critics of the miraculous had been silenced. Mrs. Humphry Ward continued to attack the arbitrary nature of the mediating compromise and its willingness to bracket the New Testament miracles from the scrutiny they merited. In her view, the compromise rested on a willingness to accept as possible things in the gospel texts that would have been rejected if recorded anywhere else. The German historian, she observed, was willing to extend the principle of uniformity to all parts of the historical record. Such a person "understands the past better, because he carries more of the present into it . . . the culture of this present provides him with sharper and more ingenious tools wherewith to understand the building of the past."[15]

The *Kernel and the Husk* (1886), published anonymously by Edwin A. Abbott, also attempted to continue the conflict. Abbott, headmaster of the City of London School and arch-critic of John Henry Newman, was convinced that the miracles recorded in the gospel were not only historically dubious but also stumbling blocks to true faith. His volume combined a critical evaluation of the gospel stories with the prediction that by the early twentieth century only retrogressive Roman Catholics would still harbor a belief in miracles.[16]

Yet these criticisms, whatever their cogency, were offered far outside the citadels of power. Ward was a novelist writing from the fringes of the church. Abbott was not associated with any university faculty. Both of their criticisms were dismissed rather than answered. Those outside the religious communities might continue to criticize the miraculous, but within these communities a belief in miracles was still seen as inseparable from a belief in historic Christianity. When one no longer could accept the former, it was one's duty to separate from the latter.

This obligation is illustrated by the career of the Cambridge philosopher Henry Sidgewick. Sidgewick began his academic career as a fellow of Trinity College, Cambridge. Like all fellows, he was obliged to affirm a religious test that included a profession of the virgin birth of Christ. By 1869 he could no longer accept the teaching and accordingly resigned his fellowship. As he explained, "Christianity, in the course of its history, has adapted itself to many philosophies . . . but there is one line of thought which is not compatible with [it], and that is the line of thought which . . . concludes against the miraculous elements of the gospel history, and in particular rejects the story of the miraculous birth of Jesus."[17] Any person who could not affirm the historic faith in the miraculous, he concluded, ought not to have a position of leadership or teaching in the church.

The Cambridge writers had done their work well. Not only had they defused the question of the miraculous for the scientific community and created a compromise in biblical interpretation, but they had also convinced many that the miraculous ought not and could not be separated from the gospel picture of Jesus.

A Breakdown of the Compromise

By the early 1890s, however, a variety of factors conspired both to weaken the cogency of the mediating position and to strengthen a more radical approach to the gospel miracles. In these forces lay the roots of the second phase of the miracle debate.

The first of these factors was the continuing attack on the gospel miracles from those outside the churches. By the late 1880s, these attacks had identified a key chink in the argument defending the dominical miracles. Jesus' miracles had been distinguished from all other miracles because of their interconnection with his character and message. In the recorded acts of healing and in the resurrection itself, the triumph of life and spirit over sickness and death had been vividly illustrated. But what of miracles that did not so easily fit into this pattern? T. H. Huxley, for example, in his debate over agnosticism with Henry Wace, questioned the distinctiveness of the gospel miracles. With his keen debater's instinct, Huxley chose to focus on one of the more problematic stories — the healing of a Gadarene demoniac. In this miracle story, Jesus commands the demons to inhabit a herd of swine, which then drown themselves in the sea. How, he asked, was this story different from medieval accounts of spirits, and how could the destruction of two thousand swine reflect a spirit of life and healing? "Everything that I know of love and justice convinces me that the wanton destruction of other people's property is a misdemeanor of evil example." Huxley concluded, "I venture to doubt whether at this present moment, any Protestant theologian, who has a reputation to lose, will say that he believes the Gadarene story."[18] Other writers pointed to the cursing of the fig tree as another example of a miracle story that was not noticeably moral or elevating.

A second factor that helped launch the second phase of the miracle debate was the gradual establishment of distinguished institutions that could provide a platform for the critique of the miraculous. One such institution was the Hibbert Trust. Robert Hibbert (1770–1849), after being barred from higher university honors as a result of his unorthodox religious opinions, amassed a fortune in the Jamaican sugar trade. His will endowed a trust dedicated to the spread of Christianity "in its most simple and intelligible form and to the unfettered exercise of the right of private judgement." In 1873 the trust began offering traveling fellowships to those dedicated to the "scientific study" and treatment of religious matters. One of the early recipients was Reginald W. Macan, a senior student at Christ Church, Oxford. Using his fellowship to study in Germany, he returned to publish *The Resurrection of Jesus Christ* (1877), which both called into question the physical resurrection, and advocated the removal of religious tests for teachers of theology. Macan's views were considered scandalous, and in 1882 he lost his studentship. But the fact that funds were now available for scientific critical study provided an alternative to the credally based theological faculties. Throughout the 1890s the trust also arranged for the translation of progressive German scholarship into English. Perhaps more significant, in the early twentieth century the trust established the *Hibbert Journal,* a leading voice in the debate over the new criticism.[19]

Likewise, one cannot ignore the role of the Scottish Gifford lectures in propagating a more radical approach. Adam Gifford's will had established a series of lectures at the Scottish universities that were to address natural theology "without reference to or reliance upon any supposed special exceptional or so-called miraculous revelation." Early lecturers used this forum not only to avoid the miraculous but also to critique it.[20]

One sees this critique clearly in Max Müller's 1891 lectures, published under the title *Anthropological Religion.* Müller used his lectures to present the fruits of comparative religious study to a popular audience. One of his topics was the miraculous. "A comparative study of religions has taught us that miracles, instead of being impossible, are really inevitable, that they exist in almost every religion, that they are the natural outcome of what Mr. Gladstone has well called 'imperfect comprehension and imperfect expression.'" Biblical miracles in this regard were no different from the miracles of the Buddha.[21]

As might be expected, Müller's lectures provoked great clerical outrage, which evidently stung him deeply. In response, when he published his lectures he added a preface in which he defended his approach and wrapped around himself the mantle of Frederick Temple. Temple's willingness to admit to the dubious nature of Old Testament miracles and to consider possible natural explanations for New Testament miracles was a tacit acknowledgment that miracles were no longer essential to Christianity. But a clean break was called for. The continuing belief in the miraculous was a source of intellectual dishonesty within Christianity. Those who were steeped in the new learning had to feign an acceptance of miracles but secretly found them incredible. Christianity, Müller prophesied, would be stronger shed of the miraculous; hence he looked forward to the day "when we shall be told, 'You are not a Christian if you cannot believe in Christ without the help of miracles.'"[22]

The question of comparative religions raised by Müller did not go away. What was the relationship between biblical miracles and non-Christian accounts? Some were willing to press the question further. The German scholar Rudolph Seydel, for example, set forth the claim that the nativity account of Jesus was in fact based upon an earlier Buddhist story. Most scholars rejected such speculations, but during these decades opponents of the virgin birth story often used this account in their arsenal of arguments.[23]

Of far greater significance were three interconnected intellectual trends that together undercut the basis of the Cambridge compromise. The first was the theological interpretation of Jesus associated with the school of Albrecht Ritschl. The second was the triumph of the theory of the Marcan priority. The last trend involved developments in psychological theory on the way in which the mind can affect the body — developments that allowed for a convincing naturalistic explanation of the healing miracles.

As H. R. Mackintosh observed (in a now-famous quote), "in the last quarter of the nineteenth century no influence in the field of theology could compare for breadth or vigour with that of Albrecht Ritschl." Ritschl's theology is undoubtedly too complex to be fully characterized in a few sentences, but some of his basic assumptions, particularly as they affect the idea of the miraculous, must be noted.[24]

Ritschl was the leading theological representative of the return to Kant (via Hermann Lotze), and of the rejection of the metaphysical predilection so dear to the nineteenth-century Hegelians. From Lotze he derived the category of "value judgement," which became crucial for him in differentiating between scientific cognition and religious cognition. A value judgment affected the ego directly; it "touches the feeling of self, [and] serves to heighten or depress it." Religious knowledge for Ritschl paralleled the concept of practical reason for Kant, and was primarily ethical.[25]

The concept of religious knowledge as practical knowledge lay behind Ritschl's interpretation of Jesus. Jesus Christ, in the fullness of his personhood, was essential for Ritschl. In rejecting Hegelianism he also rejected the attempt to turn the figure of Christ into a philosophical symbol. History, not philosophy, would reveal the true Jesus. But to get back to the authentic picture of Jesus, one must eschew not only metaphysics but also dogmatic theology, in particular the traditional understanding of Christ as human and divine. Speculative doctrine not only hid the true nature of Christ, but also possessed no value judgment. The core of the gospel for Ritschl was the kingdom of God and the reconciliation of humanity through Christ. The latter was accomplished by the loving character of Jesus, "the solidarity between Christ and God," and the "reciprocal relationship between God's love and Jesus' vocational obedience." Christ was Lord for Ritschl because he revealed to humanity both in word and deed the true nature of divine love and justice.[26]

The power of this interpretation of the person of Jesus is probably best seen in Adolph Harnack's *What Is Christianity?* which was the most popular presentation of Ritschlianism in the fin-de-siècle English-speaking world. As Harnack described Jesus, "He lived in religion, and it was breath to him in the fear of God; his whole life, all his thoughts and feelings, were absorbed in relation to God. . . . He spoke his message and looked at the world with a fresh and clear eye for the life, great and small, that surrounded him. . . . He strikes the mightiest notes; he offers men an inexorable alternative; he leaves them no escape; and yet the strongest emotion seems to come naturally to him, and he expresses it as something natural; he clothes it in the language in which a mother speaks to her child."[27]

All of these principles contributed to Ritschl's understanding of the miraculous. The miracles of Jesus had virtually no role in a true understanding of either the meaning or power of Jesus. Although Ritschl was open on the formal question of the possibility of the miraculous (albeit not if a miracle is understood to be in conflict with the uniformity of natural law), he considered miracles irrelevant to the Christian message. Faith came from the proclamation and person of Jesus, and hence "it is entirely unnecessary to ponder over the miracles which others have experienced." Accordingly, those who argued that the true nature of Jesus was to be found in a miracle such as the virgin birth missed the point of the uniqueness of Jesus. Such persons, he explained, "require us to find the essential nature of Christ not in His world-conquering will, which marks Him as the God-man, but in His physical origin, which has never yet been reconciled with His historical appearance, and never can be."[28]

Ritschl's influence on the English-speaking world was great. Students of American modernism have seen his influence in the thought of A. C. McGiffert, William Adams Brown, and Henry Churchill King, among others. His influence on the direction of British modernism is more controvertible.[29] For our purposes, the significance of Ritschl was that he offered a religiously persuasive picture of Jesus and Christianity in which the miraculous was largely irrelevant. Furthermore, Ritschl linked this picture with the fundamental nature of the Protestant heritage. Protestantism entailed a liberation from old categories and creeds and a willingness to be open to the world, in contrast to the medievalism and defensiveness that defined Roman Catholicism. The creeds that had once bound Protestants as well as Catholics to the ancient faith were shackles to the full development of the Protestant principle.

A second factor that undercut the basis of the Cambridge compromise was the gradual triumph among New Testament scholars of the hypothesis of the historical priority of the Gospel of Mark—along with the positing of an even earlier source of sayings or logia of Jesus. The question of the interconnectedness and dating of the Christian gospels had been a subject of regular debate throughout the nineteenth century. Differing solutions to the synoptic question were offered, but by mid-century a number of German scholars (most notably Heinrich Julius Holtzmann) began to argue that Mark was the oldest of the synoptic gospels and that the others were based upon it.[30]

As Stephen Neill has observed, the Marcan theory was slow in coming to Britain, in part perhaps because the Cambridge scholars wrote very little on the synoptic problem. When did the theory find an English-speaking proponent? It is impossible to be sure, but one of the earliest presentations of it was found in the ninth edition of the *Encyclopaedia Britannica* (1875–79), and the author of the fifty-four-page, double-column article was none other than Edwin A. Abbott, future author of the *Kernel and the Husk*. In the same edition of the *Encyclopaedia* were W. Robertson Smith's articles on the Old Testament, the controversy over which led to the loss of his teaching position at the Free Church College in Aberdeen. Fortunately for Abbott, he was not employed on a theological faculty, because his article on the gospels was equally as radical. In Abbott's article, the priority of Mark over the other gospels was asserted, and the theological significance of the Marcan priority was also made abundantly clear. According to Abbott's presentation, the gospel tradition emerged in stages. Lying behind all of the written gospels was a common tradition, the original gospel, which "omits the genealogies, miraculous incarnation, and the picturesque details of the infancy." Mark added to this original gospel, but this book was still largely free from supernaturalism. Indeed, the level of supernaturalism was for Abbott a means of determining the antiquity of a text. As he explained, "It might be expected when we come to the additions peculiar to each of the three synoptics, we should find some increase in the accounts of supernatural events. Now it seems to be a striking proof of the antiquity of the Second Gospel that we find in it no additions of this kind. Not that Mark does not lay stress on what appears to be the supernatural . . . but we find in Mark no mention of our Lord's birth or childhood, and only the barest prediction of his resurrection."[31]

We will return to the question of "apparent supernaturalism," but first one must reiterate what for Abbott was the theological significance of the Marcan priority. If Mark was the earliest of the gospels, then what it contained was the closest the modern world possessed to the original gospel. Conversely, that which it did not include could not be considered part of this ancient gospel. If so, then the "gospel" per se did not include either the birth narratives (and the account of the virgin birth) or postresurrection appearances. These, Abbott concluded, were to be part of the "preface" and "appendix" of the gospel. In this article he was careful not to challenge the historicity of these events (as he would later in the *Kernel and the Husk*), but he went to great lengths to show all the discrepancies that existed between the prologues of Matthew and Luke, and to suggest historical justification of why such additions might be made. Others would pick up this theme, and with the establishment of the Marcan priority a subtle but effective wedge was set between the "gospel" and the accounts of the virgin birth and empty tomb. The story of this wedge is of course more complicated and involved the large amount of new textual evidence flowing from the discovery of the papyri at Oxyrhynchus. But for our purposes we should note that one effect of this new scholarship was to succeed where Cassels in *Supernatural Religion* had failed two decades earlier. Cassels had tried to demonstrate that the supernatural was a later addition to Christianity, but had succumbed to the erudite criticisms of Lightfoot. With the triumph of Marcan priority, however, those uncomfortable with the miraculous and the supernatural had a means of separating them from the gospel.

The final intellectual factor was a new way of defining and classifying New Testament miracles. For decades scholars had noted that the miracles of Christ fell into certain broad categories (healings, exorcisms, and so forth), and a number of different schema were offered.[32] Until the 1880s this was a largely academic exercise, but by the middle of this decade the classification discussion began to take on a new meaning. The middle years of the nineteenth century were a time of great interest in the relationship between mind and body. In 1872, for example, Daniel Hack Tuke published *Illustrations of the Influence of the Mind upon the Body in Health and Disease* to elucidate those little understood forces of mind and imagination that possessed "a power which ordinary medicines have failed to exert." The question of the influence of mind on body and of the mind's role in healing, as we will see in the next chapter, became a question of great interest in both Europe and America. But what we are concerned with here is the effect of this new understanding on the interpretation of New Testament miracles. The theory gave new hope to the feasibility of interpreting the healing accounts of Jesus as being both accurate yet not contrary to nature. Of course earlier writers such as Renan had tried to provide a natural explanation of the gospel miracles, but they usually struck the reader, in F. W. H. Myers's words, as more "ingenious" than convincing. With the new theory of the power of mind and personality over the body, it was possible to posit a persuasive picture of the healing power of Jesus.[33]

Involved with this understanding was the formalization of the distinction between healing stories and "nature miracles" (or miracles that involved an intervention in the course of physical nature). This distinction had been occasionally invoked before the mid 1880s, but it now took on a particular meaning. With the new understanding of the possibility of mind and personality to influence healing, it became possible to understand the healing stories as stories of the triumph of personality (whether human or divine) over sickness. But the nature miracles were far more problematic. The power of personality could influence another person, but how could it affect nature and cause storms to cease and fig trees to wither? By the early 1890s many writers sharply contrasted "healing stories" and "miracles." Healing stories were not in fact miracles at all, but were occurrences arising from laws affecting the influence of mind on body that were only now being recognized. According to this view, the only true stories of miracles included in the New Testament were the nature miracles, and these were few in number. The healing stories made up the great majority of the works of wonder in the gospels. In Mark, for example, sixteen "miracles" were recorded, and thirteen of them were healings. The vast majority of these stories, explained Samuel McComb, "belong to . . . miracles of healing, mental and physical. These deeds of mercy are thus seen to be the most characteristic of Christ and the most frequent in his career. They are, at the same time, most in accord with well-known analogies in modern experience." The few nature miracles, it came to be argued, were curious exceptions to the general pattern of the gospel, and accordingly could be dismissed without any loss of the integrity of the picture of Jesus. Jesus could still be seen as the great healer; one need only no longer see him as the curser of a fig tree.[34]

This schema for understanding the miracles of the New Testament had a liberating quality for its adherents. It allowed them to employ confidently the principle of the uniformity of nature and law to the very center of the gospel. The history of the New Testament could also now be read like any other ancient history, and the figure of Jesus would still be preserved. The exegete was no longer required to appeal to special rules or exceptions when treating its narrative, and no extraordinary powers needed to be invoked. Just as the triumph of the Copernican world view had offered a unified view of the heavens that swept away all of the intricate exceptions necessary for Ptolemaic science, the biblical criticism of the 1890s put all of the Bible under a common exegetical law.

What I have suggested in this part of the chapter is that the position of the miraculous had been severely weakened during the last decades of the nineteenth century, but it continued to be generally defended. The earlier generation of apologists had insisted that they were not the foundation of revelation, nor were they necessary to explain the growth and triumph of the Christian community. They were at best an embarrassing but necessary heirloom of the Christian system. But until the early 1890s miracles were still viewed as so much part of the gospel record that they could not be excised without damaging the figure of Jesus. Therefore, even if they might be to historians a painful exception to the principle of uniform causality, it was nonetheless the obligation of Christian writers to defend them. If scholarly criticism can be likened to a game of solitaire, throughout the late 1880s the game was stalled for want of a "black eight." As long as no "black eight" emerged, all parties were willing, however grudgingly, to defend the miracles of Christ. The new theology, biblical criticism, and miracle classification provided the missing black eight. After this the supernatural nature of the Christian message would no longer be a point of unity. It became instead a battleground.

Born of a Virgin?

The new debate preoccupied religious communities on both sides of the Atlantic for twenty years and was distinguished in a number of ways from the earlier debate. The first distinctive feature has already been noted: it was an intra-Christian discussion. As the American George A. Gordon observed, "The significance of the new question concerning miracle is that it comes from . . . men living and potent within the Christian church." A second characteristic was that the debate was ostensibly over the question of history, not philosophy. The participants in the debate ritually abjured any dogmatic rejection of miracles on a priori grounds. Since the debate centered upon the miracle accounts in the New Testament record, the extended discussion of the distinction between natural and divine causality that so preoccupied Mozley and Tyndall was also of only secondary interest. The question to which these individuals continually returned was whether the gospels were historically reliable in their recording of the dominical miracles.[35]

Yet we should be careful about accepting this rhetoric at face value, because lying behind the appeals to historical investigation was a fundamental debate over the nature of the relationship between God and the world. Most of the participants accepted the general trend toward seeing God's relationship to the world in terms of immanence rather than intervention. The debate over evolution had left its mark, and it was largely admitted that God's activity in the world was through direction rather than disruption. Furthermore, both sides willingly quoted Augustine's famous dictum that a miracle was not something contrary to nature, but something contrary only to what is known of nature. But the two parties understood Augustine in different ways. The key issue was not nature but God's activity in it, or whether immanence exhausted the ways in which God related to the world. Did he never actively interact with it, as a boy might kick a ball? Modernists tended to say no. Such a picture of God as somehow outside of nature struck them as crude and anthropomorphic. Traditionalists, however, were convinced that some language of personal intervention in the world of physical nature as well as spirit was part of the essence of God. Particularly in the realm of salvation history, such interventions — or "kicks" — were essential. The nature miracles of the gospels became a battleground because these events could not easily be reduced to the immanent activity of God.[36]

Furthermore, there was the unspoken matter of the correct starting point for scholarly discourse. Here, too, similar definitions hid a fundamental clash in outlook. Both sides were willing to accept (at least on a theoretical level) Augustine's assertion that a miracle need not be a "violation" of a law of nature. But the different parties drew quite different conclusions from this admission. Defenders of the New Testament miracles continued to accept the fundamental veracity of the nature miracles found in the gospel text. For them the Augustinian principle was an elastic clause allowing them to hold to the biblical miracles without confronting scientific presuppositions. As Gore explained, the miracles of Jesus were no more "unnatural" when seen in the light of evolution than was the evolution from fish to amphibians. In contrast, critics of the miraculous used the Augustinian principle as a criterion for evaluating the probability of miraculous accounts. Those accounts that were in conformity with our knowledge of how nature worked were probable; those which were not were improbable. Thus the central question became: should the miracles of the New Testament be given the benefit of the doubt by Christian scholars and be judged by a special criterion, or should they be evaluated as one would any ancient historical claim?

Theoretical questions came to a head over the question of the virgin birth of Jesus. Before the end of the nineteenth century the doctrine of the virgin birth had been relatively unimportant for Protestants. It had been dutifully affirmed, but was usually viewed as only one of a number of divine miracles. For two decades, however, the virgin birth became the center of controversy. Before examining this debate we should ask why.

As might be expected, a number of factors, both spoken and unspoken, lay behind the debate. One was the prominence of the virgin birth in the ancient creeds, particularly the Apostles' Creed. The Apostles' Creed was a central document in many of the religious families of Protestantism. It had a foundational place in the Lutheran *Book of Concord;* it was the concluding part of the shorter *Westminster Catechism;* and it was part of the daily morning and evening services for Anglicans. The creed forthrightly affirmed that Jesus was "conceived by the Holy Ghost, born of the Virgin Mary." Indeed its language concerning the virgin birth was more forthright than its profession of the resurrection. If the Apostles' Creed summarized the faith, it was especially significant that embedded in it was a nature miracle.

Likewise the question of the virgin birth inevitably led to the larger question: Who and what was Jesus? For its critics, the miraculous birth served to separate Christ wrongly from the rest of humanity. If Jesus entered the world by means of a miracle rather than in the way other human beings are born, "such a being can be no possible example for us in our human nature to follow." Christian evolutionists all acknowledged that God had worked with the forces of nature to create the first human being. Hence, it was claimed, Jesus should be understood as the culmination of the evolutionary process, not as an interruption. The positing of a virgin birth presupposed a gap between God and humanity that flew in the face of divine immanence.[37]

But there were other unspoken factors both for and against the teaching. Many of its most vociferous English defenders, such as Charles Gore, were members of the Anglocatholic party of the Church of England. For them, the virgin birth was not a simple doctrine but a sign of their church's continuing catholicity. Loyalty to the creeds was central to identification with the ancient Catholic church. Furthermore, without this miracle the power of the incarnation for believers would be lost. "Half the light, the poetry, the romance, would fade out of Catholicism if the dazzling form of the Virgin Mother were to be replaced by the commonplace figure of an insignificant bourgeois matron, about whom practically nothing would be known," wrote one defender.[38] Just as the doctrine of the real presence anchored the holiness of the eucharist and prevented it from slipping into simple memorialism, so too did the virgin birth anchor the incarnation.

The virgin birth played a further role for the *Lux Mundi* writers. They had attempted to explain the limitation of Christ's earthly knowledge by a theory of kenosis, based upon the image in Philippians 2:6–7, which spoke of Christ as "emptying himself" in the act of incarnation. During his earthly ministry, Jesus' divine nature was restrained so as to allow for the existence of a genuine human consciousness. Thus it was argued that just because the gospels quoted Jesus referring to David as the author of the psalms, biblical critics need not be bound by this claim. Kenotic theologians emphasized the radical discontinuity between the earthly Jesus and the preexistent and post-resurrected Christ. Accordingly, for them, the two great miracles of the miraculous birth and miraculous resurrection served as the beginning and ends of this self-emptying, and as a guarantee of the transcendent nature of the incarnation.

But if unspoken forces made the doctrine more precious to some, they made it increasingly burdensome for others. Modernists, as a whole, viewed with suspicion the "poetry" and "romance" of Catholicism. As we have already observed, the thrust of Ritschlian theology and Modernism in general was away from Catholicism and credalism. For proponents of these views, the role of the intellectual was to remove unnecessary archaisms from the faith and to make it more understandable to the modern world. And here we must observe that lurking behind their scholarly discourse lay a strong Victorian sensibility. There was for them an uncomfortableness about talking about any conception of Jesus. The way in which these writers went about tarring the doctrine through comparisons with far more graphic pagan stories of God's siring children through mortals suggests that Victorian sexual sensibilities may have even played a role. Furthermore, the account of the virgin birth seemed to be not only crassly supernatural but also at odds with the epitome of Christian ethical institutions, the traditional family. More than one Modernist must have concurred with the observation of an American writer, "Does it not add to the significance of Jesus in our Christian faith if we can believe that his holy birth and life gave new sanctity to marriage and fatherhood, as well as to a singular and unparalleled motherhood?"[39]

The debate over the virgin birth arose in Germany, moved next to Britain, and finally emerged in America. Although its roots go back to the 1880s, the debate is usually seen as commencing in 1892.[40] In that year a licentiate in theology, Christopher Schrempf, expressed qualms about reciting the Apostles' Creed. For him the problematic affirmations were the nature miracles: the virgin birth, the ascension of Christ, and resurrection of the body. The case of Schrempf led a group of theological students at the University of Berlin to consult Adolph Harnack as to whether they ought to petition the church authorities for permission to drop the creed as a requirement for ordination. Harnack's response was to publish a small pamphlet that examined the historical roots of the Apostles' Creed. Far from being an apostolic document, he explained, it was in fact a fifth-century provincial creed emanating from southern Gaul, and reflected not the teachings of the entire church but those of the church of Rome. Furthermore it had developed over time, and a number of the most controversial clauses were later additions, in particular the virgin birth and the resurrection of the body.

Harnack's essay caused great debate in Germany, but more importantly for our story it was almost immediately translated into English, by none other than Mary A. (Mrs. Humphry) Ward, and was published in the popular journal the *Nineteenth Century*.[41] Ward translated Harnack's essay in response to a debate among members of the London school board over the nature of the religion to be taught, and in particular whether it should be modeled on the Apostles' Creed. She proudly presented Harnack's finding as true "Protestant science," a movement that "has done so much to revolutionize the religious conceptions of Europe." Such scholarship, she explained, allowed modern believers to get behind the dogmatic pronouncements of ecclesiastical Christianity: "A new consciousness of God, a new kindling of love to man, obtained through the preaching and personality of Jesus of Nazareth . . . is what it meant to be a Christian in the days before Saul was converted, or the writer of the fourth Gospel had heard the story of Christ."[42]

The details of the arguments for and against the doctrine of the virgin birth, although quite technical and involved, can be summarized briefly here. Opponents of the virgin birth appealed to the absence of the story in the New Testament in all except Matthew and Luke; the fact that Jesus never referred to it; passages in the New Testament that appeared to assume the natural birth of Jesus; and parallels between the virgin birth and non-Christian religious sources. They also maintained that the doctrine of the incarnation could be separated from the virgin birth. The doctrine's defenders, however, answered these charges and in turn appealed to the absence of any textual variation in the gospel accounts and the near universal acceptance of the doctrine in the post-apostolic period. More pointedly, defenders were dubious that any adequate doctrine of the incarnation could be put forward without the doctrine of the virgin birth.

These arguments surfaced in scores of books, pamphlets, and sermons and were regularly recycled throughout these decades. Many of the most important critical works were in fact translations of continental works, such as Walter Soltau's *The Birth of Jesus Christ* (1903), Paul Lobstein's *The Virgin Birth of Christ* (1903), and Harnack's *What Is Christianity?* (1900). The proclivity for translations was a sign not only of respect for the erudition of German scholarship but also of the theological climate in the Church of England in the early twentieth century. As Owen Chadwick has noted, throughout the first decade of the twentieth century the majority of Anglicans, including many bishops, felt that a cleric who denied the miraculous had no place in the ministry. Translation was often the better course of valor.[43]

This factor contributed to one of the distinctive aspects of the English debate: its concern with the question of credal conformity. Could a cleric in good conscience recite a creed that included the assertion of nature miracles when he no longer accepted them? The question of clerical subscription had had a long and convoluted history in England, largely because of the problems many (particularly Anglocatholic) clergy felt concerning the Reformation-era Thirty-Nine Articles of Religion. In 1865, in large part to placate high church qualms, English clerics were no longer required to subscribe to the Articles but only generally to affirm them. Anglican Modernists asked for a similar freedom regarding the creeds. The moral philosopher Hastings Rashdall challenged the claim of Henry Sidgewick that those who could not accept the virgin birth should withdraw from the ministry as he had done. Modernists, he explained, affirmed the meaning of the creed and its principles of incarnation and resurrection; all they questioned were the historical facts the early church used to explain these principles — that is, a physical virgin birth and a literal corporeal revivification. In this Modernists were taking no more liberty than those who dehistoricized the opening chapters of Genesis to respond to the challenge of evolution. Such a reconceptualiztion had shocked earlier generations, but it had become accepted that nothing essential was lost. Should not the same freedom be offered to those who desired to reconceptualize the physical miracles? As Rashdall concluded,

> To those who believe that the Church is infinitely more than a society for the provision of sermons and services on Sundays, — that is primarily a society for the promotion of the Christian ideal of life, and only secondarily "an association of persons holding certain theological doctrines" — no liberty of prophesying or hearing, no increase in theological enlightenment, could compensate the spiritual and social loss of multiple schism. . . . In comparison with the importance of maintaining and extending [the community] the non-natural interpretation of a clause or two here or there in formularies with which they feel a general sympathy will seem to them to be a very small evil.[44]

According to Rashdall, it was possible to have a symbolic or "non-natural" interpretation of the creeds and still to remain within the community.

The Traditionalists in general and Charles Gore in particular would have none of such reasoning. The Apostles' Creed and the great miracles of the virgin birth and the resurrection were foundational to the historic faith. This did not necessitate, however, that credal literalism had to take the place of an older scriptural literalism. Gore freely admitted that there were clauses in the creed that were not meant to be taken literally. No Christian need believe that God had a right hand, much less that Jesus sat upon it. Statements in the creed dealing with beliefs before or after the incarnation were human attempts to describe the indescribable, and were for that reason necessarily symbolic. But the incarnation involved the eternal God entering into history and thus entering into the world of facticity. "We must use symbolic language in the region which lies outside physical experience," Gore explained. "But the distinguishing principle of the religion of the Incarnation is that God has also manifested Himself in the body and physical events, and such events beyond all question we can describe in human language literally." Historical statements were not symbolical but reliable historical facts and had to be accepted as such. Furthermore, they were part of the essence of the gospel. Gore continued, "The whole pretension of Christianity centres upon the real occurrence of an event, the resurrection, and on . . . a series of events . . . calling attention to [God's] moral purpose in the redemption of the world." The central miracles of the gospel had to be accepted as literal.[45]

Perhaps the most dramatic contrast between these two approaches to the question of Jesus and the gospels can be seen in the Bible dictionaries each produced. The end of the nineteenth century saw the publication of two multivolume Bible dictionaries: a *Dictionary of the Bible,* edited by James Hastings, and the *Encyclopaedia Biblica* edited by T. K. Cheyne and J. Sutherland Black. Their differing approaches provided a classic battle of the books.[46]

Hastings, a Scottish Presbyterian, included scholars from both sides of the Atlantic in his undertaking. The resulting volumes were a classic statement of the cautious conservatism that marked late-nineteenth-century British biblical criticism, and in some ways it can be regarded as a last hurrah of the Cambridge mediating approach.[47]

Nowhere was this cautious conservatism more evident than in the long, fifty-page article "Jesus Christ" by the Oxford scholar William Sanday. Sanday (1843–1920), perhaps more than any other British scholar, was viewed as the successor of the triumvirate. Like the earlier Cambridge figures, he was celebrated both for the carefulness of his scholarship and the soundness of his piety. Similarly, like his predecessors he served as a gatekeeper, protecting the community from the excesses of German scholarship. Sanday was the obvious choice for the assignment, and his article lived up to his reputation. He was willing to accept the cogency of some of the new criticism. The article centers upon the public ministry of Jesus, and the nativity accounts are relegated to a section entitled "Supplemental Matters." Likewise, he admitted that the evidence for some of the miracles was not as strong as that for others. Yet as with the Cambridge scholars of a generation earlier, Sanday would bend but not break. He would not deny the fundamental historicity of the virgin birth. He also rejected as fanciful any attempt to draw a line between nature miracles and healing miracles for the purpose of preserving one and dispensing with the other. He willingly admitted that there were some miracle stories that were attested to in all three synoptic gospels, some in only two, and some found in a single gospel alone. He further acknowledged that it would not be unreasonable to assume that events attested to in one gospel rested on less historical certainty than those found in all three. But no such method could free the text of the nature miracles.

> Now if it happened that the Nature-Miracles had been confined to sections of this last kind [i.e., testified to in only one gospel], while the Miracles of Healing—and especially the Healing of Nervous Diseases—had entered largely into the Double or Triple Synopsis, or . . . if the miracles of one class had appeared only in the form of narrative, while the allusions in discourse were wholly to miracles of the other, then the inference would have lain near at hand that there was a graduated scale in the evidence corresponding to a like graduated scale in the antecedent probability of the miracle. But this is not the case. Miracles of all the different kinds occur in all the documents and sources.[48]

Sanday's essay seemed to show the continuing vitality of the Cambridge mediating approach in balancing both criticism and a respect for the integrity of the gospels. Even a conservative critic, such as Princeton Seminary's Benjamin B. Warfield, who was no friend of what he called "moderate criticism," could describe Sanday's contribution as "comprehensive, thorough, reverent, and learned."[49]

If Hastings's *Dictionary* reflected the continuing place of the mediating approach, Cheyne's and Black's *Encyclopaedia Biblica* represented a much more radical view of biblical interpretation. The *Encyclopaedia* had originally been the idea of W. Robertson Smith. When ill health forced him to withdraw from the project, he was succeeded by Thomas K. Cheyne, Oriel Professor of Biblical Interpretation at Oxford. Cheyne, who had originally been an associate of Charles Gore (and who ended his career as a Bahai), was convinced that comparative criticism was the only correct approach to the study of scripture, even the New Testament. Hence from the beginning two things differentiated Cheyne's volumes from Hastings's. The first was the explicit commitment by Cheyne of "what is commonly called advanced criticism." The second was a greater willingness to involve continental scholars. Whereas only about 3 percent of the contributors to the Hastings *Dictionary* were continental, continental scholars made up over 20 percent of the contributors to the *Encyclopaedia Biblica,* and often they were assigned very important articles. The article on "Gospels" was from the Swiss author Paul W. Schmiedel, and the German historian Hermann Usener provided the article on "Nativity." Both were among the most controversial in the volumes.[50]

Schmiedel energetically applied the most rigorous of critical methods to the gospels. His article abandoned the historicity of the Fourth Gospel, much of the historical structure of the synoptics themselves, and many of the alleged sayings of Jesus. Indeed he could only accept as reliably from Jesus five of the many sayings found in the New Testament. Turning to the miracle stories, after cautioning against any a priori dogmatic rejection of them, Schmiedel examined them with a ferocity that left few standing. Some (such as the sky turning black on Good Friday) were rejected as physical impossibilities; others were seen as misunderstood prophecies; still others (such as the cursing of the fig tree) were dismissed as misinterpreted parables. The only miracles Schmiedel was willing to consider were the healing accounts, and even these, he believed, were ultimately misinterpreted by the disciples. As he explained, "It is quite permissible for us to regard as historical only those of the class which even at the present day physicians are able to effect by psychical methods . . . [and] it is not at all difficult to understand how the contemporaries of Jesus, after seeing some wonderful deed or deeds wrought by him which they regarded as miracles, should have credited him with every other kind of miraculous power without distinguishing as the modern mind does, between those maladies which are amenable to psychical influence and those which are not."[51]

Usener, in his article "Nativity," took up where Schmiedel left off, and if anything was even more bold in his criticisms. As he calmly announced, "The oldest written forms of the gospel knew, and knew only, that Jesus was born at Nazareth as the son of Joseph and Mary." He went on to explain that Luke 1:34–35 (which referred to the virgin birth) had been "conclusively shown" to have been an interpolation in an otherwise normal account of a natural birth of Jesus. The Lucan nativity record, Usener argued, stemmed from a Jewish-Christian endeavor to invest the childhood of Christ with miracles. And the nativity account of Matthew was derived from a "pagan substratum" because it was related to an early account of the Parthian king Tiridates's homage to Nero at Rome.[52]

These were extreme analyses, and even sympathetic reviewers faulted them for their flights of speculation and their willingness to resolve debated questions when no resolution had yet been reached.[53] But one cannot fail to note how far the dismantling of the idea of a biblical dispensation had progressed. No special consideration is granted to the scriptures; they are rather held up to the same rigorous expectation as any ancient text. Furthermore, particularly in Usener's essay, there is little if any feigning of a reconciliation of scholarship and pious sensibilities. The idea of biblical study as scientific history had triumphed, and just as natural science excluded the miraculous, so too ought biblical science.

If the articles by Schmiedel and Usener were disturbing for their radicalness and lack of piety, the article "Jesus" was disturbing because of its author, Alexander B. Bruce. Bruce, one recalls, had been a leading defender of the miraculous and a vigorous opponent of Cassels's *Supernatural Religion* in the 1880s. By the end of the century he was forced to abandon the idea of the miraculous as a meaningful concept. His article, published posthumously, showed the powerful attractiveness of the new criticism. After waxing eloquent about the ethical thrust of Jesus' teachings, Bruce only reluctantly turned to the question of miracles. Avoiding any discussion at all of either Jesus' birth or resurrection, he discussed only the healing stories. Even these, Bruce admitted, posed major problems "for exegesis, for theology, and for science." The solution, he suggested, was to see the figure of Jesus not as a worker of wonders but as a compassionate soul. "Whether miraculous or not, whether the works of a mere man, or of one who is a man and more, these healing acts are a revelation of the love of Jesus, a manifestation of his 'enthusiasm for humanity'. . . . The healing ministry shows Jesus not as a thaumaturge bent on creating astonishment, but as[,] in a large, grand human way[,] the friend of men, bearing by *sympathy* their sickness as well as their sorrows and sins as a burden in his heart." Bruce wrote with a far more pious tone than either Schmiedel or Usener, but the contrast between these words and his acceptance of nature miracles just thirteen years earlier is a vivid reminder of how quickly the scholarly world was changing.[54]

It is hard to overestimate the importance of these encyclopedias in popularizing the scholarly debates and disturbing the placid lake of New Testament studies. They were widely reviewed and very often compared to each other. As encyclopaedias of the Bible they had a far wider circulation than almost all scholarly monographs. Their summary articles were for many readers a first entrance into the murky but intriguing world of the new scholarship. Finally, as encyclopaedias they possessed a stature and permanence and continued to be referred to by generations of students. The circle of ripples they created was to be far-reaching indeed.[55]

The debate over the miraculous peaked in England between 1912 and 1915. The catalyst was the continuing tension between ecclesiastical discipline and scholarship. In contrast to the situation in Germany, where the theological faculties of the universities were largely independent of the churches, in the Church of England ecclesiastical discipline could still impinge upon ordained theologians. A lay historian like Percy Gardner could write his *Exploratio Evangelica* and question the miracles of Christ with impunity, but clergy had to be more circumspect. When Charles Beeby published his essay "Doctrinal Significance of a Miraculous Birth" in the *Hibbert Journal,* it so aroused the consternation of his bishop that he was forced to resign his clerical appointment. As one modern historian has noted, "God might not work miracles, but bishops could still enforce discipline."[56]

The publication of two other books forced the issue. J. M. Thompson, dean of divinity at Magdalen College Oxford, published in 1911 *Miracles in the New Testament,* which was the most complete published critique of the miraculous in English. In Thompson the three threads of the new criticism — the Ritschlian picture of Jesus, the priority of Mark, and the distinction between healings and nature miracles — were brought to their logical conclusion. His use of biblical criticism at times almost reminds one of a great exegetical shell game — first Paul is appealed to, then Mark, then Paul again — all in order to present a portrait of the historical Jesus purged of the miraculous. He offered an elaborate pretext of Mark in order to remove the nature miracles from the original gospel. The healings were then interpreted in a nonmiraculous way. "There is sufficient evidence," Thompson explained, "drawn partly from the growing body of medical and psychological experience, that they were not originally miraculous." The end result for Thompson was a Jesus in whom divinity was understood as the culmination of humanity. "The truth of the Incarnation," he wrote, "is not that God and man, two incompatible units, somehow came together; but that it was always part of God's nature that He should be made man, and that man was always incomplete until Christ came. The Incarnation is the inevitable meeting of two natures meant for inter-communion. Without it both must remain comparatively unfruitful and unin-telligible. Through it both achieve their fullest possible existence." The incar-nation, purged of a miraculous birth, showed the fulfillment of nature and the fundamental interconnectedness of humanity and divinity.[57]

As almost all commentators at the time acknowledged, Thompson's book was second-rate; it reflected more his personal religious problems than the best of biblical scholarship.[58] But because his was an official teaching position, the question of a proper response surfaced. Eventually he was removed from his office. The result was an avalanche of controversial literature debating the question of whether one could be a minister in the Church of England and deny the miraculous.[59]

In 1912 a group of young Oxford scholars published *Foundations,* a collec-tion of essays. The thrust of this famous volume was apologetical: "The world is calling for religion, but it cannot accept a religion if its theology is out of harmony with science, philosophy and scholarship. Religion, if it is to domi-nate life, must satisfy both the head and the heart, a thing neither obscuran-tism nor rationalism can do." The willingness to reconceptualize doctrines in light of modern understandings led one of the volume's contributors, B. H. Streeter, to look afresh at that foundational event for Christians, the resurrec-tion. Streeter was one of the brightest young New Testament scholars in all of England. A protégé of William Sanday and a perceptive student of the synoptic problem, he confidently offered up possible reinterpretations of the resurrec-tion event. He willingly acknowledged that physical resurrection represented a "very difficult conception if we no longer regard the earth as flat and the centre of the solar system." As alternative theories he examined both the idea of subjective visions and an objective vision theory.[60]

The scholarly prestige and ecclesiastical status of the contributors made *Foundations* a more serious challenge than Thompson's volume. It evoked a number of responses. Perhaps the cleverest was the poem by the young Ronald Knox, who, inspired by Dryden's "Absalom and Achitofell" wrote his own poetic critique, "Absolute and Abitofhell."[61] If Knox's was among the wittiest, that of Frank Weston was one of the most passionate. Particularly in high church circles, Weston, missionary bishop of Zanzibar, was a revered figure. Others knew him for his attempt to combat European racist attitudes toward

African Christianity. Writing from the point of view of the missionary, Weston despaired over the theological divisions in the Church of England. Muslims in Zanzibar eagerly consumed the new biblical criticism because it reinforced for them the superiority of the Qur'an over the New Testament. The new criticism, he noted, seemed all too "content with the assumption of the general credibility of half of S. Mark's Gospel and of the absolute incredibility of all that is usually called the miraculous." Hence he answered *Foundations* with an open letter to the Bishop of St. Albans (whose examining chaplain was Streeter), *Ecclesia Anglicana: For What Does She Stand?,* which called for immediate clerical discipline.[62]

Weston's open letter once again raised the issue of scholarly freedom versus ecclesiastical discipline. Was the English church broad enough to include those who questioned the great dominical miracles? Charles Gore thought not. In his new position as bishop of Oxford, he observed at close range the ferment of the new scholarship. In 1914 he finally published *The Basis of Anglican Fellowship*. The *Basis* is one of Gore's most poignant statements of his vision of Anglicanism as embodying "liberal or scriptural Catholicism." In contrast to a Rome that was drowning in dogma and to a continental Protestantism that seemed moving toward unbelief, Anglicanism offered an openness to modern scholarship that maintained the credal faith. But this balance, in his view, was being upset by those within the church who, under the banner of Modernism, rejected the miraculous. "It . . . seems to me to be as clear as day that the rejection of nature miracles — even if it were possible . . . still to retain the miracles of healing — cuts so deep into the historical character of the Gospel narrative . . . that nothing like the distinctive confidence of the Christian creed could be maintained," exclaimed Gore. The rejection of the miraculous flowed not from scholarly concerns but from a dogmatic naturalism resting on a "mistaken view of natural law." Thus he called for those who could not accept the great miracles of the virgin birth and physical resurrection to follow their consciences, as Sidgewick had urged decades before, and abandon the ministry of the Church of England.[63]

One can hear in Gore the echoes of the Cambridge mediating position, particularly in his insistence that he was not closing the door on any responsible scholarship. But the uniqueness of the gospel accounts could not be rejected by scholars under the aegis of the church. Religious logic made it necessary that the gospel record be treated differently from other histories. There was "a broad difference between the Old Testament as prophecy and the New Testament as fulfillment in fact. . . . The preparatory revelation can be given as well in myth and legend, and poetry and quasi-philosophical inquiry and moral tale, as in the simple record of historical fact." But such an option was not open in the interpretation of the New Testament. The incarnation was historical. The gospel narratives were fundamentally historical. The Christian creed was based upon historical claims. Historicity was the core of the Christian message, and it could not be given up.[64]

One recalls that as a young man Gore was shaped by the creative compromise of the Cambridge triumvirate. Throughout his ministry he had attempted to combine their view of scripture with his Anglocatholic loyalty to the ancient creeds. The critical response his essay received from the scholarly community showed how far English scholarship had moved away from the Cambridge mediating compromise.[65]

The greatest blow, however, was that leveled by William Sanday, the biblical critic and successor to Lightfoot, Westcott, and Hort. More than any one else in Oxford, Sanday, both in his scholarship and in his person, was a conduit to the world of the triumvirate. His sober scholarship had been evident in his Hastings's *Dictionary* article as well as in a lifetime of publications. He had also been a loyal watchdog in defense of the miraculous, and as late as the controversy over Thompson's *Miracles of the New Testament* had sided with the defenders of the miraculous.[66] But on November 7, 1912, at a private meeting of a group of dons (known as the Theological Dinner), Sanday revealed that he could no longer accept the miraculous as something "contrary to nature." In particular, he now viewed the virgin birth as being "inconsistent with the real and complete humanity of our Lord."[67]

The publication of Gore's *Basis* compelled Sanday to make his views public in a pamphlet *Bishop Gore's Challenge to Criticism*. Playing fully on the drama of his sudden confession of the Modernist cause, Sanday artfully combined scholarly authority and Christian pathos in his apologia. As he explained it, the Modernist position did not flow from a dogmatic naturalism but from the gradual accumulation of historical knowledge. Gore's criticism was an attack upon the integrity of a group to which Sanday now finally claimed allegiance. With an air bordering on melodrama he announced, "I say 'brought against us' because I must begin by associating myself more definitely than I have hitherto done with the group of writers whom the Bishop has in mind." Speaking next as a scholar, he explained that the New Testament was more, not less, likely than the Old Testament to have its narrative shaped by theological considerations. Accordingly, the Christian scholar could no longer sweep back the sea of the uniformity of nature in order to provide a safe haven for the nature miracles.[68]

Sanday went on to describe his whole professional career as being dedicated to the evaluation of the miracle claims. Far from being impetuous or dogmatic, Sanday wrote, he had weighed thoroughly and carefully each shred of evidence, comparing miracle claims in Christianity with those in the Old Testament and antiquity to see if there was any basis for granting them special status. After a career of labor he felt compelled to report that the case could not be made any longer. Nor was he alone. The whole movement of historical research was toward a growing confidence in a uniformity of historical nature that paralleled the uniformity of physical nature. The idea of divine intervention, in Sanday's opinion, "was first given up over the whole field of profane history. There is a strong feeling that it has also given way for the Old Testament. . . . It is not likely that the general public should quite understand the real situation. It is no longer the Bible over and against all other literature and history, but the miracles of the New Testament — or rather one small group of these miracles — stand virtually alone." The nature miracles had to be abandoned. The uniform laws of nature ruled in the biblical era just as did in Sanday's time, and throughout history God did not violate these laws but worked through nature by "over-ruling" it.[69]

Finally, speaking from the authority of his celebrated piety, Sanday ended his pamphlet by claiming that a rejection of the miraculous, far from damaging Christianity, would cure it. Playing upon the biblical image of healing he concluded: "The *contra naturam* was only a part — and I may be permitted to say a small part — of these great events. It is from our modern standpoint that it becomes a small part. In ancient times it seemed necessary to the completeness of the idea, but it is no longer. The element we seem likely to lose has done its work and can be spared. It is like a lame man laying aside his crutches."[70]

The "conversion" of Sanday had a profound effect upon the English debate. Sanday's stature ensured the acceptance of the Modernist critique of the miraculous as a valid option within a comprehensive Anglicanism. It was not that the Modernist opinion became dominant, though it did shape much historical scholarship. But a belief in the nature miracles was now no longer de rigueur within Anglicanism. As one scholar has observed, the venerable Sanday stood as a "protective colossus" over the younger Modernist scholars.[71]

Sanday published at least four other defenses of the Modernist position and its critique of the miraculous.[72] The absence of a full-scale biography of Sanday has left scholars to speculate on what factors led him to his "conversion." Perhaps it is best to accept his own words. Liberalism for him meant the "unification of thought" or that the same process of thinking or modes of analysis could unite things sacred and secular. "I believe," he concluded in a work that his editors called his *Nunc Dimitis,* "it is possible for us to write, or rewrite, the History of Religion in such a way as to bring it into line with every other branch or form of History. That, I conceive, is the one step that is needed to put the final crown on the unification of thought and life." To unite thought and life, the Cambridge defense of a miraculous gospel had to be jettisoned and replaced with a new vision.[73]

Americans and the Virgin Birth Debate

The American discussion of the miraculous was transformed even more by the new debate than was the British, and followed its own pattern. Instead of a great unified national debate, the democratic nature of American intellectual life turned the discussion into a series of controversies over a varied set of issues. The result was the loss of any unifying authority for the idea of a limited age of miracles.

A number of factors contributed to the different tenor of the American debate — some obvious, some less so. The first was the dispersed nature of American theological discourse. There were no centers in America that paralleled those of Oxford and Cambridge. Nor were there figures of the stature of a Gore or a Sanday. Although, as Conrad Cherry has shown, these years witnessed the beginning of the emergence of the university-based divinity school in American theological education, there were still many loci of theological activity.[74]

This multifariousness of course reflected a second fundamental difference between the British and American debates: that the American discussion spanned a number of religious communities with disparate theological heritages as well as various types of ecclesiastical organizations. The seed of the new biblical criticism would land in very different types of soil and would take root in very different ways. This is not to deny that there were strong Protestant Christian assumptions linking these different ecclesiastical communities and creating a de facto Protestant establishment. But this interlocking set of beliefs did not have any precise theological formulation such as that offered by Apostles' Creed in England. One remembers that in the London public school controversy (that led Ward to translate and publish Harnack's "Apostles' Creed"), the issue was whether to teach the version of religion expressed in that creed. One can not imagine an American debate expressed in those terms. In America, the public concern centered on the Bible rather than the creed.

If differences in ecclesiastical structure were one factor shaping the differing developments, another was the difference in university culture. Numerous scholars have noted the influence of the German model in the modern American university, but for a variety of reasons the German model would be stronger in the field of religion than in many other disciplines. This should not be surprising, considering the Puritan and Reformed roots of American collegiate education with their inherited suspicion of the established English church. Whereas this suspicion had largely eroded within the larger academy, as American colleges rebuilt themselves to resemble Oxford and Cambridge, and a pronounced Anglophilism flourished at flagship institutions such as Yale, the American Protestant theological community was still somewhat suspicious of the religion of the English establishment. They were all too aware of a condescending attitude among English divines toward them as both Americans and Non-Conformists. The Yale scholar Benjamin W. Bacon, for example, noted that, as late as 1920, he was not allowed, as an American Congregationalist, to receive the award of D.D. from Oxford. In contrast, the pre–World War I commentators on German Protestantism regularly spoke of its openness and creativity. An interest in the new German theology and biblical studies, therefore, reflected an interest not only in progressive scholarship over traditional, but also in a form of free church independence in an increasingly Anglophilic academic culture.[75]

These factors all contributed to perhaps the greatest difference between the English and American stories: the comparative absence of the Cambridge mediating approach. In England, the Cambridge compromise was widely accepted by the early 1890s, but such was not the case in America. This, too, should not be surprising; the Cambridge position was in certain ways tailor-made for Anglicanism, but from the perspective of American Protestantism it could be criticized from both the right and the left. Those who wanted to maintain a doctrine of biblical inerrancy of course rebelled against the Cambridge willingness to accept higher biblical criticism in the Old Testament and to concentrate instead on defending the New Testament. The famous heresy trials within Presbyterianism, including those of both that of Charles A. Briggs and Henry P. Smith, involved the question of higher criticism in the Old Testament. On the other hand, the acceptance of a credal orthodoxy in interpreting the New Testament found little favor from what George Marsden has called the "low church" theological tradition of Baptists, Disciples of Christ, and many Congregationalists. For these denominations, the Bible as a practical guide to life was seen as the center of Christianity rather than any creed.[76] Furthermore, whatever their differences, both "low church" Protestants and confessionalist Presbyterians revolted against the catholicizing trends in Anglicanism. This resistance would play a subtle role in the dynamic of the American debate. We have noted that much of the defense of the miraculous in general and the virgin birth in particular was led by British Anglocatholics anxious to preserve the Catholic nature of their communion. It may be for this reason that early twentieth-century American Protestant defenders of the virgin birth so rarely made use of British sources. The doctrine's opponents often cited British Modernist writers in support of their views, but the issue of catholicism prevented any united front between British and American defenders of the dominical miracles. All of these factors conspired to center the discussion of the miraculous in America upon scripture and biblical interpretation rather than on credalism as it was in England.

The introduction of New Testament higher biblical criticism, accordingly, swiftly transformed the attitude of many scholarly Protestants toward the gospel miracles. To illustrate the rapidity of the change in some corners of American Protestantism, let us use as an example George Holley Gilbert (1854–1930), author of the popular *Student's Life of Jesus*. Originally published in 1896 while Gilbert was professor of New Testament literature at the Congregationalist Chicago Theological Seminary, the volume was perhaps the closest American counterpart of the Cambridge mediating approach, because of the way it combined "responsible" criticism and a pious attitude. Gilbert was calmly reassuring about the fundamental historicity of the biblical picture of Jesus. The synoptics, he explained, were three independent witnesses to the great events of Jesus' life and ministry, and even the historical basis of John was fundamentally accurate. He carefully affirmed the historical reliability of both the healings and the nature miracles of Jesus. But Gilbert reserved his strongest statement for the physical resurrection. He emphatically rejected any explanation appealing to either a subjective or objective vision. "The theory that the disciples had a vision of Jesus, but that he was not objectively present, is irreconcilable with the narrative. This declares that the grave of Jesus was found empty on the morning of the third day. Therefore, the body must either have risen, or have been removed with intent to deceive; but this latter alternative is simply impossible."[77]

Sixteen years later, Gilbert, then a Congregationalist pastor, returned to the subject of the life of Jesus in a volume simply entitled *Jesus*. As he frankly admitted, "A different view of the sources of our knowledge of Jesus makes necessary a different story of his life." By this date Gilbert had accepted the correctness of the Marcan priority, the existence of a logia or Q source, and the methodological presupposition that any historical portrait of Jesus must be based on these sources. Because neither the virgin birth nor the physical resurrection were to be found in either source, and because no nature miracles were found in the logia themselves, none of these could have a place in a historical portrait. Instead he relegated them to a subsequent chapter entitled, "The Legendary Jesus." But such radical criticism did not harm the religious message of the gospel. Indeed, Gilbert assured his readers that such a reconceptualizing would result in a more powerful picture of the savior: "The story of his life to be drawn from the sources after the work of criticism has been done is a story abundantly suited to inspire confidence in him as the spiritual leader of mankind, and the practice of his teaching invariably confirms that confidence."[78]

It is all too tempting to conclude that a transformation such as Gilbert's was a scholarly conversion, driven ineluctably by intellectual matters. As the weight of evidence accumulated in favor of the Marcan priority, his confidence in the great nature miracles receded. But that would be only part of the story. For Gilbert, the new picture of Jesus was not a painful necessity but an advance. One sees this in a contribution he offered to the debate over the Apostles' Creed. Any creed, he explained, derived its authority from the scriptures themselves, and had to be continually reevaluated in light of the scriptures. Hence, when the Apostles' Creed was analyzed, it was to be faulted as much for what it omitted as what it contained. Crucial parts of the gospel picture dear to American evangelicals — the messiahship of Jesus, his perfect love, and the kingdom of heaven — were ignored. Thus Gilbert offered the following reformulation:

> I believe in God as the Father of all men, who so loved the world that He gave His son to die for it, and who freely pardons every penitent sinner.
>
> I believe in Jesus as the Messiah and Savior of the World, who lived a perfect life of trust, obedience, and love; who in His character and teaching gave a perfect revelation of the will of God; who founded the kingdom of heaven upon the earth; who was glorified by the Father in his death and resurrection; who sitteth at the right hand of the Father, and who is also in vital spiritual connection with His disciples on earth.
>
> I believe in the Holy Spirit, who takes the place of Jesus with His disciples, who shows unto us the things of Jesus, and inspires to Christian service.
>
> I believe in the holy kingdom of Jesus, entered through faith in Him, manifest whenever His spirit is manifest, extended by personal witness to Jesus, triumphant and everlasting.
>
> I believe in the forgiveness of sins through Jesus, the life of consecration to the will of Jesus, the reception of believers by Jesus in the hour of death, and the perfect felicity in the perfect kingdom of God the Father.[79]

Leaving aside the touch of presumptuousness in a young Congregationalist clergyman offering to rewrite an ancient catholic creed, this is a remarkable document. Only the careful reader would have noted that missing in all of his assertions was any mention of either the virgin birth or the resurrection of the body. All of the criticisms of Harnack and the Ritschlians of the ancient creed have been incorporated in this rewriting. But the net effect was a statement that strikes the casual reader as more pious than the traditional creed. Gilbert offered an almost hypostatic union of critical theology and popular piety.

Gilbert gives us further insight into the course of the American discussion.

He was representative of what William Hutchison has described as the second generation of American liberals.[80] Whereas the first generation was trained in America and saw itself primarily as revolting against the old Calvinist views of depravity and biblicism, the second generation was largely trained in Europe and greatly influenced by the dominant current of Ritschlianism. Gilbert himself took his degree at Leipzig (a fact that he proudly advertised on the title page of his book *Jesus*), and one sees in his work how easily the Ritschlian Jesus could be combined with elements of low-church piety among American Protestants. In Gilbert's own Congregationalist Church, the liberals had successfully fought the war against credalism in the context of the Westminster Confession, and the resulting Creed of 1883 was, for example, only exemplary and not binding on any individual congregation. But even this creed affirmed neither the virgin birth nor the resurrection of the body. Its foci were faith and service. It was a creed that was "simple, clear, and modern," in the words of its most famous commentator. Thus it was possible to merge Protestant piety with the new theology far more closely in America than in England without the difficulties Anglican Modernists faced. Furthermore, it was possible for American modernists, who were not tied to debating specific credal affirmations, to engage in a more general discussion than their European counterparts, who were forced always to return to the question of the miracles in the creed.[81]

The absence of a debate over credalism meant that the American discussion focused on the interpretation of scripture and the religious validity of the immanentist vision. And on both of these subjects American writers carried on discussions that in ways paralleled the European debates. Both the Baptist Allen Hoben and the Congregationalist Benjamin W. Bacon used the new higher criticism to evaluate the veracity of nature miracle claims. Both independently brought the force of the new higher criticism against the historicity of the virgin birth.[82] Likewise, a theologian such as Henry Churchill King could argue that the new psychology of mind and the new more open view of the physical universe allowed the religious community to move beyond the distinction between natural and supernatural. Like Sanday, he argued that God's relationship to the world was both real and noninterventionist. "All's love yet all's law," King explained, and the uniformity of law was not the impediment but the way in which God operated in the world. The problem with the old supernaturalism, he went on to explain, was its presupposition that divine causality was like human causality. The old view of the miraculous — that God intervened in nature "just as a man might, putting his hand in from without, and changing conditions absolutely without means or in utter contrast with the usual relation of God in nature" — had to be rejected. King was a

personalist and believed that the person of God could touch human personality, but he argued that the idea that God affected the physical world directly
and without secondary cause was both bad science and bad theology.[83]

But two themes did distinguish the American discussion and set it off rhetorically from both the continental and British debates. The first we might call
the "progressive" motif. This motif, was not one of organic progress but of
crisis and response. The reconceptualization of the miraculous was part of the
church's response to the new challenge. New England Congregationalists,
many of whom had found the struggle of the American Civil War to be a
defining experience, framed this challenge in vivid military terms. Newman
Smyth, for example, had earlier likened the liberal defense of the figure of
Jesus against the radical criticism of D. F. Strauss "to the most difficult of
military maneuvers, to change front under fire." James Moore Whiton similarly employed martial imagery in his discussion of the miraculous. Miracles
now no longer guaranteed revelation or even the authority of Jesus. Thus what
occurred was a " transference of miracles from the ordnance department to the
quartermaster's department of the Church. Until recently they were actively
used as part of its armament, none of which could be dispensed with. Now
they are carried as part of its baggage, *impediments,* from which everything
superfluous must be removed." Both images reflected the New England interpretation of the Civil War. The war stood in the balance until the emergence of
Ulysses S. Grant, and Grant's genius was his willingness to break with convention, strike out on his own, and abandon that which was unnecessary to
achieve victory. Indeed Grant's great victory at Vicksburg stemmed precisely
from his willingness to jettison all baggage. Innovation and boldness were just
as necessary to defend Christianity, and for the cause of victory all unnecessary
and unhelpful arguments had to be set aside.[84]

If the imagination of an older generation tended to think in terms of battle,
for those coming of age in the early twentieth century the image invoked was
scientific professionalism. Allen Hoben's University of Chicago dissertation
was one of the earliest critical scholarly evaluations of the virgin birth to
appear. Not content with abstruse references to patristic commentators, he
ended his study with a touch of rhetoric. Did the church in the twentieth
century have the right to modify such ancient teachings? It depended, he
concluded, on one's evaluation of ancient versus modern knowledge.

> If the method and culture out of which the accepted interpretation sprang
> have not been improved upon . . . and a scientific culture which believed that
> certain animals, such as the vulture, conceived without intercourse, or that
> other conceived by the wind . . . if these suffice for a time where there is at least
> some knowledge of the inevitable sequences of nature and of the value of
> historical interpretation, then the understanding and doctrinal import which

the Father's attached to the virgin birth need no revision. But if . . . the Fathers were by the very nature of things incapable of interpreting correctly . . . it follows not only as a privilege, but as the duty, of the interpreter to view independently and with the most and best light available those portions of the New Testament which by tradition alone have been made to carry what they did not originally contain.[85]

Just as science and history had progressed, so too must biblical interpretation. In Hoben, one also sees another distinctive aspect of the American debate. As a Baptist, Hoben maintained that scripture was self-interpreting, and he was careful not to lay the blame for the doctrine of the virgin birth on the scriptures themselves. It was "tradition" that created the doctrine, and the role of the professional biblical critic, like that of any professional, was to scrape away tradition to reveal reality.

A second theme was the linking of the "immanentist" critique of the miraculous with the rhetoric of Transcendentalism. The Transcendentalists as early as the 1830s had warred against the miraculous because of what they saw as its insufficient view of nature. Horace Bushnell, one also recalls, attempted to answer that question in *Nature and the Supernatural.* But *Nature and the Supernatural,* we have seen, is an ambiguous work, and by the 1890s some began to argue that Bushnell's theology allowed modern Christians to transcend the impasse over miracles. No one argued this more subtly than Theodore Munger in his influential study of Bushnell. He admitted that Bushnell acknowledged the great miracles, including the virgin birth, but miracles, he argued, meant nothing to Bushnell. Rather, in his linking of nature and supernatural, Munger explained, Bushnell cut the ground out from the meaningfulness of the miraculous. Like a great pioneer, "he hewed a path — rough but not blind — into the realm of the Spirit to which [our] age is slowly opening its eyes." For Munger, Bushnell was like Moses — leading the children of Israel to the promised land but never entering it. Many others took up this theme. The Methodist Borden Parker Bowne also invoked Bushnell in his claim that God worked supernaturally through the order of nature. Nature is God's continuous deed, and in this sense it was profoundly supernatural. Just as Bushnell had described human willful response as "supernatural" (that is, affecting the course of nature), so too did God "produce a great many effects, not against general laws, but through them or accordance with them." Similarly, the Congregationalist James Moore Whiton suggested that one should reject the idea that God only occasionally intervenes and on that basis discount the old idea of the miraculous in general and the doctrine of the virgin birth in particular. Instead, a believer should favor a view "that brings the divine and the human into touch and union at all points instead of in one point."[86]

Whereas Bushnell saw *Nature and the Supernatural* as a critique of the

"Brahmanism" implicit in Transcendentalism, these writers tended to merge Bushnell and Emerson, and at times their readers could even hear the echoes of Emerson's "Divinity School Address." As Bowne exclaimed, "In some sense . . . we are in the midst of miracles all the time. As having a supernatural root, all things are miracles." Birth, life, death, and all nature reflected the ever-present will of God. A few authors, in invoking Bushnell, admitted that they were in fact correcting him. Bushnell prefigured the philosophy of the new immanent-ism in his idea that nature and supernature were part of one system, but in the words of one critic he "never succeed[ed] in overcoming the idea of an opposi-tion between the personal and the physical. Thus he consider[ed] that, in order to find the supernatural presence of God, we must find the appearance from time to time of phenomena which cannot be accounted for by previous condi-tions, and which therefore reveal a new creative act of God." Just as Christian evolution had transformed the act of divine creation to a process rather than a "fiat," so too must the modern theologian reconceptualize all divine activity in the world. Only when the idea of God's new creative activity in the world, independent of preexisting phenomena, was purged from *Nature and the Supernatural* could the volume become the platform of a miracle-free gospel.[87]

These two themes of progressivism and romanticism came together in George A. Gordon's famous *Religion and Miracle,* originally delivered as the Nathaniel William Taylor lectures at Yale Divinity School in 1909. Gordon was a leading pastor-theologian of American modernism, and he saw his min-istry as interpreting the historic faith to a generation no longer able to accept the older theology. One recalls that during the debate over *Robert Elsmere* Gordon had still held, albeit tenuously, to the gospel miracles. By the early twentieth century, believing that many of the younger clergy of Boston were no longer able to accept miracles, he called for their abandonment. *Religion and Miracles* was an apologia for a Christianity without miracles.

The current debate, Gordon explained, was unique. Heretofore the mirac-ulous had been challenged by those who desired to tear down the faith. Now it was being criticized by those who wished to defend it. The question of the age was therefore whether miracles were a necessary part of Christianity. Any discussion of the miraculous had to proceed from the "two great principles" of the times: "the scientific conception of law and the religious conception of the immanence of God." These certainties, he explained, did not make miracles impossible, but did make them improbable and superfluous. More pointedly for Gordon, miracles were irrelevant for modern Christian faith. God's power and reality were manifested in immanence and law, and all else (even scrip-ture) followed from these fundamental principles. Every believer experienced this reality personally. Miracles, by contrast, were part of the historical asser-tions of the gospel; they rested on testimony and could never be known for certain. Gordon explained, "We do not put in the same category the statement that Jesus at the wedding in Cana of Galilee turned water into wine and his great words, 'I am the light of the world: he that followeth me shall not walk in darkness, but shall have the light of life.' The statement about the turning of the water into wine we cannot verify; if we believe it, we do so on the authority of the Fourth Gospel. The statement that Jesus is the light of the world . . . is open to verification. Experience alone can determine whether the statement is or is not true." Experience could never verify miracle claims; they remained probabilities. Probabilities, he went on, might be held as private opinion, but they ought not be used as a basis for the public's faith. Even the great miracles of the virgin birth and the physical resurrection, he argued, should be relegated to private opinion.[88]

According to Gordon, an interest in miracles represented an immaturity in faith and reflected an inability to see the spirit and love that permeated the New Testament record. Appealing to the Protestant prejudices of his audience, he likened interest in the miraculous to the Roman Catholic doctrine of transubstantiation, which perverted a loving memorial and "obscure[d] with the quackery of miracle the utmost splendor in the bright domain of love." Immanence and law allowed the modern believer to recognize a higher religious vision and to view all nature as the vehicle of God. Sounding like a modern-day Emerson, Gordon concluded, "If there appears to be no room left any longer for miracle, it is that the whole creation may appear miraculous, the garment that God is weaving for himself, on the roaring looms of time."[89]

Gordon here succeeded in the challenge that had stymied liberal leaning Protestants for decades: he detached the religious significance of the life of Jesus from the details of the miraculous. But in turn he opened himself up to a very different type of question — namely, whether a historical Jesus was necessary at all. As the radical critic Frank H. Foster observed, "Has not the historical character of Christianity evaporated?" If surety is based on the immediate intuition of religious experience, Foster argued, then "a man may have . . . sufficient reason for attributing to God the inner experiences which he perceives to have their origin in influences from without himself, which are divine in their character; but what reason has he for attributing them to a distinct personality, such as Christ?" Gordon attempted to address such questions by arguing that in Jesus fact and idea are conjoined. The question, however, would not go away.[90]

The Issue Goes Public

Gordon's Taylor lectures caused a stir not only within Congregationalist circles but also within the broader theological community, though in the latter, as George H. Gilbert noted, it was due more to the celebrity of the preacher than to the success of the arguments. But it was the case involving the Episcopalian Algernon S. Crapsey that brought the question of miracles and the new biblical criticism to the general public.[91]

Algernon Crapsey was an Episcopal priest serving in Rochester, New York, at the time of his trial. What may have caught the general public's imagination was Crapsey's role as a classic modern visionary. He came to the question of the miraculous not through study but through a heartfelt belief that the church had lost its influence in the modern world. At one time it had taught and the world had listened, but now the church was irrelevant. As he explained, "In seeking the cause for this downfall of the Church, I found it in the fact that the Church was no longer in harmony with its environment. Today the world was democratic; the Church was imperial and aristocratic. The world was scientific; the Church was dogmatic. The world based its knowledge on observation and experiment; the Church rested upon what it called 'divine revelation.' " In a sermon, "The Present State of the Church," Crapsey called for the churches to adopt the spirit of democracy, science, and socialism. As part of a scientific view of Jesus, he argued, churches must emphasize a human rather than supernatural Jesus, "born as we are born, dying as we die."[92]

The intellectual coherence (or incoherence) of Crapsey's ideas is not as important here as his claim that the question of the miraculous was no mere technical problem for biblical critics or theologians, but rather an issue that lay at the very core of the church's mission to twentieth-century America. The trial of Crapsey was depicted in the general press largely as a question of freedom and modernity versus ecclesiasticism.

Church trials are always awkward. They occur so infrequently that there is a sense of nervous amateurness about them, an amateurness that is often played upon by the professional attorneys involved. The Crapsey case was no exception. He was duly found guilty and his appeal was rejected, but not before he had become a symbol of the new spirit of the twentieth century. In the trial, whereas the prosecution appealed to the patristic record, the defense appealed to leading twentieth-century authorities: Lobstein, Cheyne, McGiffert, Sanday, and so forth. For his defenders, the cause of Crapsey was that of Protestant freedom and the true relationship of creed to scripture. "We must not confuse ourselves with Rome," one authority warned. "Rome puts tradition equal to Scripture. We have the Supremacy of the Word of God."[93]

The Crapsey case showed how easily the question of the gospel miracles could be transformed into a larger discussion, and particularly how it could become a symbol for the undemocratic and reactionary nature of ecclesiastical institutions. It also showed how persons only vaguely involved with the formal issues could freely offer opinions. Andrew Dickson White, for example, offered his measured judgment that the enforcing of such canon law was "almost a crime against humanity." Finally, played out against the backdrop of the papal condemnation of Modernism, it made even individuals sympathetic with traditional beliefs uncomfortable with identifying themselves with the forces of ecclesiastical discipline.[94]

If ecclesiastical trials were not the ideal way of making the case for the necessity of the gospel miracles, the point would have to be made by persuasion. If the gospel miracles were not baggage, what purpose did they have? American Protestants contributed their share to the literature defending the dominical miracles. Two approaches are of special interest: the first was the conservative Reformed defense represented by James Orr, and the second was Charles Briggs's attempt to adapt the Cambridge mediating approach to the American context.[95]

Throughout the early twentieth century, conservative Presbyterians had grown alarmed at the growing critique of the virgin birth. For them, works like Hoben's emerged not from scholarship but as a veiled attack upon the supernatural. When Benjamin Warfield was invited to share a common forum with Hoben and B. W. Bacon concerning the virgin birth, he insisted that the issue involved the very nature of Christianity. "No one can doubt that the Christianity of the New Testament is supernaturalistic through and through," Warfield explained, and the pillars of this supernaturalism were the virgin birth and resurrection. But the fullest statement of the conservative Presbyterian response was that by the Scottish scholar James Orr. Responding to the issues raised by the Crapsey case, Orr explained, in lectures to the Bible Teacher's Training School in New York City, that the debate over the virgin birth was a struggle over the nature of Jesus and the scriptural record. "If the Virgin Birth is attacked so pertinaciously, it is because it seems to them the weakest of the Gospel facts in point of evidence, and because they feel instinctively that its overthrow would mean so much. It would be like dislodging a great stone near the foundation of a building, that would bring down much more with it."[96] The question of the virgin birth was inextricably tied to the authority of scripture.

Most of Orr's lectures involved a detailed rebuttal of the modernist critique and the assertion of the full historicity of the event as it was recorded in scripture, but in his concluding chapters he turned to the import of the doctrine. The miraculous birth, he noted, served to explain the sinlessness and uniqueness of Christ. How could a person be without sin? Christian theologians had traditionally linked Jesus' unique sinlessness to the miracle of his virgin birth. Second, the miracle served as a symbol of the supernatural nature of the incarnation. God and humanity united in a unique and supernatural way in the person of Jesus, and the virgin birth was a fitting symbol of it. "With faith in the Incarnation to start with, and the admission of a necessity of a miracle of some kind . . . we may readily perceive the fitness and credibility of the miracle as recorded," asserted Orr. Both Christ's sinlessness and the supernatural nature of the incarnation would be threatened by any abandonment of the doctrine.[97]

A very different type of argument was found in the biblical criticism of Charles A. Briggs. Briggs was perhaps the most famous of the American high biblical critics whose questioning of the inerrancy of the Bible in the 1880s had roused the ire of the Princetonians and led to his celebrated heresy trial. He has been portrayed as one of the valiant liberal figures in American religious history. One cannot deny this part of his career, but there was another part, now little remembered.[98] Like Charles Gore in England, Briggs attempted to establish an acceptable boundary for the new biblical criticism, one that would both allow an openness to historical inquiry yet preserve the figure of Jesus. Also, like Gore, he saw the keys to defining this boundary to be the authority of the creed and the idea of kenosis.

These themes came together in a series of sermons he published titled *The Incarnation of the Lord* (1902). Here one can observe the "post-liberal" Briggs. Liberals had argued, for example, that because the virgin birth was not found in the preaching of Christ it could not have been part of the original gospel. If the doctrine of kenosis were true, however, and if the preexistent Christ had emptied himself of the form of God and had assumed the form of a servant, the liberal critics erred in believing that they could rely on Christ's own self-description to describe completely his relationship with God. Briggs accordingly examined both the scriptural and early church record to plumb the meaning of the incarnation. He acknowledged (once again with the critics of the virgin birth) that there were two understandings of incarnation in the New Testament: one in Paul and John that emphasized the idea of a preexistent Logos, and the other in Matthew and Luke that spoke of the virgin birth. But he put this argument on its head. To find the true theology of incarnation, he explained, one could not look to scripture. There the evidence was mixed: liberals were right in asserting that the earliest records did not contain the doctrine of the virgin birth, whereas conservatives were right in emphasizing the irreducibility of the textual evidence of a virgin birth. One must look rather to the creeds. The great genius of the ancient creeds was the understanding that these two pictures were complementary.

But why was the virgin birth so important? Unlike Orr, who interpreted the virgin birth in terms of sinlessness and supernaturalism, Briggs described the virgin birth as the ultimate theophany; it was the way by which an immanent God took on a particular existence. The very fact that the gospels told of God choosing to begin the incarnation at conception was reflective not of ancient superstitions, but rather of the completeness of the incarnation. It implied that all human life was now sanctified. "It is sublime to think of the Son of God becoming man. . . . It is more than sublime to think of him as a babe in the Virgin's arms. That thought has been the favorite one in Christian art. . . . But vastly more sublime is that doctrine which can be only represented by the poet's art, the Son of God beginning his earthly existence as a holy thing conceived by the Virgin. The Son of God would begin at the very beginning of human substance, and so live through the whole life of man until his death and abode of the dead, that he might consecrate every moment of human existence, and redeem all that belonged to human nature."[99] The virgin birth was connected with the incarnation not because of supernaturalism but because of the fullness of divine love.

Briggs used the virgin birth debate not only to set forth the true understanding of the incarnation but also to criticize what for him was the improper use of the higher criticism. Higher criticism, he explained, was a boon to true religion, but only when it was properly circumscribed. It rightly concerned itself with four questions: the integrity, authenticity, literary features, and credibility of the text. In these ways it had helped immeasurably in the dating and classification of Old Testament texts. But the attack on the virgin birth, according to Briggs, was philosophical criticism masquerading as higher criticism. It presupposed general rules such as the uniformity of nature and historical occurrences that, whatever their validity, had nothing to do with higher criticism. Jesus Christ as the God-Man, he acknowledged, would always have to be accepted by faith, but any fair use of higher criticism affirmed that this was precisely the picture presented by the gospel records.[100]

If factors had been different Briggs might now be remembered as the American Charles Gore—as the person successful in finding an alternative to liberal immanentism and supernaturalist fundamentalism by centering the discussion on credal orthodoxy rather than the text of scripture. But this was not to be. Unlike Gore, who was viewed as the spokesperson of a vigorous movement in an established church, Briggs was a lone figure. He could never shake the notoriety of his earlier trial, and his defenses of the miraculous incarnation were largely ignored by other defenders. Perhaps his vision was always an impossible one. Whereas Gore could appeal to the acknowledged place of the ancient creeds in the life of the Church of England, Briggs found himself in a milieu that included continuing proponents of the sixteenth-century Protestant confessions and advocates of a free church liberty, but few voices in between.[101]

Conclusion

The story of the influence of the new higher criticism on the understanding of the biblical miracles has been a complicated one, but one must not lose sight of the main occurrence. One recalls that in 1890 the uniqueness of the dominical miracles was generally acknowledged by Protestant scholars, and this acceptance was the remaining tenuous leg of the old view of a limited age of miracles. By 1915, however, the uniqueness of the dominical miracles was no longer accepted by large groups within the English-speaking Protestant community. Indeed, it was argued that if they were to be accepted they must be in some ways analogous to modern events. Whereas in 1890 a person like the Methodist James Buckley had argued against faith cures because they were unlike the radically supernatural healings recorded in scripture, by 1910 critics were arguing the reverse: that biblical miracles were credible to the degree they corresponded to current healings through mind.

The distinctiveness of a biblical epoch, characterized by the direct intervention of God into the world, was no longer accepted by the scholarly community in the early twentieth century. The venerable theory of the limited age of miracles had lost its power to unite English-speaking Protestants. Of course there continued to be advocates of the limited-age position. But this position's loss of authority opened up the debate. Indeed, one of the ironies of the intellectual revolution is that if it led some individuals to look with suspicion on any biblical claim of a nature miracle, it also led others, as we shall see in the next chapter, to reconsider yet again the question of modern miracles.

The New Search for Evidences

The watchword in early-twentieth-century journalism was muckraking, and no one raked muck as effectively as did Ray Stannard Baker. Writing extensively in a number of journals, he assiduously uncovered the corruption and malfeasance that kept the body politic from achieving its due health and vigor. But by 1907 he had come to realize that not only was the political world askew, but so too was the religious. The present age was undergoing a spiritual crisis — not from a lack of belief, but rather from a loss of channels through which belief could be made real. "Religion is not decaying," Baker explained, "but only the church. More religion is to be found in our life to-day than ever before." Religion could be seen in the great fascination of the power of mind over matter and the supremacy of spirit. The churches, however, could no longer lay hold and make sense of this spiritual sensibility of the modern age.[1]

Baker's writings illustrate the way in which the literate classes of England and America seemed captivated by a search for the spiritual in the modern world. "Men to-day," observed another author, "are thinking, reading, and talking about spiritual things who awhile ago were bored of them."[2] On all points of the religious compass there emerged an interest, and indeed almost a craving, for evidences of an unseen supernatural world. Themes of the superiority of vitalism over mechanism, spirit over matter, mind over body, and life over death became the stuff of journalists and philosophers, playwrights and preachers. The central paradox of this chapter is that the same years that saw the assault on the last bastion of the limited age of miracles argument — that is, the miracles of Jesus — also witnessed a fascination with modern "miracles," and indeed the two trends occasionally appeared among the same people. These two movements served as grindstones that would reduce the supporters of the limited age of miracles to a small minority.

Sources for the New Search

Why such a concern should grip so many persons during this period cannot easily be answered. In some ways their search is simply part of the human need to perennially rediscover (as Shakespeare has written) that "there are more things in heaven and earth . . . than are dream't of in your philosophy." But what characterized the turn-of-the-century discussion was the belief not only that there was more to reveal under heaven and earth, but also that these revelations were of crucial importance. The naturalistic and mechanistic presuppositions of the great Victorian scientific popularizers like Huxley and Tyndall had offered a fundamentally warped view of reality — one that, in the words of one writer, had banished the language of mind and spirit to the "peculiar property of clergymen, professors, and women." But by century's end even many scientists admitted that materialism and mechanism could not fully explain reality. "Does anyone think that the skill of a beaver . . . arose by chance," asked the physicist Oliver Lodge, or that a "struggle for existence will explain the advent of a Beethoven?" In his Gifford Lectures, the English philosopher and psychologist James A. Ward was even more critical of naturalism. After describing the fallacies and inconsistencies in the mechanical theory of the universe (which for him undergirded naturalism), he concluded, "It is far truer to say the universe is a life, than to say it is a mechanism, even such a mechanism as Goethe describes in verses that German men of science are fond of quoting, where the Spirit of the Earth 'weaves at the rattling loom of the years the garment of Life which the Godhead wears.' " But signs were afoot of a new "intellectual reformation" that would restore the reality of spirit.[3]

The revolt against naturalism and materialism at the turn of the century is a well recognized phenomenon. From Henri Bergson's emphasis on the élan vital in philosophy, to Hippolyte Bernheim's writings on the power of hypnotism in psychology , to William Butler Yeats's themes of Celtic spirituality in literature, there arose new interests in the spiritual world. This new milieu in turn provided both an occasion and some new vocabulary for a renewed public discussion of the miraculous. New categories of analysis subtly transformed the discussion concerning two of the chief loci of the debate: healing, and psychical occurrences.

As noted in chapter 4, the faith cure movement of Charles Cullis, A. J. Gordon, and the other Protestant evangelicals was a topic of intense debate within the middle-class community. But by century's end the locus of the debate over faith healing had shifted from evangelical Protestantism toward the Catholic cures at Lourdes and the new healing cults, most particularly Christian Science. This shift is not surprising; both Lourdes and Christian Science were more visible to the general public than were the successors of Cullis. The great interest in the happenings at Lourdes has already been noted, and at century's end continued to be discussed by both Catholics and non-Catholics. Lourdes presented alleged divine cures for all to see, and did so under the scrutinizing eyes of medical examiners. Even those not converted were impressed. Many authors of non-Catholic accounts, although they carefully distanced themselves from the theological claims made by Catholics, saw in the happenings at Lourdes events that challenged the narrow world view of Victorian science. It was the blindest of dogmatisms to deny that something remarkable was happening in that place. One recalls the almost wistful view of Lourdes found in Emile Zola's fascination with the power found there. Other observers followed suit. F. W. H. Myers, writing in the *Proceedings of the Society for Psychical Research,* expressed this cautious attitude: "We on our part are prepared to believe, not indeed all that [they] . . . have *asserted,* but a good deal more than they as yet have made any attempt to *prove.*" Another non-Catholic writer, who was himself a physician, also observed, "there are qualities in the Lourdes cases which I do not understand, [and are] not to be accounted for by any explanation within our present knowledge." Catholic critics were amused at all this Protestant interest in Lourdes. As one noted, fifty years earlier Catholic miracle accounts were routinely dismissed as works of knavery and superstition and as beneath investigation, but they were now being carefully examined by non-Catholics. "Amongst the remarkable instances of a return to doctrines always held by the Catholic Church by those who for long ages derided her teaching, and who still deny her authority, there is perhaps none more curious and significant than that connected with the subject of miracles," wrote one bemused scholar.[4] The search for evidence of the divine in the world was leading persons back to Rome.

But it was leading persons in other directions as well, and in America the question of Christian Science was an even more immediate challenge than Lourdes. Although originally only one of a myriad of healing movements in postbellum New England, between its founding in 1866 and the 1890s it became one of the fastest growing religious groups in America. Particularly after the dedication of the monumental Mother Church in Boston in 1895, Christian Science was seen as a force to be reckoned with, and its growth was so dramatic that some even predicted that it would become the largest religious community in America.[5]

As students of Christian Science have argued, the theology of the movement was (and is) subtle, and healing is rightly understood as only one part of its redemptive message. But as is so often the case, the general public was little interested in the fineries of theology, and was either attracted to or affronted by what they perceived the movement to be about. Most outsiders saw Christian Science as the preeminent example of a healing movement that emphasized the power of mind to affect the body in health. Of its distinctive doctrines the public was aware of its denial of the reality of matter and disease, but not much more. The movement's critics attacked its alleged metaphysical presuppositions and viewed it as philosophical idealism run amuck: "Its ontology is a crazy-quilt patched with every crochet of philosophers from Plato to brain-fagging Hegel." More sympathetic observers, however, saw in Christian Science an important part of the message of Jesus that the Protestant churches had lost sight of. The liberal Episcopalian Richard Heber Newton, for example, praised Christian Science for its recognition that Jesus as the divine healer was not an exception but an example. Newton chided his own communion for its acceptance of the externals of apostolicity and its rejection of the idea of apostolic power. The bishops of Anglicanism might indeed be in "apostolic succession," but "not even the most sensational representative of our new journalism tells of any crowds flocking about Lambeth Palace, awaiting the coming forth of the Archbishop of Canterbury, to lay his hands upon the multitude of lame and blind and sick folk, who so sorely need some healing." Christian Science was to be gratefully acknowledged for reminding the world that within every person was the power of God.[6]

Newton, however, was nonetheless guarded in his praise, and although he affirmed Christian Science cures he distanced himself from their explanation. In his view, the healings that were recorded, albeit real, were neither unique to that community nor caused by the forces they claimed. Instead the healings of Christian Science were manifestations of a larger spiritual law, a law, indeed, that Jesus himself had employed in his own healing. They sprang from the reality of spirit and mind to effect healing, a fact that the scientific community was beginning to realize. I have already noted the importance of Daniel Tuke's book, *Illustrations of the Influence of Mind upon the Body in Health and Disease.* In France, Hippolyte Bernheim and the school of psychology associated with the city of Nancy argued in particular for the use of hypnotism in curing physical ailments. Evidence mounted in support of the idea that the mind could influence the healing of a number of maladies that did not respond to medicine. As one American writer noted, even when dubious diagnosis were factored out "there . . . remains a vast amount of material showing a powerful influence of the mind in disease."[7]

Physicians, however, were loath to give too much credence to the idea of mind cure. In America at least, the medical community at the turn of the century was not in high regard. The newly reorganized American Medical Association was involved during these years in a long process of regularizing and professionalizing the medical community, and was continuing its campaign against alternative medical models. But even doctors were forced to recognize (albeit grudgingly and guardedly) the role of mind in healing. The British Medical Society, for example, which had followed the claims of faith healers quite closely, concluded that they could not be dismissed out of hand à la the nineteenth-century scientific naturalists. Too many cases had been recorded to ignore them. But, the report continued, these events were not supernatural; rather they were part of the way in which the ordinary mind could affect the body. Furthermore the report maintained three points about these alleged cures. The first was that these cures could not be limited to any theology or community. "What are called 'miracles' are not peculiar to any religion, Christian or other, and have been wrought by 'animal magnetizers' and healers of various kinds, who are not associated with theological or spiritual formularies," the group explained. The second was that such cures were limited in their effectiveness against certain ailments. Faith could influence functional illnesses such as paralysis or depression, but not organic diseases. The British Medical Society's last claim was that such healings would decrease as medical science advanced in its treatment of functional disease. As medical science progressed and research revealed the secret spring of disease, the number of functional disorders would steadily become smaller. Therefore, "as knowledge advances 'miracles' become fewer, and such as seem to remain tend more and more on scientific analysis to resolve themselves into natural phenomena."[8]

The attitude expressed above — a willingness to accept the possibility of healing through faith on the proviso that it was an act of suggestion or auto-suggestion and that it remained within the confines of "functional" disease — was commonly heard throughout these years. These admissions created an "acceptable" venue for religious figures to talk again of religious healing. Religious groups were divided, however, on whether to accept the strictures of this compromise or to offer a bolder claim for religious healing. As we will see, many liberal defenders of religion and healing were quite willing to accept the distinction between functional and organic disease. This is not surprising because the dichotomy between functional and organic paralleled their earlier exegetical distinction between healing miracles and nature miracles. It was much easier for them to conceptualize God working through nature by means of mind and spirit rather than his intervening directly in physical nature. Other religious figures rejected the distinction between functional and organic and claimed that divine healing was possible for any malady. But for all religious groups the other limitation — that the healing came only through the human mind and not from outside of human beings — was far more problematic. It raised the recurring question of the efficacy of prayer, and almost no religious figure discussed in this chapter was willing to reduce religious healing to simple mind cure. Even among liberals what one finds is that proponents of healing spoke in a very different way when addressing physicians than when speaking to their religious communities.

The other great source of interest in the supernatural was the area of psychical research. Here too the fin-de-siècle interest built upon earlier religious trends. Spiritualism had been a strong movement since mid-century, and particularly in America developed a large following that some numbered in the hundreds of thousands. But by the 1890s, as is well known, the attempt was made to examine the spiritual world with a scientific spirit. Societies for Psychical Research were established in both England and America. The histories of both these societies have been well told elsewhere and need not be recounted here, but the religious implication of the movement bears noting.[9] Frank Turner has argued that psychical research served as a crucial avenue for those individuals, who desired to cling to the ideas of the soul and immortality while rejecting traditional Christian orthodoxy. No one represented the concerns of this group better than did the great English essayist and psychical researcher Frederic W. H. Myers. Since his youth, Myers had been obsessed with the question of the immortality of the soul. Unable to accept the creed of high Victorian agnosticism — as described in George Eliot's famous aphorism about God, Immortality, and Duty: "How inconceivable was the *first,* how unbelievable was the *second,* and yet how peremptory and absolute was the *third"* — Myers spent much of his adult life investigating the evidence for life after death and the spiritual aspects of human nature. Myers combined the spiritual and the scientific in his reasoning. Belief without evidence was impossible for him. He derided Matthew Arnold's famous definition of religion, "morality tinged with emotion," as simply "gilding the tortoise." For Myers there had to be evidence in order to believe in a spiritual reality.[10]

Myers's great contribution to the turn-of-the-century conversation was both his massive *Human Personality and the Survival of Bodily Death* and his postulation of the idea of the subliminal self. The subliminal self, he explained, was that part of the human mind lying outside the normal stream of consciousness. "Half lumber room and half king's treasury," it contained the seeds of both hysteria and inspiration. Furthermore for Myers it was the subliminal consciousness that survived after death, and it was through our own subliminal consciousness that we could communicate with these beings. The subliminal consciousness functioned like a vast psychical information superhighway interconnecting diverse souls, and it was used to explain such psychical phenomena as telepathy and the communication with departed spirits. Myers's subliminal self is at best a murky concept, and indeed some have seen it as part of the secularization of the soul. But many religious writers at the time expressed enthusiasm for the concept, because it offered a quasi-scientific category to explain a number of traditional religious categories. His paradigm furthermore offered a scientific foundation not only for the reality of the soul but also for the influence of intercessory prayer and the possibility of divine inspiration. If the subliminal consciousness could be the vehicle of telepathy, it could also be the vehicle of prayer. Some religious writers saw in the subliminal consciousness the place where the divine could affect the human. As one observed, "We know little of the law by which mind acts on mind and of the way in which the mind of man can affect the mind of God, but in view of the fact that telepathy is regarded by many sane and sober men as . . . exceedingly probable, he would be a rash man who would deny that our emotions and desires expressed in prayer can reach and help the souls of others."[11] Until it was forced out of favor by Sigmund Freud's very different schema of human consciousness, Myers's idea of a subliminal consciousness offered key "scientific" support for spiritual beliefs.

This interest in psychical research was to be a crucial impetus behind the "spiritual unrest" of the early twentieth century. It would make its weight felt in three distinct ways. The first was in a critique of the naturalist attack on the miraculous. Alfred Russel Wallace, for example, who shared with Charles Darwin authorship of the theory of evolution by means of natural selection, was both a spiritualist and a sharp critic of Tyndall, Huxley, and Hume. In his *Miracles and Modern Spiritualism* he observed that Hume had succumbed to four errors. "[He] gives a false definition of miracles, which begs the question of their possibility, 2) He states the fallacy that miracles are isolated facts, to which the entire course of human testimony is opposed, 3) He deliberately and absolutely contradicts himself as to the amount and quality of testimony in favour of miracles, 4) He propounds the palpable fallacy as to miracles connected with opposing religions destroying each other." Contrary to Hume and Tyndall, Wallace believed that miracles or supernatural intervention could be found in almost every time and every culture. Indeed proponents of psychical research took the principle of uniformitarianism, so valued by popularizers of Darwinism, and put it on its head. The earlier evolutionists had claimed that the permanency of the laws of nature ruled against any claims for a supernatural intervention into the physical world; for Wallace the universal testimony of humankind as to the existence of these supernatural occurrences, on the contrary, attested to their veracity.[12]

Second, students of psychical research proposed a reimagining of history that connected the biblical epoch with later periods. Through the discoveries of psychical research, the figure of Jesus was no longer an enigma. "It is a singular fact in the history of the Christian religion that the circumstances and events in the life of Christ which have been the greatest stumbling-blocks of scientific scepticism for eighteen centuries, are, in the last quarter of this nineteenth century, found to be the only facts in his history which can be scientifically verified," explained one commentator. No one put this confidence more vividly than did F. W. H. Myers when he extolled the good news of psychical research. The resurrection of Jesus was no longer some mysterious stumbling block, but part of the eternal law of the triumph of life over death, and it was attested to by psychical research. "I venture now on a bold saying;" proclaimed Myers, "for I predict that, in consequence of the new evidence, all reasonable men, a century hence, will believe the Resurrection of Christ, whereas in fault of the new evidence, no reasonable man, a century hence, would have believed it."[13]

Finally, psychical investigation offered for its proponents a new grounding for religious certainty. Psychical research allowed for confidence in belief in an age of doubt by offering a new type of "evidence." Empiricism and evidentialism had of course a long history in Anglo-American thought, and a number of scholars have noted the importance of Baconianism in the development of Anglo-American evangelicalism. Plain thinking, common sense, and an appeal to evidences, it has been argued, were the hallmark of evangelicalism, particularly in the face of Darwinism. But just as writers like Myers put the uniformitarianism of the Darwinians upon its head, so too did they offer a distinctive redaction of Lord Bacon. As Myers explained,

> Bacon foresaw the gradual victory of observation and experiment — the triumph of actual analysed fact — in every department of human study; — in every department save one. The realm of 'Divine things' he left to Authority and Faith. I here urge that that great exemption need be no longer made. I claim that there now exists an incipient method of getting at this Divine knowledge also, with the same certainty, the same calm assurance, with which we make our steady progress in the knowledge of terrene things. The authority of creeds and Churches will thus be replaced by the authority of observation and experiment.

Likewise Myers, along with contemporary conservative Protestants, appealed to the common sense of everyday individuals (both past and present) rather than to the theories of experts. "The best and wisest men . . . prefer to rest their practical philosophy upon a basis of ascertained facts. And for the 'hard headed artisan' . . . facts are everything, and philosophy without facts is a sentimental dream. They will never cease to desire actual evidence of another world." In order to respond to the crisis of faith, what was needed was the plain common sense of William Paley's *Evidences of Christianity.* Myers wrote, "Paley's *Evidences* is not a subtle book nor a spiritual book. But one wishes that the robust Paley with his 'twelve men of known probity,' were alive again to deal with the hypotheses like this. The Apostles were not so much like a British jury as Paley imagined them. But they were more like a British jury than like a parcel of hysterical monomaniacs." Common sense and evidence swayed the apostles, and common sense and evidence were called for in the present.[14]

One can hear the echoes of the old non-conformist or evangelical faith in a passage such as this, with its concern for experience over tradition and for the immediate reality of God over the creeds of the churches. Similarly, in the appeal to a reasonable, evidence-based faith, one can see glimpses of the old *Bridgewater Treatises,* but they are the *Bridgewater Treatises* viewed through a carnival mirror. The evidences appealed to are not those of geology or natural theology, but of parapsychology.

It is no surprise that proponents of this type of research saw in their work a renaissance of Christianity. Together with the accomplishments of the new biblical criticism, it provided a sure and certain foundation for belief. As E. Howard Grey noted, "Textual criticism fixes the authenticity of certain documents containing supernatural experience, but it does not undertake to prove those experiences to be genuine, this is the province of . . . the psychical specialist who has to deal with the observation of facts, as well as documents, and as a result of his labours in this field he finds the trances and visions of the apostle . . . were not restricted to this early church, but have become the possession of numerous Christians in the present age.' "[15] Empirical evidence could undergird not only our present faith but our confidence in the ancient record as well.

To see the appeal of this new evidence to Christian ministers, one can point to Elwood Worcester (a figure who will play a large role in this discussion). Philosophically trained and in theology a Modernist, Worcester nonetheless had great interest in psychical research. All of his philosophy and scholarship could not answer for him the fundamental questions of the reality of the super-natural and the immortality of the soul. The evidence of psychical research, however, did provide him this confidence, and this confidence transformed his ministry. As Worcester explained, "[T]hat ennui and indifference to things of the Spirit which come to so many clergymen in middle life did not come to me. My faith no longer rested merely on the faith of men of old time and of the experience of my youth, it was daily renewed by living contact with things of the Spirit."[16]

William James and "Crass" Supernaturalism

Many of these themes came together in the life and career of William James, whose *Varieties of Religious Experience* expressed so brilliantly the persuasiveness of and the problems implicit in the new evidentialism. Throughout his varied career, James was interested in such issues as abnormal psychology, mind cure, and psychical research. Like his friend F. W. H. Myers, he saw in the subconscious a connection between the self and the "more." James was furthermore an active student of psychical research; he was a member of the British Society and was one of the founding members of the American Society for Psychical Research. All of these interests would be woven into his famous Gifford lectures, *The Varieties of Religious Experience.*[17]

The *Varieties* is of course a rich book that has been widely commented upon, and many of its categories, such as the religion of healthy-mindedness and the divided self — as well as its discussion of mysticism — are well known. But for our purposes two themes of the *Varieties* are important. The first was the importance of the unseen or spiritual realm. The life of religion for James "consists of the belief that there is an unseen order, and that our supreme good lies in our harmoniously adjusting ourselves thereto." In contrast to materialists and reductionists, James argued that religion was a real, irreducible entity. In contrast to idealists, he argued that it was experienced individually and immediately. The reality of personal experience was all-important for James. In his famous phrase, "A bill of fare with one real raisin on it instead of the word 'raisin,' . . . might be an inadequate meal, but it would at least be a commencement of reality. The contention of the survival-theory that we ought to stick to non-personal elements exclusively seems like saying that we ought to be satisfied forever with reading the naked bill of fare." James's book was in large part an exercise in identifying the real "raisin," and the reality, he argued, was not in philosophy or speculation, but in the experience of the unseen. Religion was not the mere illumination of previous facts, nor a passion that puts things in a rosy light. Instead, religion was "a postulator of new facts." This was why it had always included a "miraculous" element. Common men and women, James explained, "have interpolated divine miracles into the field of nature, they have built a heaven out beyond the grave. It is only transcendentalist metaphysicians who think that, without adding any concreted details to Nature, or subtracting any, but simply by calling it the expression of absolute spirit, you make [the world] more divine just as it stands." This religious faith, based on a new knowledge that is derived from experience, he called "pragmatic."[18]

James fully recognized how controversial to some was the claim that religion rested on the "experience of fact." Many "sectarian scientists" would not accept as fact such phenomena as mind cures. "Miraculous healings have always been part of the supernaturalist stock and trade, and have always been dismissed by the scientist as figments of the imagination," James continued. But a growing awareness of the powers of hypnotism and suggestion had made some scientists begin to shy away from dogmatic science in the field of healing, and "no one can foresee just how far this legitimation of occultist phenomena under newly found scientific title may proceed."[19]

Commentators on James have noted that in his outlook he was closer to old-style evangelicalism than to either cultural Protestantism or liberalism. Not only had he little interest in a religion that was interwoven into the everyday normal life of society, characterized in his biting words as religion based on "oysters, ice cream and fun," but in the *Varieties* he also faulted liberals such as the Methodist Borden Parker Bowne for abandoning the "ancient spirit of Methodism" which he saw as a grounding in immediate religious experience. Indeed James wrote (half in jest) to Bowne and noted that in James's own willingness to place individual experientialism at the heart of religion he was "the better Methodist."[20]

If his grounding of religion on an experience of the other was one key theme of James's *Varieties,* his reflection on the nature of these experiences is even more surprising. In the "Postscript" to the *Varieties,* James explained that there were two different models for understanding the supernatural: one "refined," and one "crass." Refined supernaturalism, he explained, followed the dictates of Kantian philosophy and rejected the possibility of the supernatural or noumenal intervening within the phenomenal world. Instead the noumenal or supernatural could be seen as supporting and holding up our world. In contrast, crass or "piecemeal" supernaturalism, which James believed reigned "only among uneducated people," continued to see the world divided between a natural and a supernatural sphere. "It admits miracles and providential leadings, and finds no intellectual difficulty in mixing the ideal and the real worlds together by interpolating influences from the ideal region among the forces that causally determine the real world's details," explained James. The supernatural, far from being a ground of being, was an active player in the life of the world.[21]

In this clash between philosophers and uneducated people, James firmly placed his flag with the uneducated. Although he admitted that he could accept neither "popular Christianity" nor "scholastic theism," crass or piece-meal supernaturalism seemed superior on a variety of levels. First, refined supernaturalism surrendered too easily to naturalism and tended to reduce the supernatural to a point of view. Furthermore, on the practical level, refined supernaturalism made the supernatural largely irrelevant by confining it to the realm of idea and absolute. In this airy realm the supernatural could offer little religious solace. "It is strange, I have heard a friend say, to see this blind corner into which Christian thought has worked itself at last, with its God who can raise no particular weight whatsoever, who can help us with no private burden, and who is on the side of our enemies as much as he is on our own," pondered James. It was an odd evolution, he mused, from the God of David's psalms. A God who did not involve himself in the affairs of men and women was very little God at all. Finally, a crass supernaturalism could better make sense of brokenness in the world, and could offer hope and remedy when the fruits of nature were bad. Through the "subliminal door" in human conscious-ness, "God . . . produce[s] immediate effects within the natural world to which the rest of our experience belongs."[22]

Read in this way James offered a boon for those who desired to hold on to the idea of the miraculous, and his casual asides on the limitations of the liberal world view would have pleased a Charles Gore or a Charles A. Briggs. But James's book addressed *religious* experience, and he was insistent that this evidence of the reality of the "other" was present in all religions. For James, Buddhism, Hinduism, Islam, and all other religions were possible portholes to the divine. Religion could not be identified with any particular creed. Further-more, James anchored the "other" by divorcing it from traditional theological categories all together. As he explained, the reality of the "other" was not necessarily ultimate, but only larger than our own: "All that the facts require is that the power should be both other and larger than our conscious selves. Anything larger will do, if only it be large enough to trust for the next step. It need not be infinite, it need not be solitary. It might conceivably be only a larger and more godlike self, of which the present self would then be but the mutilated expression, and the universe might conceivably be a collection of such selves, of different degrees of inclusiveness, with no absolute unity real-ized in it at all."[23]

According to this view, supernatural occurrences were quite possible and were the stuff of religious experience, but they could just as easily (and for James more probably) be the product of a polytheistic pluralistic universe as the actions of a loving God. "Miracles" for James were always real, but were divorced from any ultimate truth. They awakened and stirred in human beings an awareness of the other, but were finally silent as to what that other might be. One could not reason from miracles to God as had earlier writers, but only to this higher reality. G. K. Chesterton, in his study of Thomas Aquinas, has a famous discussion of the nature of modern philosophical schools in which he ponders how the various schools would discuss the existence of an egg. Of James and pragmatism he wrote, "The Pragmatist may believe that we get the best out of scrambled eggs by forgetting they ever were eggs, and only remembering the scramble." Perhaps James's discussion of the miraculous is to be seen in this way. What remains of the miraculous is pure scramble, in which the egg of the divine has dropped away.[24]

What was one to make of James's bold reimagining of the question of the supernatural? To be sure there were some who were not impressed by his undertaking. James's colleague at Harvard George Santayana dismissed the volume as "religious slumming." And the English writer Harold Anson, in commenting on James's preference for dramatic emotional religious experience over that usually found in the Church of England, dryly noted, "Mr. James had never been able to distinguish between religion and delirium tremens."[25]

But the attractiveness of James was undeniable. The *Varieties* went through eighteen printings between 1902 and James's death in 1910. Part of its appeal lay in his working out of categories of classification and analysis that bridged the world of the believer and that of the academy. Likewise part of its power was the Copernican revolution it offered for the study of religion, by urging that the focus should be on the fruits of religious belief and not their roots. Finally the catholicity of James's approach, with his willingness to seek out genuine religious experience wherever it could be found, touched a responsive chord in many people of this generation of spiritual unrest. More than any other figure, James gave intellectual credibility to the new search for evidences of the spirit world, and it is little surprise that Ray Stannard Baker used James as his guide through the outgrowths of the new spirituality. But the question still remained: how would the religious communities themselves respond to the possibilities and problems of this new religious spirit?

Reopening the Question of Miracles

The practical challenge of healing and the more general problem of understanding the relationship between God and the world led many English-speaking Protestants to reconsider the idea of a limited age of miracles.[26] For example, when the Church of England published its decade-long study *Report of a Clerical and Medical Committee of Inquiry into Spiritual, Faith, and Mental Healing* one of the prominent questions asked the participants was whether they connected the spiritual healing of the present day with the gifts of healing in the apostolic church. The answer was a resounding "Yes": a great majority of participants identified spiritual healing in the twentieth century with the long dormant gifts of healing in the apostolic church. The participants differed on how they interpreted the nature of these healings, but there was an overwhelming belief that what was happening in the present was what had happened in the biblical era.[27] Similar trends were seen in America, and the long-cherished view of the limited age of miracles found less and less favor. How does one explain this sea change?

One recalls first that the argument for the limited age of miracles had been formulated to safeguard the uniqueness of biblical revelation. But no writers ever wanted to argue that the discontinuity between the biblical and postbiblical epochs had been absolute, or that God was now absent from the world and could only be found in written text. Rather, Protestant writers from the time of the Reformation, and particularly Reformed Protestants, had argued for a necessary distinction between miraculous activity and other works of providence. Providence, they explained, was God working through secondary cause or the laws of nature, whereas a miracle was a divine action outside of the sphere of secondary cause. Miracles were accordingly immediate in their effect and objectively recognizable. There could not be any doubt when a true miracle occurred. Acts of providence however, because they occurred through nature rather than outside of it, were partially hidden. There was always a degree of subjectivism in the case of providential actions. The eyes of faith might see the hand of God in the branch floating by that allowed a drowning person to be saved, but other eyes might see it as pure chance.

We have already observed how during the late nineteenth century many shifted the understanding of miracle away from an objective or scientific mooring and toward an Augustinian understanding. This trend continued, and what one finds by the early twentieth century is that the elaborate Protestant scholastic system of classification — of miracle, special providence, and general providence — was largely collapsing. The Methodist theologian Borden Parker Bowne, for example, explained that the distinction between miracle and special providence was false because it rested on an erroneous distinction between divine activity and law. Since the middle of the nineteenth century, theologians had been edging toward a definition of miracle that saw it as a reflection of a higher law of nature rather than a violation of law. If such a reconceptualization were granted, then the distinction between miracle and special providence was no longer meaningful. The older writers, explained Bowne, "were not willing to allow that answers to prayer or special providences and the like were to be viewed as miraculous," but now the theologian freely admitted that miracle, providence, and prayer were all of one class.[28] Horace Bushnell's throwing open of the definition of miracle was now increasingly accepted. If more interest began to be shown in modern miracles, it is at least in part because many things interpreted as being miracles had previously been interpreted as special providences. As we shall see, the older theology continued to have its defenders, particularly at Princeton Seminary and at other outposts of the Calvinistic subculture. But the story of the transformation of American higher education from Reformed to Christian humanist, chronicled in such detail by George Marsden and others, was to have its effect on the debate over the miraculous. The distinction between miracle and special providence was a fine theological one, greatly valued by Reformed theologians. The decline in both Calvinism and theological literacy rang the death knell for the public appropriation of this distinction, and along with it for the persuasiveness of the idea of a limited age of miracles.[29]

Bowne's criticism of the eighteenth century hints at still another factor behind this transformation, one which involved a radical reconceptualization of natural theology. The old enlightenment model had argued that human confidence in God rested upon the order and plan of nature. The heavens declared the glory of God and displayed his reality and goodness. But a recurring theme in this period was that the declaration of the heavens was nowhere near as clear as it had been. The crying need now was for particular and individual evidence rather than a mere general assurance that God was real and good. Why this became the case is an issue of speculation, but perhaps in an increasingly ordered and regularized society and economy, it became apparent to many that one could have order and regularity without love and concern.

Nowhere was this interest in evidences more striking than among many of the liberal Protestants in both England and America. For them, the concerns of Robert Elsmere to banish the miraculous from the present and the past evaporated in the new drive to find the presence of God in the world. In their quest to find God's presence, they ironically made use of the same principle that other liberals were using to further separate the world from any active involvement by God. As I noted in the last chapter, liberal exegetes and writers had made it a practice to distinguish between the healings and the nature miracles of the gospels. As we saw, some writers, such as George A. Gordon, used this understanding to deemphasize the importance of the miraculous in Christianity. Gordon would have been a classic representative of James's "refined" supernaturalism. Like the earlier natural theologians, Gordon found confidence in God's presence by reflecting on the grand design of the world and of humankind. But the redefinition of the miraculous allowed other liberal writers to emphasize the miraculous, or those evidences of "piecemeal" supernaturalism, and to see them as a way of connecting the biblical era to the present. As Richard Heber Newton proclaimed, Jesus as healer was not an exception but an example: "Those unusual gifts [of his] are not supernatural. They are all natural, orderly, under the reign of law. They are not miracles in any sense which we ordinarily use the term. They are the marvels of a marvelous personality —

the wonderful work of Him whose name is Wonderful."[30] When the concept of the miraculous was liberated from the idea of breaking a law of nature, some liberals eagerly embraced it, and saw these acts as signs and evidences not only in the past but in the present as well. Indeed, if God acted in a uniform way then there was no reason why one should not expect similar marvels in the present.

Healing, but of What Type?

If the turn-of-the-century generation could agree to reject both cessationism and *Robert Elsmere,* there was nonetheless wide variance as to how to understand these signs and wonders. The report *Spiritual Healing,* for example, noted that there was a wide division between those who saw these acts of healing as "external" and "divine" and those who considered them "ordinary" or as working through natural laws and forces.[31] The oft-repeated question of whether God worked through natural forces exclusively or whether he could also act directly, which had been central to the question of biblical miracles, also found its way into the debate over modern healings. Perhaps this division was inevitable. By its very nature, the evidence of a healing is ambiguous. Even if there might be agreement that a healing has taken place, what caused the healing always must remain a matter of conjecture. Thus the ministry of healing became the locus of the early-twentieth-century debate over how God related to the world. Three distinctive positions on this question emerged during the course of the early twentieth century: a "therapeutic" model, which saw divine action working through natural categories; a sacramental or liturgical model, which emphasized the role of grace transforming nature through regularly ordained ecclesiastical channels; and a thaumaturgical model, which argued that God intervened immediately into the lives of the faithful.

The most celebrated example of the therapeutic model was the American Emmanuel Movement, particularly as it was set forth by its founder and most persuasive advocate, Elwood Worcester.[32] The Emmanuel Movement's plea for the positive role of religion in healing was a much discussed subject during the first decade of the twentieth century, and particularly in America this healing movement received more favorable press than any other.

The life of Worcester (1862–1940) reflects the liberal attempt to bridge the gap between religion and science and to offer a new source of power for the church. Upon his graduation from Columbia University, he was convinced of two things: that he was called to a ministry in the Episcopal Church, and that the place of true learning was in Germany. Submitting to his bishop's requirement that he first graduate from an Episcopal seminary, Worcester completed his degree at General Theological Seminary in only one year, rather than the customary three. In Germany he studied philosophy at Leipzig. While there, Wilhelm Wundt and Gustav Fechner introduced him to the new and developing field of human psychology. In Germany Worcester also began to shape his intellectual development around two principles: an opposition to materialism in science, and a rejection of "dead orthodoxy" in religion. Returning to America, his ministry eventually landed him in Philadelphia. There, by the 1890s, he began to envision a marriage between the forces of medicine and religion.

Worcester got his chance to explore this possibility when in 1904 he was called as rector to the same Emmanuel Church, Boston, where Cullis had started his ministry forty years earlier. Boston seemed like an ideal place to test a marriage between religion and medicine. The success of the healing cults and particularly Christian Science convinced many in both the church and the medical guild that a new model was needed. There, along with the assistance of the Irish-born, Oxford-educated cleric Samuel McComb, and the physicians James Jackson Putnam, Richard Cabot, and Isador Coriat, Worcester began the Emmanuel Movement. At first, like Cullis, they limited their concern to the treating of victims of consumption, but quickly they too entered the broader question of religion and health.

The Emmanuel Movement was dedicated to improving the cooperation of clergy and medical professionals in the ministry of healing.[33] The role of religion in healing was primarily therapeutic. Religion, through trained counselors, could address the anxieties, fears, and moral failures that the physician could not reach. Advocates of the Emmanuel Movement often appealed to the biblical image of Paul the Apostle and Luke the Physician, united in service. Yet this cooperation required that certain tenets be in place.

The first such tenet was that such a ministry of healing had to be based on a scientific model that was grounded in both the critical study of the New Testament and the very best of modern medical theory. What had heretofore kept the spiritual resources of the church apart from the world had been the "lack of scientific method on the part of the Church," according to Worcester.[34] Hence, as McComb noted, "It is incumbent on us to study the healing ministry [of Jesus] . . . afresh, with whatever light may be thrown on it by the conclusion of psychological and medical science."[35] Both biblical criticism and medical science prescribed that religious healing be limited to functional diseases such as alcoholism and neurasthenia that seemed to have a moral or psychological root to the ailment.

A second assumption was that the new psychology offered an understanding of the true healing power of religion. Proponents of the movement peppered their writings with terms such as "suggestion," "autosuggestion," and "the subconscious mind." The psychologists' interest in the influence of mind on body, particularly in the restoration of health, implicitly affirmed the traditional religious emphasis upon the role of character and personality. "Faith and prayer imply a specific attitude of mind in which thought, feeling, and will are involved, and this activity has psychic sequences, or concomitants, which, through the nervous system, affect the whole physical organism," explained McComb.[36] Indeed the positive power that resulted from the merging of religion and psychology did not end with mere health. In an article titled "Saints Made by Psychology" one devotee of the movement claimed, "When men spend as much time in the study of their own minds and the laws which govern them as the chemists today spend in their laboratories, we will have saints such as the world never has seen."[37]

Finally the leaders of the movement acknowledged that in any such cooperative endeavor between physician and clergy the cleric must be subservient to the physician. The Emmanuel Movement was superior to all other concepts of Christian healing, according to its supporters, for this very reason. "It defers," as one writer proudly noted, "at every point to science. It accepts the judgement of the medical experts."[38] In the movement's overriding intellectualism, or belief that the only valid Christian healing was knowable and explainable, one sees it standing at arm's distance from Cullis and other proponents of thaumaturgical healing.

The defenders of the therapeutic approach, however, did not limit themselves to arguments from medicine in bolstering their position. They saw their movement as also reflective of their generation's surging interest in using idealistic philosophy as a tonic against materialism, because it emphasized the supremacy of spirit over matter and mind over matter. Worcester, for example, regularly returned to the theme of the power available to one who was "in tune" with the universal mind. He invoked an image found in Alfred, Lord Tennyson — the opening of a sluice between the "great ocean" and the "little channels" — as descriptive of the true meaning of prayer.[39] Later advocates of the therapeutic model were even more explicit. As one wrote, "The whole movement must be based upon a sound, true, practical, mysticism, that is, upon the truth that we can come into conscious intimate fellowship with God, the Eternal Spirit. . . . This truth must not be 'tacked on' a health movement, it must be its foundation rock."[40] Such a "practical mysticism," along with a confidence in modern psychology, grounded the therapeutic model.

Yet it would be wrong to view the Emmanuel Movement as merely offering physical healing. Its proponents argued that theirs was a vision of true Christianity, because the power behind the movement was nothing less than the original power of signs and wonders in the New Testament. As Worcester explained in his autobiography, "As a student of the New Testament and of early church history, I knew that something valuable had been lost from the Christian religion. . . . What has been lost is chiefly Jesus Christ, the Gospel of a Saviour's love, and a religion of the Spirit and of Power." The healing of the Emmanuel Movement was the same as that of Jesus. Furthermore, for Worcester, McComb, and the others, the Emmanuel Movement's importance lay in its offer of health not only to individuals suffering under illness but also to the church suffering under a false and archaic belief. The new psychology allowed one not only to claim the power of healing for the present but additionally to understand the place of healing in the past.[41]

Worcester's address made to the [Episcopal] Church Congress of 1903 was cast against this background. The new psychology, he argued, allowed modern individuals to see the healing miracles of Jesus in a new light and in continuity with our present age. Unlike the radical biblical scholar D. F. Strauss, who rejected the image of a healing messiah as a first-century superstition, Worcester argued that Jesus healed through the same power of character and personality as did healers of the present. The new psychology allowed for a new understanding of Jesus. Since the fourth century, he explained, the true nature of Christ's ministry had been lost, obscured by an ugly coat of supernaturalism. Now that this supernaturalism was being stripped away, the church was again realizing that Christ's powers were the same as ours, and that the weapons he used "are, in a measure, open to every Christian."[42]

Worcester was not alone in making such claims. Samuel McComb emphasized this theme of Jesus as therapeutic healer whose true message was only now being discovered. But there is an irony here. Decades before, proponents of the reconciliation of Genesis and science had made a similar type of argument — namely, that the Old Testament had embedded within it the truths of modern science, which were now only being discovered. This view of an esoteric science hidden in scripture and unknown and indeed even unthought of by the authors of the text was rejected as morally objectionable; it turned revelation into magic and trickery.[43] But this, in effect, was what Worcester and McComb saw in the gospels — Jesus acting upon and preaching a scientific reality that was only at long last beginning to be understood.

Worcester finally argued that this new understanding of the role of religion in healing could serve to empower both the church and its ministry in the twentieth century. It would bring religion down from the clouds. Ministers could now claim powers unheard of since the early days of Christianity; they could now be an "expert in dealing with moral and spiritual pathology about him." No longer would the clergy suffer from a lack of power and a sense of obsolescence in the modern world. Clergy could now heal, not merely console, and "when a minister has set men free from fear and worry, or from drink and lust, he will have an authority which no ecclesiasticism can give."[44] The lack of influence of the church in the modern world was not due to the individual failure of its ministers but to its lack of any real transformative power. As Worcester noted, "If we should promise every worshipper in Emmanuel Church next Sunday the gift of a ten dollar gold piece, no matter what the character of the preaching there would be no vacant pews."[45] Worcester went on to note that at the beginning of the nineteenth century the German theologian Friedrich Schleiermacher had recast Christian theology and in doing so had restored its power to the "cultured despisers" of his era. The Emmanuel Movement was to be seen as the new Schleiermacher for the present century, offering a way for the church to be revitalized to meet the challenges of the new age. The choice lay between the obscurantism of the old theology and the new vision offered by the modernists, but the price demanded of the new theology and new ministry was a willingness to accept the new learning.

The eschatological note in Worcester's writing was striking, but here too he was not alone. Other proponents of the therapeutic model were equally visionary. The Unitarian J. W. Winkley saw the restoration of healing to be part of the culmination of the modern age. "The gospel of healing was intended by Christ to be a part, a very essential part, of Christianity," he explained. With the loss of this gospel the Christian community had lost not only a precious gift but also a constant reminder of the power of the spirit. But Winkley believed the return of the gift of healing hinted that a new age was on its way. "Be it true that something like a new time is dawning on the world! There are 'signs of the times' that surely seem propitious," he exclaimed.[46]

A number of contemporary commentators noted the close relation of the movement to theological modernism, and in this regard it is interesting to see how Worcester, McComb, and others attempted to distance themselves from other models of healing.[47] Not only is there the expected rejection of earlier views about miracles and the distinction between nature and supernature, but there is also a continuing castigation of "fetishism." True religion was spiritual, intellectual, and personal, and accordingly these attributes should also be characteristic of any true religious healing. "We avoid all fetiches and material adjuncts as means of suggestion," Worcester proudly announced, "and rely only upon moral, spiritual, and rational means."[48] Fetishism implied some merging of the material and the spiritual in which the material carried or transmitted the spiritual. For modernists such as Worcester and McComb, it additionally bespoke the superstitious errors of paganism and catholicism, which it was the duty of the modern church to root out.

Other advocates of divine healing, however, looked not to the present but to the past, indeed to that very fetichism so decried by Worcester and McComb. They advocated the restoration of the ancient practice of anointing the sick. In the early part of the century this liturgical or sacramental approach achieved a significant degree of popularity in Britain. In America its influence was largely limited to the Episcopal Church, but its importance would grow as the century progressed.[49]

As has already been noted, the practice of sacramental anointing had arisen in the early centuries as part of the shift away from a charismatic and toward a sacerdotal view of ministry. By the time of the Reformation, anointing had largely been transformed from a ritual associated with healing to a preparation for death. The Reformers had jettisoned the practice, but by the middle of the nineteenth century Catholic-leaning members of the Church of England began to argue for its restoration. At first their appeal was largely on sacramental grounds, and was part of their agenda of reclaiming the full catholicity of the Church of England, but by the 1890s their approach shifted dramatically. The challenge of Christian Science necessitated a response, and some Anglicans began to claim that anointing did not simply console but could also heal. The power of Christ to heal, they explained, was still present in the world, but it was mediated (albeit imperfectly) through the church. The pattern of modern healings differed from biblical ones because the faith of the church was but a shadow of the faith of Jesus. Christ still did heal, "only He must do it now through the Church, and therefore He often cannot do it because, as a matter of fact, the attitude of the members of His Church has changed. They do not believe any longer in His readiness to heal, or to give them the gifts of healing . . . so that now in His Church, as at Nazareth of old, 'He can do no mighty works there because of their unbelief.' "[50]

Throughout the early twentieth century, particularly in England, a vigorous tract debate took place between proponents of the therapeutic model and advocates of the sacramental approach. The issue centered upon a number of larger questions. What connected the biblical world and the present? Did it consist of a form of knowledge that was only now being rediscovered, or was it rather a continuing presence of sacramental grace? How was healing to be brought about—through a knowledge of the new psychology, or through grace working through the sacraments? Finally wherein lay the "expertise" of clergy: in their academic training, or in their ministerial office? In this debate no one argued more vigorously or effectively the case for sacramental anointing than did the English cleric Percy Dearmer, and no volume was so influential as his *Body and Soul: An Enquiry into the Effects of Religion upon Health, with a Description of Christian Works of Healing from the New Testament to the Present Age.* Dearmer (1867–1936), who is probably better known for his musical accomplishments as well as his eccentric but enthusiastic defense of "authentic" English ceremony reflected in his *Parson's Handbook,* offered a singular defense of the role of religion in healing. Indeed one might almost liken *Body and Soul* to William James's *Varieties* garbed in proper Anglican vestments.[51]

As Dearmer argued, the Western world was undergoing a great religious revival, one that sprang not from the universities or the theologians, but from the hearts and desires of everyday men and women. The revival was not centered in dogma, which for "them means disputation about words, and the waving about of phrases," but in an intuitive understanding of the fundamental truth of reality. Twentieth-century individuals were revolting from the materialism of the Victorians, and rebelling from a false spirituality that divorced spirit and matter and considered religion as being other-worldly. It was not surprising for Dearmer that this revolt should be so strong in America, because nowhere else had materialism and false spirituality had such a strong sway. Men and women were beginning to rediscover the genius of historic Christianity, and particularly its principle that matter and spirit were rightly interconnected. True Christianity neither despised material things nor worshipped them but reconciled the material and the spiritual. "Christianity," he explained, "is the Catholic religion, that is the religion of the whole." The interconnection of spirit and matter underlie the three great Christian truths: the incarnation (God's taking on of human flesh), the miraculous (God's direct intervention in the material world), and sacrament (God's use of outward and visible matter to convey inward and spiritual grace).[52]

It was the truth of the sacramental principle—the idea that God works through the material to transform the world—that was so desperately needed by modern men and women, in Dearmer's view. The recognition that spirit clothed with matter was always present in the world transformed the human predicament. Through this lens, human beings could be seen not just as material beings, nor as bodies with a soul, but as souls clothed in a body. The body was the outward sign, whereas the soul was the inward grace.[53]

When Dearmer turned to the question of healing, one sees again how the question of miracle and sacrament were entwined in his mind. In the gospels both miracles and sacraments were properly understood as signs. A miracle was not a propositional evidence of Christ's divinity as the anti-Deist writers had argued; rather it indicated the triumph of spirit over matter and the active presence of God in the world. The reality of the spirit was now ministered through the sacraments. They were the regular, ordained conduit between the supernatural and the natural realms. But being veiled in matter, the power of the sacraments was sometimes lost sight of. To counterbalance the invisibility of sacramental grace, God continued to bring forth miracles, and their occasional occurrence served as a tangible reminder of the power of spirit in the world. At no time were such dramatic signs more needed. As Dearmer explained, "The modern world, sick with doubting hopes, needs intensely to be assured that religion is not a mere probability, nor faith a passive acceptance of conjectures; that prayer is a power producing results, that grace is real."[54]

The interconnection between sacrament and miracle also lay behind Dearmer's case for anointing. Following a traditional Catholic approach, Dearmer saw sacraments as outward, visible signs of inward grace. The spirit worked through the material in a sacrament without changing physical nature. Likewise the purpose of a sacrament was first and foremost the restoration of the health of the soul. The life of grace was invisible. Hence in anointing the primary function was the strengthening of the spirit. But the interconnection of body and soul was so close that at times an act of grace would have a physical effect, and in the case of anointing the sacramental action could lead to physical healing. Grace "when brought to bear upon a sick man must . . . strengthen his spirit, and may through that inward invigoration bring strange and wonderful recovery of the body," Dearmer explained.[55] In the case of both the sacrament and the miracle, however, the act was not an end in itself, but rather pointed to a higher reality. What distinguished religious healings was neither the success rate nor the numbers involved — in both cases, modern medicine had a far better track record than did the church. Instead, it was the truth conveyed through the healing. As Dearmer explained, "The 'mighty works' of the New Testament are signs for our instruction. . . . [W]hen a man is healed by faith of a disease which natural means have failed to move, we are in the presence of a force more important for humanity than the wonderful skill of the physician."[56]

For Dearmer, the true relationship between God and the world was a sacramental relationship, but in his view this truth had been lost. And no movement was more responsible for its demise than was Calvinism. The Calvinists of the seventeenth century had transformed the compassionate works of Christ into abstract evidences for his divinity. Furthermore, the doctrine of predestination presupposed that the experience of divine grace was the exception rather than the rule, reserved for a small number of elect instead of being poured out onto all humanity. The result was a conception of God as a distant judge as well as a loss of the sense of the divine presence in the world. The modern world was beginning to rediscover the older truth. Whatever might be said against the inner health movement, Dearmer wrote, "at least [it] is purifying Christianity from the last traces of Calvinism, and from those earlier religions of fear which had their roots in devil-worship and their last fruit in the doctrine of

Reprobation. . . . The practice of the presence of God is for all. It is not some difficult intellectual exercise to be learnt out of books: it is the gathering up of the spirit into the Silence where the dews of God may condense upon us." There was little remaining of the old *de contemptus mundi* spirituality in Dearmer. Rather than seeing the world as a burden, religion as a consolation, and sickness and suffering as the lot of humankind, he boldly proclaimed, " 'It is such fun being a Christian!' Let that sentence stand uncorrected, not unserviceable in the shock it brings."[57]

In Dearmer's evocation of fun, one can almost see the lights and colors and smell the rose petals strewn during processions in his church, St. Mary's Primrose Hill. It is likewise easy to observe that for him, as for many Edwardian English men and women, the somberness and soberness of Victorianism had been firmly put to rest. But we should be careful not to dismiss Dearmer and his *Body and Soul* as a peculiar flowering of the Edwardian religious spirit, for Dearmer linked sacramentalism and healing with the new psychology. He put great emphasis on the reality of the subliminal consciousness, and gratefully acknowledged his indebtedness to both Myers and James. In the subliminal consciousness, according to Dearmer, the divine spirit came into contact with humanity. He also observed that the new psychology confirmed the nature of the gospel miracles. Jesus in the gospels did not undermine nature but brought nature into harmony with the true purpose of God. Likewise the "miracles" of the modern world never undercut nature or "turn a man into an apple tree or a cactus," but they could bring humanity "into conformity with the whole law of God," as Jesus had promised in the gospels.[58]

Arguments such as these resonated well within some circles of the American Episcopal Church where the anti-Calvinist rhetoric was also prominent. As one writer noted, the revival of sacramental anointing helped overthrow the last remains of Puritanism within the American Episcopal Church because it had been the "Puritan" Archbishop of Canterbury, John Tillotson, who had so strongly opposed the anointing of the sick. It was by no means coincidental for the proponents of anointing that Christian Science took root in Boston, the traditional center of American Puritanism. The healing claims of Christian Science, noted another, served to fill the vacuum left by Puritan theology. A restoration of the true practice of anointing, proponents argued, would not only benefit the religious community but in turn would best answer the challenge of the healing cults "Eddyism, Dowieism, hypnotism, et al."[59]

Underlying the calls for anointing were not only the presupposition that the sacramental merging of spirit and matter was the highest form of divine activity in the world, but also a distinctive vision of the church and the ministry. The church was most basically a sacramental institution; hence the qualification or expertise of the clergy was contingent not on an ability to perform miracles or any intellectual mastery of modern psychology, but instead on their sacramental and liturgical powers. And here the advocates of anointing saw themselves as pointedly rejecting the path of the Emmanuel Movement. Theirs was not "a 'healing movement,' in which courses of psychology are an introductory requirement; which practices one of the innumerable branches of psychotherapy in a pathetically experimental way, and which, in every step, is limited by the diagnosis of medical men, and their opinion as to the possibility of benefit resulting from the 'treatment.' "[60] The healing ministry of the church was independent of the claims of modern psychology. Furthermore, the possibility of divine healing was not limited to merely functional maladies. Any type of disease could be healed through the power of grace.[61]

If liberals and modernists like Worcester found the answer to the spiritual unrest in a new therapeutic knowledge that allowed them to recapture the healing ministry of Jesus, and if persons like Dearmer found it in the sacramental principle, others argued that the outpouring of the Spirit in the modern world was nothing less than a new Pentecost. The origins of the Pentecostal movement is a long and involved story that has been well told by others, and as a movement it is only tangentially involved in this study. But the growth of the evangelical vision of faith healing from the time of Charles Cullis in 1892 is central to the early-twentieth-century search for spiritual evidences.[62]

As was noted in chapter 4, the faith cure movement had various roots and grew out of the logic of holiness and the belief that the atoning work of Jesus Christ offered not only spiritual but physical benefits. Furthermore we observed that public interest in this movement (if the indices of periodical literature are any guide) seemed to peak in the mid-1880s with the Agricultural Hall International Congress. Catholic faith cures, as well as the mind cure and Christian Science movements, seemed more to catch the public's fancy during the 1890s, and there was comparatively little public discussion of the evangelical Protestant faith cure movement.[63] By the end of the 1890s, however, the public interest changed, and the idea of thaumaturgical or miraculous healing through the direct intervention of God again burst upon the scene. If one person was responsible for this new visibility of the faith cure movement it was John Alexander Dowie. Indeed if Elwood Worcester exemplified the therapeutic approach, and Percy Dearmer the sacramental, Dowie was the leading proponent of the thaumaturgical approach to healing.[64]

If nothing else, Dowie (1847–1907) was a controversial figure. Born in Scotland, he and his family moved to Australia while he was a young man, and there he entered into the Congregationalist ministry. While ministering to his congregation during an epidemic in 1872–73, Dowie became convinced of the truthfulness of the promise of Acts 10:38 (which spoke of Jesus' power to heal "all oppressed by the devil") and the present reality of divine healing.[65] As a result of this experience, a healing mission eventually became central to his ministry. In 1888 he emigrated to America and in 1890 he began his controversial ministry in Chicago. It was not until 1893, however, when Dowie had set up his mission near the Chicago World's Fair — indeed right across the street from the camp of Buffalo Bill Cody — that Dowie's healing mission began to grow in visibility. As a result of both his healing of a number of celebrities (including the niece of Cody himself and the cousin of Abraham Lincoln), and also his highly publicized legal battle with the Chicago Board of Health, Dowie became a celebrated figure. By the turn of the century he was perhaps the best known advocate of the faith cure in America. He founded his own church — the Christian Catholic Apostolic Church — and even his own utopian community of Zion City, Illinois.

There were both fundamental continuities between Dowie and earlier proponents of healing such as Cullis, Simpson, and A. J. Gordon, and also key differences. Like them he rejected any distinction between functional and organic diseases and took pride in trumpeting claimed cures of organic diseases. Indeed, if for Worcester the paradigmatic diseases were alcoholism and neurasthenia, for Dowie it was cancer. In some ways cancer was the ideal disease for proponents of the faith cure. The medical establishment was powerless over cancer, and hence curing it through divine healing gave one the aura of Elijah on Mount Carmel triumphing over the priests of Baal.[66] But Dowie both pushed a number of elements of the earlier faith cure movement to their logical conclusion and introduced some distinctive elements as well. One new feature was his insistence on the reality of the cures themselves. Whereas A. B. Simpson had taught that it was possible to "claim" a healing for which there was not yet any physical evidence, Dowie argued that healing must be complete. More importantly, Dowie heightened the antagonism between divine healing and medicine. We saw in chapter 4 how earlier faith healers were divided over the appropriateness of the use of material medicine by believers. Dowie saw medicine as not simply wrong but diabolical. In his notorious tract *Doctors, Drugs, and Devils; or the Foes of Christ the Healer,* he charged "DOCTORS AS A PROFESSION, ARE DIRECTLY INSPIRED BY THE DEVIL." Confrontational rhetoric seemed to come easily for him. But one also notes in this claim another theme not emphasized in an earlier figure like Cullis, and that is the strong role of Satan and the demonic in sickness and health. A belief in demons was fairly common in folk Protestantism, but it had not played a major role in the earlier understanding of the nature of faith healing. For Dowie, however, the demonic was the corollary of the power of God. As one recalls, the verse from the

Acts of the Apostles that inspired Dowie in his ministry spoke of healing those "oppressed by the devil," and accordingly, explained Dowie, if Christ were still the healer then the devil must still be the defiler. Not only was all disease indirectly related to sin, but some disease was caused directly by diabolical activity. "All disease is the oppression of the Devil, but there are some which are possessions by the Devil, or by Devils." Both in his vision of sickness and in his view of healing, Dowie set forth a more sharply supernaturalist position than earlier faith healers. This may in part have stemmed from his distinctive way of reading the New Testament, which had great influence on later Pentecostalism. As others have noted, the record of the primitive church, as found in the Acts of the Apostles, became paradigmatic among Pentecostals for understanding the life of present-day Christians. And in the book of Acts both the spirit of God and the spirit of the diabolical were seen as being particularly real. The emphasis upon the demonic may have been simply a fruit of the strong sense of the reality of the spirit among Dowie and his followers. As the historian Christopher Hill has noted about the seventeenth-century fascination with the devil, when Christ was felt to be near, so too usually was Antichrist. But whatever the reason, the healing ministry of Dowie was far more radically supernatural than had been the ministry of Cullis.[67]

Dowie was of course not unique in his appeal to the vision of the primitive church. A number of scholars have noted that restorationism, or the belief that the world of the primitive church could somehow be recaptured in the present by the purified community, has been a significant theme in a number of American religious movements such as the Mormons, the Campbellites, and the Adventists. Clearly for Dowie and his followers divine healing was intertwined in this restorationist vision. The original faith of the apostles, which had been lost, was being restored in their view, and that faith entailed not only the texts of the ancient scriptures but the power that inspired them. As one convert to the movement proclaimed, "The denominations say the Bible and Bible alone is our religion. We say that the church is built on present revelation and Word of God, spoken by real Apostles who have the signs of an Apostle and the authority of an Apostle, speaking in accord with the Word of God in other ages." Secondhand knowledge and ancient stories of mighty works were not enough; only a restored faith with the power of the apostolic age could meet the religious crisis of the age. The skeptics and doubters could only be answered by real evidence. Preaching at the very beginning of the new century, Dowie proclaimed, "Robert Ingersoll may sneer at the miracles of nineteen centuries ago, but all the sayings of Ingersoll cannot alter the fact that miracles are wrought today. . . . The infidels can ask for facts, and we are stuffing them down their throats until they have to stop talking."[68]

We should linger on this last quote from Dowie. When divorced from its rather violent rhetoric, it is ironically a sentiment that could have been found in F. W. H. Myers or Elwood Worcester, because of its appeal to facts and its recognition that the battlefield over the reality of the supernatural was in the present, not the past. But for Dowie the appeal to evidences and miracles was not mediated through the new psychology but instead through a biblical matrix. In the New Testament the world was seen as a battleground between the forces of God and those of Satan; hence for Dowie this was the position in which the true church found itself.

There is one more striking implication of Dowie's emphasis on healing, and that is how it led him to reconsider Roman Catholicism. Throughout his career Dowie demonstrated his deeply bred Scottish dislike for Roman Catholicism, and rarely passed up a chance to attack that church. But whenever he compared the faith of Roman Catholics with that of the "denominations," he readily admitted that Rome was closer to the gospel faith than was contemporary American Protestantism. In 1898, for example, the Physicians Club of Chicago invited a Baptist minister (Poindexter S. Henson) and a Catholic priest to discuss the issue of faith healing. In the course of the evening the Catholic priest adamantly defended the healings at Lourdes whereas the Baptist decried the modern divine-healing movement. Commenting on the performance of these two clerics Dowie wrote, "I have more hope for the salvation of Roman Catholics than I have of . . . most of the ministers and members of the Baptist churches. I would rather take my chances before the throne of God with an earnest Roman Catholic priest . . . than with a hypocrite and liar like Dr. Henson."[69] Whatever Rome's errors might be, on the key question of God's activity in the world Catholicism was closer to the truth than was modern American Protestantism. Thus Dowie offered surprising charitableness to Roman Catholicism, in contrast to the venom he poured out on Protestant clergy. "I have received less sympathy and less help from Protestant ministers than from any other class in the community," observed Dowie, and throughout the pages of the *Leaves of Healing* he attacked the Protestant churches and clergy for their lack of faith.[70]

In turn Protestant writers sharply criticized Dowie. The rancor between Dowie and Protestant writers is not in itself surprising, but what strikes the reader of these disputes, particularly when contrasted to the situation in the 1880s, was the tone and nature of the controversy. Not only was Dowie more curtly dismissed than was Cullis, but so too were his theological and exegetical arguments. One recalls that during the 1880s the faith cure movement generated a strong but thoughtful discussion in which exegetical, theological, and pastoral issues were debated before the religious public. Cullis and Gordon might have been wrong, but critics such as Alexander B. Bruce and Marvin L. Vincent felt compelled to refute them. By the early twentieth century, however, the categories of the debate over faith healing had shifted from theology to pathology. No longer did proponents and opponents see themselves as functioning within one intellectual and religious community and as wrestling over the right interpretation of a common scripture and theology. Rather, they believed themselves to be two separate communities having little in common. James M. Buckley was something of an exception — he continued to hammer home the same themes against Dowie that he had for decades raised against all faith healers — but most critics pictured Dowie as a crazed charlatan rather than as a person who had to be refuted. As one elaborate examination of Dowie concluded, "His development toward delusion and deceit, and his assumption of the role of a conscious or unconscious imposter, was caused by his own insatiable self esteem. . . . But no less powerful has been the impulse and suggestion furnished by an overcredulous following." No longer was the error of faith healing an error in theology or exegesis; it now was seen to be a sign of a demented personality. This predisposition is perhaps most succinctly captured by a turn-of-the-century card in one university library card catalogue. Under the topic "Miraculous Cures" the researcher was instructed to "see also . . . medical delusions, quacks and quackery." The attraction of faith healing could be neither rational nor normal, but had to be some form of delusion. Accordingly, the journalist John Swain, noting the attractiveness of Dowie for "Chinese and Asiatics" suggested their might be racial explanations for Dowie's appeal. "Missionaries can preach salvation to these people till their throats give out . . . without producing the fraction of the effect on the oriental mind brought about by Dowie with the apparent cure of a single paralytic and the display of a hundred crutches. That is magic for them that even their own great men cannot excel, and the power that works it is to be propitiated."[71]

Some of this attitude can be traced to the spirit of muckraking journalism so prevalent in the early twentieth century, which took great delight in finding malfeasance and corruption. But the response of religious figures requires more of an explanation. In part it may have been a result of Dowie's violent rhetoric and questionable reputation, because even some defenders of faith healing were critics of the Australian.[72] The reaction of theologically trained commentators may also in part also illustrate their increased confidence in progressive scientific methodology. We have seen how Scottish exegete A. B. Bruce, in response to the new biblical criticism of the 1890s, gradually gave up on the idea of nature miracles, and became convinced that the New Testament record had to be interpreted in light of modern natural philosophy. The rancor between Dowie and his critics may reflect the acrimony between two very different religious trends: the increasing supernaturalism of the faith healers, and the increasing confidence in the universality of natural law and the immanence of God among the higher critics. To proponents of the latter view, Dowie, with his emphasis upon demons and prophecy, reflected an earlier and less advanced stage in the development of religion, and one that was out of step with — and detrimental to — the religious life of the age. The implication of Dowie's critics was clear: middle-class Anglo-Saxon Americans had put away such childish things as thaumaturgical healings and demons.

Faith Healing on Broadway

The overwhelmingly negative response of theologically trained critics stands in contrast with the greater degree of openness to the idea of thaumaturgical healing by some other intellectuals. As one moves further away from the confines of theological scholarship, one finds more sympathy for the admittedly nonscientific and nonrational approach to healing of a person like Dowie. Nowhere is this more clearly seen than in the 1910 Broadway play *The Faith Healer,* by the noted American poet and dramatist William Vaughn Moody.

Moody was one of the most celebrated figures in American letters before his untimely death in 1910. *The Faith Healer* was loosely based upon the career of a minor Alsatian-born faith healer, George Schlatter, known as the New Mexico Messiah. But in fact the play was an extended meditation upon the tension between the spiritual and the mundane. Moody had carefully read James's *Varieties* and had become convinced that it offered inescapable evidence for the work of the divine spirit in the world, and that human beings neglected the power of the spirit to their peril.[73]

The plot of the play takes place in the American West and concerns the travails of the Beeler family.[74] Matthew Beeler, the patriarch of the family, is a devotee of nineteenth-century science, and portraits of Darwin and Spencer hang conspicuously on the living room wall. But his wife, Mary Beeler, is an invalid, partially paralyzed and unable to walk since the accidental death of her brother almost five years earlier. Nothing has been able to help her. Into the household enters a mysterious faith healer, Ulrich Michaelis, and an Indian boy who, it was rumored, Michaelis has raised from the dead. What was one to make of Michaelis? The African-American character Uncle Abe believes that Michaelis offers the hope of a miraculous healing unlike that of medicine. His healing is "De Bible kin'. . . . De kin' what makes the lame fer to walk an de blin' fer to see" (226), but for the scientifically minded Matthew Beeler, a belief in such powers is folly. "There's nothing more [in nature] than science will account for," he explains. "You can read it up any day you like. Read that book yonder, chapter called Hallucinations. Pathological, that's what it is, pathological" (221). The conflict between scripture and science is established. But upon Mary's insistence Beeler allows Ulrich to pray over her, and a miracle takes place. For the first time in years Mary walks. In grateful recognition, Matthew Beeler removes the portraits of Darwin and Spencer from their place of honor.

Doubts about the "miracle," however, begin to emerge in Act 2. Two characters: the physician Dr. Littlefield and the cleric John Culpepper, discuss the nature of the healing. If it were truly a miracle, Littlefield observes, it would undermine both of their professions. "The brother would drive us doctors into the poor house, if he could keep up the pace. And you preachers too, as far as that goes" (280). But he asserts that the healing was no supernatural miracle. Indeed science has now rejected the very idea of the supernatural. "You can't get outside nature nowadays! Tight as a drum, no air-holes" (277). The healing of Mary Beeler, Littlefield believes, was induced by suggestion brought about by the great psychological power of Michaelis. The doctor assures the cleric that he has seen numerous cases of such healings by suggestion before. But sooner or later, he warns, the psychological exertion that such healings required would take their toll on the healer himself. The events seem to prove the doctor right. A crowd gathers to beseech Michaelis to heal them as well, and Michaelis begins to grow emotionally distraught. Finally he relents to pray for a dying baby. The doctor now chides him for overstepping the bounds of his power. Through the power of suggestion he had led Mary Beeler to heal herself from her mind-imposed illness, but suggestion could have no influence on a baby. Pointing to his brain and heart Littlefield explains, "You gave [Mary Beeler] a jog, so to speak, here, or here, and she did the rest. But you can't do the same to everybody. Above all, you can't do it to a baby in arms. There's nothing either here or here to get hold of" (271–72). The faith healer had reached the limits of the power of suggestion. Act 2 ends in crisis with the baby apparently dying, Mary Wheeler suffering a relapse, and Michaelis in despair.

Act 3, however, takes place on Easter, and there the limitations of the doctor's materialism are revealed. The materialism of the doctor is shown to be a reflection of his amoral nature. More importantly a deeper power of healing is discovered. It was a power far greater than that of Michaelis, which he did not control but could only submit to. Not only did the transforming power of spirit, as shown by the forgiving love between Michaelis and the young woman Rhoda, cure Rhoda's sick soul, but it also revived Mary Wheeler to a higher level of healing than she had heretofore experienced. Her health at this point in the play is "so different from yesterday. I was still weak then, and my limbs were heavy. Now I feel as if wings were on my shoulders" (330). The power of faith created possibilities where human consciousness could only see impossibilities. "Faith . . . makes all things possible, which brings all things to pass" (335). Indeed the play ends with the dying baby apparently recovering and the young mother ecstatically announcing, "Come here — My baby! I believe — I do believe — " (336).

In all probability Dowie, if he had still been alive, would have condemned *The Faith Healer.* Like James, Moody accepted the reality of faith healing but divorced it from any theological context. Indeed even the reviewers who lauded the play thought that it was weakened by a fundamental ambiguity about the exact nature of the spirit to which it appeals.[75] But the fact that Moody chose to use the thaumaturgical model of healing as the vehicle of his drama suggests that whatever intellectual problems such an approach might entail, he believed it nonetheless touched the imagination and kindled the desire for the reality of spirit. In his play, a belief in the power of faith that stopped cautiously at the explicable phenomenon of suggestion is cast aside, and the power and mystery of spirit is put in its place. Whatever the faults of the character Michaelis, he is nonetheless presented as a far more sympathetic and noble figure than the advocate of the theory of mental suggestion, the doctor Littlefield.

Worcester, Dearmer, and Dowie represented very different worlds, and more than likely they would have found little in common. But despite their differences in theology, they were all in their own way participants in the new search for evidences. For each the reality of the supernatural in the present was foundational to authentic faith. If there were a spiritual unrest, it could only be relieved by new signs and wonders.

Benjamin Warfield and the Defense of Cessationism

The search for evidences that might bolster belief did not of course go uncriticized. The Anglican Ronald Knox, for example, attacked the trend because its advocates collapsed the ideas of miracle and special providence and because they insisted upon anchoring religious confidence in the personal experience of the supernatural. It was a product of the modern fascination with psychology, which "is now always very much in the air; bank clerks discuss the ecstasies of S. Theresa with complete familiarity, and Mysticism is all but a breakfast-table topic in the daily Press." The current interest, however, also bespoke a crisis of religious authority in the modern world. Knox observed that popular culture was lamentably abandoning theology for apologetics. No longer did men and women accept statements without having them personally verified. The question was no longer what was true, but rather what could be believed.[76]

But no one criticized the various new movements as thoroughly nor defended the cessationist position as adamantly as did the Princeton theologian Benjamin B. Warfield. As professor of didactic and polemical theology, Warfield was heir to the long Princetonian tradition with its combination of Calvinistic orthodoxy and Enlightenment philosophy. In his volume *Counterfeit Miracles* (1918), he used both strands of influence to defend the cessationist position and to challenge all claims for modern miracles.[77]

His defense of the cessationist position rested upon two traditional principles, which he set forth in the opening chapter of his volume: the distinction between miracles and all other providential acts, and the association of miracles with revelation. Miracles, he explained, were public manifestations; there could no more be a private miracle than there could be a private revelation. Because they were instituted to authenticate revelation, miracles accordingly ceased when revelation ceased. Against those who would extend the age of miracles into the second century, he quoted the eighteenth-century writings of Conyers Middleton. Middleton might have been a "sceptic," but "he had a subject where scepticism found a proper mark." As Middleton clearly demonstrated, no persuasive evidence for postbiblical miracles could be found in the record of the early church.[78]

Most of Warfield's succeeding chapters were dedicated to dispensing with claims for ecclesiastical and modern miracles. Catholic miracles were dismissed as superstitious fetiches. He approvingly quoted Edwin A. Abbott in his critique of John Henry Newman, and along with Abbott characterized Newman's *Essay on Ecclesiastical Miracles* as "probably the most specious plea for the credibility and reality of the whole mass of ecclesiastical miracles ever penned." Claims of proponents of the faith cure were similarly rejected. A. J. Gordon, for example, was faulted for confusing miracles and special providences, and the claims of other healers were criticized in light of William James and the new psychological theory of suggestion and autosuggestion. If a healing could be explained through a category such as suggestion, it could not be a miracle. Dowie also was castigated, and even the Emmanuel Movement was attacked as offering nothing more than what had been accomplished in the faith homes of Dorothea Truedel—except in the Emmanuel Movement there was "a very much thinner religion and a more advanced medical science."[79]

The details of Warfield's individual criticisms need not detain us, because they are in large part a restatement of the classical Protestant position, but three things about Warfield's volume are striking. The first is how rooted it continued to be in the eighteenth-century debate. Clearly for Warfield the old enemies of enthusiasm and popery still loomed large and still required refutation. The memory of Edward Gibbons was still very alive for him, and only biblical Christianity could hold the line against skepticism and Rome. A second characteristic of Warfield's argument was his willingness to make use of admittedly skeptical authorities in order to combat claims for the authenticity of postbiblical miracles. Theological disputation, like politics, inevitably creates strange bedfellows, but there are few more peculiar ménage à trois than the Calvinist Warfield, the Deist Middleton, and the liberal biblical critic Edwin A. Abbott. Yet Warfield has few qualms about making common cause with them. The last point concerns the strong rationalist elements in Warfield's polemic. He has little problem dispensing with most Roman Catholic miracle accounts, but not with the best attested case of a miraculous healing at Lourdes, that of Pierre de Rudder. He admitted that the facts concerning Rudder's healing were incontestable, but he would still not concede that it might be a miracle. An extraordinary healing, he explained, did not necessarily constitute a miracle. "The healing of Pierre de Rudder's leg is not the only thing that has occurred in the world of the mode of occurrence of which we are ignorant. . . . We are only beginning to learn the marvellous behavior of which living tissue is capable, and it may well be that, after a while, it may seem very natural that Pierre de Rudder's case happened just as it is said to have happened. . . . [T]here may be forces working in nature not only which have not yet been dreamed of in our philosophy, but which are beyond human comprehension altogether."[80]

If this quotation had not been identified, many might think that these were the sentiments of Tyndall, Huxley, or Zola, rather than of the leading conservative Reformed theologian in America. Warfield's willingness to plead agnosticism as to causality when confronted with the irrefutability of evidence had also been the rhetorical device of the nineteenth-century naturalists. But it is Warfield here making such a claim. Secular journalists were somewhat amused at the circularity of his argument. "If there is no need in suggesting natural causation for the mending of de Rudder's leg," wrote C. M. Francis, "because you know in advance it cannot be of God, why is there need in suggesting any natural causation for any alleged [post-biblical] miracle . . . all of which you know in advance cannot be of God?" In Francis's view, Warfield's whole volume was an exercise in futility.[81]

For Warfield, however, *Counterfeit Miracles* was neither a futile nor circular argument; rather, it was a reaffirmation of the long-standing Protestant position. Secure in his certitude of the impregnability of the biblical miracles, he was happy to make common cause with the skeptics' attack upon postbiblical miracles. Bushnell and Newman had glimpsed over the precipice, and seeing the precariousness of belief in the modern world had opened the door for new evidences. Warfield, unruffled, continued to rest his faith upon the absolute certainty and uniqueness of the biblical record.

The Four Positions

Thus by the second decade of the twentieth century there had emerged not two but four distinctly recognizable positions vis-à-vis the miraculous. These positions offered a spectrum of interpretations of the interrelated questions of biblical and modern miracles.

On one extreme was the continuing rejection of the very idea of the miraculous, or the possibility of direct divine intervention in the world. This position involved both philosophical and religious objections to miracles. Despite the large-scale criticism of both naturalism and materialism during these years, the anti-miracle position as developed by Tyndall and Huxley continued to have its proponents. It furthermore became revitalized with the emergence of the philosophical school of logical positivism. For these philosophers the idea of a miracle or a supernatural occurrence was always to be held in suspect. "Miracle" and "supernatural" were non-explanations — an attempt to answer the question of how something occurred when the cause was not yet known. Others rejected the language of miracle or divine intervention on religious grounds. Devotees of a "refined" supernaturalism, such as George A. Gordon, were willing to see the hand of God in the order and regularity of nature but balked at the idea of piecemeal intervention. Still others argued that the problem with the miraculous was not so much that it was irrational as that it was immoral. Because they were directed to specific individuals or groups, miracles smacked of divine favoritism, and implied an image of a quixotic God who chose to intervene to help some individuals but not others. As one writer posed the question, "Can the special intervention of God at any point, in answer to the solicitation of any man or men, fail to work wrong and injustice to other men?"[82] A truly loving and moral God would only work through universal natural laws.

At the other extreme was the cessationist position of Warfield and the Princetonians. As we have noted, this position rested on a fundamental theological assumption: biblical miracles were qualitatively different from any act of grace or providence experienced in the postbiblical world. The age of miracles was over because miracles were tied to the giving of revelation. But we have also suggested that for many proponents of this position there were personal factors contributing to their attitude. In particular, some found it difficult to grapple with the inexplicable question of why God allowed suffering to go unheeded. The wife of Benjamin Warfield, for example, was an invalid during their entire marriage, and Warfield spent countless hours caring for her. She never regained health and died an invalid while Warfield was preparing *Counterfeit Miracles.* It would not be surprising if some of the sharp tone of that volume toward the confidence of faith healers reflected some of Warfield's own frustrations about losing his wife.[83]

The cessationist position also gained strength among the emerging Fundamentalists for two other reasons that I shall discuss more fully in the next chapter. One was that cessationism became an important part of the Fundamentalist critique of Pentecostalism. A second factor was that it played an increasingly larger role in the theology of dispensational premillennialism. Both of these factors moved the emerging Fundamentalists away from the idea of faith healing. This transition did not please all Fundamentalists, however. Philip Mauro, one of the contributors to *The Fundamentals,* still maintained that "God's redeemed people should look to Him, and to Him alone . . . and that they when sick in body should use the means which God has appointed, and none other," but his was fast becoming a minority position.[84]

Between these two extremes, however, were two mediating positions that were strongly interconnected. Both denied the skepticism of the positivist position and the rigid periodization of the cessationists. Both shared great interest in modern occurrences, saw a link between modern wonders and ancient ones, and showed a particular interest in faith healing. But the two positions were mirror opposites.

The first was the position that modern wonders gave us a perspective for rightly interpreting the great works recorded in the Bible. This position was aptly epitomized by William Sanday. Sanday, one recalls, rejected by the end of his life the notion of nature miracles—divine activity in the world *contra naturam.* In justifying his views he explained, "We have perhaps to translate the account of the day of Pentecost rather more into the language of our own time. . . . If the Apostolic Age was an age of the Spirit, a Welsh Revival is a lesser example of what is generally the same thing."[85] We have seen how individuals like Elwood Worcester and Samuel McComb made similar claims about modern healing movements. According to this perspective, the activities of the divine in the present world were real and were fruitful subjects of inquiry, and through the study of them one received not only confidence enough to believe in a supranatural reality, but also a criterion by which to evaluate and grant credence to the ancient claims of signs and wonders. Modern wonders allowed believers to finally understand the world of the Bible. Biblical accounts were encased, however, in a prescientific world view. Hence to be meaningful to modern believers, these ancient events had to be "translated" into the modern philosophical, psychological, and scientific categories. When this translation was accomplished, the great events of Pentecost could be understood as nothing more than a modern Welsh revival, just as the healings of Jesus were like modern spiritual healings.

It is not surprising that this position flourished during these years, because it was rooted in many of the trends I have discussed. The general spiritual unrest provided the impetus, and the currents in philosophy, psychology, and medicine provided the tools for such a reconceptualization. Likewise, because the modern experience of the supernatural was rooted in mind, personality, and humanity — rather than in physical nature — it allowed for the desire for evidences to be answered in a way that was in keeping with the cultural and intellectual currents of the early twentieth century.

The contrasting position argued the reverse. It was the biblical framework that provided an understanding of the works of the divine in the present. Its proponents agreed that the modern events of grace were indeed like those earlier ones recorded at Pentecost. But for them the events of the Welsh revival were in reality a fulfillment of biblical prophecy, particularly Joel 2:38 ("And it will come to pass that I will pour out my spirit upon all flesh."). As the evangelist and expositor G. Campbell Morgan noted concerning the Welsh revival, "It is Pentecost continued without a single moments doubt. . . . The meetings are absolutely without order, characterized from the first to the last by the orderliness of the Spirit of God."[86] For these individuals the link between the great events of the present and those of the past did not demand a translation of the past events into the language of the present but rather an interpretation of present events through the categories of the past. The biblical world and the present age were intimately connected, and biblical categories increasingly shaped the way in which they saw the world. We have seen how for Dowie the biblical language and imagery of healing became the means by which he understood his own healing ministry. This trend continued. Thus the early Pentecostals invoked the biblical metaphor of the "Latter Rain" to describe the activity of the spirit in the present. The power of the spirit that had descended onto the church at Pentecost and that had allowed its members to do mighty works was again unloosed. One aspect of this trend we have seen was the renewed emphasis on the world as a spiritual battlefield and on the role of the demonic in attempting to thwart God's will. As the immediate presence of the divine grew closer, so to did the reality of the divine adversaries.

Culturally and psychologically, this last position was far different from the previous one. It continued to maintain the relevancy of biblical categories and thought patterns, and was far less reconcilable to the trends in science, psychology, and medicine than its mirror opposite. In this sense it was a more marginal movement. The irony, however, which I shall discuss in my next chapter, is that the same characteristics that made this position marginal to the intellectual culture of the early twentieth century allowed it to flourish when the intellectual culture had changed.

The symbolic question of whether Pentecost was merely a Welsh revival or the Welsh revival was a new Pentecost divided the world views of these two middle positions on the miraculous. Both positions grew in influence and importance during the first two decades of the twentieth century, but each developed independently from the other. They existed in largely different classes and regions, and to a remarkable degree were unaware of each other, but on one key point they were nonetheless interconnected: they both rejected cessationist assumptions and would have been glad to dance on the grave of John Calvin.

Chesterton and the Ambiguity of the New Search

During these decades of spiritual unrest, many individuals revolted against the confines of both cessationism and Victorian naturalism. But if there was clarity over what was to be rejected, the question of what was to be affirmed was more problematic. Few occurrences attested both to the interest and problems concerning the miraculous than did the play *Magic,* by Gilbert Keith Chesterton. Chesterton had already established an international reputation as an essayist, novelist, and religious apologist. In 1913, after continual urging by his friend George Bernard Shaw, he turned to the stage and wrote his first (and only successful) play. Like the plays of Shaw, *Magic* was an intellectual comedy, and the subject was the reality of the miraculous.[87]

The play took place in a large country house in England, and the central characters were a mysterious conjuror and two siblings: the romantic Patricia Carleon, and her hardheaded brother, Morris. Patricia was Irish, and was enamored with the spiritual world. This fascination with the spiritual world, other characters noted, was to be expected given her Irish background. The Irish, it was claimed, were a romantic (and not particularly advanced people), and it was natural for them to still believe in the world of fairies — but the English were different. Said one such character, "I suppose it is quite correct to see fairies in Ireland. It's like gambling at Monte Carlo. It is quite respectable. But I do draw the line at their seeing fairies in England."[88] In contrast to his sister, Morris Carleon (who had spent time in America) was convinced that all talk of spiritual realities was foolish, and that all accounts of them ultimately

rested on trickery: "Most mysteries are tolerably plain if you know the apparatus. I guess I wish we had all the old apparatus of all the old Priests and
Prophets since the beginning of the world. I guess most of the old miracles and
that were just a matter of just panel and wires" (40).

The conjuror, who had been hired to provide the evening's entertainment,
was described as a young man, cultured but wearied, and through him Chesterton poked fun at the fads and foibles of upper-class English society. But
Morris Carleon's continual harping upon trickery, and his dogmatic insistence
that every trick could be explained, begins to irritate the conjuror. After each
trick Morris bursts out an explanation, and the conjuror icily admits that it
could have been done that way. Morris becomes increasingly exuberant in the
victory of scientific rationalism over mystery. Pointing to a lamp in the garden
outside, the young American triumphantly proclaims, "That red lamp is the
light of science that will put out all the lanterns of your turnip ghosts. It's a
consuming fire . . . but it is the red light of the morning. Your priests can no
more stop that light from shining or change its colour and its radiance than
Joshua could stop the sun and moon" (46). But suddenly the light changes
color from red to blue. Morris begins to rack his brain for an explanation of
how such a trick could have happened, but he cannot come up with one. He
begins to go mad.

Act 2 begins with Morris still mad and being ministered to by his sister,
Patricia. These scenes also include much philosophical discussion. As in William Vaughn Moody's *The Faith Healer,* there are in the play a physician and a
cleric, and through them much of the discussion of the relative merits of faith
and skepticism takes place. Even here in Chesterton's fantasy one sees the
shadow of William James. The cleric observes the irony of the evening: the
rationalist has gone mad and is now being ministered to by a believer in the
spirit world. The doctor, as a representative of Victorian science, had earlier
argued that belief in the unseen was a form of psychological delusion and
often reflected a weak mind and character. Confronting the doctor the cleric
asks, "Does it never strike you that doubt can be a madness as well as faith?
That asking questions may be a disease as well as doctrines? You talk of
religious mania! Is there no such thing as irreligious mania? Is there no such
thing in the house at this moment?" The doctor, in response, claims that only
by questioning beliefs can knowledge advance. Only by reducing the universe
to knowable categories can human beings be content. On the contrary, argues
the cleric, "Why can't you leave the universe alone and let it mean what it
likes? Why shouldn't the thunder be Jupiter? More men have made themselves
silly by wondering what the devil it was if it wasn't Jupiter." Religion is to be
measured by its fruits, or how it permits a person to live in the world, not by

any abstract criterion of scientific rationality. In response, the doctor can only observe, "You are a Pragmatist" (52).

Act 3 opens with Morris still mad because he is unable to discover how the trick had been accomplished. The others press upon the conjuror to reveal the secret of his trick, but he refuses on the grounds that no one will believe him. Finally he relents; he did it by . . . magic. When they respond with incredulity he lashes out and turning to the cleric says, "I say these things are supernatural. I say this was done by a spirit. The doctor does not believe me. He is an agnostic and he knows everything. . . . But what the devil are you for, if you do not believe in a miracle? What does your coat mean, if it doesn't mean that there is such a thing as the supernatural? . . . Why the devil do you dress up like that if you do not believe in it?" (62). The conjuror goes on to explain that in his younger years he had involved himself in spiritualism, which had damaged his health, and he had invoked those same spirits to perform his trick. As he explained to Patricia, "In black pride and anger and all kinds of heathenry because of the impudence of a schoolboy I called [the spirits] and they obeyed." (67–68) The trick had no natural explanation because it had been brought about by no force of nature. Finally, after agreeing to undo the trick, the conjuror retires to the garden and begins to pray fervently that the evil that he had done might be undone. Inside the house everyone senses that some great spiritual battle is taking place. Finally the conjuror returns and announces, "I am going to tell that little lad a lie. . . . I have managed to think of a natural explanation of that trick" (70). After giving the explanation privately to Morris, the latter instantly regains his composure. Preparing to leave, the conjuror is pressed by the others to share with them the explanation of the trick, but he adamantly refuses. As he explains, "Because God and the demons and that Immortal Mystery that you deny has been in this room to-night. Because you know it has been here. . . . [But] if I told you the lie I told Morris Carleon about how I did the trick . . . you would believe it as he believed it. You cannot think how that trick could be done naturally. . . . But if I tell you a natural way of doing it . . . half an hour after I have left this house you will all be saying how it was done." (71–72). For some people any natural explanation, no matter how improbable or far-fetched, was preferable to admitting a supernatural cause. Only by denying them recourse to any possible natural explanation would the members of the household be forced to wrestle with the mystery that had occurred.

As one reviewer noted, "Not Orthodoxy nor Father Brown himself is more Chestertonian than *Magic*." Perhaps this element is apparent in the play because much of Chesterton's own life is depicted. As a young man Chesterton himself had dabbled in spiritualism, and he too had fled from it. Likewise a recurring theme in Chesterton's life was that orthodox Christianity was an outline for sanity, particularly because it provided the best outlet for human natural religiosity, including the fascination with the supernatural. This religious impulse, if frustrated, would manifest itself as insanity or despair.[89]

But Chesterton's play also illustrated the unsolved problem of his generation: the reconciliation of the new supernaturalism with traditional Christianity. Chesterton, for example, was widely known as an apologist for orthodox Christianity, but in his play—which was described by one critic as a "profession of faith by England's large and genial supernaturalist"—he treats faeries and spiritualists rather than Christian miracles. Furthermore, as was the case in William Vaughn Moody's *The Faith Healer,* the spiritual sensitivity of the leading female characters stands in contrast to the skeptical attitude of the clergy. In each play women and social outcasts (in *The Faith Healer* the African-American Uncle Abe, and in *Magic* the Irish) are the true believers, as opposed to male scientific and religious authorities. Throughout the play the question simmers: who was closer to true religion, the believer in faeries or the doubting cleric?[90]

Magic was not only a successful play but also a topic for debate. Some reviewers criticized him for mixing serious questions of religion with the theater, but many more people were intrigued by the issues raised by the play. On January 14, 1914, before a packed London theater, Chesterton and others debated the question of the miraculous in the modern world. Chesterton led the side defending miracle claims and Joseph McCabe, a former Roman Catholic priest turned materialist and a noted investigator and critic of the claims of psychical research, led the opposition.[91] As Chesterton argued, the claim of the appearance of miracles was universal in human experience; it was the criticism of this claim that was exceptional. "You know from the first literature you read, and the stories you heard in the conversation of your friends, and in a thousand other places, that as you got more intimate with them, people were less and less ashamed of saying that they believed in miracles." Whether it be a belief in ghosts, seances, or planchettes, the vast majority of people recognized the reality of the spiritual manifesting itself in the natural order. Turning to the question of Christian miracle claims, Chesterton's colleague Hillaire Belloc discoursed on Lourdes, where the skepticism of Morris Carleon was acted out daily by the critics of the recorded healings. Cures were deemed impossible until the evidence was overwhelming. "Each miracle is called impossible until it takes place. When it can no longer be denied, it is given a big long name and called natural," commented Belloc.[92]

The appeal to the universal experience of humankind was a powerful one for the populist Chesterton, but it raised again the question of exclusivity. Chesterton had based his views on occult evidences; his colleague Belloc strengthened his arguments with Catholic evidences. What if anything could distinguish between these two types of evidence? This was a point made, oddly enough, by not only the opposition in the debate, but even Chesterton's own team. Arguing in favor of the miraculous in the debate was A. P. Sinnett, author of *The Occult World,* who saw in the battle over the miraculous a united front of Christians and spiritualists against materialists and skeptics. "Testimony to the experience of what is commonly called miracles has been before the world ever since spiritualism began, and that testimony cannot be disputed," Sinnett explained.[93] One of the most problematic aspects of the defense of modern miracles for many Christians was that some of the strongest proponents were the spiritualists whose arguments they had been rejecting for decades.

Conclusion

Throughout this chapter I have placed together individuals and groups — faith healers, psychical researchers, William James, Percy Dearmer, John Alexander Dowie, G. K. Chesterton, and so forth — who are almost never examined in tandem. I have done so because whatever their differences, they all participated in a new search for evidences of the divine in the modern world. All agreed that a spiritual crisis confronted modern believers and that a new basis for religious certainty was needed — one that presented God as active in the present and the past, and as vital to both the physical and intellectual realms. All moved away from the inherited world view of the Reformation with its compartmentalized view of history and its dichotomies between the biblical world and the present. And finally, all would have acknowledged that this supernatural reality was a "crass" or "piecemeal" supernaturalism (to return to William James's categories), not simply the "refined" supernaturalism of Transcendentalism and philosophical idealism.

But these individuals share one other commonality: none were trained theologians. They were pastors and professors, priests and playwrights, who sensed that some bold reconceptualization of the relationship between God and the world was necessary. Furthermore, as we have seen in Moody and Chesterton, this new religious vision is offered over the skepticism of the clergy. Theologians were not a part of the development of this new vision, but would be forced to confront the intellectual problems of this vague united front and determine whether it could be reconciled with traditional theological presuppositions. As we will see in chapter 8, the fascination with "crass" or "piecemeal" was shared by neither the Modernists nor the emerging Fundamentalists.

8

Miracles and the Crisis of the 1920s

The postwar decade was a tumultuous one in many respects, not the least of which was its religious currents. In America the Modernist-Fundamentalist controversy reached its climax. In England a surging Anglocatholic party confronted a dedicated Modernist faction over many issues, whereas figures such as Archbishop Randall Davidson attempted to keep the Church of England united as it grappled with questions of governance and liturgical reform. But it was also during these postwar years that the subject I have been tracing — the miraculous as both a biblical concept and a modern reality — also reached its boiling point. The debate over the miraculous became the stuff of sermons, pamphlets, articles, and books as English-speaking believers continued to probe the larger question of the relationship of God to the world.

One of the odd effects of a war is that it transforms theoretical religious questions into profoundly practical ones. For example, the question of the intervention of God in the physical realm had been discussed for years and had provided an occasion for many erudite ruminations by philosophers, theologians, and scientists, but it took on a new urgency when raised by an anxious mother wanting to know whether her prayers for her son in battle could be answered. Likewise, when trapped English troops during the retreat from Mons, Belgium, in the early days of the war reported being comforted and supported by celestial beings, the issue of the "Angels of Mons" became an international cause for discussion. Finally, as the historian Stuart Mews has shown, the carnage and destruction of World War I not only dampened the easy optimism of Edwardian England and Progressive America, but raised the question of religious healing to a fevered pitch. In light of the suffering that emerged from the war, the question emerged: Does Christ still heal?[1]

The "crisis" nature of the postwar decade is now almost a commonplace theme, and it is used to explain everything from the debates about morality to the popularity of the martini cocktail. Likewise religious historians have used the motif of crisis to explain the emergence of both Modernism and Funda-mentalism, which on both sides of the Atlantic tended to move the religious discussion simultaneously both to the "right" and the "left." For our purposes, however, this "crisis" had a different twist. As we suggested in the previous chapter, the broad interest in the "new evidences" of the "miraculous" and the "spiritual" that preoccupied the thought of so many individuals in the early years of the twentieth century rested upon a confluence of different factors. The loss in confidence in the assumptions of Victorian science, the popularity of philosophical idealism, a view of the human mind that posited the subliminal consciousness as a doorway to the supernatural, and a large-scale questioning of the adequacy of the materialist model for medicine all helped provide the intellectual justification for seeking earthly evidences of the divine. Together they opened the door for a broader understanding of reality. Further, as we have seen, this movement was, in the broadest sense of the term, a "lay revolt." The new search for evidences was a revolt against all specialists, whether theologians, doctors, scientists, or philosophers. But by the 1920s the door was beginning to close as a new orthodoxy began to emerge. In the sphere of Anglo-American philosophy, the slow triumph of logical positivism was beginning to shift the scope of philosophy and call into question the adequacy of long-established concepts such as a distinct, immaterial soul. Looking back, the American theologian William Adams Brown noted that by 1920 modern trends in philosophy were giving little support to religious considerations. In psychology the growing repute of Freud and Jung shifted the understanding of human consciousness far away from the paradigm posited by F. W. H. Myers. For Freud, for example, the subconscious was neither a "secular soul" nor a gateway to some higher reality, but rather an accumulation of individual experience. Finally, the medical community became increasingly more ensconced in the social fabric of the upper class, and their authority in the field of healing became more and more solidified.[2]

Indeed, even those prewar trends that in fact became more popular among the larger public declined in appeal among intellectuals. Thus, ironically, as an interest in spiritualism seemed to increase among the general public after the war (as happened after the American Civil War), it fell into more and more disfavor among scholarly commentators.[3] Spiritualism no longer reflected new scientific insight as it had in the days of Myers and James, but rather old superstition. Accordingly, most writers in religious journals urged caution: "Spiritualism, with all its paraphernalia of ouija boards, trumpets, dark cabinets, materialization, automatic writing, and spiritual photographs — . . . these are those rivers and tributaries that feed the encroaching sea of modern occultism. It is the business of the Church to take her stand upon the saying of the Master to the effect that 'an evil and adulterous generation seeketh after a sign,' that 'the kingdom of God cometh not with observation.' "[4]

This change in attitude can be seen most clearly in the declining reputation of one of the old representatives of the merging of spiritualism and science, Sir Oliver Lodge, as reflected in the pages of the American Modernist weekly, the *Christian Century*. In 1920, Lodge was still spoken of as offering new insight into religion. "He is one of the rapidly growing number of eminent men of science who stand for the scientific endorsement of the . . . supernatural," wrote one correspondent, "No one can read a page of the New Testament without feeling that he is breathing exactly the same atmosphere as that in the *Reports of the Psychical Research Society* — barring of course the critical analysis." But throughout the 1920s Lodge's star fell, and when in 1926 he was virtually asked to resign his membership in the Royal Society because of his continuing interest in spiritualism, the journal's editors applauded the action, noting "darkness and the royal society do not mix." Speculations and theories that had been respectable in 1905 and had provided a foundation for the empirical grounding of the supernatural were no longer in favor by the 1920s.[5]

These changes did much to weaken the power of the third position vis-à-vis the miraculous outlined in the previous chapter — the belief that modern wonders can unlock the meaning of biblical miracles. As we have seen, this position rested upon a precarious confluence of social and intellectual forces. The changing intellectual and cultural world meant that it would have fewer advocates during the 1920s than it had earlier.

The question of miracles would be even further complicated by a widening disparity between liberal and conservative views of the miraculous. One recalls that by the 1890s there was a tendency among religious writers to redefine the idea of a miracle in Augustinian terms rather than Thomistic — to see miracles as violations not of nature itself, but only of our present understanding of nature. This redefinition had been shared by both the *Lux Mundi* writers and their Modernist critics, albeit the former used it to include most of the dominical miracles, whereas the latter used it to exclude the nature miracles. Between 1900 and 1920, the Modernist reinterpretation of the miracle continued apace, and the discussion of miracles became part of a growing critique of the concept of the supernatural. According to this new perspective, miracles must not only conform to the laws of nature, but could have no supernatural cause. Particularly in the face of a growing Fundamentalist biblical literalism and preoccupation with eschatology, Modernists began to criticize the supernaturalism of the biblical world view. The supernaturalism of the Bible implied a dualistic universe that was no longer tenable. In the words of Shailer Mathews, the notion of supernatural intervention originated in a primitive age when it was believed that God lived in the sky, and hence a miracle was "the sky world descended to the earth-world." But the modern assumption of the regularity of the universe made the idea of supernatural intervention inconceivable. "The passing of this dualistic idea has left to us the choice between the total rejection of the supernatural, and its interpretation in a larger and more adequate sense," explained Mathews. Thus reinterpreted, the supernatural lost any objective meaning, and "miracle" became a far more subjective category than it had previously been. The meaning of a miracle was derived from the response it invoked among believers: "a miracle is an unusual, unexplained, or inexplicable occurrence which awakens within us a realization of the divine power, wisdom and beneficence."[6]

In such an atmosphere some conservative writers in America retreated to the older definition of the miraculous. If the battle line was the supernatural, argued the conservative champion J. Gresham Machen, then miracles worth their salt must be irreducibly supernatural, or else they were pointless. A miracle with a supposed natural explanation was no miracle. "It is a matter of no importance whatever that some of the wonderful works of Jesus are accepted by the liberal Church," he explained. "It means absolutely nothing when some of the works of healing are regarded as historical. For those works are no longer regarded by modern liberalism as supernatural, but merely as faith-cures of an extraordinary kind. *And it is the presence or absence of the true supernatural which is the real important thing.*" This sentiment may reflect Machen's Princetonian disdain for modern miracles as much as his dislike of Liberalism, and not all Fundamentalist champions were willing to retreat all the way back to this position. But clearly as one part of the religious spectrum drifted toward a rejection of the supernatural, others were elevating the supernatural. The result of both movements was to provide little room for earlier mediating understandings.[7]

Why is the Virgin Birth Necessary?

The controversies of the 1920s centered upon three interrelated issues. The first was a renewed debate over the question of the virgin birth. The second was a spirited discussion over the question of spiritual or faith healing.

Finally, there was a continuing reexamination of the nature of the dominical miracles themselves and their meaning for modern believers. Each was an old issue, but the social and intellectual context of the 1920s led to a number of different twists in the discussion.

As noted in chapter 6, the virgin birth had been a point of great controversy since the 1890s. Particularly in England it served as the classic battleground between Anglocatholics such as Charles Gore and Anglican Modernists. As the debate wore on, the contrasting positions became formalized. Modernists continued to emphasize the tangential nature of the doctrine to the New Testament — how it was found in neither Paul nor Mark and seemed to have played no part in the message of the first generation of believers. Likewise they emphasized the apparent factual contradictions between Luke and Matthew, in regard to both their narratives and their genealogical records, and argued that these contradictions cast doubts upon the accuracy and veracity of either account. Finally Modernists argued that the doctrine was of only secondary importance for modern believers. The virgin birth had been posited to explain the unique relationship between Jesus and the Father. As such it was only one of many possible explanations (and a late one at that), and was far more meaningful to the ancient pagan world — which expected divinity to be associated with wonders — than it was for a scientific age.

The British defenders of the doctrine, in contrast, emphasized the reliability of the historical records of Matthew and Luke. They also argued that the virgin birth bore few parallels with pagan wonder stories, and was rather in keeping with the tenor and tone of the rest of the gospel portrait of Jesus. There was a moral and spiritual interconnectedness between the nativity stories and Jesus' public ministry. They did not deny that there might be legend attached to the story; as George H. Box explained, the star and the magi might indeed be legendary. But the presence of legendary material paralleled other midrashic developments in which legends became attached to such historical events as highlighting or illumination. The legendary material, far from undermining the historicity of the birth, gave credence to it. Just as there could not be barnacles without a genuine hull of a boat, so too there could not be midrash without a historical basis in fact.[8]

Finally, and most importantly for the English Anglocatholics, the biblical argument ultimately rested upon the credal one; the issue of the virgin birth was not a question of scripture but of creed. The historic creeds raised the doctrine up as one of the key beliefs that Christians were called upon to confess, and to deny it was to cut oneself off from the historic faith. Ever since the publication of *Lux Mundi,* these writers had rejected the doctrine of plenary inspiration and biblical inerrancy. They acknowledged that the Bible undoubtedly contained myth and poetry that had to be interpreted figuratively. The creeds, however, gave a sure basis to faith, and the virgin birth was part of them.

Thus in many ways the virgin birth debate provided the ideal venue for this battle between Catholicism and Modernism. For one side it represented Catholic piety, credal loyalty, and ecclesiastical discipline. And for the Modernists the jettisoning (or at least decentering) of the doctrine reflected the triumph of both scholarship over tradition and Protestant liberty over Catholic obscurantism. Both sorts of arguments continued to be set forth in Britain in the 1920s, and cries of credal authority versus free Protestant inquiry continued to shape the discussion.[9]

But whereas the British debate followed its normal patterns, what was new in the 1920s was that the virgin birth became a hotly debated question among American Protestants. We have already seen how in the first decade of the century the issue was addressed by the scholarly community and reached the general public through the Algernon Crapsey case. Conservative Protestants were aware of the assault upon the doctrine, and as a result it had been enumerated by the Presbyterian General Assembly in 1910 as one of the "Essential and Necessary Articles" for ordination. From there the virgin birth had gradually evolved into one of the famous "Five Points" of American Fundamentalism (along with the inspiration and inerrancy of scripture, a substitutionary view of the atonement, the bodily resurrection of Jesus, and Christ's earthly miracles). Until the 1920s the doctrine had never been as central in America as in Britain, but at that time it emerged as a fundamental focus of the theological debate.[10]

Why this shift occurred is not immediately obvious. In part, as we have already observed, it reflected the larger battle over the supernatural. But there is also a simpler answer. The experience of World War I seems to have affected the dynamic of American Protestantism. The prewar years had experienced the high-water mark of Germanophilism within the American theological community. Scholars like Benjamin W. Bacon gloried in their Teutonic connection. The war experience not only put a damper on this Germanophilism but did much to reestablish the transatlantic Anglo-American theological connection. The *Christian Century,* for example, which in the early years of the century showed little interest in things English, established in 1920 a regular column "British Table Talk" to keep its readers abreast of British religious trends. English Modernists such as E. W. Barnes, Hensley Henson, and W. R. Inge featured prominently in the *Century*'s pages, and their articles and sermons were often reprinted. Even conservative American Protestants began to make use of their British counterparts. Whereas in the early part of the century

Benjamin Warfield had often excoriated Charles Gore and the *Lux Mundi* apologists, by the 1920s Warfield's successor, Gresham Machen, was far more appreciative. As Machen wrote, "I do rejoice with all my heart in the large measure of agreement that unites me with scholars like Dr. Box . . . and . . . Bishop Gore."[11] As the American Protestants drew closer to their British compatriots, they became increasingly pulled into the debate over the virgin birth.

But the adoption by American Protestant writers of the centrality of the virgin birth was to have a decided effect on the American Fundamentalist–Modernist controversy. The virgin birth debate strengthened the arsenal of the Modernists as it weakened that of the Fundamentalists. American liberals or Modernists could adopt the whole cloth of the English argument — both in its particulars concerning the technical problems of proving the doctrine from the witness of scripture, and in its general rhetorical thrust and appeal to scholarship, progress, and Protestant freedom. Furthermore the carefully crafted English Modernist position was tailor-made for popularization. Such masters of English prose as Hensley Henson and W. R. Inge had honed the scholarly arguments to a brilliant rhetorical position that had great appeal for forward-thinking laypersons.

American conservatives were not so fortunate. As representatives of the great American Protestant evangelical tradition, they could not easily adopt either of the apologetical arguments of their English counterparts. They could neither abandon the doctrine of biblical inerrancy as Box and Taylor had done, nor comfortably rest their argument on an appeal to church and creed. Rather, they had to defend the virgin birth within the larger context of biblical authority. To prove the historicity of the event on this ground was a difficult task — and to argue for the necessity of the doctrine on this ground proved almost impossible.

Considering these difficulties, what attracted conservatives to a fight over the virgin birth? One answer may lie in the continuing influence of Baconianism and Scottish Common Sense philosophy within the conservative camp. A key point in the conservative critique of liberalism was the liberal's questionable use of language. In the words of Machen, "The liberal preacher . . . is often ready to speak of the 'deity' of Christ; he is often ready to say that 'Jesus is God.' The plain man is much impressed. . . . But unfortunately language is valuable only as an expression of thought. The English word 'God' has no particular virtue in itself, it is not more beautiful than other words. Its importance depends altogether upon the meaning which is attached to it."[12] For a liberal preacher, to proclaim that "Jesus was God" was not to admit the hypostatic union but simply to imply that the life of God, which appeared in all men, was revealed with particular brilliance in the person of Jesus. Even the assertion of the resurrection was open to such ambivalence, according to Machen: "The assertion 'I believe in the resurrection of Christ' has in itself today almost as little meaning as the assertion 'I believe Jesus is God' so abysmal is the intellectual morass into which we have been flung by the modern business of 'interpreting' perfectly plain language in a sense utterly different from the sense it has always hitherto been used."[13]

The attraction of the virgin birth for conservatives was that it was ultimately a historical fact, and hence not open to "interpretation." If it could be proved, it would provide incontrovertible evidence of a miracle in the true supernatural sense, as well as ensure a view of Jesus that set him apart from the rest of humanity. For conservative apologists the attractiveness of a battle over the virgin birth was that it set the question between them and their opponents in its clearest form. On this point they were undoubtedly right. In the Presbytery of New York, for example, it was precisely on the question of the virgin birth that some ordinands balked at affirming the Essential and Necessary Articles, thus heightening the theological tension in that communion. But if the virgin birth was the clearest of the five "fundamentals," it would also prove to be the most difficult one for conservatives to defend within the American Protestant context.[14]

Hence the virgin birth debate in America involved two distinct questions. The first, or scholarly, question was over whether the event occurred. Answering this question involved issues of history and scriptural interpretation. The second, or theological, issue was whether (even if the event might have happened) it was an essential doctrine and could be required for ordained ministry.

The American debate in the 1920s was carried on at a far more popular level than the turn-of-the-century controversy. It filled the pages of secular as well as religious journals, and preachers such as Harry Emerson Fosdick and Percy S. Grant, rather than scholars and theologians, led the charge. The emphasis on popularity can also be seen in the rhetorical thrust of the Modernist spokespersons, who in many ways bypassed the denominations themselves and addressed instead a larger public. In the popular discussion the virgin birth became not so much a technical theological and exegetical issue as an emblem of the backwardness of the churches. The doctrine exemplified one of the dogmatic fixtures that tied the church to the past and prevented its participation in the intellectual ferment of the age. Employing rhetoric long used by English Modernists, Grant explained, "This doctrinal controversy involves more things than lie on the surface. It is a controversy between the old and the new; it is a controversy between tyranny and freedom; it is a controversy between democracy and the older forms of government; it is a controversy between reason and authority, between Protestantism and Catholicism, and between the supernatural and the natural." The old theology condemned the church to a smaller and smaller role in the modern world. "While the world — or rather its best men — have been seeking truth, the Church has been interested in defending tradition, with the result that the intellectual leadership, which, in the Middle Ages, belonged to the Church, has now passed to the scientist," Grant continued. The intellectual backwardness of the pulpit meant that only second-rate individuals were being attracted to the ministry, and "in the towns and cities the clergy don't measure up to the able lawyers and other intelligentsia of the places."[15]

Crying over spilt status was a long and venerable clerical tradition, and one in which Protestant liberals were particularly adept. But no one put the issue of the modern difficulties with the virgin birth more forcefully than the English female lay preacher, Maude Royden. During the 1920s Royden was one of the most celebrated, yet controversial, figures in the English-speaking religious world. Called by some "England's greatest woman," Royden was a long and tireless advocate of the role of women in the leadership of the church. In 1917 she began a preaching ministry at the City Temple in London (one of the city's leading Non-Conformist pulpits) and in 1919 shocked many in the Church of England by also "preaching" in Anglican pulpits. She began to be well known in America in the early 1920s, in large part through the influence of Joseph Fort Newton, and toured America three times during the 1920s. Some in the religious public were shocked by her scandalous willingness to smoke cigarettes in public, but many others looked at her (nonetheless) as a breath of fresh air. She was christened "the greatest woman preacher of our generation."[16]

Royden argued that women belonged in the pulpit not for reasons of equal rights but rather because they brought a unique understanding to the gospel message — one that had been hidden by centuries of male domination. One place in particular where a woman's insight was needed concerned the virgin birth. Royden had been preaching on this theme from as early as 1919, but in 1921 her sermon, "A Woman's View of the Virgin Birth" appeared in the *Christian Century,* and it created a storm.[17] According to the journal's editors, requests for the article were so overwhelming that they felt justified in reprinting it, which they did in 1924 at the height of the controversy between Fundamentalists and Modernists. The first part of her sermon simply catalogued the standard criticisms of the biblical evidence, but she quickly turned to a feminist critique of the doctrine that focused on both the idea of the Marian secret, the doctrine of sin presupposed by the virgin birth, and the implications of the doctrine concerning human sexuality.[18]

Previous defenders of the doctrine had explained the absence of the teaching in the first generation as a result of "feminine modesty." Mary, they argued, did not want the knowledge of the miraculous birth to be made known, so she had kept it a secret, and out of respect for her the evangelists did not include it in the gospels until after her death. Such an explanation, Royden explained, might satisfy Victorian male theologians, but anyone with a knowledge of how women really thought and felt would view it as ludicrous. Would "modesty" have been enough to keep any woman, much less one of the character of Mary, from proclaiming such a remarkable wonder? Royden asked. Such an explanation presupposed that "modesty" was a more powerful motivating force among women than truth. "There are limits," she chided, "to the follies into which 'feminine modesty' will carry the silliest of women, let alone the greatest and best who ever breathed, the mother of our Lord." No woman would act in this way; if the event had occurred in the way in which it was represented in Matthew and Luke, Mary would not have kept silent for sixty years but rather would have proclaimed it as one of the greatest acts of God, whatever the personal consequences for speaking out might have been. The absence of the doctrine of the earliest records accordingly could not be explained away by "feminine modesty."[19]

Furthermore, Royden explained, the doctrine presupposed a patriarchal view of sin. Because Christians believed that all humans participated from birth in the original sin of Adam, the early church had to explain how Jesus was exempted from this stain. The doctrine had evolved to explain how Jesus was free from the curse of original sin. But to say that a virgin birth liberated one from original sin implied that the male was the creator of life, and that the female was merely a passive instrument. It assumed that the child was the offspring of the male alone. Could any modern woman accept this? "Is there any mother in this congregation," she asked, "who dreams that if, by a miracle, her child had been born without a father, it would by that fact alone, have been exempted from human frailty?" Male theologians might so speculate, but women knew better. "I wish women had more to do with the building up of our theology. They would never have fallen into so extravagant an error as to suppose a child's mother had no portion in the nature of her child."[20]

Finally Royden argued that the doctrine rested upon a perverse view of human sexuality. As early as 1919 she had proclaimed, "One cannot resist an uneasy suspicion that [the virgin birth] arose in the minds of men out of a sense that there is something fundamentally base about sex, that for God to be born of the ordinary love of an ordinary man and woman . . . was impossible, because the human desire of men and women for each other is ignoble, is even base." She often reiterated this criticism.[21] In her 1921 sermon she related how she had personally been advised by a [male] cleric to abstain from sexual intercourse before receiving communion, because such actions were a "concession to our lower nature." The view that human sexuality was somehow low and tawdry permeated the idea of the virgin birth and its presupposition that God could not enter the world through the normal love of a man and women but only in an unnatural way.

Royden's criticisms are significant because they pushed the virgin birth debate into two of the most sensitive areas of the postwar world: sexuality and the role of women. As one popular journal noted, Royden's ideas were important because they gave "a woman's view on an issue that, in a peculiar sense, belongs to womanhood." Still another commentator observed that the real question in the virgin birth was not one of doctrine but rather one of morality: "who organized the family, God or the devil?" The issues Royden raised could not be easily ignored. Even the conservative apologist Gresham Machen had to admit that Protestant defenders of the doctrine had paid little attention to the person of Mary. "We are indeed as far as anyone from accepting the Roman catholic picture of the Blessed Virgin. But we also think that Protestants, in the reaction against this picture, have failed to do justice to the Mother of our lord. . . . The virgin Mary is no lifeless automaton, but a person who lives and moves — a person who from that day to this had the power to touch all simple and childlike hearts." Although Machen refused to ally himself with the traditional Catholic emphasis on the centrality of the Virgin Mary, he nonetheless recognized that a plausible scenario of the virgin birth, as Roman Catholics had long known, had to include a persuasive picture of the Mother Mary.[22]

The American debate over the virgin birth was a central part of the great Modernist-Fundamentalist debate that engulfed American Protestantism during the 1920s. It raged most intensely among American Episcopalians and Presbyterians, but was found among Baptists and Methodists as well.[23] The details of the controversy in the differing denominations need not concern us; what is important for our purposes is how the doctrine was attacked and defended, because this sheds light on the contours of religious sensibilities. We can take as representative a public debate over the doctrine held at Carnegie Hall in New York City, which featured the Fundamentalist John Roach Straton and the Unitarian Charles F. Potter. During 1924, Straton and Potter engaged in a series of debates on the key issues dividing Fundamentalists and Modernists: the Bible, evolution, the deity of Christ, and the virgin birth. These were decorous affairs, and the mantle of the still strong Protestant establishment hung proudly. Presidential opinions were invoked by both sides. The daily press eagerly reported on their outcome. The debates even involved judges, who were to determine a winner — judges who were not theologians but distinguished persons of the community such as justices, journalists, bankers, and the president of the Sons of the American Revolution. These august individuals strove to adjudicate which of these two versions of the great American Protestant faith was the authentic one.

Straton and Potter had split the first two debates: Straton had "won" the debate on the Bible, and Potter had "won" the one on evolution. Hence Straton carefully mounted his case for the virgin birth on the possibility, probability, and positive proofs of the doctrine. Because science could never disprove a miracle (or any other possible event), nothing made the doctrine inherently impossible. On the question of probability, he argued that the alternative explanations of the textual evidence were more improbable than the doctrine itself. Finally he attempted to address that question with which American Protestants had the most difficulty: why was it necessary to maintain the doctrine? On this third question Straton offered four answers: two theological (namely, that the virgin birth undergirded both the atonement and the deity of Christ), and two of a broader nature. In the first of these broader arguments, Straton argued that an acceptance of the doctrine preserved the authority of scripture: "To deny or reject it is to deny the integrity of the Bible and to reject its authority." To eschew one part of scripture was to impugn the entirety. Such an argument appealed to the long-standing place of the Bible in American Protestant culture. Straton's final defense was a new one, however. To reject the doctrine, he explained, was to reject an "essential Christian doctrine . . . of all the great branches of the Christian church." Protestants and Catholics, Anglicans and Orthodox all united in attesting to the virgin birth, and for American Protestants to reject it was to go against this universal voice. "Here is one doctrine upon which Protestants, Roman Catholics, and Greek Catholics stand together," he wrote. Such was not an argument typical of conservative American Protestantism, much less of the Baptist tradition in which Straton was trained. Yet the crisis of the 1920s saw the Protestant Fundamentalist Straton appealing to the universal voice of Christendom, and citing as support for his views the writings of Anglocatholic Charles Gore and the Roman Catholic archbishop Patrick Hayes.[24]

In light of the events of the hour, however, such an appeal was less surprising. In New York City, for example, both the Episcopal bishop William Manning and the Roman Catholic archbishop Patrick Hayes were strong and vocal defenders of the doctrine of the virgin birth. Indeed American Catholics, in many ways for the first time in their history, were being increasingly drawn into the religious debates of Protestants. The Paulists of New York in early 1924 were having a series of public lectures on the contested doctrines, and Archbishop Hayes pronounced that March 25, Annunciation day (when Catholic Christians traditionally celebrated the appearance of the angel to the

Virgin Mary), would be set aside as a day of support for the doctrine of the virgin birth and of contrition for the "thoughtless insults and blasphemous denials" of the doctrine.[25]

The judges, however, were not persuaded by Straton's eloquence; they awarded the debate to Potter. Potter's speeches included references to all of the traditional textual problems concerning the virgin birth. Furthermore he appealed to Maude Royden's argument that the doctrine undermined the family by "degrading holy wedlock." Yet in the conclusion of his address Potter countered Straton's appeal to the great branches of the Christian church with his own brand of ecumenical appeal, one that was pan-Protestant in nature. To declare that the virgin birth was an essential doctrine, or that to deny it was to separate oneself from the Christian flock, Potter argued, was to imply that some of the most respected persons in American society were not real Christians. "Will my opponent dare to say," he challenged, "that the entire Unitarian denomination . . . which has twenty-two names in the Hall of Fame out of sixty-five there, and the . . . liberal Quakers, . . . containing some of the best people alive today, will he dare to say that these are not Christians?"[26] In particular, to draw the line in this way was to call into question the Christianity of persons such as Charles Eliot, the Unitarian president of Harvard, and William Howard Taft, former president and current chief justice of the supreme court.

Potter's appeal to Unitarians and Quakers may seem odd to us at the end of the twentieth century, but in the early 1920s these groups still held an important place in the hearts of American Protestants. They uniquely represented those key Protestant principles of free intellectual inquiry and benevolence to the world. Furthermore, an appeal to these two groups inevitably touched an ancient memory of those in the audience. If anything bound together the English-speaking northern American Protestant community, it was the memory of the Civil War. Lincoln and the war hung heavy upon this decade as the war generation slowly died away. It was only in 1922 that the Lincoln Memorial was finally dedicated, and throughout these years books and articles about Lincoln flowed from both the religious and secular presses. Indeed, Ida Tarbell's popular and influential study of Lincoln, *In the Footsteps of the Lincolns,* was at the time avidly discussed. As the *New York Times* had editorialized, Tarbell's biography reminded the American people once again of the martyred president's "liberty loving heritage" and strong commitment to freedom. Lincoln and the war represented the very best of the nation, and by implication, the very best blending of Protestantism and civil religion. And few groups were more associated with the great old cause than Unitarians and Quakers.

The ironic unspoken subtheme of the Straton-Potter debate was the question: who were one's allies? Historically, whatever their differences, American Protestants had seen themselves as having more in common with each other than with Roman Catholics. They might disagree on theology or interpretation of scripture, but they were on one side of the line and Catholics were on the other. The virgin birth debate potentially undermined this confidence. If the doctrine were an essential mark of Christianity, then conservative Protestants were in fact closer to Roman Catholics than they were to their liberal brethren, and the pope was more of a Christian than Charles Eliot and William Howard Taft. There may indeed have been more than a hint of rhetorical posturing when newspapers like the *New York Times* used the term "Fundamentalist" to describe Roman Catholics as well as conservative Protestants like Straton. When the issue became framed in such categories, it is small wonder that the august and establishmentarian judges, far more attune with culture than theology, awarded the debate to Potter.

As Americans debated the virgin birth throughout the 1920s, they always returned to the thorny question of why the belief was necessary. Since the 1860s other alleged teachings of the Bible, particularly those addressing creation and evolution, had been modified, and yet the faith seemed to survive. Why was a belief in this particular miracle essential? Even those who professed a belief in the virgin birth were unsure of its necessity. "There are laymen of high standing, and clergymen of great distinction, and professors of undoubted piety and wide influence who have become agnostics on the doctrine of the Virgin Birth, and some of them reject it," wrote the popular Congregationalist preacher, Charles Jefferson. Even though he could profess the doctrine, he nonetheless had come to believe that although what the doctrine symbolized — the unique relationship between Jesus and God — was essential, the doctrine itself was not, and individuals who could no longer affirm it had a place in the community and even the ministry. Jefferson was not alone. A 1929 survey of Chicago-area Protestant clergy, conducted by the psychologist George Herbert Betts, testified to a wide and growing disparity over the belief in the virgin birth. Almost one in five of the ministers surveyed denied the doctrine, whereas one in ten was agnostic. Of Episcopal clergy, 25 percent either rejected or doubted its veracity, as did 31 percent of the Presbyterians, 46 percent of the Methodists, and an overwhelming 76 percent of the Congregationalists. The future of the doctrine seemed even more dubious. The survey included data from "five theological schools" representing "three large denominations," and among these individuals there was a dramatic rejection of the traditional teaching. Three out of four seminarians surveyed either rejected or doubted the doctrine.[27]

Betts's poll was anything but scientific, but it did suggest that the traditional assumptions regarding the miraculous were increasingly doubted and that the virgin birth was the weak link in the Protestant Christian faith. There was overwhelming agreement on the reality of God and the sinlessness of Christ; and even the claim that Jesus rose from the dead continued to have broad support. But the survey revealed doubts not only about the miraculous conception, but also about biblical authority. Only a small majority of those surveyed could agree "that the Bible was written by men chosen and supernaturally endowed by God . . . and by him given the exact message they were to write."[28] Furthermore, over two-thirds of those surveyed accepted at least in principle the fundamental presupposition of higher biblical criticism — that the "criticism and evaluation applied to other literature and history should be applied to the Bible." It is little wonder that the attempt to anchor the doctrine of the virgin birth solely on the authority of the scriptural text was not universally persuasive. Hence the problem confronting the doctrine's defenders: why was it a necessary belief to hold?

No one wrestled with this question with more vigor than did Gresham Machen. From his position at Princeton Theological Seminary, Machen was the leading intellectual Fundamentalist spokesman, as well as one of the leading advocates of the conservative theological tradition within American Presbyterianism. Perhaps the capstone of his intellectual career was his erudite *The Virgin Birth of Christ,* published in 1930. Machen had been studying the infancy narratives since his seminary days, and his volume was the product of prodigious effort and research.[29]

Machen's *Virgin Birth* was both an impressive defense of the cogency of the biblical narrative and a piercing criticism of some of the more fanciful modern theories to explain it away. As we have already seen, for Machen the key question was the supernatural nature of the event. Accordingly he had little patience with attempts to salvage the religiosity of the event by suggesting a natural cause such as parthenogenesis: "If the virgin birth is reduced to the level of biological triviality, it becomes quite unbelievable. . . . But if the virgin birth represents the beginning of a new era in the course of the universe, a true entrance of the creative power of God, in sharp distinction from the order of nature, then we think, when it is taken in connection with the entire phenomenon of Jesus's life and particularly in connection with the evidence of His resurrection, it is no longer a meaningless freak, but becomes an organic part of the mighty redeeming work of God."[30]

Machen's volume moved powerfully toward its culminating "Conclusions and Consequences." As might be expected, he linked the acceptance of the doctrine primarily to the issue of the authority of scripture: "If therefore the virgin birth be rejected, let us cease talking about the 'authority of the Bible' or the 'infallibility of Scripture' or the like." But at this point Machen stumbled. Perhaps he inadvertently looked over his shoulder to glance at his Anglo-catholic supporters, but in any event a noticeable break in his rhetorical stride occurs. One recalls that Charles Gore and others had anchored the necessity of accepting the virgin birth on their catholic view of credalism — that the church rightly defines the nature of the faith and that individual believers are called to submit to its authority. While approaching his conclusion, Machen attempted to side-step this conclusion and avoid soiling his Protestant sandals with Catholic ideas. "We are in little agreement," he assured his readers, "with those who make the Apostles' Creed, in which the virgin birth is contained, the be-all and end-all of their Christian profession. Just as important is the Christian doctrine of redemption — the Christian doctrine of sin and grace — about which the Apostles' Creed says scarcely a word." One must avoid at all cost the catholic error. But as a Protestant, why was the doctrine essential, and could one be a Christian without professing it?

Protestants (particularly English Reformed Protestants) and Catholics had been divided for centuries over the question of what made one a true believer. Part of the Puritan revolution of Elizabethan England, out of which evangelicalism emerged, was the assertion that an external profession of faith was not sufficient evidence — rather there had to be signs of divine grace working within the soul. The tension between form and spirit, externals and internals, had long been a subject of debate within American Protestant evangelicalism. But there had always been an awareness that to reject this tension, and to say that it was the externals that were definitive, was to separate oneself from the Protestant world. The specter of credalism swung Machen back, and his long treatise ended in a surprisingly modest way. Christianity, he affirmed, was ultimately the relationship of the soul to God, and God alone was to be the judge. "Who can tell exactly how much knowledge of the facts of Christ is necessary to have a saving faith? None but God can tell. Some knowledge is certainly required, but exactly how much is required we cannot say." What was apparent was that one's denial of the doctrine could indicate that one's soul was not in right relationship with God. "Perhaps not one man out of a hundred of those who deny the virgin birth today gives any real clear evidence of possessing saving faith," he argued. Even for Machen, the necessity of holding the belief in the miraculous birth was to be held in check by the fundamental Protestant principle that internals and not externals were the mark of the Christian.[31]

The debate over the virgin birth in America during the 1920s was of course far more involved, and this analysis fails to do it full justice. But for our purposes we may conclude that the debate awakened for the first time an awareness of a new fault line in the Christian world. Machen, Straton, and the other conservative defenders of the virgin birth began to sense that they were in fact drawing closer to some of their long-standing Anglican, Roman Catholic, and Orthodox opponents than they were to fellow Protestants. One saw within some places in the conservative movement a tentative reaching out for support from these traditional adversaries. But the loyalty to the Protestant ideal was strong, and the ties of culture and history were stronger still. In the end, these bonds hindered any fundamental reevaluation.

The Question of Healing

Although the virgin birth debate is occasionally remembered as a key part of the religious controversy during the 1920s, the vexing question of religious healing is now almost forgotten. Yet at the time, healing generated dozens of books and scores of pamphlets, and in the early part of the decade it was discussed across the Atlantic even more than was the debate over the virgin birth.

As one recalls, the question of religious healing had elicited a wide spectrum of responses in the early years of the century. The discussion abated somewhat during the war years, but immediately after the war it began with a new intensity. It is of course not surprising that an interest in healing would arise in the wake of the war. Just as with spiritualism, the possibility of faith healing offered both practical benefit and theodicean comfort to those suffering the wounds of war. Furthermore, as students of Pentecostalism have shown, there continued to be a wide interest in the gift of healing among members of the young Pentecostal community, even though the Pentecostal movement rarely entered into the larger public discussion.

But by the early 1920s the English-speaking world was abuzz with the question of faith healing, and if one were to designate an agent provocateur for this phenomenon it would have to be the Anglican layman James Moore Hickson. Although little remembered today, Hickson (1867–1933) was arguably the most famous proponent of Christian healing in the English-speaking world. Hickson's early life gave hints of his later ministry. His grandfather was a doctor, and as a young boy Hickson was torn between a desire to be either a doctor or a priest "that I might help people who were sick and in trouble." At age fourteen, however, he healed a cousin of neuralgia through the laying on of hands. Other healings followed. His mother became convinced that he possessed a special gift and urged him "to pray that [he] might be guided as to its use." For reasons never made explicit, however, the young Hickson first chose a career in business rather than healing, and accordingly dedicated himself to wealth rather than health. But by the turn of the century the evidence of his healing charism became too strong, and after studying physiology, anatomy, medical electricity, and massage, he entered into the ministry of healing. In 1905 he founded the Society of Emmanuel to advance the ministry of healing in Britain. During the first decade of the new century, Hickson gained a certain amount of notoriety. His volume *The Healing of Christ in His Church,* which was published in 1908, so impressed Archbishop of Canterbury Randall Davidson that he gave copies of it to all of the bishops attending the Lambeth Conference.[32]

It was not until a decade later, however, that Hickson became an international figure. In 1919 he made a tour of the United States. His mission began in Boston, and there his success was dramatic. Starting from historic St. Paul's Cathedral, he set forth his evangel of spiritual healing. Thousands attended, and according to news reports hundreds had to be turned away daily. He then took his message on the road, and visited over thirty-three cites from Boston to San Francisco, lecturing in Episcopal churches.[33] Hickson's tour became a much discussed event in the daily press, but even more important a factor in his rise to popularity Hickson caught the attention of William Manning, Episcopal rector of Trinity Church, Wall Street. Manning, who in a few years would be elected bishop of New York and who would dedicate himself to the dual mission of maintaining true doctrine and constructing the largest cathedral church in the world (St. John the Divine), was rector of the wealthiest and arguably the most prestigious church in America. His embrace of Hickson had tremendous consequences. As one journalist at the time observed, Manning opened the doors of "the most exclusive religious edifices in America" for Hickson, and in doing so introduced the question of faith healing to many who had theretofore been unaware of it. Furthermore Manning convinced the General Convention of the Episcopal church, which was then meeting in Detroit, to establish a commission to investigate the question of faith healing. A few months later, at the worldwide meeting of Anglican bishops (the Lambeth Conference), a resolution was passed to study the question of faith healing, and in 1920 Randall Davidson established a committee to likewise investigate the phenomenon. The Church of Scotland (though with less fanfare) also began to study the question of faith healing.

It is hard to overemphasize the impact of these events. The social, cultural, and intellectual status of the Church of England legitimated a discussion of the question of faith healing on both sides of the Atlantic. Indeed, even advocates of Pentecostal-style faith healing acknowledged the importance of Hickson and the Anglican interest in healing. The American Pentecostal faith healer F. F. Bosworth gleefully cited Hickson and the American Episcopal interim report on healing as testimony from "the most godly and able teachers of the Church" in support of divine healing.[34] As we have shown, an interest in healing within Anglicanism was neither new, nor, on a theological level, surprising. The sacramental focus of their theology made Anglicans sensitive to the question of the spiritual effect upon the material, and sacramentalism offered a framework for interpreting a continuing divine activity in healing.

Catholic-leaning Anglicans furthermore believed that a revival of the practice of anointing the sick allowed the church to compete with healing movements like Christian Science and Mind Cure while reclaiming its Catholic sacramental heritage. As we saw in chapter 7, healing was a key point of conflict between Catholics and Modernists, and indeed was far more critical than were issues such as biblical inerrancy or eschatology.

But for the great American religious public, the eruption of concern over religious healing among Episcopalians seemed exotic, and somewhat alluring. The appeal can be seen in an article by Mabel Potter Daggett's article "Are There Modern Miracles?" published in the *Ladies Home Journal*. As Daggett explained, "The denomination that is the most established and conservative of all indorsed the efficacy of prayer as an instrument in the cure of disease. . . . It is the old time religion but with a new content that makes it as secular as it is sacred: Christ the Redeemer of the world from sickness as well as sin; a faith as valuable for here as the hereafter." Those attracted to the new evangel were from the heart of the American establishment. People were now opening "their Bibles to Psalm ciii, 3 and point[ing] to you a God 'who forgiveth all thine iniquities, who healeth all thy diseases.' . . . Are they crazy? But Smith is a judge perhaps, and Brown is, say, a member of the Republican campaign committee. They are as regular as that." Clearly for judges and Republicans to take the promises of the Bible seriously was big news.[35]

In other ways as well, Daggett's article reflected the heightened class structure of American denominationalism. Although focusing on the movement within the Episcopal church, she also included discussion of both Aimee Semple McPherson and Paul Rader. Both are now better known to scholars than is Hickson—McPherson is remembered as the most flamboyant (if not important) American faith healer of the 1920s, and Rader is known as the successor of A. B. Simpson in the Christian and Missionary Alliance. But for Daggett both were validated because their cause was now being taken up by more mainline clergy. "For a few years past," she explained, "it has been happening in city after city, that some important Main Street minister has put on his hat and gone across the town to investigate what the little obscure Christian and Missionary Alliance was doing to draw such crowds." By the early 1920s, Daggett confirmed, the healing movement had spread far and wide:

"[It] is sweeping over America [and] is challenging the attention of as excited throngs as watched the aeroplanes ten years ago." Proponents of the movement could now be found among the Congregationalists, Methodists, and Presbyterians.[36]

As had been the case earlier in the century, fundamental disagreements continued to exist over the understanding of a healing ministry, and the three models that emerged at the turn of the century — the thaumaturgical, the sacramental, and the therapeutic — all had their supporters. Similarly the question over whether religious healing could affect organic as well as functional diseases also continued to be debated. Hickson, for example, tended to appeal to the thaumaturgical model. He and his supporters saw the gift of healing as being that promised in 1 Corinthians 12, where healing is listed as one of the gifts of the Spirit. Hickson explained the working of this gift in sacramental language, but it was a sacramental language with a difference.

> Healing by touch in the name of Jesus is sacramental in nature. . . . The human instrument is but a channel through which Christ heals. Even though the instrument may possess the gift of healing from God, he still has no power in himself to heal, but only to mediate the divine healing. . . . To claim any power of his own would be to cut himself off from the Source, and his work would cease to be spiritual healing in a sacramental sense and would become only suggestion or magnetism. . . . Spiritual healing is thus the transference of healing virtue from Christ to man through man by the laying on of hands, Holy Unction, or other means of grace through which He works. We may describe the method as an extension of the Incarnation.

The church as the body of Christ healed because Christ healed, and in the same direct manner. But the gift of healing was given to select individuals in the church and not necessarily to the ordained ministry. Only a certain few received this charism. These individuals were the material means through which divine healing was brought into the world.[37]

Like earlier proponents of the thaumaturgical model, Hickson believed the restoration of this spiritual gift linked the present age with the power of the biblical age. Through it, the "atmosphere of Galilee" was reclaimed. "The Ante-Nicene Church was a healing Church," he wrote, "Will the same be said of the Church in the twentieth century, or will Christ be among us as our healer still despised and rejected of men, a man of sorrows and acquainted with disease?" A healing ministry was foundational for the unchanging message of the church. It reflected God's benevolence, displeasure with illness, and power over matter as well as spirit. Healing had been a key gift of the ancient church, and the loss of this gift robbed the church of its power. "The Church will never be a life-giving Church again," he warned, "until she goes back to the glow and enthusiasm of the early days . . . and becomes a healing Church."[38]

Hickson and his supporters, however, hinted that Christian healing further gave to the church an authority of power that transcended the authority of mere knowledge. In the Bible the church was called to heal but not necessarily to understand how the healing worked, because ultimately God was the healer. For proponents of this view, herein lay the key difference between medical healing and religious healing. In medicine, healing rested on knowledge and was correspondingly dependent upon it. In religion, however, healing came from promise alone and was hence independent of knowledge. To be sure, Hickson and his supporters were respectful of the medical profession and acknowledged that spiritual healing could come through spiritual doctors as much as through anyone. Yet they nevertheless emphasized the uniqueness of religious healing. In the words of one supporter, "If we depend upon our experience, if we insist upon scientific investigations to prove the validity of healings, if we wait upon tabulations and testimonials, we shall found our work upon a false ground."[39]

The gift of healing for Hickson had two other important functions. First it emphasized the practical nature of the gospel message. "It gives to the Church a point of contact with the 'man on the street' which nothing else can give," he explained. In a world in which the reality of the spiritual was being lost, divine healing reminded all that God was still active. Second, the revival of the gift of healing would help restore one final aspect of the ancient church, its sense of unity. It offered hope for ecumenical cooperation, because divine healing "breaks down all barriers and helps to unite all communions of the Church of Christ." For Hickson the divisions of Christianity were tied to the Christian community's emphasis upon tradition or human reason, rather than trust in the Spirit. Accordingly to reclaim the gift of healing might be a first step toward restoring the unity of the ancient church.[40]

Most of the debate over healing, however, occurred between advocates of the sacramental and the therapeutic approaches. Sacramentalists claimed that physical healing came through sacramental grace, whereas those who believed in the therapeutic approach linked healing to advancing knowledge of modern psychology. Indeed in both England and America these two camps were represented by competing organizations. The Guild of Health reflected the therapeutic ideal in both nations, and the Guild of St. Raphael and the Society of the Nazarene represented the sacramental and liturgical approach in English and American Anglicanism, respectively. The scope of the debate was more clearly defined in England than in America, because in England a well-defined group of advocates for the sacramental model squared off against proponents of the therapeutic. In America, however, the sacramentalists were few and were largely limited to the Episcopal church. The sacerdotal and liturgical presuppositions of the sacramentalist approach failed to resonate among American Protestants. Yet the few American spokespersons for the sacramentalist position argued passionately for it.

The sacramentalists contended that the healing ministry was central to the Christian task and played a key part in the restoration and redemption of humankind. Like Hickson, they claimed that healing was rightly the unifying thread connecting the ancient church and the present. "Spiritual healing," explained J. Wilson Sutton, "is one of the normal activities of the church, for which it is commissioned today as it was over nineteen hundred years ago. . . . If God be what we know Him to be, miracles are not only possible today but they are the most natural thing in the world." Only by restoring a healing ministry could the present-day church reclaim the power of the ancient church. Sacramentalists noted that in the ancient world Christian apologists, when arguing for the reality of their message, did not appeal to the miracles of Christ, but to the great wonders that God continued to perform in the church. Such an appeal to modern evidences was desperately needed if the church was to maintain its position in the twentieth century.[41]

Proponents of the therapeutic healing in turn offered a different model for understanding both healing and the relationship between God and the world. For them, the nature of Christian healing was fundamentally the reintegration of the harmony between body and soul. Health, according to Frank Cole Sherman, the president of the American Guild of Health, was based upon a "sound, true, practical mysticism" through which believers come "into conscious intimate fellowship with God the Eternal Spirit." Inner harmony was the tonic that restored health.[42]

One finds reflected in these advocates the same ambiguity concerning the miraculous that one saw earlier in the Emmanuel Movement. On the one hand they were willing to reject any idea of a miracle (either as a biblical or modern concept) as an isolated exhibition of divine power. They willingly affirmed the uniformity of nature and its laws, and that God worked through the uniformity of nature and not against it. To seek the miraculous was somehow gauche, and any person who could not see the presence of deity in "the life activity of the cell or in the autumn coloring of the leaves" had an injured soul. However, they still believed that prayer unlocked a power that could affect physical nature. Invoking the authority of William James, Sherman affirmed, "energy which but for prayer would be bound is by prayer set free and operates in some point . . . of the world of experienced phenomenon or fact."[43] At least on this minimal level, Sherman affirmed that spirit could intervene and transform the physical.

Yet here one sees a subtle retreat from the more expansive language of an earlier year. One recalls that in the earlier part of the century advocates of the therapeutic view of healing saw in it a reclaiming of the lost power of the gospel. Elwood Worcester and Samuel McComb viewed this power as a source of the revitalization of the church. Indeed even during the 1920s McComb saw in the uniting of "medical power, psychic power and a strong religious faith" not only a means to reclaim the healing power of Jesus but also a way of bringing about a "New Reformation" that the world desperately needed. In contrast, the language of the Guild of Health on both sides of the Atlantic was far more reserved. Members preferred to speak of the role of faith in maintaining health rather than in healing. In McComb's words, "The primary stress of a constructive movement must be placed on 'health' and not on 'healing.' The word 'health' implies 'wholeness'. It covers every part of man's being, body, mind, and spirit, all of which are to be brought into harmonious relationship with each other. The whole is to be made healthful."[44]

This rhetorical change may stem from the erosion by the 1920s of categories that earlier proponents had assumed. Worcester, one recalls, had suggested that the subliminal self was a sluice opening the individual to the great ocean of the universal spirit. He in turn used this psychological category to give scientific justification for religious healing and to distinguish it from mere autosuggestion. The subliminal mind as sluice was a concept no longer available to proponents of the Guild of Health in the 1920s, and they tended to explain their endeavor in very different terms, much more in keeping with William James's typology of "refined supernaturalism." Sherman, for example, grounded his philosophy of healing on a combination of "devotionalism, modernism, and uplift." The prayer he advised persons to recite daily was "God is Infinite Creative Life. I am a conscious individuated center of that One Life that is always creating, healing, sustaining, and perfecting. Spirit is supreme over matter. Evil is impotent." The line between religious healing and mind cure was subtly shrunken. Furthermore Sherman claimed that the mark of true spirituality was that each must bear his or her own burden. It was a sign of weakness to seek out another as a healer. "We want someone to do for us what we are loath to do for ourselves."[45]

This idea that through the power of knowledge one could achieve inner harmony had significant implications for how the ministry of Jesus was to be understood. If Christ's ministry was spiritual and didactic, and if the core of his message was that the right ordering of spirit brought health, what purpose did the passion serve? According to Harold Anson, head of the English Guild of Health, the crucifixion of Jesus, instead of being the culmination of his mission, was a regrettable faux pas. "The heart of the problem is reached when we ask whether the crucifixion of Jesus was a necessity for the salvation of the world or not," Anson wrote. "I have always believed that an even greater good might have resulted if . . . the Jews had accepted instead of rejecting Him, and Christianity had evolved in a healthy way out of Judaism, instead of being tinged with . . . the adoration of suffering and death." An understanding of the true nature of healing revealed the true heart of the gospel.[46]

As was the case earlier, sacramentalists and therapeuticians often pointedly disagreed about the true nature of healing. For those who took the therapeutic approach, it was rank superstition to believe that the power of spirit worked through sacrament and ritual. "Will the Church be content with a mere 'laying on of hands' or the administration of 'the rite of unction' or the exercising of a supposed 'gift of healing?'" asked Sherman. "Must we not be ardent and sincere in our search for the truth, ever unwilling to accept as fact what does not have solid evidence behind it, and, keeping our poise and balance, never be led astray by our zeal and enthusiasm?" In contrast, the sacramentalists likened opposition to the church's ministry of healing to the rejection of Christ's own healings by the Pharisees: "The modern Pharisee objects that the healing work was done by one technically unqualified — though such a one might be eminently well qualified by faith and personal holiness. Or they will insist that a simple obedience to Christ's command to heal breaks the unwritten law of professional etiquette and is an infringement upon the rights and prerogatives of the medical profession."[47]

The question of religious healing was hotly debated in the first half of the decade, but the debate was not limited to these three positions. Significant voices within the religious communities asserted that the churches ought to take no role in the sickroom other than that of consolation and support.

Typical of this attitude was Charles Reynolds Brown, dean of Yale Divinity School. Although he fully acknowledged that the new psychological insight regarding the power of mind over body allowed for a more persuasive picture of Jesus as a healer, he nonetheless cautioned his ministerial colleagues from embracing healing. Healing ministries might be popular, but this popularity hid two pitfalls. First, embracing faith healing would lead to a loss of social status for clergy. Those interested in faith healing were found "on the frontiers of discriminating intelligence, in foreign missionary work among people just in process of entering upon higher modes of thought, and among less fortunate people in the cities where the Salvation Army officers and the rescue missions are at work." Second, indulging in healing threatened the intellectual and professional expertise of the clergy. For decades liberal Protestants had attempted to bolster their status in a changing America by professionalizing their theological education, and now some ministers appeared willing, in Brown's view, to abandon this professional status for a mess of mystical pottage. The average minister had no medical training and almost no psychological training. All he or she brought was common sense, but "good intentions and ordinary common sense are not sufficient for many of the responsibilities which confront us." When clergy ignored the division of labor between themselves and doctors, they undermined the claims of their own expert knowledge. By implication, if through simple common sense a minister could claim the right to heal, could not a simple layperson through common sense rightly interpret the scripture and do theology? Brown advised those ministers who were interested in the issue of health to rededicate themselves to the Social Gospel and root out those social forces and destructive appetites that were the breeding ground of sickness.[48]

Brown was of course not alone in seeing the movement toward healing as a retreat by the churches, and his criticisms would be echoed by many. No one elaborated more eloquently upon the dangers of intellectual retrogression implicit in healing ministries than did the English Modernist bishop H. Hensley Henson. Henson was perhaps the most notorious of the English Modernist bishops, and his views on the virgin birth and miracles were well known on both sides of the Atlantic. But by the 1920s he turned his ire against spiritual healing. Whether in its thaumaturgical form (proposed by Hickson, whom he particularly disliked), its sacramental form, or even its therapeutic form, religious healing was detrimental to the reconciliation of the church and the modern age. The fascination with healing, Henson explained, was grounded in the allure of the wonderful, and as such always tied to superstition: "Sickrooms are the breeding-places of superstition, as marshes are of the mosquitoes which carry malaria." True Christian spirituality had nothing to do with the base belief that one invokes the spirit world to benefit or change the material: "the prayerwheel is not a Christian instrument." According to Henson, the idea of spiritual healing was a corruption of the original gospel message that entered the Christian world during periods of ignorance such as the Middle Ages. It had been purged at the time of the Reformation but was now threatening to return. Crude demonology, false biblical exegesis, and "preposterous science" buttressed the medieval interest in exorcism and unction, and these should not be recaptured. Henson likened talk of spiritual healing to the superstitions of Italian peasants carrying images of saints in procession hoping that these might influence God. The choice for Henson was clear:

Protestantism and progress or Catholicism and superstition. Like Charles Reynolds Brown, he urged that those interested in health should eschew spiritual healing and take up a more practical cause, which for him was organized athletics. Healing should be left to physicians.[49]

The question of superstition, I should emphasize, was troublesome even for persons sympathetic with the possibility of healing. It was all well and good to claim for the present age the healing power of scripture, but how much else of the biblical world view had to go along with it? As we saw with John Alexander Dowie, once one accepted a thaumaturgical view of healing there was a tendency to accept literally more and more of the biblical world view. James Moore Hickson, for example, might have been an attractive figure, but he too fell victim to this tendency, particularly concerning the idea of the demonic. He argued that demons and departed spirits attached themselves to material objects, including the hair that was used to fashion the wigs and hairpieces of many of his wealthy matrons. As one writer noted, "After one of his healing missions in New York he told one of his attendants that he felt much of the trouble with a great many women was due to the spirits of departed persons, whose hair they were wearing." Indeed evil spirits, according to this view, could cause not only sickness but other evils, and Hickson allegedly suggested that the problems then confronting Ireland stemmed from that land being in bondage to evil spirits. Such speculations cast a shadow upon the divine healing movement and posed the question of whether one could accept the idea of spiritual healing without agreeing to its effects on hairstyling and international relations.[50]

The issue of professionalization was even more critical, particularly in America. American Protestants confronted an apparent upswing of interest in healing, but they had fewer options than their English compatriots. Except among some Episcopalians, sacramentalism was not a real alternative. Thus one observes a distinct dichotomy between clerical and lay reaction to healing. All sorts of healing fads flourished during the 1920s, from Christian Science to Mind Cure, to Emil Coué's famous mantric advice "Day by day in very way I am getting better and better," but many American Protestant clerical intellectuals were skittish of them. Despite the popularity of healing ministries, it was argued, they should be rejected. As one writer noted, it was "better to lose thousands of communicants to Mrs. Eddy's church than to assume the liability of Mrs. Eddy's medical and religious heresies. . . . [We] can afford to wait for fuller knowledge of psychotherapy, the new psychology, the new medicine, but [we] cannot afford to endorse medical and religious quackery." In part clerical reticence may have been a reaction to the sharp criticism of many physicians. As one nerve specialist wrote, "As things are now, medical men would look no more kindly on the entrance of the clergy into the field of healing than if the day laborers invaded it." Another writer noted, "Let the shoemaker stick to his last. Let the clergyman heal the soul. Leave to the physician the attempt to cure disease." Still others urged that the idea of "miraculous healing" be categorically rejected and be regarded as a "crime against the laws of the Church, of religion, and of society." Any healing ministry that a cleric might wish to undertake, they argued, must be in a clinical situation "under the direction of a trained physician who is also a psychiatrist."[51]

Language of quackery was of course not new; we had encountered it in the 1880s. But the issue of professional status was expressed far more sharply in the 1920s than it had been forty years earlier. As historians of the medical profession in America have noted, these years saw a rapid advance in the socioeconomic level of physicians, particularly during the Progressive era, and this elevation in status had in large part left the ordained ministry in its wake. Furthermore, the language used by physicians (and I should emphasize that these were on the whole physicians who were also church members) minced no words about status and professionalization: a minister was not welcome in the sickroom. The paradox of professionalism had turned on the liberal proponents of the therapeutic model. They had argued that social status should be based on education and an openness to new ideas, but clearly physicians were more educated and more "modern" than clergy could ever hope to be. Moreover, as gatekeepers to the sickroom, physicians determined access to medical healing techniques. Although sacramentalists could challenge the presumptuousness of physicians and claim a uniquely clerical role in healing, advocates of the therapeutic found this response more difficult.

Reports from the established commissions on the question of faith healing finally came out in both the Church of England and the American Episcopal Church, and in both churches the pattern of the discussion and the eventual outcomes were the same.[52] Both churches had established commissions in the wake of the great popular excitement about healing (particularly the dramatic healings of Hickson), yet in the end the reports were lukewarm at best toward either the propriety or possibility of spiritual healing. Both reports held up the therapeutic model as more correct than the other alternatives. The English report noted that its investigations turned up no case of healing that was certifiably "miraculous" or unique. In all the alleged cases, one could find similar cases of healing wrought by "psychotherapy without religion," or by instances of "spontaneous healing." Both reports affirmed that the physician was the primary healing agent: the role of religion in healing was supportive. As the English authors affirmed: "The best and sanest form of healing by spiritual methods appeared to us to be when the aim was to relate the whole personality of the patient to the will of God, believing that physical harmony would normally result as a by-product of this harmony, but laying little stress upon merely physical results, or any ecclesiastical techniques."

The final report of the American Episcopalians followed in this pattern. It relied most heavily upon Sherman and the Guild of Health, and even borrowed from them the phrase "sound true practical mysticism." It likewise rejected both the thaumaturgical and sacramental models. "A sane, constructive health movement cannot be based upon the use of consecrated oil," the authors explained. "The same may be said of 'a gift of healing' . . . no movement could be based upon that!" Both reports recommended that the proper venue for clerical entrance into healing was through psychological training in order to ensure cooperation with "physician, surgeon, and psychiatrist."[53]

How does one explain this phenomenon of large-scale popular interest in healing coupled with a decidedly cool official position? Inevitably, many factors contributed to this outcome. The issue of ecclesiastical politics played a role, and the refusal of either commission to endorse sacramental anointing reflected broader ecclesiastical issues. Likewise the ground rules that the commissions established in order to validate a healing as miraculous — that is, that it could not merely be inexplicable, but also had to be unique and not found in the annals of either medicine or other religions — almost ensured that no healings would be deemed "miracles." But one should also note that perhaps the disparity between the reports and the public excitement stemmed from fundamentally different concerns. The popular excitement over healing in the early 1920s occurred because of the events themselves — events that seemed to make real religious ideas that had theretofore had often been merely words. As Mabel Daggett wrote, "Does Christ still heal? Let the doctrinal discussion wage. Suppose you lift your eyes and look on those who say he does. See! From the cook's cousin to the society lady and the man on the street, there's a shining in their face, there's a radiance in their whole personality. Something has happened to them."[54] The primary focus for Daggett and others attracted to the new healings was the vitality and transformation of individual lives. The commissioners, however, were acutely concerned with the theological debate that Daggett easily dismissed. They felt obliged to make intellectual, theological, and ecclesiastical sense of these claims and to reconcile them with the concerns of physicians, psychologists, theologians, and philosophers.

It is of little surprise that there should have been this discrepancy between clergy and lay believers on the topic of faith healing. As I suggested earlier, the generation of believers studied in this book were confronted with two questions. One was intellectual: How could one understand religious claims in the new intellectual environment? But the second was based on belief: How was one to ground faith in a world that no longer seemed to show the footprints of God? The interest in healings may be indicative of the continuing relevance of the belief-based query for persons in the 1920s, whereas the ambivalence of the official reports may reflect the continuing concern for the intellectual question.

Jesus and His Miracles

Beginning in the 1880s, as we have seen, efforts to distinguish between healing miracles and nature miracles gave new vitality to a rationalized view of the life of Jesus. Scholars like Adolph Harnack could argue for the fundamental historical reliability of the gospel narratives while seeing the alleged miracles contained there as having natural explanations. This new scholarly tack in turn encouraged advocates to link the biblical miracles and modern "wonders" and to use their understanding of miracles to provide insight into these wonders. This trend continued to find favor during the 1920s. Modernists continued to link the present with the past through the uniformity of nature, and claim that the expanding understanding of psychological nature made the miracles of Jesus more and more exoteric. As Frederick C. Grant explained, "If the healing miracles of the Gospels and of the early days of the Church — and of Mr. Hickson and other spiritual healers to-day — are perfectly natural results, under given conditions of the power of the power of God released by faith, then we have a clue to the meaning of other Gospel miracles."[55]

But as a knowledge of the possible natural means of gospel miracles became clearer, the opposite question ironically surfaced. Was there anything unique about the wonders of Jesus? One recalls that the rationalizing agenda had been developed by Modernists to better hold on to the figure of Jesus. Perhaps, however, they had succeeded too well. By the 1920s Jesus and his miracles were in danger of being reduced to the level of the human realm.

E. R. Micklem attempted to address this question in *Miracles and the New Psychology*, one of the most detailed and sophisticated (not to mention oft-quoted) treatments of the dominical miracles to appear during the decade. Micklem's argument had two parts. The first was that although Jesus' miracles could not be reduced to suggestion, they were nonetheless in conformity with the laws of nature and could be understood through the use of the new psychology. Jesus healed through the power of his personality, Micklem explained: "Jesus cured by bringing to the sufferers life, and His contact with them, whether physical or psychical, was a life giving contact; that is to say He brought them into touch with God." The second part of Micklem's thesis, however, was that Jesus was unique, and accordingly his works were qualitatively different from those of any other person. "If the argument in the discussion above is valid it follows that modern scientific psychotherapy, while it may (and I think it does) very considerably help our understanding of the cures in the N. T., yet does not supply us with the complete explanation of them."[56] The new psychology was helpful in setting the healing miracles of Jesus within a broad framework of law and uniformity, but the miracles themselves remained an unfathomable mystery.

Another author to play upon this theme of regularity yet mystery was the Modernist American Congregational minister Lloyd C. Douglas. Douglas was a regular contributor to the *Christian Century* throughout the 1920s. He published in 1927 a volume titled *Those Disturbing Miracles,* which offered a Modernist pastoral interpretation of the miracles of Jesus because "those who while deeply revering the Bible as an unsurpassed record of a great race's spiritual evolution, are not prepared to accept its stories of magical deeds." Many believed that it was impossible to enter into the world of naive superstition while being faithful to the modern outlook. Accordingly Douglas offered imaginative retellings of the great events. In his hands the miraculous wine at Cana became a story of the transforming power of Jesus' presence; the stilling of the storm became an account of the power of Christ to calm the stormy breast; and the feeding of the five thousand (where he notes that the crowd was subdivided into groups of fifty) a story of how charity and brotherhood is easier in small groups than in large.[57]

But when he turned to the miracles of healing, Douglas chose not to allegorize them. Instead he displayed them as signs of the transforming power of Jesus. He cautioned his fellow Modernists from purging these stories of their profound mystery: "We self-confessed Modernists must have a care lest, in our honest and commendable endeavor to relieve the Galilean story of its magical features — in the interest of reconciling it to *what we think we know* about the orderly outworking of natural laws in a law abiding universe under the direction of an apparently law-loving God — we fail to take account of the fact that the Jesus personality so overwhelmingly transcends any other personality ever known in the world that comparisons drawn between him and other men only make the others, however useful and dynamic, seem mere pygmies dwarfed to insignificance in his presence."[58]

Douglas's writings on the miracles of Jesus would be of only minor importance except for the fact that upon retiring from the pulpit he took up novel writing. His two biblical novels, *The Robe* and *The Big Fisherman,* became two of the most popular American novels of his time. Furthermore, in their own way, Douglas's novels are classic statements of the Modernist portrait of Jesus: in them the nature miracles are subtly relativized. In *The Robe,* for example, he had an observer at the marriage feast at Cana note that the new wine of Jesus was delicate and white rather than potent and red as the original wine had been, which raises the possibility that it could have merely been water flavored by the residue of the older wine. He had other characters admit that the storm did not immediately cease and that the feeding of the five thousand could also be given a natural explanation.

But in the climax of *The Robe*, Douglas returned to the question of healing and here there is an interesting scene. The Christian slave Demetrius has been severely wounded and lay near death. The finest Roman physician, Sarpedon, had been summoned, yet despite all of his skills he admits that the case was hopeless. But to the death bed comes Simon Peter, who asks to be alone with the dying slave. After a while the weary Peter emerges, announcing that Demetrius will recover. A number of elements of this scene are noteworthy. The first was that it suggested that the healing power of Jesus was not his alone, but was part of the community. The second is that Demetrius suffered from real wounds and not just a functional illness, yet he received healing. But perhaps most interesting is the reaction of the physician Sarpedon. The doctor is angry at the apostle and jealous that he has succeeded where the learned skills of the physician have failed. The reaction of Sarpedon infuriates the hero, Marcellus. "You and your Hippocratic oath!" Marcellus shouts. "You are supposed to be interested in healing! Has it come to pass that your profession is so jealous — and wretched-of-heart — that it is enraged when a man's life is restored by some other means than your futile remedies?"[59] The jealousy of the physician indeed even leads him to betray the Christian hero to the emperor Caligula.

It is conceivable that Douglas in this scene was offering a subtle comment on some of the controversies of the 1920s. On the one hand the healing of Demetrius comes at the end of a long book and stands alone in the story. Most of *The Robe* is about the healing of souls, not bodies. It was an event neither called for nor expected. But it was nonetheless real despite the inability of medical professionals to understand it.

An Ebbing of the Debate

Among the reviewers of Douglas's *Those Disturbing Miracles* was a young Reinhold Niebuhr, who found the author's solution more disturbing than the miracles themselves. In Niebuhr's opinion, Douglas glibly believed that there was an allegorized "truth" embedded in each miracle story that could be ferreted out and lifted up, but he missed the real religious significance of these stories. "Religion is essentially an insistence that personal values have priority over physical fact," Niebuhr explained. The old religion justified "this insistence by making physical fact obviously and historically subject to the needs of men." For believers of the old religious paradigms, miracles meant that God ruled the world. Modern believers, however, were confronted with maintaining this confidence without the physical assurance. To this task the rationalizing and allegorizing of Douglas was little help.[60]

As we have seen, the great debate over the miraculous was facilitated by a variety of forces that thrust the question of miracles (both scriptural and current) into the intellectual consciousness of the age. By the early 1930s, however, another combination of forces began to form that would defuse the question and allow it to recede from public discussion.

The first influence involved a new way of interpreting the scriptures. As has been suggested, the distinction between healing and nature miracles was part of a broader late-nineteenth-century attempt to present a persuasive picture of the historical Jesus. Only when a natural explanation for the healing miracles could be posited did English-speaking Christian exegetes on the whole begin to criticize the nature miracles. The ultimate agenda of this attempt was to recapture a portrait of the original Jesus free from both ecclesiasticism and superstition. Despite the criticism of the historical Jesus school leveled by Albert Schweitzer in *The Quest of the Historical Jesus* (ET 1910), this approach continued to find favor until the 1920s. There were, of course, some who recognized the precarious scaffolding upon which the liberal quest for the historical Jesus rested. As the English biblical critic Edwyn Clement Hoskyns observed, the approach rested "upon a series of brilliant and attractive intuitive judgements rather than upon a critical and historical examination of the data supplied by the documents." Thus, for example, Mark was regarded as a primary and historically reliable source except when he included nature miracles such as Jesus' stilling of the storm or walking upon the waters. Theological difficulties were curtly relegated to later history. "What is supernatural is transferred to the period of growth, what is human and merely moral and philanthropic and anti-ecclesiastical is assumed to be primitive and original. The miracles and the Christological passages are, therefore, treated primarily as presenting literary and historical rather than religious problems," explained Hoskyns. These assumptions told one more about modern theological liberalism than about the meaning of scripture.[61]

If scholars like Hoskyns could find fault with some of the methodological assumptions of the rationalizing interpreters, a much more serious blow was leveled by proponents of the *Formgeschichte* — the form criticism school of interpretation. Form criticism emerged in Germany through the writings of Johann Weiss, Martin Dibelius, and Rudolph Bultmann, and it was first presented in detail in English by Burton Scott Easton in *The Gospel Before the Gospels* (1928).

Form criticism shifted the focus of biblical (and particularly gospel) criticism away from the literary sources and to the preliterary forms that lay behind the text. Furthermore, as Easton noted, the focus shifted from authors to communities. Form criticism studied "the history of certain pre-literary forms not consciously created by individuals but developed by constant oral repetition." These forms constituted the earliest message of the Christian community and consisted of various types. The four main classes were "paradigms" (stories with a universal application useful for preaching), sayings of Jesus, miracle stories, and historical narrative or legend.[62]

The significance of the rise of form criticism for our purposes was twofold. First, this paradigm recognized that miracle stories were part of the original proclamation and not a later tradition. But more importantly, form criticism shifted the focus of biblical criticism from the historical Jesus to the faith of the first generation. The gospels were not history but the record of faith. Even Mark interpreted the life and ministry of Jesus through the transforming prism of the resurrection. Accordingly, the question of historical veracity seemed singularly inappropriate. As Easton himself admitted, "Form-criticism is not in itself a historic tool; by itself it can tell us nothing of the truth or falsity of the events narrated." This bracketing of the historical question seemed puzzling to English-speaking scholars, and even Easton, who on the whole was sympathetic to the new approach, was uneasy with the unwillingness of the form critics to raise historical questions. But for the form critics the gospels were a testimony of faith and not a record of history. Throughout the 1930s form criticism gained increasing sway in theological faculties, and with this development the question of the miraculous was largely defused. Unlike the earlier critics who emphasized the continuity between the life and ministry of Jesus and the present, and who accordingly found it imperative to distinguish between rational miracles (such as, healings) and irrational ones (such as nature miracles), form critics emphasized the preaching, or *kerygma,* of the ancient community. Many thought it was impossible to probe behind this expression of belief to discover a historical foundation for the faith. When the question then became *kerygma* and not biography, the miracle accounts ceased being the stumbling block to a belief in Jesus.[63]

Form criticism was not the only factor in this transformation. From the 1920s onward a new trend emerged related to the presentation of the figure of Jesus. Broadly speaking, whereas the trend in earlier years was to emphasize the connectedness between Jesus and other human beings, by the late 1920s some were arguing that it was the otherness or strangeness of Jesus that was crucial. The American expatriate and Kierkegaard scholar Walter Lowrie, for example, returned to the source of liberal theology, the gospel of Mark, and found there a very different picture of Jesus than that which he had learned in seminary. One did of course find there the humanity of Jesus, but that was an "easy discovery": the "fact that Jesus was a man is not the new discovery. What distinguishes our age is the failure to discover that God is God. We are naturally enough at a loss to conceive how the 'Absolute' of the philosophers might become man. And the immanent God, the Soul of the universe, cannot be incarnate in one man any more really than he is with every man — or that he is incorporate with a stone." According to Lowrie, modern thinkers, so infatuated with the immanence of God in nature, failed to do justice to the radical transcendence of God found in the gospel narrative. The Jesus of the gospel of Mark was a strange and intimidating figure — one who was not an ethical teacher but an awesome presence. To ignore this fact was to miss the crux of the story. As Lowrie continued, "It must be evident . . . that one who approaches the Gospels with the presumption that it is ridiculous to fear Jesus had better not open the book." A crucial part of that awesomeness stemmed from Jesus' ability to do mighty works. As Lowrie observed, the response of the apostles to many of the great nature miracles — the calming of the sea, the walking on water, the immense catch of fish — was fear. Modern believers had lost the idea of the fear of God. "We will not allow that even the Christ is to be feared. The Pantocrator, that most worthy Judge eternal, has no place in our Christian art, and we have few pictures which represent Jesus as an awe-inspiring figure." But the sense of godly fear was an overriding theme in the gospel of Mark, according to Lowrie: "The feeling prompted in the disciples was a religious feeling, the very stuff out of which religion is made, i.e., a sense of the numinous. . . . 'Who can he be?' they said — and they knew no answer."[64]

Both Traditionalists and Modernists, according to Lowrie, misread the function of the miracle stories of the gospel. Traditionalists saw them as proofs of Christ's divinity, whereas Modernists dismissed them as mere baggage. They were neither of these, however; they were signs. They aroused attention that the Kingdom of God was breaking into the world, but their meaning was religious, not rational, and their force was not automatic. People could see them and still not believe. Christ's awesome works did not persuade everyone in his own day, nor do they persuade everyone in any age, wrote Lowrie: "Jesus was evidently wise in not encouraging people to regard his miracles as a proof of his right to the sublime title of Messiah. But then neither was his moral grandeur sufficient to prove this. The high priest did not recognize his claim — but neither did his Apostles when all forsook him and fled. There was one miracle at Jerusalem — the resurrection of Jesus from the dead. Without that this miracle-worker would not have been accounted the Christ." Lowrie firmly placed himself with a reading of the gospels found in Kierkegaard, Dostoyevski, and Karl Barth.[65]

Lowrie's invocation of Kierkegaard, Dostoyevski, and Barth reflected not only a new view of the gospels but a new trend in theology, namely the Neoorthodox revolt against Modernism. Neoorthodoxy is a complicated and multifaceted theological phenomenon, but in many of its broad themes it too would contribute to defusing the debate over the miraculous. One recalls that at least from the 1890s the debate over the miraculous was tied to the larger question of historical continuity. No matter how much modernists, sacramentalists, positivists, and faith healers might disagree, they were united in seeing a fundamental continuity between the biblical epoch and the present. The biblical world and the present age were linked by common laws that served to connect present-day experiences with those recorded in scripture. Some used the present as a lens to interpret the biblical events, whereas others used biblical categories to understand present events, but a connectedness was assumed by all. Furthermore, as we have seen in chapter 7, there was another common theme of evidentialism. Howsoever Elwood Worcester and John Alexander Dowie differed, they would have agreed that it was present personal experience upon which faith was grounded. Neoorthodoxy challenged both of these assumptions.

On the theological level, Neoorthodoxy can be seen as elevating the sovereignty and otherness of God over a century-long endeavor to anchor theology on human experience. Thus it rejected (or at least downplayed) both natural and philosophical theology in favor of grounding theology on the word of God. According to proponents of Neoorthodoxy, in the Bible God was revealed, and it was—to use Karl Barth's famous phrase—"the strange new world of the Bible" to which the believer must turn. Furthermore that "strange new world" was radically different from our own. The Bible led us beyond ourselves and our categories, weighing and judging all human constructs. As Barth explained,

> The Bible says to us, in a manner candid and friendly enough, with regard to the "versions" we make of it, " 'These may be you, but they are not I!' They may perhaps suit you, meeting the demands of your thought and temperament, of your era and your 'circle' of your religious and philosophical theories. . . . But now I bid you come to seek me as well. Seek what is here." It is the Bible itself, it is the straight inexorable logic of its onmarch which drives us beyond ourselves and invites us . . . to reach for the last highest answer, in which all is said that can be said, although we can hardly understand and only stammeringly express it. And that is: A new world, the world of God.[66]

In that strange new world the miraculous played a key role. Miracles testified to the sovereignty and freedom of God and the reality of grace. For Barth, grace was the secret hidden meaning behind nature, and just as revelation made known the hidden God, so too did biblical miracles make visible the hidden grace. "Miracle must not be reduced to the level of God's other and general being and action in the world," he warned. "[Their] miraculous nature must not be denied. . . . For it is miracle alone which opens for us the door to the secret that the Creator's saving opposition to us does not confront us only at individual points and moments, but throughout the whole range of our spatio-temporal existence."[67] To domesticate the signs and wonders of the Bible, or to explain them through analogies from nature or human experience, was to abandon their power. They were irreducibly dramatic and supernatural events because the God who performed them was sovereign and above nature.

But if the new supernaturalism of the Neoorthodox writers served to support the religious value of biblical miracles, their view of faith undercut an interest in modern miracles. As we have seen, since the time of Horace Bushnell Protestant writers had been suggesting that in modern signs and wonders one could ground a confidence in the reality of a personal God — a belief that might be a substitute for the older natural theology. Neoorthodox writers looked askance on this agenda. They emphasized instead the Kierkegaardian distinction between faith (which was believed) and knowledge (which was rationally appropriated). Religious confidence and commitment were grounded rightly on faith, not knowledge. As Lowrie had observed, even the biblical miracles could not convince nonbelievers; only when viewed through the eyes of a resurrection faith were they convincing. As another popular Neoorthodox writer explained, "Faith is therefore the very opposite of proof. Proof means the security of thought, the secure casting of the anchor of new knowledge in that which is already known. . . . Faith cannot be established on a settled basis. It does not stand, it depends. It depends on the Word of God alone, which can be trusted because it is the Word of God. He who does not trust this Word, does not see it as God's Word and does not believe. It is impossible to believe and at the same time ask for proofs. Faith is pure dependence upon revelation."[68] In the Neoorthodox elevation of faith over knowledge, one gleans a return to the distinctly Pauline theology that surfaced in the Reformation, encapsulated by those verses in 1 Corinthians: "For Jews demand signs and Greeks seek wisdom, but we preach Christ crucified, a stumbling block to the Jews and folly to the Gentiles." Many a Neoorthodox preacher in the succeeding decades returned to this theme of the "foolishness of the cross," and emphasized that the true gospel was independent of philosophical categories and the demand for signs. Instead, these proponents argued, the gospel centered upon the miraculous revelation of God in Christ.[69]

The spread of Neoorthodoxy in English-speaking circles began in the late 1920s, and by the 1950s it had largely become the official theology of mainline

American Protestant clergy. It had a lesser but significant influence in Britain.[70] Where it triumphed, the old debate over the miraculous melted away, as shown by the figures of William Temple in England and Edwin Lewis in America. Early in his career, Temple had problems with the miraculous, and for a time these qualms even threatened to prevent his ordination. As a contributor to *Foundations,* he participated (at least tentatively) in the Modernist attempt to rethink the idea of the miraculous and the supernatural. But by the late 1930s Temple had come to see the miraculous not as an unnecessary stumbling block but as part of the essence of the gospel. In the introduction to his *Readings in St. John's Gospel,* he dismissed out of hand the old attempt to locate a nonsupernatural "Jesus of history." "Why anyone should have troubled to crucify the Christ of Liberal Protestantism," he mused, "has always been a mystery." He concluded, "It is now recognized that the only Christ for whose existence there is any evidence at all is a miraculous figure making stupendous claims."[71]

Even more dramatic was the transformation of the American Methodist theologian Edwin Lewis. During the 1920s, Lewis was one of the leading proponents of theological liberalism within American Methodism, and his *Jesus Christ and the Human Quest* (1924) attempted to reconstruct a Christology on the philosophy of personal idealism. In it he argued that Christ, although he revealed the true nature of God, remained fully human. Along the way Lewis discussed the vexing question of the virgin birth and emphasized the ambivalence of the textual evidence. The inconclusive nature of the scriptural record justified the position of those modern believers who had troubles with the doctrine. He concluded, "While the Virgin Birth is part of historic Christianity, the unquestioning acceptance of it is not, if we take Luke as our guide, so wholly indispensable to Christian discipleship that those who reserve judgement on it must be denied membership in the church." Lewis's position provoked great controversy, and there was serious talk of trying him for heresy.[72]

By the end of the 1920s, however, Lewis had undergone a theological conversion, and by the 1930s he was one of the leading American Methodist exponents of Neoorthodoxy. He returned to the question of the virgin birth in 1940 in *A Philosophy of the Christian Revelation.* If his earlier volume had emphasized personal idealism, here he emphasized faith. The core of faith was choice, or the accepting of not only a set of facts but also the meaning of those facts. "Reason can go no farther than to say respecting Jesus that he was the Son of Mary: faith adds to his Sonship to Mary the claim of his Sonship to God" explained Lewis. Scripture contained both facts and meaning, and one could accept the former without the latter. But true Christian faith combined both; it was the "process whereby objectively given truth becomes tied to the very structure of our life, to accomplish there that redeeming and sanctifying purpose which alone brings life to its fulfillment."[73]

No two claims were more important for the Christian faith than were the virgin birth and the resurrection. The central issue concerning these claims was neither scientific nor historical, but one of faith and the integrity of Christian life. Lewis preached, "The Christian faith no more asks for scientific corroboration of the Virgin Birth or the Resurrection than it asks for scientific corroboration of the Fatherhood of God. . . . Science as such is equally impotent to prove or disprove Christian truth." On the theological level Christ's birth and resurrection anchored the doctrine of the historical person of Christ and therefore could not be jettisoned. Thus for Lewis, as for other Neoorthodox theologians, the great miracles flowed from theology and faith; they were not empirical evidences. He noted in passing the failure of Gresham Machen's defense of the virgin birth. Machen had attempted to anchor the virgin birth in the historical reliability of the scriptural record, but if the question were a historical one then it would have to be judged on historical or textual grounds. "If the only reason we have for our faith is the story in Matthew and Luke, it is little enough and uncertain enough," argued Lewis. Faith in the virgin birth rested not upon the testimony of the Matthean and Lucan narratives but upon faith in God and Christ.[74] Neither Machen nor the Modernists had gotten it right.

The new biblical criticism and Neoorthodox theology transferred the question of the miraculous out of the fields of history and philosophy and ensconced it in the language of faith. In doing so, the miraculous became a religious category — existing within the language of the community as a way to describe the true nature of the divine sovereignty. During the heyday of Neoorthodoxy, there was a substantial consensus that the theological problem of the miraculous had been solved.[75]

Although the new theology and biblical criticism did their part to defuse the debate, two other factors must be mentioned in passing. The first was the triumph of the therapeutic model as the answer to the question of the church's role in healing. In the fifty years after the revival of faith healing within English-speaking Protestantism, the thaumaturgical, sacramental, and therapeutic models struggled for ascendency. By the early 1930s, as both Brooks Holifield and Allison Stokes have shown, the therapeutic model had clearly triumphed in the mainline Protestant churches in America.[76] The great popular excitement in the possibilities of psychoanalysis undergirded the development of the Clinical Pastoral Education movement. The rise of this movement is not part of our story, but it is important to emphasize how this movement profoundly differed from that of even the earlier advocates of the therapeutic approach. The American clinical traditions, both in the Boston- and New York–based movements, saw psychology and counseling as key tools for ministerial involvement in healing. They did not, however, as Elwood Worcester and Samuel McComb had done in the beginning of the century, stress the interconnectedness of modern techniques and the biblical precedents, nor did they emphasize the centrality of physical healing. The contrast between Worcester and a representative of the new clinical traditions, such as the psychologist Rollo May, is illuminating. May was famous for many of his volumes on religious counseling, in particular *The Art of Counseling* (1939) and *The Springs of Creative Living* (1940). Particularly in the latter, where he expressed his indebtedness to theologians such as Reinhold Niebuhr and Paul Tillich, May showed that he was influenced by the new theological trends. But the effect of May's works was to move the therapeutic tradition into a more professional model. The new clinical-professional training might help shed crucial light on the human predicament, but it did not illumine the scriptural record.

Finally, among conservative Protestants one finds a parallel hardening of the rejection of modern miracles, particularly healings. A belief in the cessation of the miraculous, we have found, had always been a core belief among many Protestant theologians, but the emergence of Pentecostalism — and with it the belief in the restoration of the Pauline spiritual gifts — raised the question in a far more immediate manner. Healing was perhaps the most troubling case, because almost no conservative Protestant wanted to deny that God could heal. As Edith Blumhoffer has noted in her study of Aimee Semple McPherson, conservative American Protestants, although agreeing in the condemnation of glossolalia, were ambiguous about healing ministries. Reuben Torrey, for example, one of the leading Fundamentalist spokesmen, condemned the practices of modern faith healers (including explicitly John A. Dowie and implicitly Aimee Semple McPherson), but nonetheless accepted the promise found in James 5:13–14, "Not only does the Bible teach it, but experience demonstrates it." Indeed, although the evidence is sketchy, there seemed to be some interest in healings within conservative congregations. The *Christian Century* recorded that an interest in faith healing had even surfaced in the congregation of the Fundamentalist John Roach Straton.[77]

But the continuing development of dispensational theology and exegesis began to solidify the a priori rejection of evidence for modern miracles. Lewis Sperry Chafer, president and professor of theology of the dispensationalist stronghold Dallas Theological Seminary, dismissed any appeal to James 5:14 as anachronistic. The anointing was a Jewish holdover rather than a Christian practice, he argued, and one could no more intuit a general guideline for

Christian healing from it than from any other passage of the New Testament. "Peter cast a shadow and some were healed," he wryly noted, "but he never went into the shadow casting business." The age of miracles was clearly over. John Walvoord, also of Dallas Theological Seminary, argued as well that there was no longer any gift of healing. God may occasionally heal, but he did so out of his own volition, not from any promise. The gift of healing that the ancient church possessed had been withdrawn. "No one today, however filled with faith and powerful in prayer, is able to heal in virtue of an abiding gift," Walvoord asserted. Thus the Reformed cessationism of Warfield and dispensational cessationism triumphed in conservative Fundamentalist circles, and by 1948 the Neo-Evangelical theologian Edward J. Carnell could write, "The doctrine that miracles could no longer occur is one of the fundamental canons which separate Protestantism from Roman Catholicism."[78]

All this in no way denies that popular interest in the possibility of miracles continued to thrive. Often it was a view divorced from any theological content, as when Fred Astaire in "A Foggy Day in London Town" asked the musical question, "How long, I wondered could this thing last? / But the age of miracles hadn't passed." When he wrote these lines for *A Damsel in Distress*, Ira Gershwin was probably not hoping to initiate a disputation with Benjamin Warfield.[79]

On a more serious level, the miraculous continued to surface as a religious question in the general culture. Usually this was in the context of Catholicism. In Bruce Marshall's popular novel *Father Malachy's Miracle*, a priest prays for a miracle (the moving of a noxious pub), and it occurs. The novel, while poking fun at Protestant Modernists who refuse to accept the evidence (or in this case, the lack of evidence) right in front of their noses, nonetheless raised the serious question of what exactly would happen if a dramatic nature miracle did take place in the modern world. On an even larger scale, the story of Lourdes reached millions in the popular novel and even more popular movie, *The Song of Bernadette*. On all sorts of levels an interest in the miraculous continued to be evident.

On the intellectual level, however, the question of the miraculous appeared to be solved for Protestants by the new theology, by biblical criticism, and by a clinical approach to counseling. The great debate that had arisen in the wake of the new science and biblical criticism of the mid-nineteenth century had reached a denouement.

Epilogue

The cease-fire in the debate over the miraculous lasted a little more than a generation, from the 1930s until the 1960s. It was never, of course, absolute, and particularly in England discussion of the miraculous continued, albeit in a lower key. But where the principles of form criticism, Neoorthodoxy, and a therapeutic approach to the question of religion and healing held sway, the "problem" of miracles appeared to be largely defused. The mighty acts of God continued to have a religious and theological significance while being bracketed from scientific or historical scrutiny.[1]

But the solution was only a temporary one because, to borrow Sydney Ahlstrom's phrasing, it offered only a "very thin sheet of dogmatic asphalt" over the problem. By the 1960s the asphalt had begun to crack. Many became aware that Neoorthodoxy and form criticism had seen their day and that their elaborately worked out compromise vis-à-vis miracles was intellectually indefensible. A number of theological voices began to grow dissatisfied with the bracketing of biblical language and categories, and on both sides of the Atlantic individuals took up the cause of "demythologizing" the Bible by translating biblical categories into modern modes of discourse. In the famous words of John A. T. Robinson, these scholars became "convinced that there is a growing gulf between the traditional orthodox supernaturalism in which our Faith has been framed and the categories which the 'lay' world . . . finds meaningful today."[2]

The mid-century solution, however, was not only breaking down from the "left"; the same decade in which demythologizing scholars argued that modern individuals could no longer accept the outdated biblical world view witnessed a tremendous growth of interest in Pentecostalism, including a fascination with the charismatic gifts. Although the chief historian of the charismatic and healing revival in modern America rightly notes that the movement emerged after the World War II, it was in the 1960s that Neo-Pentecostalism — or the charismatic movement — began to flourish in both old-line Protestantism and Roman Catholicism.[3]

The popular interest in the miraculous has only increased over the last three decades. During these years Americans have found themselves engaging in passionate discussions on a variety of topics involving the reality of the miraculous. The questions of angels, demons, and miraculous healings have all been debated. Some of these questions, such as the discussion of the Shroud of Turin and the allegation that it provided evidence not only for the historicity of Jesus but for the miraculous resurrection, have generated a spate of publications. By 1995 a *Time* magazine poll recorded that 69 percent of all Americans believed in miracles. All of this has been somewhat disconcerting to many theological writers. As Martin Marty wrote in the *Christian Century*, this searching after evidences such as the Shroud of Turin in order to "prove" scientifically that the resurrection occurred abandons the true nature of the gospel faith: "An unbelieving generation seeks signs from science and, we are told, these signs will compel faith. . . . [But] the Christian circle will not grow an inch because of such 'proof' . . . it is idol not testimony."[4]

The passion of Marty's language, however, betrayed the fact that the older mid-century compromise was now at best a minority position, even among believers. The rapid breakdown of the Neoorthodox compromise and the new polarization of religious thought — with critics of the miraculous on one side and proponents of modern miracles on the other — have been some of the most remarkable occurrences of the last thirty years. Few if any at mid-century would have predicted that within thirty years the American public would be engaged in resuscitating both the agenda of the *Encyclopaedia Biblica* and the old "prayer gauge" challenge. Yet as a self-constituted "Jesus Seminar" of biblical critics whittles away the gospel miracles and modernist clerics call once again for a "rethinking" of the virgin birth, medical journals publish studies on the effect of prayer on healing.[5]

The task remains to summarize where we have been and to offer some suggestions for the present. Although this story has involved many characters and a number of sub-plots, one should not lose sight of its basic outline. As we have seen, the long-cherished Protestant view of a limited age of miracles became increasingly attacked by the middle of the nineteenth century. In response, scholars on both sides of the Atlantic attempted to preserve the New Testament miracles by tying them to the character of Jesus. This strategy proved successful until the 1890s when, despite the labors of such persons as Charles Gore in England and Charles Briggs in America, there arose key voices who argued that it was possible to maintain a Christian self-identity while rejecting the miraculous. The mid-century challenge to biblical miracles, however, led other individuals like Horace Bushnell and John Henry Newman to argue that biblical miracles could only be preserved if the question of post-biblical miracles were reopened. The interest in modern signs and wonders inspired many of the early proponents of faith healing. Both of these trends came together in the early twentieth century. The collapse of the hegemonic role of the cessationist view of miracles, led, as we have seen, to sharp conflicts over the question of miracles during the early decades of the century. The ascendency of Neoorthodoxy and other factors allowed for a lessening of the conflict by mid-century, with the collapse of Neoorthodoxy in the 1960s the conflict has resumed.

Suggestions for the present are a more daunting task. Although the epilogue of a long work is not the place to take on such an enormous question as the origin and meaning of the post-1960s interest in the miraculous, it is appropriate to reflect on what insights modern-day readers might gain from this study. Most fundamentally, it is clear that the growing criticism of the miraculous and its corollary, the deepening interest in miracles, are not unique to the late 1900s. Since the collapse of the hegemonic position of the limited age of miracles, the simultaneous appearance of both groups has been a recurring pattern. Indeed it may not be the late twentieth century that is anomalous, but rather the mid-century interlude.

Second, not only has the debate over the miraculous emerged, but the four views of the interrelationship of biblical signs and wonders and modern signs and wonders (identified in chapter 7) have also resurfaced. As one recalls, these four positions were (1) that the concept of miracle should be abandoned, (2) that miracles occurred during a "limited age," (3) that "miracles" are important and occur in all ages, and one must use the understanding of the modern spiritual wonders to properly interpret the nature of biblical miracles, and (4) that miracles are common to both biblical times and the present day but one must use the biblical miracles to understand modern wonders. Over the last few decades each position has found its supporters. Once again "progressive" clergy are calling for an abandonment of the category of the miraculous and are reinterpreting the great gospel miracles, whereas some conservative Protestants continue to maintain the cessationist position.[6] But what seems to characterize the present religious world is the tremendous growth in popularity of positions three and four. Most modern advocates of miracles can be seen as dividing along these two positions. Thus whereas advocates of New Age healing attempt to interpret the healings of Jesus in light of their distinctive metaphysic, individuals like John Wimber and other advocates of sign ministry continue to emphasize the relevancy of biblical categories for the present.[7] As with other groups during the early twentieth century, however, a closer look at the two movements may reveal intriguing overlaps and more commonality than either would be willing to admit.[8]

Third, one observes that the new discussion has emerged in a sociointellectual milieu similar to that which framed the earlier debate. The modern discussion has moved into the larger community for the same reasons as did the early-twentieth-century "search for evidences": a confluence of the religious desire to ground the reality of the "other" in personal experience, and the loss of confidence in scientific theory and medical practice. Once again one also sees the interest in wonders and healings reflected in drama and literature as well as religion. And it is perhaps not coincidental that in both eras the loss of confidence in the scientific model was rhetorically connected to an assault upon the Enlightenment. The often-voiced late-twentieth-century attack of the Enlightenment—to which such diverse groups as Postmodernists and Neo-Evangelicals have contributed—has perhaps provided an acceptable atmosphere for raising anew questions regarding miracles and healing.[9]

But if this study has allowed me to suggest possible points of continuity between the early-twentieth-century discussion of miracles and the current interest in the miraculous, it also isolates key differences. As I noted in the discussion of William James, the attempt to ground the reality of the transcendent upon religious experience inevitably made it difficult to confine these experiences to the historic Christian tradition. Cultural inertia and a continuing reverence for the figure of Jesus nonetheless led many early-twentieth-century individuals to continue to elevate the significance of the New Testament and the figure of Jesus in the spiritual quest. Modern-day proponents of the belief that "miracles" are important and occur in all ages but should be interpreted in light of the present, however, have been less likely to confine the new spiritual reality in the old wineskins of the gospel framework. An increased awareness of the cultural and religious diversity of the human race has necessitated a rethinking of narrowly Christian categories. As one Jesuit devotee of New Age spirituality has noted, "The time is past when I can present myself as a Christian without placing my faith in the context of Hinduism, Buddhism, African and Oceanic religion, Taoism, and Confucianism. God is great and one, and the plenitude and diversity of creation . . . expresses that greatness." Although there continues to be an interest in signs and wonders among Christians, there seems to be a tendency to interpret them within a broader framework.[10]

A second equally noticeable trend has taken place among conservatives who believe that miracles are common throughout history but biblical miracles inform our understanding of modern wonders. As we observed, the necessity of defending the miraculous led English-speaking Protestants again and again to the brink of joining in common cause with Roman Catholics. Always, however, this movement was frustrated, from the Roman Catholic side by a reluctance to engage in any ecumenical dialogue with Protestants, and from the Protestant side by an ultimate unwillingness to give up the idea of a pan-Protestant unity. The religious changes of the 1960s altered this stalemate. Among American Protestants, the loss of quasi-established status reduced the importance of a pan-Protestant unity; meanwhile, among Roman Catholics, the new ecumenical spirit flowing from the Second Vatican Council opened up a new possibility for rapprochement. Furthermore the religious debates of the 1970s and 1980s, in which conservative-liberal questions have replaced Protestant-Catholic ones as the central point of controversy, have also brought conservative Protestants and Catholics closer together. Catholics and Protestants frequently join forces to defend the reality of miracles, and the new debate over miracles is far more ecumenical than any of the earlier discussions. Figures like Killian McDonnell and Francis Macnutt and topics such as the Shroud of Turin are appealed to by both Catholics and Protestants. Catholics and Protestants still have different view of miracles—in particular, Roman Catholics believe that miracles function within the broader context of sacramentalism, whereas Protestant Pentecostals do not—but an interest in modern signs and wonders seems nonetheless to be a unifying element in lay Protestant and Catholic piety.[11]

Perhaps, too, the issue of the miraculous has become a unifying position for many modern traditional believers for another reason—one that is also related to the inherent limitation of the old idea of a limited age of miracles. The traditional cessationist position was always in some ways "artificial"—that is, it rested necessarily upon the artifice of Reformation Protestant (and particularly Calvinistic) theology. As we have seen, it presupposed an elaborate set of theological categories such as special providence to distinguish miracles from actions of God in the world. The period we have explored witnessed the large-scale collapse of this theology in America, and its parallel transformation in England. Few if any modern-day English-speaking lay Protestants are aware of the old theology, and fewer still could intelligibly distinguish between a miracle and a special providence. With the collapse of the old Protestant theological superstructure, the issue of miracles has moved away from the older division, taken up by Protestants and Catholics — that between a limited age of miracles and continuing ecclesiastical miracles. Instead, a more basic question is being asked: Does God actively intervene in the world? When the question becomes framed in this manner, the religious community finds itself divided in fundamentally new ways.

All of these observations are at best conjectures, and they must be tested by a detailed study of the new discussion of the miraculous. Such a study will undoubtedly also address even more intriguing questions such as why the use of religious ritual in healing, which had been so vigorously rejected in the earlier story, seems to have become so accepted. Likewise the influence of a developing Neo-Pentecostal theology on the nature of the modern debate will also undoubtedly be addressed.

But whatever the outcomes of a future study, one conclusion is certain: the modern debate stands upon the shoulders of the early twentieth-century one. The decline of the idea of a limited age of miracles transformed English-speaking religious life and thought. This fundamental shift in how we think of miracles has moved the religious discussion off a Reformation axis and has raised the question of how God relates to the world. This question continues to confront all believers.

Notes

Introduction

1. See W. E. H. Lecky, *History of the Rise and Influence of the Spirit of Rationalism in Europe,* 2 vols. (New York, 1900), 1:152.

2. See Horace Bushnell, *Nature and the Supernatural, as Together Constituting the One System of God* (New York, 1871), 447.

3. I regret that I have not been able to include in my study the strong African-American tradition of faith healing and interest in signs and wonders. This was largely a separate and independent movement, however, with complexities of its own. On the interest in supernatural healing in the African-American context, see Albert Raboteau, *Slave Religion: The "Invisible Institution" in The Antebellum South* (New York, 1978); and his essay "The Afro-American Traditions" in *Caring and Curing: Health and Medicine in the Western Religious Traditions,* ed. Ronald L. Numbers and Darrel W. Amundsen (New York, 1986).

4. My use of "crass supernaturalism" here differs in one key way from James's. As I will discuss in chapter 7, James would have denied that these interventions of crass supernaturalism could necessarily be attributed to the divine.

Chapter 1: A Limited Age of Miracles?

1. Surveys of the miraculous tend to fall into two chronological periods. The extended debates over the miraculous in the period between 1880 and 1930 generated a flurry of volumes. I have found most helpful C. J. Wright, *Miracle in History and in Modern*

Thought . . . (New York, 1930); Johannes Wendland, *Miracles and Christianity,* trans. H. R. Mackintosh (London, 1911); and Frederick C. Grant, "The Place of Miracles in Religion," in *Problems of Faith and Worship: A Record of the Church Congress of the United States* . . . (New York, 1926), 120–46. Since the 1960s a new wave of interest in the miraculous has produced a very different scholarly oeuvre. See Colin Brown, *Miracles and the Critical Mind* (Grand Rapids, Mich., 1984).

2. On the question of the miracles of the New Testament, see R. H. Fuller, *Interpreting the Miracles* (London, 1963); Gerd Theissen, *The Miracle Stories of the Early Christian Tradition,* trans. Francis McDonagh (Philadelphia, 1983); and for background, Howard Clark Kee, *Miracles in the Early Christian World: A Study in Sociohistorical Method* (New Haven, Conn., 1983).

3. Robert M. Grant, *Miracle and Natural Law in Graeco-Roman and Early Christian Thought* (Amsterdam, 1952), 190–98.

4. Rowan A. Greer, *The Fear of Freedom: A Study of Miracles in the Roman Imperial Church* (University Park, Pa., 1989), 115–16.

5. Grant, *Miracle and Natural Law,* 215–20; Greer, *Fear of Freedom,* 170–78; and Benedicta Ward, *Miracles and the Medieval Mind: Theory, Record, and Event, 1000–1215* (Philadelphia, 1982), 3–5. For a different interpretation of Augustine, see John A. Hardon, S.J., "The Concept of Miracle from St. Augustine to Modern Apologetics," *Theological Studies* 15 (1954): 230–31.

6. Augustine, "Of True Religion," as quoted in Greer, *Fear of Freedom,* 170; see also *The City of God,* trans. Marcus Dods (New York, 1950), 820.

7. On the interconnection of holiness and miracles, see Peter Brown, *The Cult of the Saints: Its Rise and Function in Latin Christianity* (Chicago, 1978). On the transformation of anointing, see F. W. Puller, *Anointing the Sick in Scripture and Tradition* . . . (London, 1910); and Reginald M. Woolley, *Exorcism and the Healing of the Sick* (London, 1932).

8. For a more complete discussion of the miraculous in Aquinas, see chapter 5.

9. Thomas Aquinas, *Summa Theologiae,* pt. 1, ques. 110, art. 4. (This and all subsequent quotations from Aquinas are from the Blackfriar's edition of the *Summa*)

10. "De Notis Ecclesiae" in *Roberti Cardinalis Bellarmini Opera Omnia* . . . , 6 vols. (Naples, 1856–62), 2:132. My translation.

11. Luther, *Sermons on the Gospel of St. John: Chapters 14–16,* in *Luther's Works,* ed. Jaroslav Pelikan and Daniel E. Poellet, 55 vols. (St. Louis, Mo., 1958–86), 24:181. See, too, D. P. Walker, "The Cessation of Miracles," in *Hermeticism and the Renaissance: Intellectual History and the Occult in Early Modern Europe,* ed. Ingrid Merkel and Allen G. Debus (Washington, 1988), 111–24.

12. Calvin, "Prefatory Address to King Francis," in *Institutes of the Christian Religion,* ed. John T. McNeill, trans. Ford Lewis Battles, 2 vols. (Philadelphia, 1960), 1:16. For an extended discussion of Calvin's views, see John Mark Ruthven, "On the Cessation of the Charismata: The Protestant Polemic of Benjamin B. Warfield" (Ph.D. diss., Marquette University, 1989), 21–62.

13. On Calvin and the spiritual gifts, see *Commentary on the Epistles of Paul the Apostle to the Corinthians,* trans. John Pringle (Grand Rapids, Mich., 1979), 402, 427–28; and Ruthven, "Cessation," 26–37. The Calvin quote is from the commentary on Acts of the Apostles, cited in Ruthven, "Cessation," 32.

14. D. P. Walker, *Unclean Spirits: Possession and Exorcism in France and England in the Late Sixteenth and Early Seventeenth Centuries* (Philadelphia, 1981), 72–73.

15. Ward, *Miracles and the Medieval Mind*, 89, 169.

16. *The Works of John Jewel*, ed. John Ayre, 4 vols. (Cambridge, Eng., 1845–50), 3:197–98; *Later Writings of Bishop Hooper . . .* , ed. Charles Nevinson (Cambridge, Eng., 1852), 44–45. For a sense of the preoccupation of the English Reformers with the miracle question, see Henry Gough, ed., *A General Index to the Publications of the Parker Society* (Cambridge, Eng., 1845), 541–43. Walker, in *Unclean Spirits*, 66–73, argues that there a distinction between Anglicans and Puritans emerged by the early seventeenth century. Whereas Anglicans began to use the cessationist view to reject the idea of demon possession, Puritans attempted to hold on to demon possession and exorcism by differentiating these events from miracles.

17. E. W[orsley], *A Discourse of Miracles Wrought in the Roman Catholic Church . . .* (Antwerp, 1670), 35.

18. [John Digby], *Miracles Not Ceased. To His Grace George Duke of Buckingham . . .* (London, 1663), 18. J. O. F. may be the same healer identified by Keith Thomas as "Blake." The two cases are parallel, but differ in some details. See Keith Thomas, *Religion and the Decline of Magic: Studies in Popular Beliefs in Sixteenth- and Seventeenth-Century England* (Middlesex, Eng.: 1973), 240. See pp. 209–51 for the broader context of religious healing in seventeenth-century England.

19. For discussions of the idea of providence from the classic Reformed perspective, see Heinrich Heppe, *Reformed Dogmatics: Set Out and Illustrated from the Sources*, rev. and ed. Ernst Bizer, trans. G. T. Thomson (Grand Rapids, Mich., 1978), 251–67; William Sherlock, *A Discourse Concerning the Divine Providence* (London, 1694) shows how the subject was interpreted by late-seventeenth-century Anglicans. For an analysis of the implications of providence, see Perry Miller, *The New England Mind: The Seventeenth Century* (Boston, 1961), 227–31. For a discussion of its role in popular religious thought, see Thomas, *Religion and the Decline of Magic*, 90–132.

20. Turner includes an account of the African confessors. See his *A Compleat History of the Most Remarkable Providences, Both of Justice and Mercy Which Happened in this Present Age . . .* (London, 1697), 12 [pagination erratic]. Beard includes an account of the death of Arius; see his *The Theatre of God's Judgements. Wherein Is Represented the Admirable Justice of God Against All Notorius Sinners . . .* (London, 1612), 98–99. Both of these events were taken up by John Henry Newman in his celebrated *Two Essays on Biblical and Ecclesiastical Miracles* (London, 1907), discussed in chapter 5. On the popularity of such volumes in Puritan New England, see David D. Hall, *Worlds of Wonder, Days of Judgement: Popular Religious Belief in Early New England* (Cambridge, Mass., 1990), 73–81.

21. On the early Quakers, see H. J. Cadbury, *George Fox's Book of Miracles* (Cambridge, Eng., 1948), and in particular Cadbury's introduction, which discusses the historical context of the seventeenth-century sectarian and Quaker interest in miracles.

22. Increase Mather, *An Essay for the Recording of Illustrious Providences . . . Especially in New-England* (Boston, 1684), x. On the interchangeable use of the terms, see esp. pp. 16 and 19. For a discussion of this volume, see Hall, *Worlds of Wonder*, 83–90; and Jon Butler, *Awash in a Sea of Faith: Christianizing the American People* (Cambridge, Mass., 1990), 71–72.

23. Mather, *Essay,* 127. Mather's account is based on book 5 of Pontanus's *Historia Belli, quod Ferdinandus Rex Neapolitanus Senior Contra Ioannum Andegaviensam Ducan Gessit,* found in *Ioinnis Iovani Pontani Opera Omnia . . . ,* 3 vols. (Venice, 1518–19), 3:306–7. What Mather fails to note, however, is that Pontanus, far from being a disinterested observer of Catholic practices, was rather a partisan historian of Naples, and included this account to show how wicked and corrupt (*"scelestissimi"*) the opposing Sicilians were.

24. Mather, *Essay,* 259–72.

25. Hall, *Worlds of Wonder,* 108. See, too, Thomas's *Religion and the Decline of Magic,* 767–800, and Peter Burke, *Popular Culture in Early Modern Europe* (London, 1978), 241 ff. On the continuing interest in magic and the occult, see the evidence cited in Butler, *Awash in a Sea of Faith,* 71–91. On evidence of continuing interest in miracles and healing from a very different venue and theological context, see J. C. D. Clark, who linked the interest with continuing Jacobitism in his *English Society: 1688–1832* (Cambridge, Eng., 1985), 161–73. See, too, Eamon Duffy, "Valentine Greatrakes, the Irish Stroker: Miracle, Science and Orthodoxy in Restoration England," in *Studies in Church History: Religon and Humanism,* ed. Keith Robbins 17 (1981): 251–74. On Fleetwood, see William Fleetwood, *An Essay upon Miracles in Two Discourses* (London, 1701), particularly discourse 1. Fleetwood's *Essay* was controversial on other grounds and provoked John Locke to write his *Discourse on Miracles.*

26. Francis Bacon, *Novum Organum,* trans. and ed. Peter Urbach and John Gibson (Chicago, 1994), aphorism 46, p. 57. On Willard, see Ernest Benson Lowrie, *The Shape of the Puritan Mind: The Thought of Samuel Willard* (New Haven, Conn., 1974), 71–74. The Wesley quotation is from Thomas, *Religion and the Decline of Magic,* 765, who also discusses the shift away from special providence.

27. On the debate over Robert Merton's linking of Puritanism with the rise of modern science, see I. Bernard Cohen, ed., *Puritanism and the Rise of Modern Science: The Merton Thesis* (New Brunswick, N.J., 1990). On one scholar's attempt to link the question of modern miracles with differing Protestant and Catholic theories of science, see Peter Dear, "Miracles, Experiments and the Ordinary Course of Nature," *Isis* 81 (1990): 663–83. I wish to thank Douglas Jesseph and Reginald Savage for these references.

28. Hugo Grotius, . . . *Discourses, I: Of God and His Providence, II: Of Christ, His Miracles and Doctrines,* trans. Clement Barksdale (London, 1652) 39. (Emphasis added.) This volume was a popular abridgement of *De Veritate Religionis Christianae.* On the appeal of this apologetic, see Margaret Jacob, *The Newtonians and the English Revolution: 1689–1720* (Ithaca, N.Y., 1976), 22–71.

29. John Locke, "A Discourse on Miracles" in *The Reasonableness of Christianity,* ed. and abr. I. T. Ramsey (London, 1958), 80; Locke, *An Essay Concerning Human Understanding . . .* comp. Alexander Campbell Frazier, 2 vols. (New York, 1959), 2:382. For a discussion of Locke, see R. M. Burns, *The Great Debate on Miracles: From Joseph Glanvill to David Hume* (Lewisburg, Pa., 1981), 57–69. Much of my discussion of eighteenth-century issues has been illuminated by Burns's excellent volume, though the questions we ask are somewhat different.

30. Locke, *Reasonableness,* 82, 81.

31. Thomas Chubb, *A Discourse on Miracles Considered as Evidences to Prove the*

Divine Original of a Revelation (London, 1726), 83–93. On the Deist debate, see Burns, *Great Debate,* 70–96 (the Annet quotation is taken from p. 75), and Hans J. Hillebrand, "The Historicity of Miracles: The Early Eighteenth-Century Debates Among Woolston, Annet, Sherlock, and West," *Studies in Religion* 3 (1973): 132–51.

32. See Abraham Lemoine, *A Treatise on Miracles* . . . (London, 1747); and John Leland, *A View of the Principal Deistical Writers* . . . , 2 vols. (London, 1755), 2:134, who discusses Le Moyne (*sic*) and Chubb.

33. Jonas Proast was chaplain of All Souls Oxford. For background on the debate, see Ramsey's Introduction to Locke, *Reasonableness,* 88–90; and Mark Goldie, "John Locke, Jonas Proast and Religious Toleration 1688–1692," in *The Church of England c.1689–c.1833: From Toleration to Tractarianism,* ed. John Walsh, Colin Haydon, and Stephen Taylor (Cambridge, Eng., 1993), 143–71. On the nature of the Anglican appeal to antiquity, see Owen Chadwick, *From Bossuet to Newman: The Idea of Doctrinal Development* (Cambridge, Eng., 1957), 1–20; and G. V. Bennett, "Patristic Tradition in Anglican Thought," in *Oecumenica: An Annual Symposium of Ecumenical Research, 1971–72* (Minneapolis, Minn., 1972), 63–87.

34. *The Works of John Locke in Nine Volumes* (London, 1794), 5:443, 455.

35. Conyers Middleton, *A Free Inquiry into the Miraculous Powers Which Are Supposed to Have Subsisted in the Christian Church* . . . (1749; reprint ed., New York, 1976), xxxi–xxxii.

36. On Middleton as an eighteenth-century Latitudinarian, see Norman Sykes, *From Sheldon to Secker: Aspects of English Church History, 1660–1768* (Cambridge, Eng., 1959), 167–74. Leslie Stephen saw an even more radical agenda in the *Free Inquiry* and classified him as a covert Deist. See Stephen's *History of English Thought in the Eighteenth Century,* 2 vols. (1876: reprint ed., New York, 1949), 1:253–73.

37. William Dodwell, *A Free Answer to Dr. Middleton's Free Inquiry into the Miraculous Powers of the Primitive Church* (London, 1749); Thomas Church, *A Vindication of the Miraculous Powers Which Subsisted in the Three First Centuries of the Christian Church* . . . (London, 1750). Both faulted Middleton for surrendering the entire witness of the early church to Rome. Both men also received honorary degrees from Oxford University for their labors.

38. Middleton plays an important role in Benjamin B. Warfield's *Counterfeit Miracles* (New York, 1918), which will be discussed in chapter 7. The argument above is based upon negative evidence and is of course open to empirical refutation, but I have found no appeal to the miracles recorded in the first three centuries published in antebellum America, even among American high church Episcopalians who revived the appeal to the primitive church. Methodists proved to be something of an exception to this broader tendency. John Wesley was critical of Middleton, and Methodists more than other groups continued to have a strong interest in the world of wonders. On Wesley, see Ted A. Campbell, "John Wesley and Conyers Middleton on Divine Intervention in History," *Church History* 55 (1986): 39–49. Methodist exceptionalism is discussed in chapter 4.

39. *The Life of Edward Gibbon* . . . , ed. Rev. H. H. Milman (Paris, 1840), 45. Gibbon discusses the African confessors in chapter 37 of the *Decline and Fall.* See *The Decline and Fall of the Roman Empire,* 3 vols. (New York, [1932]) 2:377–78.

40. *An Inquiry Concerning Human Understanding,* ed. Charles W. Hendel (Indianapo-

lis, Ind., 1955), 122–23, 133. On Hume's argument, see Burns, *Great Debate*, 131–246, who also provides much bibliography.

41. Leland, *View,* 2:117. George Campbell makes a similar claim in *A Dissertation on Miracles* (Edinburgh, 1757), 232. The evidence of Abbé Pâris is also attacked in William Adams, *An Essay on Mr. Hume's "Essay on Miracles"* (London, 1752), 83 ff.

42. William Paley, *View of the Evidences of Christianity* in *The Works of William Paley, D. D.* (Philadelphia, 1853), 321–22, 326.

43. It is of course true that in America Paley's reputation was beginning to fade by the 1820s. But this had more to do with reevaluation of his third major work, *Principles of Moral and Political Philosophy.* On this latter shift, see E. Brooks Holifield, *The Gentlemen Theologians: American Theology in Southern Culture* (Durham, N.C., 1978), 134–37.

44. On the interrelationship between science and theology in antebellum America, see Theodore Dwight Bozeman, *Protestants in an Age of Science: The Baconian Ideal and Antebellum American Religious Thought* (Chapel Hill, N.C., 1977); and Herbert Hovenkamp, *Science and Religion in America: 1800–1860* (Philadelphia, 1978).

45. Timothy Dwight, *Theology Explained and Defended in a Series of Sermons,* 4 vols. (New York, 1850), 2:262; William Ellery Channing, "The Evidence of Revealed Religion," *The Works of William Ellery Channing,* 6 vols. (Boston, 1848), 3:106–7; Charles P. McIlvaine, *The Evidences of Christianity in Their External or Historical Division* (New York, 1832), 165. It is interesting that neither Channing, Dwight, nor McIlvaine address the problem of postbiblical miracles. In this sense they were not unique. Although refutation of Hume's essay became something of a cottage industry among American evangelicals, they paid almost no attention to the second half of the essay, even when their arguments were based on British models, which did include extended discussions of the question of modern miracles. See, for example (among many), Samuel Stanhope Smith, *A Comprehensive View of the Leading and Most Important Principles of Natural and Revealed Religion* (New Brunswick, N.J.: 1815); the refutations included in vol. 14 of the American Tract Society's *Evangelical Family Library*(New York, n.d.), 439–49, and Henry Ruffner, ed., *Lectures on the Evidences of Christianity, Delivered at the University of Virginia* (New York, 1852).

46. Charles Babbage, *The Ninth Bridgewater Treatise: A Fragment* (London, 1837), 134. His calculations are found on pp. 128–29.

47. The senior Emerson recorded this lament in *A Sermon, Preached at the Ordination of the Rev. Robinson Smiley.* It is quoted and discussed in Wesley T. Mott, *"The Strains of Eloquence": Emerson and His Sermons* (University Park, Pa., 1989), 75; E. G. Sanford, ed., *Memoirs of Archbishop Temple by Seven Friends . . . ,* 2 vols. (London, 1906), 1:18.

48. Andrew L. Drummond, *Edward Irving and His Circle* (London, 1938), 137–45. Thomas Boys, *The Suppressed Evidence: Or Proofs of the Miraculous Faith and Experience of the Church of Christ in All Ages* (London, 1832); and Baptist W. Noel, *Remarks on the Revival of Miraculous Powers in the Church* (London, 1831) offer two very different interpretations of these claims. Among the Americans interested in these occurrences was Horace Bushnell, as discussed in chapter 3.

49. On early Mormons and the miraculous, see Butler, *Awash in a Sea of Faith,* 242–45; and D. Michael Quinn, *Early Mormonism and the Magic World View* (Salt Lake City,

Utah, 1987), 192, 221–22. The question of Mormon miracles was to play a role in Theodore Parker's *Discourse of Religion,* to be discussed later in this chapter.

50. Of the many studies of antebellum American Unitarianism, I have found most helpful: Conrad Wright, *The Liberal Christians: Essays on American Unitarian History* (Boston, 1970); Daniel Walker Howe, *The Unitarian Conscience: Harvard Moral Philosophy, 1805–1861* (Cambridge, Mass., 1970); and Sydney E. Ahlstrom's introduction to *An American Reformation: A Documentary History of Unitarian Christianity,* ed. Sydney E. Ahlstrom and Jonathan S. Carey (Middletown, Conn., 1985).

51. Andrews Norton, *The Evidences of the Genuineness of the Gospels,* 2d ed., 3 vols. (Cambridge, Mass., 1846), 1:96. His argument against biblical infallibility is also set forth in his *Internal Evidences of the Genuineness of the Gospels* (Boston, 1855), 14 ff. Norton as exegete is discussed in Jerry W. Brown, *The Rise of Biblical Criticism in America, 1800–1870: The New England School* (Middletown, Conn., 1969), 75–93.

52. The literature on Transcendentalism is enormous, but among the best general surveys are Octavius Brooks Frothingham, *Transcendentalism in New England: A History* (1876; reprint ed., New York, 1959); William R. Hutchison, *The Transcendentalist Ministers: Church Reform in the New England Renaissance* (New Haven, Conn., 1959); Paul F. Boller, *American Transcendentalism: 1830–1860: An Intellectual Inquiry* (New York, 1974); and Catherine L. Albanese, *Corresponding Motion: Transcendental Religion and the New America* (Philadelphia, 1977). On the issue of biblical criticism, see John Edward Dirks, *The Critical Theology of Theodore Parker* (New York, 1948); and William Adler, "Theodore Parker and D. F. Strauss's *Das Leben Jesu* . . . ," *Unitarian Universalist Christian* 30 (1975): 19–30.

53. The classic account of the dispute is Hutchison, *The Transcendentalist Ministers,* 52–137. Many of the documents of the debate can be found in Perry Miller, ed., *The Transcendentalists: An Anthology* (Cambridge, Mass., 1960).

54. Emerson, "Divinity School Address," in *Theology in America: The Major Protestant Voices from Puritanism to Neo-Orthodoxy,* ed. Sydney E. Ahlstrom (Indianapolis, 1967), 302–3, 299.

55. Theodore Parker, *A Discourse of Matters Pertaining to Religion* (Boston, 1907), 10–11, 183–84, 215–16.

56. Ibid., 186–87; Theodore Parker, *Theism, Atheism, and Popular Theology, Sermons* (London, 1853), 181.

57. Parker, *Discourse,* 250, 251.

58. Parker *Discourse,* 39–58; Parker, *Theism,* 143.

59. Andrews Norton, *A Discourse on the Latest Form of Infidelity,* in Ahlstrom and Carey, *American Reformation,* 449; Norton, *Evidences of the Genuineness of the Gospels,* 1: 258–59, 260.

60. Indeed at least in one key way they had the reverse effect of drawing Unitarians and evangelical Protestants closer together. Norton published *Two Articles from the "Princeton Review," Concerning the Transcendental Philosophy God the Germans and of Cousin, and its Influence on Opinion in this Country* (Cambridge, Mass., 1840). The authors of these articles were Charles Hodge, James W. Alexander, and Albert B. Dod. The Boston reprint omitted an attack upon Norton's willingness to give up biblical infallibility, but this note was included in the British edition. See pp. 96–97.

61. This phrase was originally coined by Henry S. Commager. See "Tempest in a Boston Tea Cup," *New England Quarterly* 6 (1933), 651–52. I borrow it not to disparage the intellectual importance of the debate, but to substantiate my thesis that the great debate over miracles that engulfed English-speaking Protestantism at the end of the nineteenth century was distinct from the Transcendentalist-Unitarian debate.

Chapter 2: The Rise of the New Debate over Miracles

1. *Letters of the Rev. J. B. Mozley, D. D. . . . Edited by His Sister* (New York, 1885), 261–62. Emphasis added.

2. For twentieth-century attitudes about Mozley's writings, see Owen Chadwick, *The Victorian Church,* 2 vols. (London, 1966–70), 2:31–32; L. E. Elliott-Binns, *English Thought, 1860–1900: The Theological Aspect* (London, 1956), 53–54; John Stewart Lawton, *Miracles and Revelation* (London, 1959), 135–37; and B. M. G. Reardon, *From Coleridge to Gore: A Century of Religious Thought in Britain* (London, 1971) 155–57.

3. Perhaps the most recent and complete study of the controversy surrounding *Essays and Reviews* is Ieuan Ellis, *Seven Against Christ: A Study of 'Essays and Reviews'* (Leiden, Neth., 1980). See, too, Josef L. Altholz, "A Tale of Two Controversies: Darwinism and the Debate over 'Essays and Reviews,'" *Church History* 63 (1994): 50–59. On Powell and his contribution, see Pietro Corsi, *Science and Religion: Baden Powell and the Anglican Debate, 1800–1860* (Cambridge, Eng., 1988).

4. Baden Powell, "On the Study of Evidences of Christianity," in *Recent Inquiries in Theology . . . Being . . . "Essays and Reviews"* (Boston, 1860 [reprinted from the 2d London ed.]), 150.

5. Ibid, 124. As Ellis notes, Powell's essay is based upon his larger, more nuanced discussion of the scientific method, *Essays on the Spirit of Inductive Philosophy, The Unity of the Worlds, and the Philosophy of Creation* (London, 1855).

6. Ibid., 127.

7. On William E. Channing's influence, see William H. Channing, *The Life of William Ellery Channing, D. D.* (1880; reprint ed., Hicksville, N.Y., 1975), esp. 332–50. See also Corsi, *Baden Powell,* 215 ff.; and Martin Murphy, *Blanco White: Self-Banished Spaniard* (New Haven, Conn., 1989), 181 ff.

8. Powell, for example, alludes to them in his discussion of the problem of miracles. See p. 122 of his essay.

9. See Frank Podmore, *Modern Spiritualism: A History and a Criticism,* 2 vols. (London, 1902); John J. Cerullo, *The Secularization of the Soul: Psychical Research in Modern Britain* (Philadelphia, 1982); Logie Barrow, *Independent Spirits: Spiritualism and English Plebians, 1850–1910* (London, 1986); and on the connection between Spiritualism and feminism, Ann Braude, *Radical Spirits: Spiritualism and Women's Rights in Nineteenth Century America* (Boston, 1989).

10. See, for example, G. H. Forbes, *No Antecedent Impossibility in Miracles . . . By a Country Clergyman,* 2d ed. (London, 1861), 16–19.

11. Newman's arguments, and the response they elicited, will be discussed in detail in chapter 5.

12. On Froude's authorship of the *Life of St. Anthony* and its role in his abandonment

of the Christian faith, see Thomas Mozley, *Reminiscences: Chiefly of Oriel College and the Oxford Movement*, 2 vols. (Boston, 1884), 2:35–37.

13. On Max Müller's influence, see *The Life and Letters of the Right Honorable Friedrich Max Müller*, 2 vols. (London, 1902). For a recent discussion (with bibliography) of the problem of other religions in Victorian England, see Terence Thomas, "The Impact of Other Religions," in *Religion in Victorian Britain*, Vol. 2: *Controversies*, ed. Gerald Parsons (Manchester, Eng., 1988), 280–98.

14. Chadwick, *Victorian Church*, 2:31.

15. Mozley, *Eight Lectures on Miracles Preached Before the University of Oxford* (London, 1865), 9 ff.

16. Ibid., 209. In his discussion of special providence (pp. 9 ff.), Mozley discusses a number of the ecclesiastical miracles (e.g., the Thundering Legion, the death of Arius) that Newman invoked in his volume on ecclesiastical miracles.

17. Ibid., 283.

18. Ibid., 58.

19. Ibid., 68. For Mozley's application of this argument to a critique of Powell's essay, see pp. 294–95.

20. On the parallels between Mozley and Hume, see Alexander B. Bruce, *The Miraculous Elements of the Gospels* (New York, 1886), 44–46.

21. See Mozley, *Eight Lectures*, 275–92. In particular he acknowledged his indebtedness to William Whewall's criticism of John Stuart Mill.

22. *Letters of Mozley*, 262.

23. Mozley, *Eight Lectures*, 167.

24. Ibid., 75.

25. Ibid., 107, 114. Mozley went on to argue that the separation of the qualities of omnipotence and personality was also characteristic of the religions of the east.

26. On Mansel's argument and its effects, see (in addition to the standard secondary literature already cited in n. 2) W. R. Matthews, *The Religious Philosophy of Dean Mansel* (Oxford, 1956); and K. D. Freeman, *The Role of Reason in Religion: A Study of Henry Mansel* (The Hague, 1969). For the most celebrated response to Mansel (though by no means the most intellectually astute), see Frederick D. Maurice, *What Is Revelation? Letters to a Student of Theology on the Bampton Lectures of Mr. Mansel* (Cambridge, Eng., 1859).

27. See *Letters of Mozley*, 238–39.

28. Ellis, *Seven Against Christ*, 2–5.

29. On Tyndall's life, see A. S. Eve and C. H. Creasey, *Life and Work of John Tyndall* (London, 1945). For thoughtful observations on class antagonisms in the conflict between science and the churches, see Frank Turner, "John Tyndall and Victorian Scientific Naturalism," in *John Tyndall: Essays on a Natural Philosopher*, ed. W. H. Brock, N. D. McMillan, and R. C. Mollan (Dublin, 1981), 169–80.

30. Tyndall, "Miracles and Special Providences," in *Fragments of Science*, 2 vols. (New York, 1897), 2:23, 31. The essay had originally appeared in the *Fortnightly Review*.

31. Ibid., 19.

32. T. H. Huxley, *Hume* (New York, [1879]), 130. The philosophical groundwork for this new argument had been laid earlier by John Stuart Mill in a discussion of miracles in

his *A System of Logic: Ratiocinative and Inductive* . . . , *New Impression* (London, 1925), 407–18. For a contemporary critique of this "new Humean argument," see Benjamin B. Warfield, "The Question of Miracles," in *Selected Shorter Writings of Benjamin B. Warfield*, ed. John E. Meeter, 2 vols. (Phillipsburg, N.J., 1973), 2:178. For a modern discussion of this move, see R. M. Burns, *The Great Debate on Miracles: From Joseph Glanvill to David Hume* (Lewisburg, Pa., 1981), 84–85.

33. Tyndall, "Miracles and Special Providences," 2:16.

34. See, in particular, Daniel L. Pals, *The Victorian Lives of Jesus* (San Antonio, Tex., 1982), 31–50.

35. Tyndall, "Reflections on Prayer and Natural Law," in *Fragments of Science*, 2:5. As with his discussion of miracles, Tyndall here linked his opposition to the superstitions of Catholic peasants.

36. Ibid., 4.

37. Tyndall, "On Prayer as a Form of Physical Energy," in *Fragments of Science*, 2:41–42.

38. Tyndall, "The Prayer For the Sick," *Contemporary Review* 20 (1872): 209. Tyndall in this article quotes from an anonymous letter sent to him that proposed the prayer test. But he clearly supported the proposal, and during the controversy that it provoked it was always associated with Tyndall himself. On the prayer test controversy, see Stephen G. Brush, "The Prayer Test," *American Scientist* 62 (1974): 561–63.

39. J. W. Reynolds, *The Supernatural in Nature: A Verification by Free Use of Science* (London, 1878), 353.

40. On the public reaction to the American tour, see Brock, McMillan, and Mollan, *Tyndall*, 168–71; E. Brooks Holifield, *Health and Medicine in the Methodist Tradition: Journey Toward Wholeness* (New York, 1986), 39; and articles in the *New York Times*, Dec. 28, 1872, and Dec. 30, 1872. Among Tyndall's more thoughtful critics was Mark Hopkins, president of Williams College; his position will be discussed in detail in chapter 3.

41. For an elaboration of the theme of the connectedness between Protestantism and the orderly universe, see James Turner, *Without God, Without Creed: The Origins of Unbelief in America* (Baltimore, Md., 1985).

42. John Morley, "A Recent Work on Supernatural Religion," *Fortnightly Review* 16 (1874): 505–6.

43. [W. R. Cassels], *Supernatural Religion: An Inquiry into the Reality of Divine Revelation*, 2d ed., 2 vols. (London, 1874), 1:xiv.

44. Ibid., 1:xvi.

45. Ibid., 1:193. The categories of evaluation alluded to here are those set forth by Paley in his *View of the Evidences of Christianity*. See *The Works of William Paley, D. D.* (Philadelphia, 1853), 313–26.

46. *Supernatural Religion*, 1:202–3. These two spots were associated with Roman Catholic miracles. La Salette, a village near Grenoble, was where the Virgin Mary was said to have appeared in 1846. Naples was where the blood of St. Januarius appeared to liquefy. This recurring miracle was a continuing point of discussion; see chapter 5.

47. Ibid., 2:486.

48. For an amusing account of the controversy, see Henry Chadwick, *The Vindication of Christianity in Westcott's Thought* (Cambridge, Mass.., 1961), 20–23. Westcott himself offered his own defense in his preface to the fourth edition of *A General Survey of the History of the Canon of the New Testament* (London, 1875).

49. J. B. Lightfoot, *Essays on the Work Entitled "Supernatural Religion"* (London, 1889), 30–31.

50. Owen Chadwick, *Victorian Church,* 2:71. For a similar interpretation, see Henry Chadwick, *Vindication,* 22–23; and Pals, *Victorian Lives of Jesus,* 128–32.

51. Morley, "Recent Work on Supernatural Religion," 504, 506. In this essay he referred to the silencing of Bishop J. W. Colenso, who had earlier questioned the Mosaic authorship of the Pentateuch.

52. Ward, *A Writer's Recollection,* 2 vols. (London, 1918), 1:220.

53. Ibid., 1:222. For the life of Ward, see John Sutherland, *Mrs. Humphry Ward: Eminent Victorian, Pre-eminent Edwardian* (Oxford, 1990); on her religious developments, see William S. Peterson, *Victorian Heretic: Mrs. Humphry Ward's Robert Elsmere* (Leicester, Eng., 1976).

54. Mary A. Ward, *Robert Elsmere* (London, 1921), 277–78. All succeeding references are to this edition.

55. Peterson, *Victorian Heretic,* 132–33.

56. William Gladstone, "Robert Elsmere and the Battle of Belief," *Nineteenth Century* 23 (1888): 766–88.Oscar Wilde's comments can be found in Wilde, *Intentions,* (New York, n.d.), 15.

57. Sutherland, for example, entitles his chapter on the public reception of the book "Elsmere Mania;" see his *Ward,* 106–24.

58. This conversation was recounted by Ward. See Mrs. Humphry Ward to T. Humphry Ward, 9 Apr. 1888, Mary Ward Papers, Pusey House Library, Oxford, Eng. It is perhaps ironic that the papers of the author of *Robert Elsmere* now reside in the library of one of the leading Anglocatholic institutions in the world.

59. For this figure see Peterson, *Victorian Heretic,* 159. Sutherland, in his *Ward* (pp. 129 ff.), gives a lower figure.

60. Peterson, *Victorian Heretic,* 163, 178.

61. For two of the more extensive critiques, see Reynolds, *Supernatural in Nature*; and C. A. Row, *The Supernatural in the New Testament: Possible, Credible, and Historical* (London, 1875).

62. Peterson, *Victorian Heretic,* 181. Holmes quoted in Ward, *Writer's Recollection,* 2:92.

63. See, for example, William Newton Clarke, *Sixty Years with the Bible: A Record of Experience* (New York, 1912), 137–73; and Jerry Campbell, "Biblical Criticism in America, 1858–1892: The Emergence of the Historical Critic" (Ph.D. diss., University of Denver, 1982).

64. Julia Ward Howe et al., "Robert Elsmere's Mental Struggle," *North American Review* 148 (1889): 110, 111.

65. On this conflict, see Robert Bruce Mullin, "Biblical Critics and the Battle over Slavery," *Journal of Presbyterian History* 61 (1983): 210–26.

Chapter 3: The Miracle Question in America

1. On the role of nature in American religious thought at the time, see Conrad Cherry, *Nature and Religious Imagination: From Edwards to Bushnell* (Philadelphia, 1980), 66–133.

2. These essays were collected in *Faith and Philosophy: Discourses and Essays by Henry B. Smith . . .* , ed. George L. Prentiss (Edinburgh, 1878). On Smith, see George M. Marsden, *The Evangelical Mind and the New School Presbyterian Experience* (New Haven, Conn., 1970), 157–82.

3. *Faith and Philosophy,* 168.

4. Ibid., 189.

5. Ibid., 194.

6. Ibid., 439.

7. On these trends, see Claude Welch, *Protestant Thought in the Nineteenth Century,* 2 vols. (New Haven, Conn., 1972–85), 1:108–27, 269–73. The influence of the mediating theologians in America is discusssed in Walter H. Conser, Jr., *God and the Natural World: Religion and Science in Antebellum America* (Columbia, S.C., 1993).

8. Praise for these writers can be found in a number of places. See, for example, Smith's praise of Ullmann in "The Relation of Faith and Philosophy," reprinted in *Faith and Philosophy,* 36–37. Bushnell also praised Ullmann; see the letter reprinted in Mary B. Cheney, *Life and Letters of Horace Bushnell* (New York, 1903), 219. The subject of the influence of Schleiermacher is more complicated, particularly vis-à-vis the question of the miraculous. Schleiermacher's suggestion that miracles were only apparently supernatural, but were in fact in accordance with laws of nature not then fully understood, found no support among evangelical writers during mid-century, and was often pointedly attacked. See Richard Trench, *Notes on the Miracles of our Lord* (New York, 1853), 64 ff.

9. Trench, *Notes,* 78. See, too, p. 81. Trench was professor of theology at King's College, London, and later would become Archbishop of Dublin.

10. George P. Fisher, *Essays on the Supernatural Origin of Christianity, with Special Reference to the Theories of Renan, Strauss, and the Tübingen School* (New York, 1866), iii, 493. For the historical context of Fisher, see Louise L. Stevenson, *Scholarly Means to Evangelical Ends: The New Haven Scholars and the Transformation of Higher Learning in America, 1830–1890* (Baltimore, Md., 1986).

11. Fisher, *Supernatural Origin,* 496–507.

12. Ibid., 477. The philosopher to whom he directed his criticism was the Cambridge idealist John Grote, although in the 1871 edition of *Supernatural Origin* the name is misspelled as Grove.

13. Ibid., 510–11.

14. See McCosh's discussion in his *The Ulster Revival and Its Physiological Accidents* (London, [1859]). For background to the revival, see Peter Brooke, *Ulster Presbyterianism: The Historical Perspective* (New York, 1987).

15. James McCosh, *The Supernatural in Relation to the Natural* (New York, 1862), 103. The broader context of McCosh's intellectual system is discussed in J. David Hoeveler, Jr., *James McCosh and the Scottish Intellectual Tradition: From Glasgow to Prince-*

ton (Princeton, 1981); as well more generally in William M. Sloane, ed., *The Life of James McCosh* (New York, 1896).

16. McCosh, *Supernatural,* 246.

17. The literature on Bushnell is enormous, though comparatively few writers have addressed his treatment of the miraculous. See the bibliography of Bushnell studies in James O. Duke, *Horace Bushnell on the Vitality of Biblical Language* (Chico, Calif., 1984), 110–26.

18. See, for example, "The Immediate Knowledge of God," in *Sermons on Living Subjects* (New York, 1910), 114–28.

19. Cheney, *Life of Bushnell,* 358.

20. Bushnell, *Nature and the Supernatural as Together Constituting the One System of God,* new ed. (New York, 1871), v.

21. The ball example is from Bushnell, *Nature and the Supernatural,* 253. His linking of human will to the supernatural was by no means a unique argument to Bushnell. Over a decade earlier Trench had made a similar claim. See his *Notes on the Miracles of our Lord,* 21.

22. Bushnell, *Nature and the Supernatural,* 254, and 251–75. Bushnell quoted from Agassiz's *An Essay on Classification,* which was originally published as the introduction to *Contributions to the Natural History of the United States.* On Agassiz's view of evolution, see Edward Lurie, *Louis Agassiz: A Life in Science* (Chicago, 1960), 252–303; and Peter J. Bowler, *Evolution: The History of an Idea,* rev. ed. (Berkeley, Calif., 1989), 126–29. On Bushnell and evolution, see Thomas Paul Thigpen, "On the Origin of Theses: An Exploration of Horace Bushnell's Rejection of Darwinism," *Church History* 57 (1988): 499–513.

23. Theodore T. Munger, *Horace Bushnell: Preacher and Theologian* (London, n.d.), 224.

24. Bushnell, *Nature and the Supernatural,* 316–17. For a parallel of this emphasis on the character of Jesus, see McCosh, *Supernatural,* 246.

25. See, for example, George A. Gordon, *Religion and Miracle* (Boston, 1909), 83–92. Gordon's reworking of Bushnell is discussed in chapter 6.

26. Bushnell, *Nature and the Supernatural,* 350.

27. Ibid., 447.

28. Ibid., 448.

29. Ibid., 453, 451.

30. Ibid., 468, 457. The Scottish miracles involving the brothers James and George MacDonald and a "Miss Fancourt" were a great issue of debate within evangelical circles in the early 1830s. Their integrity was upheld by the *Irvingite Morning Watch or Quarterly Journal on Prophecy, and Theological Review* (which was Bushnell's source). The criticism of them was led by the *Christian Observer,* which was the source Bushnell alluded to in the text. See *Christian Observer* (American ed.) 41 (1831): 99 ff.

31. Bushnell acknowledged that John Henry Newman was attempting much the same endeavor in England, yet the Protestant Bushnell was clear in distinguishing the miracles he was defending from those "ecclesiastical" miracles of Newman. These for Bushnell were to be dismissed because they did not reflect the high moral character that was necessary for a true miracle.

32. John Howie, *Biographia Scoticana: or A Brief Account of . . . Scots Worthies*, 2d ed. (Glasgow, 1827).

33. Bushnell, *Nature and the Supernatural*, 467. At the very end of his life Bushnell hoped to return to this theme of glossolalia. See Bushnell, *The Spirit of Man: Sermons and Selections* (New York, 1903), 27–28, 34–35.

34. Bushnell, *Nature and the Supernatural*, 475–90.

35. For a summary of the criticism, see Robert Bruce Mullin, "Horace Bushnell and the Question of Miracles," *Church History* 58 (1989): 468–71.

36. Munger, *Bushnell*, 216.

37. On the widespread interest in the experience of religious reality, see Grant Wacker, "The Holy Spirit and the Spirit of the Age in American Protestantism, 1880–1910," *Journal of American History* 72 (1985): 54–57.

38. Bushnell, *Nature and the Supernatural*, 68–69. The critique of pantheism is found throughout the volume, but it is not always directed against Emerson.

39. Ibid., 506, 507, 515.

40. Ibid., 499, 521. Second emphasis added.

41. *Biblical Repertory and Princeton Review* 31(1859): 155.

42. Bushnell, *Nature and the Supernatural*, 486–89. Bushnell used this account in the culmination of his chapter on modern miracles. For its importance for Bushnell, see Cheney, *Life of Bushnell*, 466–67.

43. The liberal appropriation of Bushnell is discussed at length in chapter 6. For an appeal to Bushnell by an early proponent of faith healing, see A. J. Gordon, *The Ministry of Healing, or Miracle Cures in All Ages* (Boston, 1882), 110–15.

44. Francis Galton et al., *The Prayer Gauge Debate . . .* (Boston, 1876), 135–36.

45. Mark Hopkins, *Prayer and the Prayer Gauge, A Discourse . . .* (Albany, N.Y., 1873), 6, 9–11.

46. Even the heresies theologians accused each other of were different after the Civil War. The mid-century emphasis upon the supernatural had given to theology a tendency of focusing on its coming from above, and thus always leaving itself open to the charge of Sabellianism by underemphasizing the independence of the second person of the trinity. See, for example, Henry Boynton Smith, *Faith and Philosophy*, 39 ff. For a historical discussion of this phenomenon, see Fred Kirschenmann, "Horace Bushnell: Orthodox or Sabellian?" *Church History* 33 (1964), 49–59. After the 1870s the emphasis shifted to the humanity of Jesus, and the charges of Sabellianism disappeared.

47. The literature on the influence of Darwin is legion. The best, and most provocative, biography is Adrian Desmond and James Moore, *Darwin* (New York, 1991). Still one of the most thoughtful of studies is Gertrude Himmelfarb, *Darwin and the Darwinian Revolution* (New York, 1959). On the effect of Darwinism on religion, James R. Moore, *The Post-Darwinian Controversies: A Study of the Protestant Struggle to Come to Terms with Darwin in Great Britain and America* (Cambridge, Eng., 1979) is the best general study, and Jon H. Roberts, *Darwinism and the Divine in America: Protestant Intellectuals and Organic Evolution, 1859–1900* (Madison, Wis., 1988) is the most complete account of the American debate.

48. On this see George Harris, *A Century's Change in Religion* (New York, 1914), 87–95.

49. *Progressive Orthodoxy: A Contribution to the Christian Interpretation of Christian Doctrines, by the Editors of "The Andover Review"* ed. Egbert C. Smyth, William J. Tucker, J. W. Churchill, George Harris, and Edward Hinks (Boston, 1885). Many of the contributors were associated with Andover Seminary and these essays had appeared earlier in the *Andover Review.*

50. The best study of this work is still Daniel Day Williams, *The Andover Liberals: A Study in American Theology* (New York, 1941). See, too, William R. Hutchison, *The Modernist Impulse in American Protestantism* (Cambridge, Mass., 1976); and Bruce Kuklick, *Churchmen and Philosophers: From Jonathan Edwards to John Dewey* (New Haven, Conn., 1985).

51. *Progressive Orthodoxy*, 213. Emphasis added.

52. Theodore T. Munger, "Notes on Robert Elsmere," *Christian Union* 38 (Dec. 6, 1888): 644.

53. George A. Gordon, *"Robert Elsmere"* (Boston, 1888), 12. This was a review published in pamphlet form.

54. H. A. Westall, *Robert Elsmere: Was He a Unitarian?* (Bloomington, Ill., 1888), 5.

55. John Burroughs, "Dr. Munger on *Robert Elsmere*," *Christian Union* 39 (Jan. 3, 1889): 9. The wider context of Burroughs's religious views is discussed in Clifford Hazeldine Osborne, *The Religion of John Burroughs* (Boston, 1930).

Chapter 4: The Question of Healing

1. The above account is taken from George Cubitt, *The Life of Martin Luther . . .* (New York, 1844), 311–12. Cubitt's book was a publication of the Methodist Episcopal Church. This story was picked up by the defenders of faith healing and used as a historical antecedent for their movement. See Adoniram J. Gordon, *The Ministry of Healing, or Miracle Cures in All Ages* (Boston, 1882), 94–96. Martin Marty offers a modern interpretation of the account in *Health and Medicine in the Lutheran Tradition: Being Well* (New York, 1983), 88.

2. W. R. Greg, "Realisable Ideals," in *Enigmas of Life* (Boston, 1873), 30–36. The literature on the transformation of the medical profession during these years is legion, and the transformation has been variously interpreted. See, for example, John Duffy, *The Healers: A History of American Medicine* (New York, 1976); William G. Rothstein, *American Physicians in the Nineteenth Century: From Sects to Science* (Baltimore, Md., 1972); John S. Haller, *American Medicine in Transition, 1840–1910* (Urbana, Ill., 1981); and George Rosen and Charles E. Rosenberg, ed., *The Structure of American Medical Practice, 1875–1941* (Philadelphia, 1983). One testimony of the interest in medicine and healing during this period is found in Poole's *Index to Periodical Literature*, which records almost as many articles on medicine published between 1882 and 1892 as had been published during the preceding eighty years.

3. David D. Hall, *Worlds of Wonder, Days of Judgement: Popular Religious Belief in Early New England* (Cambridge, Mass., 1990), 196–210; Geoffrey Marks and William K. Beatty, *The Story of Medicine in America* (New York, 1973), 45–47.

4. The subject of alternative healing in nineteenth-century America is enormous. Among the many sources, I have found most useful Norman Gevitz, ed., *Other Healers:*

Unorthodox Medicine in America, From the Civil War to World War 1 (Baltimore, Md., 1988); Gail T. Parker, *Mind Cure in New England* (Hanover, N.H., 1973); Catharine L. Albanese, "Physic and Metaphysic in Nineteenth-Century America: Medical Sectarians and Religious Healing," *Church History* 55 (1986): 489–502; also Albanese, *Nature Religion in America: From the Algonkian Indians to the New Age* (Chicago, 1990); and Robert C. Fuller, *Alternative Medicine and American Religious Life* (New York, 1989).

5. William A. Muhlenberg, *A Plea for a Church Hospital in the City of New York* (New York, 1850), 13–14. In this regard one also cannot discount the challenge provided by the increasing Catholic presence in the United States. Commentators at the time regularly praised the Catholic Church for its works of charity, including its care for the sick.

6. Muhlenberg, *Plea,* 7. Emphasis in original.

7. On the rise of the modern hospital, see John D. Thompson, *The Hospital: A Social and Architectural History* (New Haven, Conn., 1975); and Charles E. Rosenberg, *The Care of Strangers: The Rise of America's Hospital System* (New York, 1987). Morris J. Vogel, *The Invention of the Modern Hospital: Boston 1870–1930* (Chicago, 1980) is an excellent discussion of one hospital that also includes an interesting treatment of the conflict between the new hospitals and faith healing homes.

8. Muhlenberg, *Plea,* 11.

9. On St. Luke's Hospital, see Anne Ayres, *The Life and Work of William Augustus Muhlenberg* (New York, 1880); and Alvin W. Skardon, *Church Leader in the Cities: William Augustus Muhlenberg* (Philadelphia, [1971]). On Presbyterian Hospital see Albert R. Lamb, *The Presbyterian Hospital and the Columbia Presbyterian Medical Center, 1868–1943 . . .* (New York, 1955). On Methodist hospitals, see E. Brooks Holifield, *Health and Medicine in the Methodist Tradition: Journey Toward Wholeness* (New York, 1986); and George Preston Mains, *James Monroe Buckley* (New York, 1917).

10. Ayres, *Muhlenberg,* 277, 298, 214. Ayres herself was the first American nun of the Anglican tradition and was actively involved in St. Luke's Hospital as well. Presbyterian Hospital seems not to have followed this pattern.

11. George M. Marsden and Bradley J. Longfield, *The Secularization of the Academy* (New York, 1992), 13–25. For an example of this trend, see Lamb's *Presbyterian Hospital,* which pointedly downplays the hospital's religious roots.

12. Cited in Donald Dayton, *Theological Roots of Pentecostalism* (Grand Rapids, Mich., 1987), 120. A. J. Gordon appealed to Bengel's example and exegesis. See his *Ministry of Healing,* 100.

13. On the role of these writers, see Peder Olsen, *Healing Through Prayer,* trans. John Jensen (Minneapolis, Minn., 1962); and Marty, *Health and Medicine in the Lutheran Tradition.* Gordon referred to Stockmayer in *Ministry of Healing* (p. 165) as the "theologian of the doctrine of healing by faith," and his works in English translation, particularly *Sickness and the Gospel,* went through multiple editions.

14. *Dorothea Trudel, or The Prayer of Faith,* 3d ed., revised and enlarged (Boston, 1872), 20. English-speaking writers would refer to her as either Trudel or Truedel.

15. "A Letter to the Right Reverend Lord Bishop of Gloucester . . ." in *The Works of John Wesley,* 14 vols. (1872; reprint ed., Grand Rapids, Mich., 1978): 9, 124. Wesley went on in this tract to deny that he ever personally laid claim to possessing miraculous

gifts, and that there was any connection between these works, including healings and individual faith. For Wesley's view on the issue of supernatural intervention, see Ted A. Campbell, "John Wesley and Conyers Middleton on Divine Intervention in History," *Church History* 55 (1986): 39–49.

16. Harold Y. Vanderpool, "The Wesleyan-Methodist Tradition," in Ronald L. Numbers and Darrel W. Amundsen, *Caring and Curing: Health and Medicine in the Western Religious Traditions* (New York, 1986), 320–30; and Holifield, *Health and Medicine in the Methodist Tradition,* 28–47.

17. John Wesley, *A Plain Account of Christian Perfection,* in John A. Hardon, S.J., *The Spirit and Origins of American Protestantism: A Source Book in Its Creeds* (Dayton, Ohio, 1968), 233.

18. The classic account of this revival and the role of the doctrine of the Holy Spirit in interpreting it is still Timothy L. Smith, *Revivalism and Social Reform: American Protestantism on the Eve of the Civil War* (Nashville, Tenn., 1957).

19. See Diana Butler's study of Charles P. McIlvaine on this increased concern for the doctrine of the holy spirit, *Standing Against the Whirlwind: Evangelical Episcopalians in Nineteenth-Century America* (New York, 1995), 158 ff.

20. This is not to deny that the phenomenon had older roots. The Methodist faith healer Ethan O. Allen claimed that within Methodist circles it could be traced back to the 1840s. But it is noteworthy that Allen's defense of faith healing was not published until 1881. See *Faith Healing: or What I Have Witnessed of the Fulfilling of James V:14, 15, 16* (Philadelphia, 1881).

21. The best accounts of Cullis's life are still probably W. E. Boardman, *Faith Work: or the Labours of Dr. Cullis in Boston,* 2d ed. (London, 1875); and W. H. Daniels, *Have Faith in God: Dr. Cullis and His Work* (Boston, 1885). The most complete contemporary studies are those of Raymond J. Cunningham, "Ministry of Healing: The Origins of the Psychotherapeutic Role of the American Churches," (Ph.D. diss., The Johns Hopkins University, 1965); Paul G. Chappell, "The Divine Healing Movement in America," (Ph.D. diss., Drew University, 1983); and Dayton, *Theological Roots of Pentecostalism.*

22. The board was listed in the annual report of the Consumptives' Home. On Huntington's involvement, see Arria S. Huntington, *Memoirs and Letters of Frederic Dan Huntington* (Boston, 1906), 241.

23. Even persons who were to break with Cullis over faith healing continued to defend his work as an example of practical Christian charity. See William I. Gill, "The Faith Cure," *New England Magazine* 5 (1887): 438–48.

24. Müller and his orphanage were a topic of great interest among English-speaking Protestants, particularly among those critical of the overly rational policies of the religious and benevolent societies of the period. On the appeal of Müller, see H. Lincoln Wayland, ed., *The Life of Trust: Being a Narrative of the Lord's Dealings with George Müller . . .* (Boston, 1864); and William Henry Harding, *The Life of George Müller* (London, 1914).

25. Daniels, *Have Faith in God,* 116.

26. Charles T. Cullis, *Faith Cures* (Boston, 1879), 5.

27. Daniels, *Have Faith in God,* 126–27.

28. The following is based on the writings of ten individuals: Cullis, W. E. Boardman,

A. J. Gordon, R. Kelso Carter, R. L. Marsh, Robert L. Stanton, Samuel Gracey, Daniel Steele, Carrie Judd [Montgomery], and A. B. Simpson.

29. R. Kelso Carter, *The Atonement for Sin and Sickness; or a Full Salvation for Soul and Body* (Boston, 1884), 23.

30. The Rev. D. D. Smith in *Record of the International Conference on Divine Healing and True Holiness Held at the Agricultural Hall, London, June 1 to 5, 1885* (London, 1885), 91–92. In their reconceptualizing of Christian history, they even rediscovered the seventeenth-century Irish healer Valentine Greatrakes. See Ibid., 155.

31. Gordon, *Ministry of Healing,* 75.

32. Carter, *Atonement for Sin and Sickness,* 66.

33. Cited in Boardman, *Faith-Work,* 23.

34. R. L. Marsh, *Faith Healing: A Defense* (New York, 1889), 145.

35. Robert L. Stanton, "Healing Through Faith," *Presbyterian Review* 5 (1884), 50.

36. Marsh, *Faith Healing,* 80–81.

37. Charles T. Cullis, *Faith Cures* (Boston, 1879), 5.

38. Carter, *Atonement for Sin and Sickness,* 5.

39. Carrie Judd [Montgomery], *The Prayer of Faith* (New York, 1880), 37. Emphasis added.

40. Gordon, *Ministry of Healing,* 195. See also Grant Wacker, "The Holy Spirit and the Spirit of the Age in American Protestantism, 1880–1910," *Journal of American History* 72 (1985): 54–57.

41. Carter, *Atonement for Sin and Sickness,* 90.

42. See contributions in *Divine Healing and True Holiness,* 31–32.

43. Simpson's speech is recorded in *Divine Healing and True Holiness,* 80; Gordon's quote is from his *Ministry of Healing,* 10. On Simpson and healing, see A. W. Tozer, *Wingspread: Albert B. Simpson — A Study in Spiritual Altitude* (Harrisburg, Pa., 1943).

44. D. D. Smith in *Divine Healing and True Holiness,* 92. A. B. Simpson made a similar appeal. See *Divine Healing,* 69.

45. Judd, *Prayer of Faith,* 28.

46. Gordon, *Ministry of Healing,* 193.

47. Charles T. Cullis, *Other Faith Cures* (Boston, 1885), vii.

48. Cited in Daniels, *Have Faith in God,* 162–63.

49. Gordon, *Ministry of Healing,* 116.

50. Ibid., 205.

51. A. B. Simpson, *The Gospel of Healing* (Harrisburg, Pa., 1915 [1885]), 69.

52. Gordon, *Ministry of Healing,* 202.

53. Simpson, *Gospel of Healing,* 40 ff.

54. On this question R. Kelso Carter provides an interesting example. In his early writings he followed this line of reasoning to its logical conclusion, rejecting medicine as a sign of a lack of faith. After the publication of *Atonement for Sin and Sickness,* he suffered another serious ailment and was helped by medicine. This experience led him to reassess his early position. See *"Faith Healing" Reviewed* (Boston, 1897).

55. This lack of interest was typical. A survey of the literature suggests that the great concern over Christian Science (to be discussed in chapter 7) did not begin until the middle of the 1890s, and did not peak until the first decade of the twentieth century. On

Gordon's alleged attraction to Christian Science, see James M. Buckley, *The Fundamentals and Their Contrasts* (New York, 1906), 151. As we will see, however, Buckley is not a disinterested source.

56. Carter, *Atonement for Sin and Sickness*, 176–79.

57. Holifield, *Health and Medicine in the Methodist Tradition*, 40ff. Buckley, it should be noted, did not limit his attacks to faith healing, but also criticized Spiritualism, Christian Science, and eventually the Emmanuel Movement. See James M. Buckley, *Faith-Healing, Christian Science and Kindred Phenomena* (New York, 1892).

58. The following is based on the anti-faith healing writings of James M. Buckley, Marvin R. Vincent, George Hepworth, L. T. Townsend, Alfred T. Schofield, Walter Moxon, Leonard W. Bacon, W. McDonald, Clyde W. Votaw, A. F. Schauffler, Alexander B. Bruce, Samuel T. Spear, and a number of unsigned articles in various periodicals of the period.

59. Buckley, *Faith-Healing*, 40, 36–37; Marvin R. Vincent, "Modern Miracles," *Presbyterian Review* 4 (1883): 479. Vincent was later to become professor of Sacred Literature at Union Theological Seminary, New York.

60. Marvin R. Vincent, "Healing Through Faith," *Presbyterian Review* 5 (1884): 329.

61. George Hepworth, "The Faith Cure," *Independent* 34 (Oct. 19, 1882): 1. See, too, Samuel T. Spear, "The Faith Cure," *Independent* 34 (Sept. 14, 1882): 7–8; and Leonard W. Bacon, "The Faith Cure Delusion," *Forum* 5 (1888).

62. Both Buckley and L. T. Townsend use this term. See Buckley, *Faith-Healing*, 8; and L. T. Townsend, *"Faith Work," Christian Science, and Other Cures* (Boston, 1885), 28.

63. See James G. Burrow, *Organized Medicine in the Progressive Era: The Move Toward Monopoly* (Baltimore, Md., 1977;, and Martin Kaufman, *Homeopathy in America: The Rise and Fall of a Medical Heresy* (Baltimore, Md., 1971).

64. Alfred T. Schofield, *A Study of Faith Healing* (New York: n.d.), 11.

65. Alexander B. Bruce, *The Miraculous Elements of the Gospel* (New York, 1886), 317. These were lectures originally given at Union Theological Seminary in New York.

66. Samuel L. Gracey and Daniel Steele, *Healing by Faith: Two Essays* (Boston, 1882), 45.

67. Almost all the leading New England liberals argue this, and almost unanimously they trace their argument from Bushnell. See, among many, George Harris, *A Century's Change in Religion* (New York, 1919), 42–46; and Theodore T. Munger, *Horace Bushnell: Preacher and Theologian* (London, [1899]), 68 ff.

68. On the assassination, see James D. McCabe, *Our Martyred President . . . The Life and Public Services of Gen. James A. Garfield* (Philadelphia, 1881).

69. Townsend, "Faith Work," 120–29. On the Garfield assassination, see also Vincent, "Healing Through Faith," 326. The argument for the prayer instinct had already been made vis-à-vis Tyndall a decade earlier. See Leonard W. Bacon, "Prayer, Miracle, and Natural Law," *Fraser's Magazine* n.s. 8 (1873): 340 ff.

70. For one of the earliest and most influential popularizations of this argument in America, see Newman Smyth, *The Religious Feeling: A Study for Faith* (New York, 1877).

71. Gordon, *Ministry of Healing*, 219.

72. R. L. Stanton, *Healing Through Faith Again* (Buffalo, N.Y., 1884), 29.

Chapter 5: Catholics and the Question of Miracles

1. James Kent Stone, *The Invitation Heeded* (New York: Catholic Publication Society, 1870), 73, 76, 77. This work went through multiple editions during the end of the nineteenth century and was favorably compared with Newman's own *Apologia*. On Lecky and Protestantism, see W. E. H. Lecky, *History of the Rise and Influence of the Spirit of Rationalism in Europe*, 2 vols. (New York, 1900), 1:79–82. The conversion of Stone was seen as a scandal among American Episcopalians. See W. Hubert Smythe, *The Invitation Answered: A Reply to J. Kent Stone's "Invitation Heeded"* . . . (New York, 1871).

2. [Augustine F. Hewit] "The Reality of the Supernatural Order," *Catholic World* 29 (1879): 482. See also Aquinas, *Summa Theologiae*, 1a. 105, 8. For the invoking of Thomas, see (among many) John Gilmary Shea, ed., *The Catholic Educator: A Library of Catholic Instruction and Devotion* (New York, 1889); Paul Schanz, *A Christian Apology* (E.T.: New York, 1891); and J. J. Quinn, "Miracles . . ." *American Ecclesiastical Review* 6 (Jan. 1892). Other Catholic writers, most notably the future Benedict XIV, were willing to admit that members of the created order could in a secondary sense perform miracles. See John A. Hardon, "The Concept of Miracle from St. Augustine to Modern Apologetics," *Theological Studies* 15 (1954): 229–57. English-speaking writers commenting on miracles seemed on the whole to emphasize the Thomistic point of view.

3. Aquinas, *Summa Theologiae*, 1a. q.105, a.7. Shea also makes this distinction. See his *Catholic Educator*, 298–99.

4. The classic statement of these themes in English was that of George Hay. See his *The Scripture Doctrine of Miracles Displayed*, 2 vols. (New York, 1851), 2:216.

5. On the insistence that no Catholic could ever claim a miracle see John England, "Report . . . upon the Miraculous Restoration of Mrs. Ann Mattingly, of Washington D.C." in *The Works of the Right Rev. John England* . . . , 5 vols. (Baltimore, Md., 1849), 3:415.

6. John Milner, *The End of Religious Controversy* . . . (New York, n.d.), 137–38.

7. Ibid., 146.

8. *The Life of St. Francis Xavier, of the Society of Jesus* . . . (Philadelphia, 1841), 138–39. As it will be shown, this account was a source of controversy throughout the nineteenth century. This English translation also reprints Milner's defense of the historical veracity of the miracles of Francis Xavier.

9. England, *Examination of Evidence and Report to the Most Rev. James Whitfield, D. D.* . . . *upon the Miraculous Restoration of Mrs Ann Mattingly* (Charleston, S.C., 1830), [2]; James A. Corcoran, "Miraculous Powers in the True Church," *American Catholic Quarterly Review* 1 (1876): 350.

10. See, for example, Acts 19:6 and James 5:14–5. This, as we have seen, was an old argument. Calvin had used it to reject the sacramental nature of confirmation and anointing. See *Institutes of the Christian Religion,* ed. John T. McNeill, trans. Ford Lewis Battles, 2 vols. (Philadelphia, 1960), 2:1453–56, 1465–67.

11. James Cardinal Gibbons, *The Faith of Our Fathers: Being a Plain Exposition and Vindication of the Church Founded by Our Lord Jesus Christ,* 88th ed. (New York, 1917), 281–82.

12. "Two Miraculous Conversions from Judaism," *Catholic World* 39 (1884): 613.

13. Johannes Jorgensen, *Lourdes* (E.T.: London, 1914), 182.

14. [Augustine F. Hewit], "Christianity and Positivism," *Catholic World* 14 (1871): 4.

15. Ibid., 14.

16. Andrew Dickson White, *A History of the Warfare of Science with Theology in Christendom*, 2 vols. (New York, 1929), 2:20.

17. Thomas F. Hughes, "History at Cornell University: Some Canons of Criticism for Dr. White's Legends," American Ecclesiastical Review 17 (1897), 251.

18. See the following articles by Thomas F. Hughes: "*The Popular Science Monthly* on the Miracles of St. Francis Xavier," *Catholic World* 53 (1891): 837–49; "Dr. A. White on St. Francis Xavier's Gift of Tongues," *Catholic World* 54 (1891): 20–32; "Dr. A. D. White on the Warfare of Science with Theology," *American Ecclesiastical Review* 17 (1897): 597–615; "The Cornell Historian: or Dr. A. D. White's Legend About St. Francis Xavier," *American Ecclesiastical Review* 17 (1897): 46–60; and "Dr. White's Evolution: The Genesis and Structure of His Legend," *American Ecclesiastical Review* 17 (1897): 184–206. See also A. F. Hewit, "The Warfare of Science," *Catholic World* 54 (1891). White added substantially to his *Popular Science Monthly* article to answer some of the Catholic objections. Cf. *Warfare* and *Popular Science Monthly* 39 (1891), 1–10.

19. See, for example, "A Miraculous Cure in St. Louis," *Ave Maria* 3 (1867), 136; and "Mary Immaculate," *Ave Maria* 4 (1868) 505. Ann Taves, *The Household of Faith: Roman Catholic Devotions in Mid-Nineteenth Century America* (Notre Dame, 1986), 56–69; and Jay P. Dolan, *The American Catholic Experience* (Garden City, N.Y., 1985), 233–35. I wish to thank Jay Dolan for the *Ave Maria* references.

20. The standard account of the miracle is England's *Examination of Evidence . . .* (which is also included in his *Works*). For a modern discussion of the healing, see Taves, *Household of Faith*, 57.

21. England, *Works*, 3:408, 410. The healing was alleged to be through the intercession of a German healer and priest Prince Hohenloe. For a discussion of the healing, see Taves, *Household of Faith*, 57.

22. James Parton, "Our Roman Catholic Brethren," *Atlantic Monthly* 21 (1868), 451.

23. Ibid., 451–52.

24. The following account is based on a number of sources. In addition to the nineteenth- and early-twentieth-century accounts discussed below, see Rene Laurentin, *Bernadette of Lourdes: A Life Based on Authenticated Documents* (Minneapolis, Minn.: c. 1979); Edith Saunders, *Lourdes* (New York, 1940); Alan Neame, *The Happening at Lourdes: The Sociology of the Grotto* (New York, 1967); Richard Fredericke Clarke, *Lourdes, Its Inhabitants, Its Pilgrims and Its Miracles* (London, 1888); John W. Lynch, *Bernadette — The Only Witness* (Boston, 1981); and Michel Agnellet, *I Accept These Facts: The Lourdes Cures Examined* (London, 1958).

25. For this figure, see Patrick Marnham, *Lourdes: A Modern Pilgrimage* (New York, 1980), 185–91.

26. Lasserre's account was translated and serialized in *The Catholic World* in 1870 and 1871. The translation was published in book form in 1884. Lasserre's work was also used as a major source for the account of Lourdes by Denys Shyne Lawler, serialized in *Ave Maria* in 1870 and 1871.

27. Lasserre, "Our Lady of Lourdes," *Catholic World* 11 (1870): 758; 12 (1870): 397, 264.

28. Ibid., 12:542.

29. According to the faithful, the Virgin Mary appeared at Knock in County Mayo in Ireland in 1879. See Peter O'Dwyer, *Mary: A History of Devotion in Ireland* (Dublin, 1988), 267. For a critique of the apparition, see Michael P. Carroll, *The Cult of the Virgin Mary: Psychological Origins* (Princeton, N.J., 1986), 202–11.

30. Tyng's sermon caused a sensation at the time, but I have still not been able to locate a surviving copy of the text. These quotations are from the articles in the *New York Herald*, Nov. 22, 1880, and the *New York Times*, Nov. 23, 1880. The sermon was also commented upon in other New York newspapers. For other comments on the sermon, see Marvin R. Vincent, "Modern Miracles," *Presbyterian Review* 4 (1883): 492; and "Dr. Tyng's Sermon on 'The Mountain Movers,'" *Catholic World* 33 (1881): 1–8.

31. See, for example, Stephen Bonsal, "A Pilgrimage to Lourdes," *Century Illustrated Monthly Magazine* 47 (1893–94): 659–70; or Edward Berdoe, "A Medical View of the Miracles at Lourdes," *Nineteenth Century* 38 (1895): 614–18. Nor was this sympathy limited to Lourdes alone. See the surprising response of Edward Benson, then archbishop of Canterbury (and no friend of Roman Catholicism) to his visit to La Salette recorded in Arthur Christopher Benson, *The Life of Edward White Benson*, 2 vols. (London, 1899), 2:691. This is not to deny that there were still negative accounts of Lourdes that criticized the superstition there, but what is striking is the surprising open-mindedness of many of the commentators.

32. Robert Hugh Benson, *Lourdes* (London, 1914), 57–58.

33. *The Works of Joseph Addison*, 3 vols. (New York, 1845), 3:340–41; White, *Warfare*, 2:80; James Jackson Jarves, *Italian Sights and Papal Principles Seen Through American Spectacles* (New York, 1856), 202. See, too, William Furniss, *The Land of the Caesar and Doge* . . . (New York, 1853); Charles Dickens, *Pictures from Italy* (New York, 1974); Octavian Blewitt, *Handbook For Travellers in Southern Italy* . . . (London, 1853); and Mozley, *Letters*, 278–79.

34. *Addison*, 3:341. The most detailed defense of the miracle by an English-speaking Catholic was by Patrick N. Lynch (bishop of Charleston). His *The Liquefaction of the Blood of St. Januarius at Naples* (New York, 1872) was the republication of his articles published in *Catholic World* in 1871.

35. Newman's essay was part of his larger work, "The Life of Apollonius Tyanaeus . . .," which appeared in *Encyclopaedia Metropolitana*, 1825–26.

36. Sheridan Gilley, *Newman and His Age* (London, 1990) discusses the importance of Hume for Newman; see p. 57. See also Robert Pattison, *The Great Dissent: John Henry Newman and the Liberal Heresy* (New York, 1991), 152–56. On Newman's disappointment with the reaction of even his friends to the *Lives of the Saints*, see Ian Ker, *John Henry Newman: A Biography* (Oxford, 1988), 282 ff. The influence of Hume on Newman was not missed by contemporary critics. See A. M. Fairbairn, *Catholicism: Roman and Anglican* (London, 1899).

37. John Henry Newman, *Two Essays on Biblical and on Ecclesiastical Miracles* (London, 1907), 116, 151. Newman made the same points also in the notes, which he provided for the 1865 edition of the *Apologia Pro Vita Sua*. See his note B.

38. Ibid., 184.

39. This tendency was not missed by his contemporaries, who accused him and other Tractarians of undermining the authority of biblical miracles. See Charles Daubeny, *Christianity and Rationalism in their Relation to Natural Science* . . . (London, 1867).

40. Gilley, *Newman and His Age,* 213; Edwin A. Abbott, *Phylomythus: An Antidote Against Credulity,* 2d ed. (London, 1891), lxi. Charles Kingsley had also raised this issue in the pamphlet warfare that precipitated Newman's *Apologia.* See "What, Then, Does Dr. Newman Mean?" in John Henry Newman, *Apologia Pro Vita Sua: An Authoritative Text* ed. David J. DeLaura (New York, 1968).

41. John Henry Newman, *Fifteen Sermons Preached Before the University of Oxford* (London, 1900), 195, 196.

42. These observations are found in the preface of the third edition of *Lectures on the Prophetical Office of the Church,* reprinted in John Henry Newman, *The Via Media of the Anglican Church,* 2 vols. (London, 1891), 1:xiv, lxvi, lxviii.

43. There were a few exceptions. H. T. Henry in "The Centenary of the Prodigies of Mary," *American Ecclesiastical Review* 15 (1896): 32–61; and John Hogan in "The Miraculous in Church History," *American Catholic Quarterly Review* 23 (1898): 382–98, both use arguments that parallel Newman's, as does Robert Hugh Benson. See Benson, *Lourdes,* 38. But even positive reviews of Newman's *Ecclesiastical Miracles* such as "Newman on Miracles," *Catholic World* 15 (1872): 133–34 did not look at Newman's understanding of the miraculous in light of all of his writings. An exception to the above is H. I. D. Ryder, "On Certain Ecclesiastical Miracles," *Nineteenth Century* 30 (1891): 217–36.

44. On these trends, see Roger Aubert et al., *The Church in the Age of Liberalism* (E.T.: New York, 1981), 228–47; Roger Aubert et al., *The Church in the Industrial Age* (E.T.: New York, 1981), 311–18; and Gerald A. McCool, *Catholic Theology in the Nineteenth Century: The Quest for a Unitary Method* (New York, 1977).

45. *Dei Filius,* chap. 3. This translation was published in *Ave Maria* 6 (1870): 363. The American bishop Thaddeus Amat was influential in the final wording of *Dei Filius* and also in making sure that the place of internal experience was defended. See James Hennesey, S.J., *The First Council of the Vatican: The American Experience* (New York, 1963), 150–52.

46. Norman P. Tanner, S.J., ed., *Decrees of the Ecumenical Councils,* 2 vols. (Washington, D.C., 1990), 2:810.

47. Maurice Blondel, *The Letter on Apologetics and History and Dogma* (E.T.: New York, 1964), 135. This passage is also cited in Gabriel Daly, *Transcendence and Immanence: A Study in Catholic Modernism and Integralism* (Oxford, 1980), 37. Much of my interpretation of Blondel is indebted to Daly. On Blondel, see also Marvin R. O'Connell, *Critics on Trial: An Introduction to the Catholic Modernist Crisis* (Washington, D.C., 1994), 83–90, 155–65.

48. See Gabriel Daly, *Transcendence and Immanence*; and Alec R. Vidler, *A Variety of Catholic Modernists* (Cambridge, Mass., 1970), 79–87. On the question of the relationship of Newman to Blondel, see also Vidler's earlier *The Modernist Movement in the Roman Church* (Cambridge, Eng.: 1934).

49. In addition to the articles cited below, see the discussion of this debate in Michael J. Devito, *The New York Review (1905–1908)* (New York, 1977), 114–25.

50. F. F. Siegfried, "The Old Method of Apologetics," *American Ecclesiastical Review*

19 (1898): 9. See, too, Joseph Selinger, "Why a New Method in Apologetic Theology?" *American Ecclesiastical Review* 30 (1904): 36–45.

51. A possible exception to this trend is William Turner's "A Contemporary French School of Pragmatism," *New York Review* 2 (1906–7): 27–36. On this point see R. Scott Appleby, *"Church and Age Unite": The Modernist Impulse in American Catholicism* (Notre Dame, 1992), 130.

52. Henry H. Wyman, "The Old Apologetic," *American Ecclesiastical Review* 32 (1905): 31. Wyman, in his defense of the old apologetic against the new, claimed that this appeal to certainty was influential not only in his own conversion from Protestantism but that of Isaac Hecker was as well.

53. Daly argues that Blondel is foundational to Catholic Modernism. Vidler, however, is persuaded that Blondel does not rightly belong in the category of Modernist. See Vidler, *Variety*, 79ff.

54. Gabriel Oussani identified only three Catholic critics of the virgin birth in contrast to a voluminous number of Protestant critics. See "The Virgin Birth of Christ and Modern Criticism," *New York Review* 3 (1907), 328–30. For the *New York Review*'s defense of the category of the miraculous against the French writer Eduourd Le Roy, see Walter McDonald, "A New Theory of Miracles," *New York Review* 2(1907): 675–90.

55. For this claim, see Appleby, *"Church and Age Unite,"* 1–2.

56. The Tyrrell letter is found in G. L. Prestige, *The Life of Charles Gore* (London, 1935), 271; On Driscoll's agenda, see De Vito, *New York Review,* 62 ff.

57. Sullivan, *The Priest* (Boston, 1911), 230, 235.

58. The career of Sullivan is discussed in Appleby, *"Church and Age Unite,"* 169–89.

59. For background to the novel and a discussion of its popularity, see Graham King, *Garden of Zola: Emile Zola and his Novels for English Readers* (Surry, Eng., 1978); and F. W. J. Hemmings, *Emile Zola* (Oxford, 1966).

60. *Lourdes,* trans. Ernest A. Vizetelly, 2 vols. (New York, 1897).

61. Ibid., 1:229.

62. Ibid., 1:273.

63. Ibid., 1:118–19.

64. Ibid., 2:388, 392, 393.

Chapter 6: What About Jesus?

1. Adolph von Harnack, "The Present State of Research in Early Church History," *Contemporary Review* 50 (1886): 221–24; The quotation is from William Higgs, "The Balance of Authorities: A Criticism of Mrs. Humphrey [*sic*] Ward's Article in the *Nineteenth Century*," *New Englander* 52 (1890): 39.

2. Charles Gore, *The Clergy and the Creeds* (London, 1887), 25.

3. Frederick Temple, *The Relation Between Religion and Science* (New York, 1884).

4. Temple, *Religion and Science*, 31, 194–95. On Temple's lectures, see Owen Chadwick, *The Victorian Church, Part II* (London, 1972), 23–24.

5. Temple, *Religion and Science*, 207–8.

6. Ibid., 219.

7. A. T. Lyttelton, *The Place of Miracles in Religion* (London, 1899), 51. These were the Hulsean Lectures of 1891.

8. Temple, *Religion and Science,* 212.

9. Charles Gore, "Miracles" (lecture delivered Feb. 23, 1885) Dixie Papers, Pusey House, Oxford, Eng.

10. *Lux Mundi: A Series of Studies in the Religion of the Incarnation . . .* (New York: n.d.), 274. Peter Hinchliff discusses the influence of both Westcott and Jowett on Gore; see his *God and History: Aspects of British Theology: 1875–1914* (Oxford, 1992), 105 ff.

11. See, for example, the manuscript "Christianity and Miracles" (lecture delivered Oct. 22, 1888), Dixie Papers, Pusey House, Oxford, Eng. See, too, H. S. Holland, *Christ and Ecclesiastes: Sermons Preached in St. Paul's Cathedral* (London, 1888), 56–81.

12. R. C. Moberly, "The Incarnation as the Basis of Dogma," in *Lux Mundi,* 223.

13. Adrian Desmond and James Moore, *Darwin* (New York, 1991), 566–86; Peter J. Bowler, *Evolution: The History of an Idea,* rev. ed. (Berkeley, Calif., 1989), 246–81.

14. Holland, *Christ and Ecclesiastes,* 79.

15. Mary A. Ward, "The New Reformation," *Nineteenth Century* 25 (1889): 458.

16. Edwin A. Abbott, *The Kernel and the Husk: Letters on Spiritual Christianity* (London, 1886), 3–6.

17. Henry Sidgewick, "The Ethics of Religious Conformity," *International Journal of Ethics* 6 (1896): 289. He also included this essay in his collection of essays *Practical Ethics* (London, 1898).

18. Huxley, "Agnosticism," in *Science and Christian Tradition: Essays* (New York, 1896), 215, 220. The essay was originally published in the *Nineteenth Century* (Feb. 1889). For Wace's response, see his *Christianity and Agnosticism: Reviews of Some Recent Attacks on the Christian Faith* (New York, 1895), 13–61.

19. Jerom Murch, *Memoir of Robert Hibbert, Esquire, Founder of the Hibbert Trust, with a Sketch of Its History* (Bath, Eng., 1874), 32–3, 60, and Reginald W. Macan, *The Resurrection of Jesus Christ: An Essay in Three Chapters* (London, 1877). On Macan, see his obituary notice in the *Times* (London), Mar. 25, 1941, and his own account of the events of his day, *Religious Changes in Oxford During the Last Fifty Years* (London, 1918).

20. On the lectures, see Stanley L. Jaki, *Lord Gifford and His Lectures: A Century Retrospect* (Macon, Ga., 1986). In addition to Max Müller, Otto Pfleiderer's lectures, *Philosophy and the Development of Religion,* attacked the idea of the miraculous and aroused great controversy. See Robert Rainy et al., *The Supernatural in Christianity* (Edinburgh, 1894), and Patrick Carnegie Simpson, *The Life of Principal Rainy,* 2 vols. (London, 1909), 2:131–37.

21. F. Max Müller, *Anthropological Religion* (London, 1892), 13–14.

22. Ibid., xix–xx. On the controversy, see Willim P. Dickson, *Professor Max Müller's Preface on 'Miracles'* (Glasgow, 1892), and for a typical American response, see W. B. Greene's review in *Presbyterian and Reformed Review* 2 (1891): 158.

23. See, among many, Percy Gardner, *Exploratio Evangelica: A Survey of the Foundations of Christianity,* 2d ed. (London, 1907), 240–41. The theory continues to have supporters. See Zacharias P. Thundy, *Buddha and Christ: Nativity Stories and Indian Traditions* (Leiden, 1993).

24. H. R. Mackintosh, *Types of Modern Theology* (London, 1937), 138.

25. Bernard M. G. Reardon, ed., *Liberal Protestantism* (Stanford, Calif., 1968), 102.

In addition to Mackintosh and Reardon, my understanding of Ritschl has been shaped by John Kenneth Mozley, *Ritschlianism: An Essay* (London, 1909); Alfred E. Garvie, *The Ritschlian Theology: Critical and Constructive* (Edinburgh, 1899); and James Orr, *Ritschlianism: Expository and Critical Essays* (London, 1903).

26. "Instruction in the Christian Religion" in *Albrecht Ritschl: Three Essays*, trans. Philip Hefner (Philadelphia, 1972), 229.

27. Adolph Harnack, *What Is Christianity?* trans. Thomas Bailey Saunders (New York, 1901), 34–37.

28. *Three Essays*, 270, n. 46; Albrecht Ritschl, *The Christian Doctrine of Justification and Reconciliation*, trans. and ed. H. R. Mackintosh and A. B. Macaulay (1900; reprint ed., Clifton, N.J., 1966), 467–68. On the ambiguity of Ritschl on the miraculous, contrast the passages on pp. 227 and 270 of *Ritschl: Three Essays* and the fundamentally differing assessments of Orr and Mozley.

29. William R. Hutchison argues persuasively for the influence of Ritschl and Harnack on American Modernists. See *The Modernist Impulse in American Protestantism* (Cambridge, Mass., 1976), 122–32. Bernard M. G. Reardon, Alec R. Vidler, and Alan M. G. Stephenson all acknowledge Ritschlian strands in Anglican Modernism, but see it as only one theological root of the movement. See Reardon, *Liberal Protestantism,* 51–65; Vidler, *20th Century Defenders of the Faith* (London, 1965), 123–24; and Stephenson, *The Rise and Decline of English Modernism* (London, 1984), 86–87.

30. On the triumph of the Marcan priority, see Hans-Herbert Stoldt, *History and Criticism of the Marcan Hypothesis*, trans. and ed. Donald L. Niewyk (Macon, Ga., 1980).

31. E. A. Abbott, "Gospels," *Encyclopaedia Britannica . . . , Ninth Edition*, 24 vols. (New York, 1878–79): 10:801. Neill is vague about the introduction of the Marcan priority into England, and merely sees it as post-1881. See Stephen Neill and Tom Wright, *The Interpretation of the New Testament: 1861–1986*, 2d ed. (Oxford, 1988), 122 ff. This is the basis for my tentative claim for Abbott as being the first. It is intriguing to question both why Abbott (as a nonacademic) was assigned the project and also why it was ignored then and later. Perhaps Abbott's nonacademic status contributed to its lack of prominence.

32. Although the question of the precise origin of the healing miracle–nature miracle distinction in English-speaking scholarship is not central to my argument, it is compelling. Friedrich Schleiermacher does employ something like it in *The Life of Jesus,* ed. Jack C. Verheyden (Philadelphia, 1975), 202–9, which was published in German in 1864. No English-speaking writer whom I have found, however, cites Schliermacher as an authority. A. B. Bruce, for example, in his *The Miraculous Elements of the Gospels* (New York, 1886) employs the distinction and attributes it to B. F. Westcott. Other English scholars also cite Westcott; e.g., J. H. Bernard, "Miracle" in *A Dictionary of the Bible . . . ,* ed. James Hastings, 5 vols. (New York, 1898–1904), 3:390, also attributes it to Westcott. Westcott, however, has a fairly elaborate classification schema for the New Testament miracles, and the distinction between healing miracles and nature miracles is only part of his schema. See his *Introduction to the Study of the Gospels,* 4th ed. (London, 1872), 312–13, 395–97.

33. Daniel Hack Tuke, *Illustrations of the Influence of the Mind Upon the Body*

in Health and Disease Designed to Elucidate the Action of the Imagination, 2d ed. (London, 1884), xiv; F. W. H. Myers, "Ernest Renan," in *Essays: Modern* (London, 1908), 206 ff.

34. Samuel McComb, *Christianity and the Modern Mind* (London, 1910), 135.

35. George A. Gordon, *Religion and Miracle* (Boston, 1909), 12.

36. On the English Modernist-Conservative debate over miracles, see John Stewart Lawton, *Miracles and Revelation* (London, 1959), 167–216. Lawton's is a thorough discussion, but my interpretation of the debate is different.

37. See C. E. Beeby, "Doctrinal Significance of a Miraculous Birth," *Hibbert Journal* 2 (1904): 138.

38. N. P. Williams, *Miracles* (London, 1914), 33.

39. William H. Ryder, "Review of The Birth and Infancy of Jesus Christ According to the Gospel Narratives," *Biblical World* 31 (1908): 396.

40. On the controversy, see Harnack's own account recounted in Mary A. Ward's introduction, "The Apostles' Creed: A Translation and Introduction," *Nineteenth Century* 34 (1893): 153–55 ; G. W. Fritsch, "Harnack on the Apostles' Creed," *Quarterly Review of the Evangelical Lutheran Church*, n.s. 26 (1896): 116–18 ; and A. Zahn, "The Conflict in Germany over the Apostles' Creed," *Presbyterian and Reformed Review* 4 (1893): 267–71; "Professor Harnack on the Apostles' Creed," *Church Quarterly Review* 35 (1892–93): 472 ff. For a discussion of the issues involved, see G. Wayne Glick, *The Reality of Christianity: A Study of Adolph von Harnack as Historian and Theologian* (New York, 1967), 50–58.

41. It also provoked a protracted scholarly debate about the accuracy of his claims. In England scholars such as Henry B. Swete criticized him for the radical nature of his claims, but in America, the Ritschlian A. C. McGiffert was basically supportive. See H. B. Swete, *The Apostles' Creed: Its Relation to Primitive Christianity* (Cambridge, Eng., 1894); and A. C. McGiffert, *The Apostles' Creed: Its Origin, Its Purpose, and Its Historical Interpretation* (New York, 1902).

42. Ward's introduction to "The Apostles' Creed," 157.

43. Chadwick, *Victorian Church*, 2:143. A number of the more technical volumes, such as Karl Wezsacker's *The Apostolic Age,* were translated under the auspices of the Hibbert Trust. For a fairly comprehensive list of the major publications, see the bibliography of Charles R. Tucker, "The Problem of the Virgin Birth in Contemporary Theology (Since 1900)" (Th.D. diss., Southern Baptist Theological Seminary, 1951), 210–32.

44. Hastings Rashdall, "Professor Sidgewick on the Ethics of Religious Conformity: A Reply," *International Journal of Ethics* 7 (1897): 165–66.

45. Charles Gore, "The Place of Symbolism in Religion," *Constructive Quarterly* 2 (1913), 64.

46. *A Dictionary of the Bible . . . ,* ed. James Hastings, 5 vols. (New York, 1898–1904); *Encyclopaedia Biblica . . . ,* ed. T. K. Cheyne and J. Sutherland Black, 4 vols. (New York, 1899–1903). For some insightful observations about this battle, see Daniel L. Pals, *The Victorian "Lives" of Jesus* (San Antonio, Tex., 1982), 165 ff.

47. To be sure not everyone was pleased with the project. Although he himself was a contributor, Benjamin Warfield faulted the volumes for their willingness to compromise on higher biblical criticism and for the paucity of contributions by Americans and conser-

vative critics. Yet even he admitted that it was "tolerably conservative" vis-à-vis the New Testament. See his review in *Presbyterian and Reformed Review* 9 (1898): 516–18.

48. Sanday, "Jesus Christ" in *A Dictionary of the Bible* . . . , ed. James Hastings, 5 vols. (New York, 1898–1904), 2:625–26. Sanday's article was later published as a separate book entitled *Outlines of the Life of Christ* (Edinburgh, 1905).

49. Warfield, "Hastings' Dictionary of the Bible," *Presbyterian and Reformed Review* 11 (1900): 174.

50. Quoted from "Preface," *Encyclopaedia Biblica* . . . , ed. T. K. Cheyne and J. Sutherland Black, 4 vols. (New York, 1899–1903), 1:ix.

51. Schmeidel, "Gospels," *Encyclopaedia Biblica*, 2:1885.

52. Usener, "Nativity," *Encyclopaedia Biblica*, 3:3348, 3349.

53. The American Modernist Shailer Mathews, for example, was critical of Schmiedel's essays for their extreme skepticism. See his reviews in the *American Journal of Theology* 4 (1900): 384 ff., and *American Journal of Theology* 5 (1901): 732–51.

54. "Jesus" 2:2445–46. Emphasis added. Contrast these passages with his *Miraculous Elements of the Gospels* (New York, 1886), 119 ff. A factor that might help explain (or at least further illuminate) the change in Bruce's attitude toward the miraculous is that he translated Adolph Harnack's *History of Dogma* into English during the 1890s.

55. As I write this, the well worn copies of both sets that are before me are the library copies of my public, technological university. Almost a hundred years old, they are still being used. One can only wonder how many students have consulted them over the years.

56. K. W. Clements, *Lovers of Discord: Twentieth Century Theological Controversies in England* (London, 1988), 51. For an account of the Beeby case, see G. L. Prestige, *The Life of Charles Gore* (London, 1935), 243–45. As Prestige admits, however, this was more a result of the force of Gore's will than of the clarity of the legal case against Beeby.

57. Thompson, *Miracles in the New Testament* (London, 1912), vii, 213.

58. For criticism of Thompson, see Prestige, *Gore*, 343; F. L. Cross, *Darwell Stone: Churchman and Counsellor* (London, 1943), 100–2; Hinchliff, *God and History*, 229; and Clements, *Lovers of Discord*, 51 ff. Thompson was later to abandon the ministry and become a virtual agnostic. He did gain fame in a second career as a historian of revolutionary and Napoleonic France.

59. Some of the more significant of these were Walter Lock et al., eds., *Miracles: Papers and Sermons Contributed to the Guardian* (London, 1911); T. Fields, *Did It Happen? An Open Letter to the Rev. J. M. Thompson, M.A.* (London: n.d.); Philopais, *Some Notes on the Rev. J. M. Thompson's Recent Book "Miracles in the New Testament"* (London, 1913); and H. Hensley Henson, *The Creed in the Pulpit* (London, 1912).

60. Streeter et al., *Foundations: A Statement of Christian Belief in Terms of Modern Thought* . . . (London, 1912), vii, 132. On Streeter and *Foundations*, see Hinchliff, *God and History*, 223–47.

61. Knox continued his combination of humor and orthodox criticism of *Foundations* (the title of which he found pompous) in another volume, which he entitled *Some Loose Stones* (London, 1913).

62. Frank Weston, *The Christ and His Critics* (London, 1918), 10. On the controversy, see H. Maynard Smith, *Frank Bishop of Zanzibar* (London, 1926); and G. K. A. Bell, *Randall Davidson: Archbishop of Canterbury*, 3d ed. (Oxford, 1952), 671–89.

63. Charles Gore, *The Basis of Anglican Fellowship* (London, 1914), 4, 10, 8.

64. Ibid., 18.

65. Some of the more significant responses (not including those of William Sanday to be discussed in detail) were H. M. Gwatkin, *The Bishop of Oxford's Open Letter* (London, 1914); Cyril W. Emmet, *Conscience, Creeds, and Critics: A Plea for Liberty of Criticism within the Church of England* (London, 1918); B. H. Streeter, *A Plea for Liberty: A Letter to the Bishops in Reference to Dr. Gore's Pronouncement* (N.p.: [1914]); and J. F. Bethune Baker, *The Miracle of Christianity* . . . (London, 1914). Each was a Modernist and a noted scholar in his own right.

66. Sanday contributed a sermon "The Meaning of Miracle" to the volume *Miracles,* edited by Lock.

67. The most complete account of this meeting is found in Cross, *Darwell Stone,* 106. Prestige discusses Gore's reaction in *Gore,* 347.

68. William Sanday, *Bishop Gore's Challenge to Criticism* (London, 1914), 17.

69. Ibid., 23.

70. Ibid., 27–28.

71. Hinchliff, *God and History,* 225.

72. William Sanday and N. P. Williams, *Form and Content in the Christian Tradition* (London, 1916); William Sanday and T. B. Strong, *Spirit, Matter, and Miracle* (Oxford, 1916); William Sanday, *Divine Overruling* (Edinburgh, 1920); and William Sanday, *The Position of Liberal Theology* (London, 1920).

73. Sanday, *Position,* 32.

74. Conrad Cherry, *Hurrying Toward Zion: Universities, Divinity Schools, and American Protestantism* (Bloomington, Ind., 1995).

75. See B. W. Bacon, "Enter the Higher Criticism," in Vergilius Ferm, ed., *Contemporary American Theology: Theological Autobiographies,* 2 vols. (New York, 1932), 1:45–46. The interconnection of Puritanism and Teutonism in Bacon are also noted in Roy A. Harrisville, *Benjamin Wisner Bacon: Pioneer in American Biblical Criticism* (Missoula, Mont., 1976).

76. George M. Marsden contrasts Princeton and the University of Chicago in this regard. See his *The Soul of the American University: From Protestant Establishment to Established Nonbelief* (New York, 1994), 196–248.

77. Gilbert, *The Student's Life of Jesus,* 3d ed. (New York, 1924), 331.

78. Gilbert, *Jesus* (New York, 1912), vii, viii.

79. Gilbert, "The Apostles' Creed Revised by the Teaching of Jesus," *Biblical World* 12 (1898): 160–61.

80. William Hutchison, ed., *American Protestant Thought: The Liberal Era* (New York, 1968), 7–8.

81. Text and commentary are found in Williston Walker, *The Creeds and Platforms of Congregationalism* (New York, 1893), 577–82. See, too, William E. Barton, *Congregational Creeds and Covenants* (Chicago, 1917), 247 ff., for a distinctively Congregationalist view of the ethics of credal subscription.

82. Allen Hoben, *The Virgin Birth* (Chicago, 1903); Benjamin W. Bacon's contributions were in articles. See those listed in Harrisville, *Bacon,* 48–59. Both also contributed to a roundtable on the subject, see B. W. Bacon et al., "The Supernatural Birth of Jesus,"

American Journal of Theology 10 (1906): 1–30. Another Baptist contributor to the scholarly debate was Nathaniel Schmidt, who authored *The Prophet of Nazareth* (New York, 1905). Another leading critic was the Disciples scholar Herbert L. Willett. See Ferenc Morton Szasz, *The Divided Mind of Protestant America, 1880–1930* (University Place, Ala.: 1982), 25–26.

83. Henry Churchill King, *Reconstruction in Theology* (New York, 1901), 62, 72–73.

84. Newman Smyth, *The Reality of Faith* (New York, 1884), 86; James M. Whiton, *Miracles and Supernatural Religion* (New York, 1903), 41. William M. King has noted the same tendency toward crisis progressivism in much of the social gospel rhetoric. See "'History as Revelation' in the Theology of the Social Gospel," *Harvard Theological Review* 76 (1983), 109–29.

85. Hoben, *Virgin Birth*, 80.

86. Theodore T. Munger, *Horace Bushnell, Teacher and Theologian* (London: n.d.), 231; Borden Parker Bowne, "Concerning Miracle," *Harvard Theological Review* 3 (1910): 155; Whiton, *Miracles and Supernatural Religion*, 113. Whiton was usually considered part of the "school of Bushnell." See Frank H. Foster, *The Modern Movement in American Theology* (1939; reprint ed., Freeport, N.Y., 1969), 69–79. Munger's contemporaries were well aware that his was an interpretation of Bushnell that "saw clearly what was incidental and passing in his writings" and chose to emphasize "the new path on which he was moving." See George A. Gordon, *My Education and Religion* (Boston, 1925), 311–12.

87. Bowne, "Concerning Miracle," 156; Edward S. Drown, "What Is the Supernatural," *Harvard Theological Review* 6 (1913): 150.

88. Gordon, *Religion and Miracle*, 164, 34.

89. Ibid., 94–95, 153.

90. Foster, *Modern Movement*, 133–34.

91. George H. Gilbert, "Religion and Miracle," *American Journal of Theology* 14 (1910): 271–79. There were other heresy trials as well involving at least in part the issue of the miraculous, in particular that of the Methodist philosophical theologian, Borden Parker Bowne. The second charge against Bowne involved the question of the miraculous. Bowne, however, was acquitted. See Francis John McConnell, *Borden Parker Bowne: His Life and Philosophy* (New York, 1929), 179–206, and Harmon L. Smith's article on Bowne in George H. Shriver, ed., *American Religious Heretics* (Nashville, Tenn., 1966). In 1910 Presbyterians enacted an even more stringent position than did Episcopalians by establishing five "Essential and Necessary Articles," which included an affirmation of both the virgin birth and physical resurrection. But the controversy over these did not erupt until the 1920s.

92. See Algernon Sidney Crapsey, *The Last of the Heretics* (New York, 1924), 250, 251–52. Crapsey both quotes parts of his sermon and comments on the controversy.

93. Henry S. Nash in *Appeal by the Rev'd Algernon S. Crapsey, S.T.D. to the Court of Review of the Protestant Episcopal Church* (New York, 1906), 93; A. V. G. Allen made many of the same points; see his *Freedom in the Church* (New York, 1907). On the trial as well as on Crapsey's memoirs, see also Elwood Worcester, *Life's Adventures: The Story of a Varied Career* (New York, 1932), 243 ff. The chief scholarly discussion of the trial is

Hugh M. Jansen, "Algernon Sidney Crapsey: Heresy at Rochester," in Shriver, *American Religious Heretics.*

94. White's letter is printed in Crapsey, *Last of the Heretics,* 267. See also Ralph Albertson, "The Trial of Dr. Crapsey," *Arena* 37 (1907): 94 ff. It is true that White occasionally attended Episcopal worship service, but as one scholar has noted his faith consisted in "ethics, dignity, and acoustics." See Paul Carter, *The Spiritual Crisis of the Gilded Age* (Dekalb, Ill., 1971), 41.

95. A number of the articles in the early volumes of the [Baptist] *Review and Expositor* defended the virgin birth. For a Methodist defense, see S. M. Merrill and Henry W. Warren, *Discourse on Miracles* (Cincinnati, Ohio, 1902). In many ways the most impressive scholarly defense of the virgin birth produced by an American was that by the Presbyterian Louis M. Sweet; see his *The Birth and Infancy of Jesus Christ According to the Gospel Narratives* (Philadelphia, 1906). But because its chief strength was its treatment of technical questions, and because Orr's work would be summarized in his contribution to *Fundamentals,* I have chosen to discuss him. One could also mention Gresham Machen's *Princeton Theological Review* articles, but Machen will be discussed in chapter 8.

96. B. B. Warfield, "The Supernatural Birth of Jesus," *American Journal of Theology* 10 (1906): 24; James Orr, *The Virgin Birth of Christ* (New York, 1907), 10.

97. Ibid., 227.

98. For two recent studies of Briggs, see Mark S. Massa, *Charles Augustus Briggs and the Crisis of Historical Criticism* (Minneapolis, Minn., 1990); and M. James Sawyer, *Charles Augustus Briggs and Tensions in Late Nineteenth-Century American Theology* (Lewiston, N.Y., 1994).

99. Charles A. Briggs, *The Incarnation of the Lord* (New York, 1902), 234. Briggs returned to these themes in *The Fundamental Christian Faith* (New York, 1913).

100. Charles A. Briggs, "Criticism and Dogma," *North American Review* 182 (1906): 868. This article reflected Briggs's argument that the church must hold the doctrine of the virgin birth but could be charitable toward those members who did not.

101. His views were appreciated by English defenders of the virgin birth, who also acknowledged the relationship between his views and that of Gore. See G. H. Box, *The Virgin Birth of Jesus* (London, 1916).

Chapter 7: The New Search for Evidences

1. Ray Stannard Baker, *The Spiritual Unrest* (New York, 1910), 47. This volume was a collection of earlier articles from the *American* magazine, and it highlighted such diverse figures as the evangelist Jerry McAuley, Elwood Worcester of the Emmanuel Movement, and Walter Rauschenbusch. For the background to these articles, see John E. Semonche, *Ray Stannard Baker: A Quest for Democracy in Modern America, 1870–1918* (Chapel Hill, N.C., 1969), 215–19.

2. Lyman P. Powell, *The Emmanuel Movement in a New England Town* (New York, 1909), 1.

3. *Hamlet,* 1.5.166; Stow Persons, *American Minds: A History of Ideas* (New York, 1958) 421; Oliver Lodge, *Science and Immortality* (New York, 1909), 35; James A. Ward, *Naturalism and Agnosticism,* 2 vols. (London, 1899), 1:180, 166. On the general

phenomena, see Frank M. Turner, *Between Science and Religion: The Reaction to Scientific Naturalism in Late Victorian England* (New Haven, Conn., 1974); and Bernard Lightman, *The Origins of Agnosticism: Victorian Unbelief and the Limits of Knowledge* (Baltimore, Md., 1987).

4. See A. T. Myers and F. W. H. Myers, "Mind Cure, Faith Cure, and the Miracles of Lourdes," *Proceedings of the Society for Psychical Research* 9 (1894): 175; and William Frederic Cobb, *Spiritual Healing* (London, 1914), 103. Cobb cites an observation of an unnamed physician. See Sir Bertram C. A. Windle, "Miracles — Fifty Years Ago and Now," *Catholic World* 101 (1915): 38. For another typical Protestant account of Lourdes, see H. H. Bashford, *The Corner of Harley Street: Being Some Familiar Correspondence of Peter Harding, M.D.* (Boston: n.d.).

5. On Christian Science, see Stephen Gottschalk, *The Emergence of Christian Science in American Religious Life* (Berkeley, Calif., 1973); and Stuart E. Knee, *Christian Science in the Age of Mary Baker Eddy* (Westport, Conn., 1994).

6. Meredith Clymer, "Creed, Craft, and Cure," *Forum* 5 (1888): 198. Clyde W. Votaw makes the same claims in his "Christian Science and Faith Healing," *New Englander and Yale Review* 54 (1891): 249–58. See also Richard Heber Newton, *Christian Science: The Truths of Spiritual Healing and their Contribution to the Growth of Orthodoxy* (New York, 1898), 15. For other clerical responses to Christian Science, see Raymond J. Cunningham, "The Impact of Christian Science on American Churches, 1880–1910" *American Historical Review* 72 (1967): 855–905. For a lay evaluation of Christian Science healings that also involved a criticism of the Protestant position of a limited age of miracles, see Frank J. Ryan, *Protestant Miracles: High Orthodox and Evangelical Authority for the Belief in Divine Interposition in Human Affairs . . .* (Stockton, Calif., 1899). Both Gottschalk and Knee argue convincingly that Christian Science theology is distinctive from other healing movements.

7. Daniel Hack Tuke, *Illustrations of the Influence of the Mind Upon the Body in Health and Disease Designed to Elucidate the Action of the Imagination,* 2d ed. (London, 1884); Henry H. Goddard, "The Effects of Mind on Body as Evidenced by Faith Cures," *American Journal of Psychology* 10 (1899): 463. See also Frank S. Hoffman, *Psychology and the Common Life* (New York, 1903), 159–86.

8. British Medical Society, "The Anglican Church and Faith Healing," *British Medical Journal* (Dec. 16, 1911), 1609.

9. On the British Society for Psychical Research, see John J. Cerullo, *The Secularization of the Soul: Psychical Research in Modern Britain* (Philadelphia, 1982); on the American movement, see R. Laurence Moore, *In Search of White Crows: Spiritualism, Parapsychology, and American Culture* (New York, 1977). The most recent study of spiritualism in America is Ann Braude, *Radical Spirits: Spiritualism and Women's Rights in Nineteenth-Century America* (Boston, 1989).

10. F. W. H. Myers, "Autobiographical Fragment," in *Collected Poems* (London, 1921), 6–7 ; Turner, *Between Science and Religion,* 108–17; Frederic W. H. Myers, *Human Personality: And Its Survival of Bodily Death,* 2 vols. (1903; reprint ed., New York, 1975), 2:284.

11. Elwood Worcester, Samuel McComb, and Isador H. Coriat, *The Subconscious Mind: Its Nature and Value for the Cure of Nervous Disorders by Means of Suggestion*

and Autosuggestion (London, 1920), 315. Percy Dearmer also emphasized the role of subliminal consciousness as the conduit of prayer. For a critical view of Myers's idea of the subliminal consciousness, see Cerullo, *Secularization of the Soul,* 88–108.

12. Alfred Russel Wallace, *Miracles and Modern Spiritualism* (1896; reprint ed., New York, 1975), 13. See too F. W. H. Myers's essay "Ernest Renan," in *Essays: Modern* (London, 1908), where he attacked both skeptics and Protestant proponents of the limited age of miracles argument.

13. Thomson Jay Hudson, *A Scientific Demonstration of the Future Life* (Chicago, 1895), 151; Myers, *Human Personality,* 2:288.

14. Myers, *Human Personality,* 2:279; and "Renan," 224, 222.

15. Grey, *Visions, Previsions, and Miracles in Modern Times* (London, 1915), 11.

16. Worcester, *Life's Adventure: The Story of a Varied Career* (New York, 1932), 330.

17. William James, *The Varieties of Religious Experience: A Study in Human Nature* (New York, 1961). The literature on James is legion, but I have found particularly useful Ralph Barton Perry, *The Thought and Character of William James,* 2 vols. (Boston, 1935); Henry Samuel Levinson, *The Religious Investigations of William James* (Chapel Hill, N.C., 1981); Gerald E. Myers, *William James: His Life and Thought* (New Haven, Conn., 1986), 470–74; William Clebsch, *American Religious Thought: A History* (Chicago, 1973), 162–68; and Bennett Ramsey, *Submitting to Freedom: The Religious Vision of William James* (New York, 1993).

18. James, *Varieties,* 388, 401.

19. Ibid., 388n.

20. Ibid., 289, 389n. The letter to Bowne is found in Perry, *Thought and Character,* 2:331.

21. James, *Varieties,* 403.

22. Ibid., 404, 404n, 405, 406.

23. Ibid., 407.

24. G. K. Chesterton, *Saint Thomas Aquinas: "The Dumb Ox"* (New York, 1956), 147.

25. Santayana is quoted in Myers, *James,* 462; Harold Anson, *Looking Forward* (London: n.d.), 72.

26. The emphasis here is on Protestant. As with the debate over the virgin birth, Roman Catholic commentators watched bemusedly from the sidelines. Although they might have applauded the jettisoning of the cessationist argument, they showed almost no sympathy for the constructive ideas of people like Myers. As one Catholic writer observed, "Regarding its theory or philosophy one can say little, if anything, in its favor." (J. Godfrey Raupert, "Review of Human Personality," *American Ecclesiastical Review* 31 [1904]: 316). Catholic writers saw in the new Baconianism an assault on sacerdotalism and authority. Whether the Catholic Modernists would have moved in this direction if they had not been condemned is of course a matter of speculation.

27. *Spiritual Healing: Report of a Clerical and Medical Committee of Inquiry into Spiritual, Faith, and Mental Healing* (London, 1914), 3. This report stemmed from the Lambeth Conference of 1908, and among the participants were Samuel McComb and Percy Dearmer.

28. Borden P. Bowne, "Concerning Miracle," *Harvard Theological Review* 3 (1910): 149–51.

29. George M. Marsden, *The Soul of the American University: From Protestant Establishment to Established Nonbelief* (New York, 1994).

30. Newton, *Christian Science,* 12.

31. *Spiritual Healing,* 13–14.

32. The standard source of the life of Worcester is his autobiography, *Life's Adventure.* One should be careful, however, about seeing Worcester and the Emmanuel Movement in isolation. The interest in Worcester and the Emmanuel Movement has often hidden the fact that the latter was but a piece of a more general phenomenon. Loring Batten, professor of Old Testament at General Theological Seminary, was yet another proponent of the therapeutical paradigm. For others and a discussion of the wider liberal and modernist interest in religion and healing, see Alison Stokes, *Ministry After Freud* (New York, 1985), 29–32. As I suggest in chapter 8, one can also see clear parallels between the Emmanuel Movement and the later American Guild of Health.

33. In addition to Stokes on the Emmanuel Movement, see John G. Greene, "The Emmanuel Movement, 1906–1929," *New England Quarterly* 7 (1934): 494–532; Raymond J. Cunningham, "Ministry of Healing: The Origins of the Psychotherapeutic Role of the American Churches (Ph.D. diss., The Johns Hopkins University, 1965); and E. Brooks Holifield, *A History of Pastoral Care in America: From Salvation to Self-Realization* (Nashville, Tenn., 1983).

34. Worcester, *The Christian Religion as a Healing Power: A Defense of the Emmanuel Movement* (New York, 1909), 30.

35. Samuel McComb, "Christ's Theory and Treatment of Disease," *Independent* 66 (1909):574.

36. McComb, "Spiritual Healing and the Church," *Contemporary Review* 119 (1921): 672. For a cultural discussion of the role and meaning of neurasthenia in turn-of-the-century upper-middle-class American culture, see Tom Lutz, *American Nervousness, 1903: An Anecdotal History* (Ithaca, N.Y., 1991).

37. The person quoted was S. S. Marquis, the leading apostle of the Emmanuel Movement in Detroit. See "Scrapbook on the Emmanuel Movement," Episcopal Divinity School Library, Cambridge, Mass.

38. Powell, *Emmanuel Movement,* 8–9.

39. Elwood Worcester, Samuel McComb, and Isador H. Coriat, *Religion and Medicine: Moral Control of Nervous Disorders* (New York, 1908), 307.

40. Frank Cole Sherman, *The Inner Chamber: A Manual of Devotion* (Cleveland, Ohio, 1929), 199. Sherman was head of the American Guild of Health, which during the 1920s was the leading proponent of the therapeutic model of healing within the Episcopal Church.

41. Worcester, *Life's Adventure,* 276.

42. *Papers, Addresses, and Discussions at the Twenty-Second Church Congress in the United States . . .* (New York, 1903), 131–39. See also Worcester, *Christian Religion as a Healing Power,* 86–90.

43. See the discussion of this point in Jon H. Roberts, *Darwinism and the Divine in America* (Madison, Wis., 1988), 151 ff.

44. Powell, *Emmanuel Movement,* 160.

45. Elwood Worcester, Samuel McComb, and Isador H. Coriat, *Religion and Medicine*, 12.

46. J. W. Winkley, "Christianity's Next Step," *Arena* 25 (1901): 31, 34. Like a number of those interested in the therapeutic model, Winkley saw it as a corollary to the Social Gospel movement, one that transformed the spiritual life as the Social Gospel did the social.

47. See, for example, Robert McDonald, *Mind, Religion, and Health,* . . . (New York, 1908). Worcester himself was quite cognizant of the interconnection. See his *Life's Adventure.*

48. Worcester, McComb, and Coriat, *Religion and Medicine,* 54.

49. See, for example, Bryan Crandell Epps, "Religious Healing in the United States, 1940–1960: History and Theology of Selected Trends" (Ph.D. diss., Boston University, 1961). Baptists in early-twentieth-century Boston also seemed to be somewhat interested in the anointing of the sick. See "A Proposed Revival of 'Faith Healing' in the Churches," *Current Literature* 41 (1906): 680.

50. See Robert C. L. Reade, *Spiritual Healing and the Anointing of the Sick* (London, 1911), 26. Contrast this attitude with the absence of interest in the healing power of anointing in Orby Shipley, *Tracts for the Day* . . . *No. 7.: Unction of the Sick* (London, 1867); and H. J. Pye, *Ought the Sick to be Anointed? A Theological Essay* (Oxford, 1867).

51. Percy Dearmer, *Body and Soul: An Enquiry into the Effects of Religion upon Health, with a Description of Christian Works of Healing from the New Testament to the Present Age* (New York, 1909).

52. Ibid., 1, 12.

53. Ibid., 11–22.

54. Ibid., 334.

55. Ibid., 330.

56. Ibid., 334–35.

57. Ibid., 348, 350.

58. Ibid., 95. Chapters 5 and 6 of *Body and Soul* dealt extensively with the role of the subconscious or "undermind" and its relationship to healing.

59. These quotations are both from letters appearing in *Living Church,* Sept. 8, 1906. On anointing and healing, see also *The Works of the Rt. Rev. Charles C. Grafton* . . . , 8 vols. (New York, 1914), 8:236.

60. Henry B. Wilson, *Does Christ Still Heal?* (New York, 1917), 134. Wilson was the head of the Society of the Nazarene.

61. This debate between Modernists and their critics had an exegetical aspect as well, and a number of writers denied that the healings recorded in the gospels could be explained through the power of personality to affect functional disease. See R. J. Ryle, "The Neurotic Theory of the Miracles of Healing," *Hibbert Journal* 5 (1906–7): 572–86.

62. On the origins and development of twentieth-century Pentecostalism, see Donald W. Dayton, *Theological Roots of Pentecostalism* (Peabody, Mass., 1994); Edith Blumhofer, *Restoring the Faith: The Assemblies of God, Pentecostalism, and American Culture* (Urbana, Ill., 1993); Robert M. Anderson, *Vision of the Disinherited: The Making of*

American Pentecostalism (New York, 1979); Vinson Synan, *The Holiness-Pentecostal Movement in the United States* (Grand Rapids, Mich., 1971); Grant Wacker, "Pentecostalism," in *Encyclopedia of the American Religious Experience: Studies of Traditions and Movements,* ed. Charles H. Lippy and Peter W. Williams, 3 vols. (New York, 1988), 2:933–45; and Wacker, "Playing for Keeps: The Primitivist Impulse in Early Pentecostalism," in *The American Quest for the Primitive Church,* ed. Richard T. Hughes (Urbana, Ill., 1988). Although I have chosen to discuss Dowie, a number of the same themes can be seen in the life and ministry of Charles F. Parham, often considered to be the father of American Pentecostalism. See James R. Goff, Jr., *Fields White unto Harvest: Charles F. Parham and the Missionary Origins of Pentecostalism* (Fayetteville, Ark., 1988).

63. This may be a point of perception. Writers from within the faith cure tradition such as Paul Chappell in "The Divine Healing Movement in America" (Ph.D. diss., Drew University, 1983) have argued vigorously that there was a continuity between Cullis and the later advocates of faith healing. In contrast, outsiders to the tradition, such as Raymond Cunningham in "Ministry of Healing," have emphasized a discontinuity. My position is a mediating one: it is undoubtedly true that within certain sections of the religious public there continued to be an interest in faith healing; the movement was largely ignored by the larger public until near the turn of the century when it was taken up again.

64. The two best modern published treatments of Dowie's life and ministry are Grant Wacker, "Marching to Zion: Religion in a Modern Utopian Community," *Church History* 54 (1985): 496–511; and Edith L. Blumhofer, "The Christian Catholic Apostolic Church and the Apostolic Faith: A Study in the 1906 Pentecostal Revival," in *Charismatic Experiences in History,* ed. Cecil M. Robeck, Jr. (Peabody, Mass., 1985).

65. This narrative is based on Dowie's own account, *The Gospel of Divine Healing and How I Came to Preach It* (Zion City, Ill.: [1903]). This account originally appeared in his journal *Leaves of Healing,* and was often reprinted in tract form.

66. In Dowie's letter to the International Conference on Divine Healing, for example, all of the cases he cited were cures of cancer. See *Record of the International Conference on Divine Healing and True Holiness . . .* (London, 1885), 172–75. On the psychological importance of cancer at the end of the nineteenth century, see James T. Patterson, *The Dread Disease: Cancer and Modern American Culture* (Cambridge, Mass., 1987), 12–35.

67. John Alexander Dowie, *Doctors, Drugs, and Devils; or the Foes of Christ the Healer* (Zion City, Ill., 1901), 13, 11. *Leaves of Healing* cataloged the types of diseases Dowie claimed to heal, and cancers were always at the top of the list. On the emphasis upon the demonic in Dowie, see Rolvix Harlan, *John Alexander Dowie and the Christian Catholic Apostolic Church in Zion* (Evansville, Wis., 1906), 157 ff. On the folk belief in demons, see Grant Wacker, "The Pentecostal Tradition," in *Caring and Curing: Health and Medicine in the Western Religious Traditions,* ed. Ronald L. Numbers and Darrel W. Amundsen (New York, 1986), 523–24. Numerous scholars have noted the centrality of the Book of Acts for Pentecostal self-understanding. See Dayton, *Theological Roots,* 23–24, and J. R. Michaels, "Luke-Acts," in *Dictionary of Pentecostal and Charismatic Movements,* ed. Stanley M. Burgess, Gary B McGee, and Patrick H. Alexander (Grand Rapids, Mich., 1988), 544–61; Christopher Hill made his observation in *Antichrist in Seventeenth Century England* (New York, 1971), 167–68. One should perhaps be cautious about ascribing any simple cause for the interest in the diabolical during this period.

Dowie and the Pentecostals were not alone, and even the English Anglocatholic mission-ary bishop Frank Weston was convinced of the reality of the demonic. See H. Maynard Smith, *Frank Bishop of Zanzibar* (London, 1928), 114–18.

68. On the themes of restoration or primitivism, see Hughes, *American Quest for the Primitive Church*; and Richard T. Hughes and C. Leonard Allen, *Illusions of Innocence: Protestant Primitivism in America, 1630–1875* (Chicago, 1988). Convert's quotation is from Harlan, *Dowie,* 143; the Dowie quotation is from *Leaves of Healing* 8 (Jan. 12, 1901): 364.

69. John Alexander Dowie, *"You Dirty Boy!" A Reply to the Rev. Dr. Henson . . . with Some Remarks upon "Dining with the Doctors"* (Zion City, Ill., 1898), 27–28.

70. Dowie, *Leaves of Healing* 8 (Dec. 1, 1900): 169.

71. Harlan, *Dowie,* 202–3; John Swain, "John Alexander Dowie: The Prophet and His Profits," *Century Magazine* 64 (1902): 938. Harlan's study was a dissertation from the University of Chicago. For another negative evaluation, see Edward E. Weaver, *Mind and Health: With an Examination of Some Systems of Divine Healing* (New York, 1913). The library catalogue card is found in the Old Widener Library of Harvard University.

72. See, for example, H. T. Davis, *Modern Miracles* (Cincinnati, Ohio, 1901), 12–14.

73. The influence of James on Moody is acknowledged in the standard biography of Moody, Maurice F. Brown, *Estranging Dawn: The Life and Works of William Vaughn Moody* (Carbondale, Ill., 1973), 225, 247. For biographical details on Schlatter, see Goddard, "Effects of Mind on Body," 440–41.

74. All the quotations are from the play as printed in *The Poems and Plays of William Vaughn Moody,* vol. 2: *Prose Plays* (Boston, 1912).

75. "Mr. Moody's Play of the Power of the Spirit," *New York Times,* Jan. 20, 1910, p. 11.

76. Ronald A. Knox, *Some Loose Stones* (London, 1913), 181, 54.

77. The volume had its origins as a series of lectures at Columbia Theological Seminary in South Carolina. On Warfield and the question of miracles, see Jon Ruthven, *On the Cessation of the Charismata: The Protestant Polemic on Post-Biblical Miracles* (Sheffield, Eng., 1993).

78. Benjamin B. Warfield, *Counterfeit Miracles* (New York, 1918), 28–29.

79. Ibid., 55, 161, 90, 194, 205.

80. Ibid., 118–20.

81. C. M. Francis, "Miracles," *New Republic* 17 (Jan. 18, 1919): 347–48. This was a review of *Counterfeit Miracles.*

82. S. D. McConnell, "The Ethics of Miracles," *North American Review* 197 (1913): 834.

83. This observation is made by Ruthven, *On the Cessation of the Charismata,* 56.

84. Philip Mauro, *By What Means?* (London, 1910), 5. He also wrote *Sickness Among Saints: To Whom Shall We Go?* (Swengel, Penn., 1915) and *Trusting God in Sickness* (Williamsport, Penn., 1910).

85. T. B. Strong and William Sanday, *Spirit, Matter, and Miracle* (Oxford, 1916), 59.

86. Morgan is quoted in Edith Blumhofer, *Restoring the Faith,* 58. Blumhofer also discusses the influence of the Welsh revival on the imagination of early Pentecostalism.

87. Patricia H. Keats, "An Analysis of Chesterton's First Play, *Magic*" *Chesterton*

Review 20 (1994): 449–61. See, too, William B. Furlong, *Shaw and Chesterton: The Metaphysical Jesters* (University Park, Pa., 1970), 11–22.

88. G. K. Chesterton, *Magic: A Fantastic Comedy in a Prelude and Three Acts* (London, 1914), 16. The play was produced in America on Broadway in February of 1917, and was frequently revived. My textual references are to page numbers in the printed version of the play.

89. "A Miracle Play by G. K. Chesterton," *New York Times*, Feb. 13, 1917, 9. On the relationship between *Magic* to Chesterton's own life, see Dudley Barker, *G. K. Chesterton: A Biography* (New York, 1975), 57–58.

90. "Second Thoughts on First Nights," *New York Times*, Feb. 18, 1917, sec. 2, p. 6.

91. On McCabe, see Joseph McCabe, *Twelve Years in a Monastery,* 3d ed. (London, 1936).

92. G. K. Chesterton et al., *Do Miracles Happen?* (London, 1914), 4, 11. This debate was excerpted and reprinted verbatim in the *New York Times,* July 4, 1915. The reviewer for the *Times* of London criticized Chesterton's play as "opinions in the wrong place." See *Times,* Nov. 8, 1913.

93. Ibid., 17.

Chapter 8: Miracles and the Crisis of the 1920s

1. Stuart Mews, "The Revival of Spiritual Healing in the Church of England, 1920–26," in *The Church and Healing: Papers Read at the Twentieth Summer Meeting and Twenty-First Winter Meeting of the Ecclesiastical History Society,* ed. W. J. Sheils ([Oxford, Eng.]: 1982), 307 ff. On the question of whether prayer could stop a bullet, see the discussion in Harold Anson's memoirs, *Looking Forward* (London: n.d.), 195 ff. On the "Angels of Mons," see "Angelic Intervention at Mons," *Literary Digest* 51 (July 31, 1915): 214; "Miracle at Mons," *Independent* 83 (Sept. 20, 1915): 381–82 ; "Those Angels at Mons," *Literary Digest* 51 (Sept. 25, 1915): 669–70; and Harold Temperley, "On the Supernatural Element in History: With Two Examples from the Present Day," *Contemporary Review* 110 (1916): 188–99.

2. William Adams Brown, *A Teacher and His Times* (New York, 1940), 303 ff. Brown dates the shift in American philosophy to the 1912 publication by Ralph Barton Perry et al. of *The New Realism.* On the general trends in philosophy, see J. O. Urmson, *Philosophical Analysis: Its Developments Between the Two World Wars* (Oxford, 1971); and on the effect of these trends upon religious thought, see James Patrick, *The Magdalen Metaphysicals: Idealism and Orthodoxy at Oxford, 1901–1945* (Macon, Ga., 1985). On the contrasting ideas of Myers and Freud, see John J. Cerullo, *The Secularization of the Soul: Psychical Research in Modern Britain* (Philadelphia, 1982), 160–67. On the advancement of the social status of physicians in America, see James G. Burrow, *Organized Medicine in the Progressive Era: The Move Toward Monopoly* (Baltimore, Md., 1977).

3. On the rise of popularity of Spiritualism as a result of the war, see J. M. Winter, "Spiritualism and the First World War," in *Religion and Irreligion in Victorian Society,* ed. R. W. Davis and R. J. Helmstadter (New York, 1992), 185–200.

4. *The Churchman* 133 (May 15, 1926): 7, quoting Robert Norwood, rector of St. Bartholomew's Episcopal Church in New York.

5. H. D. C. MacLachlin, "Sir Oliver Lodge and Religion," *Christian Century* 37 (Feb. 19, 1920): 13–14 ; Editorial, "Divorcing Science from Spiritualism," *Christian Century* 43 (Apr. 8, 1926): 436.

6. Shailer Mathews, *The Faith of Modernism* (New York, 1924), 110–11; and "The Supernatural," *Christian Century* 44 (Dec. 21, 1922): 1581. See too Frederick Grant's essay in *Problems of Faith and Worship: A Record of the Church Congress in the United States . . .* (New York, 1926), 122–40; and "The Miraculous," *Christian Century* 44 (Dec. 14, 1922): 1545. For a slightly later example of a Liberal-Modernist evaluation of the supernatural, see Shirley Jackson Case, *Experience with the Supernatural in Early Christian Times* (New York, 1929).

7. J. Gresham Machen, *Christianity and Liberalism* (1923; reprint ed., Grand Rapids, Mich., 1972), 107. (Emphasis added.) Significantly John Roach Straton (to be discussed below), second only to Machen as the intellectual leader of American Fundamentalism, was not willing to retreat to an absolute definition of miracle. See John Roach Straton and Charles Francis Potter, *The Virgin Birth — Fact of Fiction? Third in a Series of Fundamentalist-Modernist Debates* (New York, 1924), 17–20.

8. Box, *The Virgin Birth of Jesus* (London, 1916), 12, 19, 20. See too Vincent Taylor, *The Historical Evidence of the Virgin Birth* (Oxford, 1920).

9. Contrast, for example, Charles Harris, *Creeds or No Creeds: A Critical Examination of the Basis of Modernism* (London, 1922), with Jocelyn Rhys, *Shaken Creeds: The Virgin Birth Doctrine, A Study of its Origins* (London, 1922). Both are reflective of the vast amount of literature on the subject.

10. The origin of the "Five Point" statement and its connection with American Fundamentalism is a complicated story. See George M. Marsden, *Fundamentalism and American Culture* (New York, 1980), 277–78, n. 3.

11. J. Gresham Machen, "The Virgin Birth: Is the Doctrine Crucial?" *British Weekly* 88 (Aug. 21, 1930): 418.

12. Machen, *Christianity and Liberalism,* 109.

13. J. Gresham Machen, *The Virgin Birth of Christ* (1930; reprint ed., Grand Rapids, Mich., 1965), 110.

14. On the controversy within the Presbyterian Church, see Bradley J. Longfield, *The Presbyterian Controversy: Fundamentalists, Modernists, and Moderates* (New York, 1991), 100, and Lefferts Loetscher, *The Broadening Church: A Study of Theological Issues in the Presbyterian Church Since 1869* (Philadelphia, [1954]), 126–7.

15. Percy Stickney Grant, *The Religion of Main Street* (New York, 1923), 61, 20. "Dr. Grant Queries 'Is the Bishop Right?' " *New York Times,* Feb. 18, 1924, p. 15. Grant was the Episcopal rector of the New York, Church of the Ascension. For background to Grant as a Modernist, see Terence Blackburn, "Neither Fundamentalism Nor Modernism: An Examination of the Relationship Between William Thomas Manning and Percy Stickney Grant," (Honors thesis, General Theological Seminary, 1988). Fosdick included a critique of the virgin birth in his famous sermon "Shall the Fundamentalists Win?" reprinted in *Christian Century* June 8, 1922, and later reissued as a tract under the title *The New Knowledge and the Christian Faith.* On the background to these events, see Robert M. Miller, *Harry Emerson Fosdick: Preacher, Pastor, Prophet* (New York, 1985), 112–17.

16. On Royden, see Sheila Fletcher, *Maude Royden: A Life* (Oxford, 1989). On her

reputation in America as a preacher, see Joseph Fort Newton, "Maude A. Royden," *Christian Century* 38 (May 12, 1921): 9–11; and "A Woman's View of the Virgin Birth," *Current Opinion* 76 (Mar. 1924): 698 ff. Newton, who had headed the City Temple when Royden had served there, was probably the person who introduced her to the American audience. On Newton, see Bill J. Leonard, "Joseph Fort Newton: Minister and Mystic" (Ph.D. diss., Boston University, 1975).

17. Editors' Preface, "A Woman's View of the Virgin Birth," *Christian Century* 41 (Feb. 21, 1924): 234. An earlier sermon was "Can We Believe in the Virgin Birth?" in *City Temple Sermons,* ed. Joseph Fort Newton (London, 1919), 93 ff.

18. Maude Royden, "A Woman's View of the Virgin Birth," *Christian Century* 38 (Oct. 20, 1921): 12–15.

19. Ibid., 13.

20. Ibid., 13–14.

21. Quoted in Fletcher, *Royden,* 199. She was to make the same point also in *The Church and Women* (London, 1924), 90 ff.

22. "A Woman's View of the Virgin Birth," *Current Opinion* 698; William E. Barton, "A Common Sense View of the Virgin Birth," *Christian Century* 41 (Feb. 28, 1924): 266; Machen, *Virgin Birth,* 134.

23. Harry Emerson Fosdick and Shailer Mathews were probably the two most noted American Baptist questioners of the doctrine. Among Methodists, the issue was raised in an article circulated by Edgar Blake, bishop resident in Paris. See "Virgin Birth Issue Now Plagues Methodist," *Christian Century* 43 (Apr. 15, 1926): 487.

24. Straton and Potter, *Virgin Birth,* 48, 50.

25. "Call Pontifical Mass to Protest Modernism," *New York Times,* Feb. 10, 1924, sec. 1, pt. 2, p. 6; "Catholics to Defend 'Fundamental' Views," *New York Times,* Feb. 17, 1924, sec. 2, p. 15; "To Honor the Virgin Birth," *New York Times,* Mar. 17, 1924, p. 3.

26. Straton and Potter, *Virgin Birth,* 66.

27. George Henry Betts, *The Beliefs of 700 Ministers and Their Meaning for Religious Education* (New York, 1929), 44–48, 52–56.

28. Ibid., 27. The actual figures were: 55 percent agree, 2 percent uncertain, 43 percent disbelieve. These figures are probably lower than if the wording had been slightly altered, because the wording implied an idea of dictation that even many conservatives rejected.

29. On the background to Machen and the virgin birth, see D. G. Hart, *Defending the Faith: J. Gresham Machen and the Crisis of Conservative Protestantism in Modern America* (Baltimore, Md., 1994), 20–24, 88ff.

30. Straton and Potter, *Virgin Birth,* 217.

31. Ibid., 391, 396. The surprising ending of the volume was not missed by astute theological critics at the time. See the review of Machen's work by the Scottish theologian H. R. Mackintosh, "The Virgin Birth: Is the Doctrine Crucial?" *British Weekly* 88 (July 17, 1930): 313–14.

32. There is no biography of Hickson and the above account has been pieced together from a variety of sources. For biographical data, see James Moore Hickson, *Heal the Sick* (New York: n.d.); T. W. Crafer, ed., *The Church and the Ministry of Healing* (London, 1934); Mews, "Revival of Spiritual Healing"; Morris Maddocks, *The Christian Healing Ministry* (London, 1981); Kenneth MacKenzie, "The Hickson Mission to the Church,"

American Church Monthly 7 (1920): 38 ff.; and Charles W. Gusmer, *The Ministry of Healing in the Church of England: An Ecumenical-Liturgical Study* (Great Western Wakering, Eng.,: 1974), 12. James H. Hyslop includes a number of press reports on the Hickson mission in "Mr. Hickson's Spiritual Healing," *Journal of the American Society for Psychical Research* 14 (1920): 266–72.

33. The itinerary is found in James Moore Hickson, *Heal the Sick,* 15–46.

34. Bosworth, *Christ the Healer: Sermons on Divine Healing* ([Racine, Wis.]: 1924), 29–31.

35. Daggett, "Are There Modern Miracles?" *Ladies Home Journal* 40 (June, 1923): 20.

36. Daggett, "Are There Modern Miracles?" 20, 167. She cites J. Wilson Lundy and Matthew Holderby among Presbyterians; Edwin L. House among Congregationalists; and J. S. Bitler, W. I. Gates, and Charles Shreve among Methodists. On McPherson, see Edith Blumhoffer, *Aimee Semple McPherson: Everybody's Sister* (Grand Rapids, Mich., 1993); and Daniel Mark Epstein, *Sister Aimee: The Life of Aimee Semple McPherson* (New York, 1993). On Rader, see R. L. Niklaus, J. S. Sawin, and S. J. Stoesz, *All for Jesus: God at Work in the Christian and Missionary Alliance over One Hundred Years* (Camp Hill, Pa., 1986).

37. James Moore Hickson, "Laying on of Hands," in Crafer, *Church and the Ministry of Healing,* 48–49.

38. James Moore Hickson, *The Healing of Christ in His Church* (New York, 1919), 38; and "Laying on of Hands," 47–48.

39. Kenneth MacKenzie, "The Hickson Mission to the Church," *American Church Monthly* 7 (1920): 38.

40. Hickson, "Laying on of Hands," 53. On the ecumenical implications of the thaumaturgical view of healing, see also the "Pastoral Letter of the Archbishops and Bishops of the Anglican Church in Australia," reprinted in "Laying on of Hands," 53–54.

41. Sutton quoted in Daggett, "Are There Modern Miracles?" 165. Henry B. Wilson, *Does Christ Still Heal?* (New York, 1917), 156; Claude O'Flaherty, *Health and Religion* (London, 1923), 152. See, too, James Robert Pridie, *The Church's Ministry of Healing* (London, 1926), vii; A. J. Gayner Banks, *The Healing Evangel* (Milwaukee, Wis., 1925), 166–67.

42. Sherman, *The Inner Chamber* (Cleveland, Ohio, 1929), 199.

43. Ibid., 59, 69.

44. Samuel McComb, "The New Reformation," *Contemporary Review* 125 (1924): 759; Sherman, *Inner Chamber,* 198.

45. Sherman, *Inner Chamber,* 2, 193, 109.

46. Anson, *Looking Forward,* 207.

47. Sherman, *Inner Chamber,* 202–3; Banks, *Healing Evangel,* 126. Some predicted the division would lead to a schism in the Episcopal Church. See "Topics of the Times," *New York Times,* Aug. 30, 1922.

48. Charles Reynolds Brown, *Faith and Health* (New York, 1924), 60–61, 142.

49. Herbert Hensley Henson, *Notes on Spiritual Healing* (London, 1925), xxiii, 106, 193; "Spiritual Healing," *Hibbert Journal* 23 (1925): 399. On the background for Henson's opposition, see Mews, "Revival of Spiritual Healing," 327–30.

50. Henry B. Wilson, *Ghosts or Gospels: The Methods of Spiritualism in Healing Compared with the Methods of Christ* (Boonton, N.J.: n.d.), 62, 57. See, too, Hyslop, "Mr. Hickson's Spiritual Healing," 271–72. Other negative criticisms of Hickson can be found in L. W. Grensted's Bampton Lectures, *Psychology and God: A Study of the Implications of Recent Psychology for Religious Belief and Practice* (London, 1930), 97–126.

51. Egbert H. Grandin quoted in Daggett, "Are There Modern Miracles?," 167; David Orr Edson cited in *Literary Digest* 75 (Oct. 28, 1922): 30; Edward Cowles, *Literary Digest* 75 (Oct. 28, 1922); Cowles, *Religion and Medicine in the Church* (New York, 1925), 92.

52. The best account of the politics of the English debate is found in Mews, "Revival of Spiritual Healing," and my interpretation is based upon his findings. On the debate within the Episcopal church, see Robert Bruce Mullin, "The Debate over Healing in the Episcopal Church, 1870–1930," *Anglican and Episcopal History* 60 (1991): 213–34.

53. *The Ministry of Healing: Report of the Committee Appointed in Accordance with Resolution 63 of the Lambeth Conference, 1920* (London, 1924), 16; "Report of the Joint Commission on Christian Healing," app. 20, *Journal of the General Convention of the Protestant Episcopal Church* (1931), 557, 558. The American report did include a minority report that defended the use of sacramental anointing.

54. Daggett, "Are There Modern Miracles?" 171.

55. Grant, *Problem of Faith and Worship*, 137.

56. E. R. Micklem, *Miracles and the New Psychology: A Study in the Healing Miracles of the New Testament* (London, 1922), 135, 136.

57. Lloyd C. Douglas, *Those Disturbing Miracles* (New York, 1927), vii.

58. Ibid., 189. Emphasis added.

59. Lloyd C. Douglas, *The Robe* (Boston, 1943), 666.

60. Reinhold Niebuhr, "Allegorizing the Miracles," *Christian Century* 44 (Oct. 13, 1927): 1203.

61. Edwyn C. Hoskyns, "The Christ of the Synoptic Gospels," in *Essays Catholic and Critical: By Members of the Anglican Communion*, ed. E. G. Selwyn (London, 1934), 166, 168. On Hoskyns see also Michael Ramsey, *An Era in Anglican Theology: From Gore to Temple* (New York, 1960), 131–40.

62. Burton Scott Easton, *The Gospel Before the Gospels* (New York, 1928), 31.

63. Ibid., 60.

64. Walter Lowrie, *Jesus According to St. Mark: An Interpretation of St. Mark's Gospel* (New York, 1929), 13, 213, 212.

65. Ibid., 336, ix.

66. Karl Barth, *The Word of God and the Word of Man*, trans. Douglas Horton (New York, 1957), 33–34.

67. Karl Barth, *Church Dogmatics* 2:1, trans. T. H. L. Parker et al. (Edinburgh, 1957), 509.

68. Emil Brunner, *The Mediator: A Study of the Central Doctrine of the Christian Faith*, trans. Olive Wyon (New York, 1934), 301. English-speaking scholars reacted favorably to such appeals. See R. Birch Hoyle, *The Teaching of Karl Barth: An Exposition* (London, 1930), 187–91.

69. See, for example, Reinhold Niebuhr's essay "The Foolishness of the Cross and the Sense of History," in *Faith and History: A Comparison of Christian and Modern Views of History* (New York, 1949), 139–50.

70. On the role of Neoorthodoxy in America, see William A. Silva, "The Expression of Neo-Orthodoxy in American Protestantism, 1939–1960" (Ph.D. diss., Yale University, 1988).

71. William Temple, *Readings in St. John's Gospel: First and Second Series* (1939, 1940; reprint ed., Wilton, Conn., 1985), xxvii. On Temple's earlier difficulties, see F. A. Iremonger, *William Temple, Archbishop of Canterbury: His Life and Letters* (London, 1948), 112–22.

72. Edwin Lewis, *Jesus Christ and the Human Quest: Suggestions Toward a Philosophy of the Person and Work of Christ* (New York, 1924), 305. On the controversy the volume provoked in American Methodism, see *The History of American Methodism*, ed. Emory Stevens Bucke et al., 3 vols. (Nashville, Tenn., 1964), 3:272 ff.

73. Edwin Lewis, *A Philosophy of the Christian Revelation* (New York, 1940), 181, 182.

74. Ibid., 184, 188.

75. Among the many volumes representative of this confidence, see in particular Alan Richardson, *The Miracle Stories of the Gospels* (London, 1941).

76. E. Brooks Holifield, *A History of Pastoral Care in America: From Salvation to Self-Realization* (Nashville, Tenn., 1983), 231–58; Allison Stokes, *Ministry After Freud* (New York, 1985).

77. Reuben A. Torrey, *Divine Healing: Does God Perform Miracles Today?* (1924: Grand Rapids, Mich.: n.d.), 12–13, 31, 52; Blumhoffer, *McPherson*, 221 ff. The note on faith healing in Straton's church is found in *Christian Century* 44 (Nov. 24, 1927): 138–39.

78. Lewis Sperry Chafer, *Systematic Theology*, 8 vols. (Dallas, Tex., 1947–48), 7:184–85; John F. Walvoord, *The Holy Spirit* (Grand Rapids, Mich., 1954), 180; Edward J. Carnell, *An Introduction to Christian Apologetics: A Philosophical Defense of the Trinitarian Theistic Faith* (Grand Rapids, Mich., 1948), 272, cited in Colin Brown, *Miracles and the Critical Mind* (Grand Rapids, Mich., 1984), 203.

79. On the background to the song, see Ira Gershwin, *Lyrics on Several Occasions* (New York, 1973), 65–66.

Epilogue

1. The attempt by the English Modernist bishop E. W. Barnes to free Christianity of supernaturalism provoked a number of responses. See E. W. Barnes, *The Rise of Christianity* (London, 1947); and on the controversy it provoked, John Barnes, *Ahead of His Age: Bishop Barnes of Birmingham* (London, 1979). Another person who kept the discussion alive was the English lay apologist C. S. Lewis. Indeed, Lewis continued to defend the early-twentieth-century Anglican mediating position not only in his volume *Miracles*, but also in his periodic references to the virgin birth question, the Angels of Mons, and the Augustinian understanding of miracle. See his *God in the Dock: Essays on Theology and*

Ethics (Grand Rapids, Mich., 1970), 25–34, 80–89. Considering Lewis's influence on evangelical thought in post–World War II America, it is intriguing to consider his role as a conduit between the earlier and later miracle debates.

2. Sydney E. Ahlstrom, *A Religious History of the American People* (New Haven, Conn., 1972), 947; John A. T. Robinson, *Honest to God* (Philadelphia, 1963), 8. For an early critique of the unintelligibility of the mid-century compromise, see Langdon Gilkey's celebrated essay, "Cosmology, Ontology, and the Travail of Biblical Language," *Journal of Religion* 41 (1961): 194–205. Still other contributors to this critique were the American Paul Van Buren and the Englishman J. S. Habgood. See Van Buren, *The Secular Meaning of the Gospel, Based on an Analysis of its Language* (New York, 1963); and Habgood, "The Uneasy Truce Between Science and Theology," in *Soundings: Essays Concerning Christian Understanding,* ed. A. R. Vidler (Cambridge, Eng., 1964), 23–41. Brevard S. Childs chronicled the collapse of the Neoorthodox biblical theology; see his *Biblical Theology in Crisis* (Philadelphia, 1970). On the crisis in biblical theology, see also Carl Braaten, *New Directions in Theology Today: History and Hermeneutics* (Philadelphia, 1966). All acknowledged that the intellectual roots of this movement stemmed from the theology of Rudolph Bultmann and Dietrich Bonhoffer. As Mary Kathleen Cunningham has shown, the tendency to reinterpret biblical categories had long been present in the theology of Rudolph Bultmann, and was part of a fundamentally different hermeneutical theory dividing him from Karl Barth. See Cunningham, *What Is Theological Exegesis? Interpretation and Use of Scripture in Barth's Doctrine of Election* (Valley Forge, Pa., 1995), 68–77.

3. David E. Harrell, *All Things Are Possible: The Healing and Charismatic Revivals in Modern America* (Bloomington, Ind., 1975). The literature on the growth of Pentecostalism and the spread of charismatic movement into historically non-Pentecostal churches is immense and continually growing, but two older but still useful works are Richard Quebedeaux, *The New Charismatics II* (San Francisco, 1983); and Edward D. O'Connor, *The Pentecostal Movement in the Catholic Church* (Notre Dame, 1971); as well as the recent Harvey Cox, *Fire from Heaven: The Rise of Pentecostal Spirituality and the Reshaping of Religion in the Twenty-First Century* (Reading, Mass., 1995).

4. *Time* 145 (Apr. 10, 1995): 64. Martin Marty, "Proof-Shroud," *Christian Century* 97 (Apr. 2, 1980): 391. The *Time* poll did not distinguish between believers in biblical miracles and believers in modern miracles, but for the past six years my colleague David Austin has been polling over four thousand Philosophy of Science students concerning their attitudes towards the miraculous. Defining a miracle as "an event caused by the direct intervention by God, who temporarily suspends the laws of nature" he has found that 17 percent of his students believe that miracles never happen; 77 percent believe they occur at present; and only 6 percent maintain that they happened in the past but have ceased. Because the student body at North Carolina State University is overwhelmingly Protestant, this last figure is some indication of the decline of the classic Protestant cessationist position. For other statistics on the continued interest in miracles, see George Gallup, Jr. and Jim Castelli, *The People's Religion: American Faith in the 90s* (New York, 1989), 56–58.

5. Since its inception in 1985, the controversial Jesus Seminar has attempted to identify (as Paul W. Schmiedel had attempted in the *Encyclopaedia Biblica*) the authentic

sayings and actions of Jesus. In the autumn of 1994 they voted to reject the biblical account of the virgin birth, and their decision was widely reported in both secular and religious presses. For a somewhat jaundiced (but amusing) account of the decision, see Charlotte Allen, "Away with the Manger: Scholars Tackle the Historical Jesus," *Lingua Franca* 5 (Feb. 1995): 22–30. On the renewed medical discussion of the role of prayer and healing, see (among many): L. B. Bearon and H. G. Koenig, "Religious Cognitions and the Use of Prayer in Health and Illness," *Gerontologist* 30 (1990): 249–53; T. L. Saudia et al., "Health Locus of Control and Helpfulness of Prayer," *Heart and Lung*, 20 (1991), 60–65; and "Prayer and Health During Pregnancy: Findings from the Galveston Low Birthweight Survey," *Southern Medical Journal* 86 (1993): 1022–27. I wish to thank Ronald Numbers for these medical references.

6. As in the earlier period, one again finds Anglican bishops popularizing this message of rethinking the virgin birth. See, for example, John Shelby Spong, *Born of a Woman: A Bishop Rethinks the Birth of Jesus* (San Francisco, 1992); and David L. Edwards, *Bishops and Beliefs* (Kidderminster, Worcestershire: [1987]). On the continuation of the cessationist position, see the sources listed in Jon Ruthven, *On the Cessation of the Charismata: The Protestant Polemic on Postbiblical Miracles* (Sheffield, Eng., 1993), 15–16, n. 3. Even Benjamin Warfield's *Counterfeit Miracles* was reissued in 1976.

7. For an example of a New Age attempt to reinterpret Jesus and his healings, see John White, *The Meeting of Science and Spirit: Guidelines for a New Age* (New York, 1990), 98–106. Wimber's view of the interrelationship between Jesus' healing ministry and modern healings can be found in John Wimber with Kevin Springer, *Power Healing* (New York, 1987). On the evangelical controversy over Wimber, see Grant Wacker, "Wimber and Wonders—What About Miracles Today?" *Reformed Journal* 37 (1987): 16–19.

8. One such point of intersection is the interest among both orthodox Christians and New Age devotees in the Shroud of Turin. Contrast David Vaughan's "New Light Upon the Empty Tomb: The Turin Shroud and Mediumistic Evidence," and "Frank Tribbe Responds to Mr. Vaughan," *Journal of Religion and Psychical Research* 9 (1986): 98–105, with Kevin E. Stevenson and Gary R. Habermas, *Verdict on the Shroud: Evidence for the Death and Resurrection of Jesus Christ* (Ann Arbor, Mich., 1981). On the general theme of the convergence of New Age and Charismatic concerns, see Philip C. Lucas, "The New Age Movement and the Pentecostal/Charismatic Revival: Distinct Yet Parallel Phases of a Fourth Great Awakening?" in *Perspectives on the New Age*, ed. James R. Lewis and J. Gordon Melton (Albany, N.Y., 1992), 189–211.

9. For applications of a critique of Enlightenment presuppositions from fundamentally different religious systems, see Catharine L. Albanese, *Nature Religion in America: From the Algonkian Indians to the New Age* (Chicago, 1990); and Colin Brown, *Miracles and the Critical Mind* (Grand Rapids, Mich., 1984).

10. David Toolan, *Facing West from California's Shores: A Jesuit's Journey into New Age Consciousness* (New York, 1987), 307.

11. Conversely, a major difference between the story we have related and the present debate is the changing role of Anglocatholicism. Before Vatican II, Anglocatholicism was an important conduit of Catholic ideas into English-speaking Protestantism. In the years since, its intellectual importance has declined.

Index